THE ART OF USELESS

GLOBAL CHINESE CULTURE

The Art of Useless

FASHION, MEDIA, AND CONSUMER CULTURE IN CONTEMPORARY CHINA

Calvin Hui

Columbia University Press

New York

Columbia University Press wishes to express its appreciation for assistance given by the Wm. Theodore de Bary Fund in the publication of this book.

Columbia University Press
Publishers Since 1893
New York   Chichester, West Sussex
cup.columbia.edu

Library of Congress Cataloging-in-Publication Data
Names: Hui, Calvin, author.
Title: The art of useless : fashion, media, and consumer culture in contemporary China / Calvin Hui.
Description: New York : Columbia University Press, [2021] | Series: Global Chinese culture | Includes bibliographical references and index.
Identifiers: LCCN 2020057649 (print) | LCCN 2020057650 (ebook) | ISBN 9780231192484 (hardback) | ISBN 9780231192491 (trade paperback) | ISBN 9780231549837 (ebook)
Subjects: LCSH: Consumption (Economics)—China. | Fashion—Social aspects—China. | Middle class—China. | Consumption (Economics) in motion pictures. | Fashion in motion pictures. | Middle class in motion pictures. | Documentary films—China—History and criticism. | China—Economic conditions—1976–2000. | China—Economic conditions—2000–
Classification: LCC HC430.C6 .H85 2021 (print) | LCC HC430.C6 (ebook) | DDC 306.30951—dc23
LC record available at https://lccn.loc.gov/2020057649
LC ebook record available at https://lccn.loc.gov/2020057650

Columbia University Press books are printed on permanent and durable acid-free paper.
Printed in the United States of America

Cover design: Milenda Nan Ok Lee
Cover image: Francois Guillot/AFP © Getty Images

For my parents and my brother

CONTENTS

ACKNOWLEDGMENTS

I am extremely grateful to the following institutions and individuals for providing generous support for my research. In terms of external funding, I sincerely acknowledge the financial support of the American Council of Learned Societies fellowship (2019); Design Trust Hong Kong Seed Grant (2018); Chiang Ching-kuo Foundation for International Scholarly Exchange Scholar Grant (2016); University of Alberta's China Institute Postdoctoral Fellowship (2016), which I was not able to accept; and China Times Cultural Foundation Young Scholar Award (2013). In terms of internal funding from the College of William and Mary, where I worked as an assistant professor from the fall of 2013 to the spring of 2019 and as an associate professor from the fall of 2019 to the present, I am grateful for the funding and support from the Chinese Program, Department of Modern Languages and Literatures, Confucius Institute, Arts and Sciences, and Provost's Office. I am very thankful for a junior scholar leave before applying for tenure and a scheduled semester research leave after receiving tenure. I sincerely thank my wonderful colleagues for their warmth, generosity, trust, and encouragement. I also appreciate my students for showing interest in my work on uselessness, dirt, garbage, and the copycat.

When I pursued my doctoral trainings in the Program in Literature at Duke University, I received very generous financial support from the Graduate School. I am especially obliged for an International Research Travel

Fellowship (2011); a Special Collections Library Internship (2011), which I was not able to accept; and a Women's Studies Dissertation Fellowship (2010). The ten-plus other awards and grants, from the Program in Literature, Department of Asian and Middle Eastern Studies, Program in Women's Studies, Asia and Pacific Studies Institute, John Hope Franklin Humanities Institute, Center for International Studies, and other academic units, enabled me to conduct research in China and Hong Kong and to present my works in academic conferences in the United States, Canada, China, Hong Kong, and the United Kingdom. I must emphasize that I have been extremely fortunate to be able to study and closely work with professors Rey Chow, Michael Hardt, Fredric Jameson, Leo Ching, and Robyn Wiegman. Their teaching and mentoring greatly expanded my intellectual horizon and made me realize that theory can be so powerful and thought-provoking. I am indebted to Rey, as she has been the most important influence on my intellectual development as a scholar. I appreciate that she continued to mentor me after I had graduated from Duke. While in graduate school, I was greatly inspired by the many interesting conversations I had with my classmates, friends, and colleagues in such venues as talks, seminars, conferences, colloquia, reading groups, and writing groups. I still vividly remember the dialogues we had about new, cutting-edge research projects in modern Chinese humanities, Western Marxism, feminist and sexuality studies, and postcolonial and transnational studies. I owe special thanks to Hongsheng Jiang and Koonyong Kim, respectively, for teaching me to see China and Asian America in new and interesting ways. I enjoyed the writing group with Gerry Canavan, Lisa Klarr, and Timothy Wright at Elmo's Diner on Ninth Street in Durham. I also appreciated the writing group with John Stadler, Chase Gregory, and Carolyn Laubender at the many coffee shops in Durham. I have very fond memories of Duke.

I sincerely thank the senior and junior faculty for inviting me to present my research in academic conferences and their home institutions. I have greatly benefited from our intellectual conversations. My special thanks go to Shuang Shen, who has read several drafts of the introduction and offered very useful feedback and suggestions. I also thank Su-ching Huang and Yu Zhang for reading my work and sharing their ideas with me. I am indebted to Dr. Qingsheng Tong for teaching and mentoring me when I was an undergraduate student at the University of Hong Kong. An earlier version of chapter 1, "Dirty Fashion: Ma Ke's Fashion 'Useless,' Jia Zhangke's

ACKNOWLEDGMENTS

Documentary *Useless*, and Cognitive Mapping," was published in *Journal of Chinese Cinemas* 9, no. 3 (2015): 253–70. A very small part of chapter 2 was published as "Socks and Revolution: The Politics of Consumption in *Sentinels under the Neon Lights* (1964)" in *The Cold War and Asian Cinemas*, coedited by Poshek Fu and Man-Fung Yip (New York: Routledge, 2020). A very early version of chapter 3 was published as "Mao's Children Are Wearing Fashion!" in *The Changing Landscape of China's Consumerism*, edited by Alison Hulme (Oxford: Chandos, 2014). I am thankful for the permission to reprint these materials here.

At Columbia University Press, I am grateful to Christine Dunbar, Christian Winting, Leslie Kriesel, and the other professional staff for their editorial wisdom, guidance, and patience. I also want to thank Patricia Bower for working with me. Importantly, I need to express my deep gratitude to the anonymous reviewers of my book manuscript. My revisions have greatly benefited from their questions, comments, and suggestions. Any errors are mine alone.

I dedicate this book to my parents and my brother. Without their love, patience, and support, there is no way I could have finished this book.

INTRODUCTION

The Trouble with Naming: Middle-Class Culture, Petty-Bourgeois Sensibility, and *Zhuang* (裝)

Culture, I argue, is central to understanding the unprecedented political-economic, social, and historical transformations of the People's Republic of China (PRC). In the 1960s the proletariat —an alliance of workers, peasants, and soldiers—was the dominant subject of socialist China. In Maoist cultures, they were shown to be engaging in class struggles, national liberations, and socialist revolutions. In the 1980s the petty bourgeoisie, such as intellectuals and small-scale business owners (*getihu* 個體戶), was recruited by the party-state. In the early stage of China's economic reforms and opening up (*gaige kaifang* 改革開放), the petty-bourgeois cultures were mobilized to advocate China's modernization and promote "socialism with Chinese characteristics" (*zhongguo tese de shehui zhuyi* 中國特色的社會主義). In the 2000s the Chinese public sphere featured the economically empowered and aspirant middle class—that is, the white-collar and professional-managerial class. However, somewhat unique to China's post-socialist and neoliberal conditions, the Chinese middle class has eluded a proper name and definition. This new social actor has been labeled in different ways, for example, the bourgeoisie (*zichanjieji* 資產階級), the petty bourgeoisie (*xiao zichanjieji/xiaozi* 小資產階級/小資), the middle-propertied class (*zhongchanjieji* 中產階級), the middle-income class (*zhongdeng shouru jieceng* 中等收入階層), and its variations, such as middle (*zhongjian* 中間), middle-range (*zhongdeng* 中等), as well as class (*jieji* 階級), stratum (*jieceng* 階層), and group (*qunti* 群體). It can also include the modestly prosperous or well to do (*xiaokang* 小康). A symbol of China's rise on the global stage in the twenty-first century, the figure of the Chinese middle class embodies overwhelmingly positive connotations: education, professionalization, consumption, leisure, cultural taste, symbolic capital, and a tacit sense that the long-cherished desire to become like the United States is close to being realized.

To be sure, the emergence of the middle class in postsocialist and neoliberal China has been a heated topic of academic debates.[1] Questions arise: What is the Chinese middle class? Who belongs to this new social stratum? What is its population? What is the cultural expression of this new social actor? In the social sciences, Chinese sociologists and political scientists in China and abroad have used quantitative methods to dissect social stratifications in contemporary China. Although their mappings are detailed and meticulous, their research projects seem to rest on the premise that the Chinese middle-class culture is a belated response to the Chinese middle-class subject. Their assumption appears to be that the Chinese middle class has already come into being and that their culture, which is still in the process of becoming, reflects the appearance of this new social actor. Diverging from this social sciences approach, my work deploys a humanities and cultural studies methodology to argue that cultural productions—in particular, media and popular cultures—can potentially call into being and construct this new social subjectivity. Indeed, it is the middle-class consumer culture that helps anticipate and expect the middle-class subject as much as the other way around.

The Art of Useless: Fashion, Media, and Consumer Culture in Contemporary China draws on a variety of media and popular cultures—fiction film, documentary film, and fashion—to track the emergence of middle-class consumer culture in China's encounter with global capitalism. Through the methodologies of cultural studies and the practices of critical theory, I explore the massive reorganization of national culture that has accompanied the economic reforms since 1978. How, I ask, has middle-class consumer culture replaced proletarian culture and become the dominant imaginary of China today? How does culture contribute to the country's changing social relations and class hierarchies? In addition, what are the conditions of possibility of Chinese middle-class consumer culture? By considering these questions in terms of the cultivation of new identities and sensibilities, I trace China's changing social and cultural formations through media productions. The project is organized into three parts, each of which attends to a particular constellation of ideologies and subjectivities. Chapter 1 engages with the transmedial dialogue between Ma Ke's (馬可) fashion exhibit *Useless* (*Wuyong* 無用) (2007) and Jia Zhangke's (賈樟柯) documentary film *Useless* (*Wuyong* 無用) (2007) in order to stage an analysis of a commodity chain of fashion involving production, consumption, and disposal on a transnational scale. Chapters 2–4 focus on the representations of fashion and consumption in Chinese cinema in the 1960s (i.e., the socialist period), the 1980s (i.e., the economic reforms period), and the 2000s (i.e., the globalization period). By analyzing fiction films such as Xie Tieli's (謝鐵驪) *Never Forget* (*Qianwan buyao wangji* 千萬不要忘記) (1964), Huang Zumo's (黃祖模) *Romance on Lu Mountain* (*Lushanlian* 廬山戀) (1980), and Xu Jinglei's (徐靜蕾) *Go! Lala Go!* (*Du Lala shengzhi ji* 杜拉拉升職記) (2010), I argue that the cinematic representations of fashion, gender, and consumption constitute a productive site for deciphering the symptoms of otherwise imperceptible political-economic, social, and historical contradictions of contemporary China. These depictions can also be seen as a screen onto which the emerging middle-class desires and fantasies are projected, worked out, and negotiated. Turning to the undersides of consumption, chapters 5–6 discuss production and labor (i.e., what comes before consumption) and disposal and waste (i.e., what comes after consumption). By examining recent documentary works, such as Ho Chao-ti's (He Zhaoti 賀照緹) *My Fancy High Heels* (*Wo'ai gaogenxie* 我愛高跟鞋) (2010), Qin Xiaoyu (秦曉宇) and Wu Feiyue's (吳飛躍) *Iron Moon* (*Wode shipian* 我的詩篇) (2017), and Wang Jiuliang's (王久良) *Beijing Besieged by Waste* (*Laji weicheng* 垃圾圍城) (2010), and ethnographic reports written by sociologists, anthropologists, and communication studies scholars, I explain how the migrant factory workers, the scavengers, and garbage are rendered invisible in the process of consumption. This book demonstrates the relevance of cultural studies, Western Marxism, and poststructuralist theory in investigating the complexities of contemporary Chinese media and popular cultures.

In this introduction I present three major ways of naming the culture of the Chinese middle class: (1) the middle-class culture (*zhongchan jieji wenhua* 中產階級文化); (2) the new petty-bourgeois culture or sensibility (*xin xiaozichanjieji wenhua/xiaozi qingdiao* 新小資產階級文化/小資情調); and

(3) *zhuang* (裝). In addition, I suggest that culture can have the potential to construct social class as much as the other way around. In fact, "the middle class" is a term more situated in the West, especially the United States, whereas the petty bourgeoisie has its historical roots in twentieth-century China. I see the merits of using the middle-class culture and the new petty-bourgeois culture/sensibility to signify my object of study. Both of them can be used to explore the cultural formation of this new social actor. Adding to the existing discussions about the Chinese middle class and culture, I propose to use the Chinese word 裝 to name and analyze my object of study. Indeed, 裝 has multiple meanings. It can refer to fashion as clothes and dresses. It can also signify the process of fashioning, making, composing, forming, and producing. It exemplifies a desire for upward mobility and individual betterment; it is about fantasy and imagination. Therefore, 裝 is a useful device to investigate how fashion and culture can help construct the Chinese middle-class and new petty-bourgeois subjectivity. Moreover, 裝 can mean to act, pose, simulate, pretend, fake, fabricate, conceal, disguise, deceive, and lie. It emphasizes storytelling, fictionalizing, narrativizing, and the process of creating an artifice. Furthermore, 裝 involves work and labor. By dwelling on the multifaceted meanings of 裝, I relocate the conditions of possibility to track the making of the Chinese middle-class and new petty-bourgeois consumer cultures. I end this introduction with a summary of the book chapters.

THE FORMATION OF THE CHINESE MIDDLE CLASS AND CULTURE

In a 2005 Chinese TV program titled "The Century Forum" (*Shiji dajiang-tang* 世紀大講堂) on Phoenix TV (*Fenghuang weishi* 鳳凰衛視), Chinese sociologist Zhou Xiaohong (周曉虹) delivers a talk titled "The Chinese Middle Class: Reality or Illusion?" (*zhongguo zhongchan jieji xianshi yihuo huanxiang* 中國中產階級現實抑或幻想). In this talk he affirms that a new social stratum called the middle class has already come into being in early twenty-first-century China. However, he maintains that China is far from being a middle-class society. By the middle class, he refers to white-collar workers and professionals. He calls such a group the new middle class as opposed to the old middle class. By the old middle class, he refers to owners of small farms, small enterprises, and shopkeepers. Then Zhou explains the composition of this new Chinese middle class. He provides six job-related categories for this social group: first, owners of private enterprises and village enterprises; second, owners of small businesses and self-employed individuals, or in Chinese, the *getihu*; third, state cadres, intellectuals, and managers of state-owned enterprises; fourth, white-collar workers in transnational business companies; fifth, managers of other enterprises and organizations (for example, those who have received masters of business administration or public administration, and other professional degrees); and, sixth, professionals such as architects, lawyers, accountants, businessmen, and others. According to Zhou, the new middle class is a product of China's economic reforms and social transformations (*shehui zhuanxing* 社會轉型).

Zhou points out the major differences between the American and Chinese middle classes. According to him, the American middle class has existed for more than one generation. Individuals in the United States can learn how to be middle class from family members. If parents are middle class, he claims, their children are likely to be middle class too. On the contrary, the Chinese middle class is distinct because it is the first generation. In the PRC, due to the political upheavals of the socialist and revolutionary period, it is more difficult for Chinese individuals to learn how to become middle class at home. In addition, Zhou emphasizes the fact that in the United States, the old middle class appeared in the mid-nineteenth century whereas the new middle class appeared in the mid-twentieth century; their historical formations were a hundred years apart. In the United States, the rise of the new middle class accompanied the fall of the old middle class. Nevertheless, in postsocialist and neoliberal China, the old and new middle classes co-emerged at more or less the same time, with the old middle class—namely, the small business owner—appearing slightly earlier in the 1980s. According to Zhou, the Chinese middle class includes blue- and white-collar workers rather than simply white-collar workers.[2] Finally, Zhou points out three major challenges confronting the expansion of the new middle class in twenty-first-century China. First, the gap between rich and poor has not been properly solved; second, the modernization of peasantry has not been completed; and third, the ideological obstacles surrounding the middle class have not been fully eliminated.[3]

In 2005 Zhou and his sociological research team published two Chinese-language edited volumes, *Survey of the Chinese Middle Classes* (*Zhongguo zhongchan jieji diaocha* 中國中產階級調查) and *Report of Middle Classes in the World* (*Quanqiu zhongchan jieji baogao* 全球中產階級報告), both published by the Social Sciences Academic Press (*shehui kexue wenxian chubanshe* 社會科學文獻出版社) in China. According to the *Survey of the Chinese Middle Class*, in the first six months of 2004, by surveying more than three thousand individuals in five major Chinese cities (Beijing, Shanghai, Guangzhou, Nanjing, and Wuhan) and by interviewing more than one hundred middle-class individuals in these five cities and in Shenzhen and Suzhou, Zhou's research team defined the Chinese middle class as the "middle propertied stratum" or simply the "middle stratum" (*zhongchan jieceng* 中產階層). They also acknowledge other related terms such as the "middle-level income stratum" (*zhongdeng shouru jieceng* 中等收入階層), "middle-level income group" (*zhongdeng shouru qunti* 中等收入群體), and "middle stratum" (*zhongjian jieceng* 中間階層). These terms are also used in the official discourse. In addition, they approach this new social stratum from eight different angles, including identity recognition, consuming behaviors, leisure modes, social interaction, education and cultural inheritance, cultural taste, political participation, and media contacts. In many ways, Zhou's sociological research in 2005 is a continuation of the work pursued by Chinese social scientist Lu Xueyi (陸學藝), who published *Research Report on Contemporary Chinese Social Strata* (*Dangdai zhongguo shehui jieceng yanjiu baogao* 當代中國社會階層研究報告) in 2002. In the first part of this report, Lu suggests that the contemporary Chinese society consisted of ten different strata based on one's occupation, coupled with one's access to organizational or institutional resources, economic resources, and cultural resources. These ten strata include, first, state and social administrators; second, managers; third, private entrepreneurs; fourth, individual business owners; fifth, professional and technical personnel; sixth, office workers; seventh, employees of commercial services; eighth, industrial working class; ninth, agricultural laborers; and tenth, unemployed and semi-employed in urban and rural areas. In the second part of this report, Lu acknowledges the emergence of the new middle stratum (*zhongjian jieceng* 中間階層) in the contemporary Chinese society.[4] This paves way for Zhou's description of the new middle class in China.

To see the specificity of these sociological reports concerning the Chinese middle class, it is useful to compare them with Mao Zedong's (毛澤東)

political essays regarding the Chinese petty bourgeoisie before the founding of the PRC. In Mao's early writing "Analysis of the Classes in Chinese Society" (*Zhongguo shehui gejieji de fenxi* 中國社會各階級的分析) (1926), Mao argues that in the 1920s, the Chinese petty bourgeoisie can be considered a friend, but not the principle agent, of the Chinese revolution.[5] By the petty bourgeoisie, Mao refers to the class fraction uneasily situated between the bourgeoisie and the proletariat. It mostly refers to the shopkeepers and owners of small businesses as well as to the intellectuals. (In Mao's other essays, he suggests that the petty bourgeoisie mostly identifies with the bourgeoisie; this class fraction may exhibit petty-bourgeois sensibility [*xiaozi qingdiao* 小資情調]. However, through cultural revolutions and ideological reforms, the petty bourgeoisie can attain proletarian consciousness. According to Mao, the petty bourgeoisie needs to disidentify from the bourgeoisie in order to identify with the proletariat.)

In his 1926 essay Mao identifies five classes in mid-1920s China; he also analyzes to what extent each class can be considered a friend or an enemy of the Chinese revolution. He argues: "Our enemies are those in league with imperialism—the warlords, the bureaucrats, the comprador class, the big landlord class, and the reactionary intellectuals. The leading force in our revolution is the industrial proletariat. Our closest friends are the entire semi-proletariat and petty bourgeoisie. As for the vacillating middle class [i.e., the national bourgeoisie], their right wing may become our enemy and their left wing may become our friend." According to Mao, the first group refers to the landlord class and the comprador class. Because their existence is structurally dependent on feudalism, imperialism, and international capital, they are the most reactionary toward the Chinese revolution. They are the enemy of the Chinese revolution. The second group is the middle class or, more accurately, the national bourgeoisie. According to Mao, the national bourgeoisie's attitude toward the Chinese revolution is contradictory. On the one hand, "when they are smarting under the blows of foreign capital and the oppression of the warlords, . . . they feel the need for revolution and favor the revolutionary movement against imperialism and the warlords." On the other hand, they can become reactionary and counterrevolutionary because their economic interest is structurally tied to the imperialists and the international bourgeoisie. This is especially true "when they sense that . . . the revolution is threatening the hope of their class to attain the status of a big bourgeoisie." The third class is the petty bourgeoisie. It includes the middle-peasants, the artisans and handicraftsmen, and the lower stratum of the intellectual class such as the students and teachers of primary and secondary schools, lower government functionaries and administrators, office clerks, small lawyers, small merchants, and trades-men.[6] According to Mao, the petty bourgeoisie is a friend of the Chinese revolution. The fourth group is the semiproletariat or the peasants, who are a trusted friend of the Chinese revolution. The fifth group refers to the proletariat or industrial workers. Despite its small size, Mao argues that "the industrial proletariat represents China's new productive forces, is the most progressive class in modern China, and has become the leading force in the revolutionary movement."

Both Zhou's and Lu's sociological reports and Mao's political essay provide social mappings of their contemporary Chinese societies. In comparison, Zhou's and Lu's reports are more descriptive, perhaps even prescriptive, whereas Mao's essays are more political—even friends and enemies are political concepts—and more analytical. Zhou's and Lu's descriptions are based on social stratum (*jieceng* 階層) whereas Mao's analysis focuses on social class (*jieji* 階級). In fact, the stratum and the class refer to different ways of understanding and interpreting social structure and organization. The discourse of stratum regards social struc-ture and hierarchy as independent, nonrelational, and non-antagonistic. This social theory diverges from the Marxist view of class. For Marx, class is defined by production rather than consumption and by one's structural position in relation to capital. (However, it does not necessarily mean that Marxist critics do not provide a critique of consumer society.) According to Marxism, class is relational and, in times of crisis, antagonistic; hence, class struggle.

Similar to his Western Marxist counterparts, Mao considers culture as fun-damentally constitutive of the production and reproduction of class sub-jectivity. Through cultural revolutions and ideological reforms, proletarian consciousness can help construct the proletariat subject. This is the role of culture and ideology in the Great Proletarian Cultural Revolution (1966–1976). Inspired by this utopian or, some may say, idealist thinking, I note that culture can have the potential to help construct and interpellate the Chinese middle-class and new petty-bourgeois subject. The middle-class or new petty-bourgeois culture can attempt to summon the middle-class and new petty-bourgeois identity as much as the other way around.

Let me provide an example to illustrate how middle-class and new petty-bourgeois culture can attempt to construct middle-class and new petty-bourgeois subjectivity. According to a popular saying in the 1980s, the two Dengs ruled China: "In the morning, Deng Xiaoping (鄧小平) rules; in the evening, Teresa Teng (Deng Lijun 鄧麗君) rules." A singer from Taiwan, Teng is famous for her sweet, feminine singing. During the economic reforms period, Chinese people were given opportunity to listen to Teng's songs, such as "The Moon Represents My Heart" (*Yueliang daibiao wodexin* 月亮代表我的心), "As Sweet as Honey" (*Tianmimi* 甜蜜蜜), and "When Will You Return?" (*Heri junzailai* 何日君再來).[7] These songs were a stark contrast to the revolutionary songs, such as "We Are the Successors of Communism" (*Women shi gongchan zhuyi de jiebanren* 我們是共產主義的接班人), "We the Workers Have Power" (*Zamen gongren you liliang* 咱們工人有力量), and "Glory to the Red Sun" (*Hong taiyang song* 紅太陽頌), that Chinese people listened to during the Cultural Revolution. Indeed, what is attractive about Teng's music is that she conveyed such personal feelings as love, nostalgia, sadness, sorrow, and other sentiments that had been either repressed or sublimated during the revolutionary era. Moving beyond the motifs of continuous class struggle, national liberation, and socialist revolution, such "decadent music" (*mimi zhiyin* 靡靡之音) taught the new Chinese generation how to express themselves in a more individualized manner. It emphasized the "I" rather than the "we."[8] In retrospect, in the 1980s this kind of popular music helped constitute the cultural foundation for the Chinese middle-class and new petty-bourgeois subjects to emerge in the 1990s and 2000s. It helped build the milieu for the soft landing of the Chinese middle class and new petty bourgeoisie in the coming decades.

I suggest that the middle-class culture has the potential to anticipate and expect the middle-class subject in the context of postsocialist and neoliberal China. In fact, this view has been briefly mentioned by cultural critic Dai Jinhua (戴錦華). In the beginning of her essay "Invisible Writing: The Politics of Mass Culture in the 1990s" in the edited book *Cinema and Desire* (2002), she draws the reader's attention to the changing connotations of the Chinese words *guangchang* (廣場) from the socialist to postsocialist eras. In the socialist context, the *guangchang* referred to a venue where political events were held. For instance, the Tiananmen Guangchang (Tiananmen

Square) is the place where the ceremony celebrating the founding of the PRC took place on October 1, 1949. It is also the place where Mao, during the Cultural Revolution, greeted the Red Guards. Nevertheless, since the 1990s the referent of *guangchang* has been coopted by commercial forces and is used to denote shopping malls or other spaces of consumption. Dai uses the *guangchang* anecdote to explain how the commercial cultures depoliticize the socialist revolutions, downplay class relations and hierarchies, and begin to signify middle-class ideas. Adding to Dai's observation, I suggest that the signifier of the petty bourgeoisie has undergone a similar metamorphosis. The old petty bourgeoisie, understood in terms of production, is subjected to politicization (e.g., Chinese revolutions) from the 1930s to 1960s. However, the new petty bourgeoise is subjected to depoliticization (e.g., consumer culture) at the turn of the millennium. Dai continues: "What the cultural discourse of the nineties calls for is the creation of a Chinese middle class . . . popular culture and the mass media in the nineties (at least, from 1993 through 1995) defined marketing targets in terms of allegedly middle-class taste and consumption levels. It is a matter of cultural imagination rather than actual needs . . . the Chinese media is attempting to sustain a middle-class community."[9]

According to Dai, the Chinese and foreign media attempt to nurture and construct the Chinese middle class. The example that she uses to illustrate her observation is the Chinese edition of French fashion magazine *Elle*. She explains how the Chinese and foreign middle-class consumer cultures repress or overshadow the unequal distribution of wealth, bureaucratic corruption, and the gap between rich and poor.[10]

Similarly, in the Chinese-language chapter "An Anonymous Leader: The Cultural Meaning of *Fashion* Magazine" (匿名的引导者—《时尚》杂志的文化意味) (2000), cultural critic Mei Yuanmei (梅園粿) mentions how consumption-oriented fashion magazines in the 1990s attempted to call into being the new middle class.[11] She writes:

> Luxurious lifestyle magazines like *Fashion* are infused with consumerist flavor. Through refined pictures and brief descriptions, they construct a consumption-oriented mindset and lifestyle. When consumerism is being developed in China, when global capital enters the country, and when the middle class is being constructed, luxurious lifestyle magazines play an important role. They simultaneously reflect and participate in these processes.[12]

Mei suggests that the middle-class magazines such as *Fashion* (*Shishang* 時尚) and *Elle* (*Shijie shizhuang zhiyuan* 世界時裝之苑) are trying to call into being and construct as well as to reflect the new Chinese middle class. Indeed, these fashion and lifestyle magazines are ahead of their time. Targeting the emerging Chinese middle class, they display to them how lives can be lived; they also encourage them to imagine what their futures can potentially be like.[13] Indeed, both Dai's and Mei's views confirm my argument concerning how the Chinese middle-class culture attempts to conjure and anticipate the new Chinese middle-class subject.[14] The cultural imaginary comes first and then the social group comes afterward; they are dialectically related. However, what is missing in Dai's and Mei's cultural criticism is a theoretical engagement with how culture helps to constitute this new social actor. I fill this conceptual lacuna in chapter 4, in which I analyze Li Ke's (李可) workplace novel *Chronicle of Du Lala's Promotion* (*Du Lala shengzhi ji* 杜拉拉升職記) (2007) and Xu Jinglei's film *Go! Lala Go!* (*Du Lala shengzhi ji* 杜拉拉升職記) (2010). The latter is a filmic adaptation of Li's popular novel.

In his book *Distinction: A Social Critique of the Judgement of Taste* (1984), French sociological theorist Pierre Bourdieu argues that culture is not a domain of objectivity, impartiality, and what Immanuel Kant calls "disinterestedness." Rather, it is a crucial site where social hierarchies and class ideologies are actively constructed, perpetuated, and maintained. In addition, Bourdieu discusses how family and education are two key institutions where unequal social relations are reproduced and sustained. According to Bourdieu, culture can be conceptualized as capital—hence, cultural capital. Furthermore, different forms of capital, such as economic capital, social capital, and cultural and symbolic capital, can be converted and reinforce each other. For example, upper-class and middle-class parents have the resources to endow their children with cultural and linguistic competency, which ultimately enable their children to perform well in school. If their children are successful in school, that is, if their children own more cultural capital, they are more likely to have higher-paying jobs when they enter the workforce. Lower-class parents may not be able to do this, and their children may not be able to secure better jobs. Economic capital can be converted to cultural capital, which can be converted back to economic capital.

Whereas Bourdieu focuses on the private and familial aspect of the formation of the French middle class, I emphasize the public dimension of the making of the Chinese middle class. Extending Bourdieu's analysis to postsocialist and neoliberal China, I think the family is not a primary domain where the Chinese middle-class subject is (re-)produced and nurtured. Rather, it is through higher education, such as university and college (most of which are public) that the middle-class taste and sensibility are fostered and cultivated. More importantly, in the PRC, it is through consumption, particularly the consumption of (Westernized) popular and media cultures, that the middle-class subjectivities are produced and the middle-class values are transmitted. In fact, numerous examples from contemporary China's popular fiction, entertainment films, and television dramas can illustrate my argument. Concerning popular fiction, one can think of workplace novels, such as *Chronicle of Du Lala's Promotion* (2007) and *Floating and Sinking* (*Fuchen* 浮沉) (2008). Regarding entertainment films, one can refer to *Go! Lala Go!* (2010), *Love Is Not Blind* (*Shilian 33 tian* 失戀 33 天) (2011), and *Tiny Times* (*Xiaoshidai* 小時代) (2013). Considering television dramas, one can turn to *Struggle* (*Fendou* 奮鬥) (2008); *Ode to Joy* (*Huanlesong* 歡樂頌) (2016), and *The First Half of My Life* (*Wode qianbansheng* 我的前半生) (2017). And the list goes on. Indeed, these (Westernized) popular and media productions resemble self-help books. They teach the Chinese readers and viewers to recognize the symbols of the middle class, acculturate them to look at the world through a middle-class perspective, and instruct them to act and perform in a distinctively middle-class manner. These popular and media cultures also educate them to distinguish themselves from the other social groups, such as the nouveau riche (*baofahu* 暴發戶/*tuhao* 土豪) who have economic capital but not cultural capital. Meanwhile, the middle class is supposed to have sufficient economic and cultural capitals.

THE MIDDLE CLASS AS THE NEW PETTY BOURGEOISIE

There is a political-economic, objective, and materialist dimension of the Chinese middle class, or what Marxist critics call the new petty bourgeoisie. The latter refers to the white-collar and professional-managerial class. This new petty bourgeoisie is structurally dependent on the party-state as well as on the transnational and national capitals. Rejecting the idea that the new petty bourgeoisie is an independent, autonomous, and self-determining class, I suggest that this class fraction is actively tempered and sustained by the state and the capitals. Discussion among three former student participants of the 1989 Tiananmen Square movement illustrates the political economy of the formation of this new petty bourgeoisie in China. In March 1999 Wang Dan (王丹), Li Minqi (李民騏), and Wang Chaohua (王超華) spoke in a forum called "A Dialogue on the Future of China" and shared their views about the economic, political, social, and cultural transformations of postsocialist China.[15] The forum's moderator, Leo Ou-fan Lee (李歐梵), asked them whether it is "realistic to pin most hopes for the future of democracy in China on an emerging middle class." Although my work does not directly or explicitly deal with democracy and freedom, these former students' responses to this question reveal China's social structure.

In the beginning, Wang Dan identifies the Chinese middle class as what I call the "bureaucratic bourgeoisie." He says: "[Social scientist] He Qinglian [何清漣] has shown the way state properties were divided up by these people. They secretly acquired assets through their power, then cut their official connections, took off their red hats and changed the property into their own private firms."[16] Wang Dan reasons that these bureaucrats' economic and material interests inform their political positions. He thinks this group of people is highly invested in maintaining the existing social order and will not move in any democratic directions. Li Minqi agrees with Wang Dan's claim that the bureaucratic bourgeoisie will not provide any contribution to the democratic movement in China. However, he is hesitant to accept Wang Dan's definition of the middle class. Li Minqi inquires whether this concept should be used to refer to the private capitalistic class, or the professionals and intellectuals, within the Chinese context.[17] Concurring with Wang Dan's definition, Wang Chaohua also identifies the Chinese middle class as the bureaucratic capitalists who have converted public property to private wealth. She highlights the distinction between, on the one hand, the bourgeoisie whose members own capital or have direct control of the means of production and, on the other hand, the professionals and intellectuals who perform mental labor. She points out that "the historic bourgeoisie of early modern Europe is not the same kind of force as the middle-income class in America today, buying cars and houses."[18]

If the bureaucratic bourgeoisie's material interests prevent them from genuinely embracing democracy, the private capitalistic class is also unlikely to be a devoted supporter of liberal democracy. Li Minqi perceptively underlines the contradictory character of the private capitalistic class's relation to the bureaucratic capitalistic class. On the one hand, the private capitalistic class opposes the bureaucratic capitalistic class and seeks to share in political power. On the other hand, the private capitalistic class is hesitant to oppose the bureaucratic capitalistic class because it needs the existing political dictatorship to exploit labor, create surplus value, and generate profits in the processes of production and exchange.[19] In response, Wang Chaohua emphasizes that the local private entrepreneurs' ideology has not been fully constituted yet.[20] However, Li Minqi replies by saying that even if the private capitalistic class had a coherent set of ideologies and was transformed from a class-in-itself to a class-for-itself, it was still implausible for members of this class to lead the democratic movement. He explains: "Historically, it has not been unusual for clearly defined private property to coexist with political dictatorship, so even a very moderate hope for a progressive middle class in China might prove unrealistic."[21] Indeed, there is no causal and direct relationship among capitalism, the private bourgeoisie, and democracy. It is possible for capitalism and the private bourgeoisie to coexist with political dictatorship.

To be sure, Wang Dan, Li Minqi, and Wang Chaohua maintain conflicting standpoints regarding the democratic potential of the Chinese middle class. The liberal-minded Wang Dan believes in free markets and thinks the bureaucratic bourgeoisie does not have any significant democratic potential. The new left and critical intellectual Li Minqi points out the limitation of the free market ideology and adds that the private bourgeoisie cannot be the primary agent of the democratic movement either. Wang Chaohua brings up the professional-managerial class, or the middle class, who performs mental labor rather than manual labor. This is a more accurate understanding of the middle class I have in mind. However, she does not express her view concerning the democratic potential of this Chinese middle class. To what extent can their divergent viewpoints be reconciled? I propose the following model: There are two major contending classes—the bourgeoisie (the capitalists) and the proletariat—that exist in relational, hierarchal, and antagonistic relation with each other. Their confrontation can be revealed in times of crisis. The bourgeoisie can be subdivided into the bureaucratic and private bourgeoisies. The private bourgeoisie can be further segmented into the transnational and national bourgeoisies. The petty bourgeoisie, which is not a class on its own but a fraction of a class, is structurally dependent on the private bourgeoisie, including the transnational and national bourgeoisies, and on the bureaucratic bourgeoisie. There are two kinds of petty bourgeoisie in post-socialist China—namely, the old and new petty bourgeoisies. The old petty bourgeoisie refers to small business owners (*getihu*). The new petty bourgeoisie refers to the white-collar and professional-managerial class. The *getihu*, and the white-collar and professional-managerial class, co-emerged at more or less the same time, with the *getihu* appearing in the 1980s and the white-collar and professional-managerial class appearing in the 1990s and 2000s. The middle-income class that Wang Chaohua brings up denotes the white-collar and professional-managerial class.

Let's focus on the bourgeoisie first. The bureaucratic bourgeoisie refers to the governmental officials who have political power in the party-state. It is said that they have converted the collectively owned (*gongyou* 公有) properties to state-owned (*guoyou* 國有) assets and to private (*siyou* 私有) possessions. Therefore, Wang Dan is correct to feel pessimistic. This class will not decentralize its economic and political power to the people. It does not have democratic potentials. Meanwhile, the private bourgeoisie—comprising the transnational and national bourgeoisies—is not part of the ruling class and does not have political power. This class makes money by exploiting labor. To do this, it needs the support of the bureaucratic bourgeoisie. Therefore, Li Minqi is correct to reason that the private bourgeoisie, similarly, is unlikely to support democracy.

Concerning the petty bourgeoisie, the old petty bourgeoisie has some control over the means of production. In some cases it relies on family labor; in other cases it hires a few laborers to help out due to the small size of its business. Indeed, the figure of shopkeeper personifies the old petty bourgeoisie. In the 1980s, the figure of *getihu*, which refers to small business owners, emerged onto the social scene. In fact, contemporary Chinese films, such as Zhang Liang's (張良) *Yamaha Fish Stall* (*Yamaha yudang* 雅馬哈魚檔) (1984), Xu Tongjun's (許同均) *Zhenzhen's Hair Salon* (*Zhenzhen de fawu* 珍珍的髮屋) (1987), Wang Binglin's (王秉林) *Erzi Has a Little Hotel* (*Erzi kaidian* 二子開店) (1987), Chen Peisi (陳佩斯) and Ding Xuan's (丁喧) *Father and Son Open a Bar* (*Yeliang kaigeting* 爺倆開歌廳) (1992), Zhang

Liang's (張良) *A Woman's Street* (*Nürenjie* 女人街), Huo Jianqi's (霍建起) *Life Show* (*Shenghuoxiu* 生活秀) (2002), and Feng Gong's (馮鞏) *Eat Hot Tofu Slowly* (*Xinji chibuliao redoufu* 心急吃不了熱豆腐) (2005), gave visual expressions to the lived experience of the small business owners.[22] While some small business owners made a fortune and became bigger business owners (*wanyuanhu* 萬元戶) or even nouveau riche (*baofafu* 暴發戶), a strange phenomenon called "the reversal of brain and body" (*naoti daogua* 腦體倒掛) occurred in 1980s and 1990s China. This phrase connotes the fact that with the same input of labor power, what one can earn through manual labor exceeds what one can earn through mental labor. Interestingly, a popular saying at that time is as follows: "Repairing the brain [i.e., being a brain surgeon] is not as good as shaving the head [i.e., being a barber]" (*xiu danaode buru titoude* 修大腦的不如剃頭的), "holding a medical scalpel is not as good as holding a shaving blade" (*na shoushudaode buru na titoudaode* 拿手術刀的不如拿剃頭刀的), and "doing research on nuclear bombs is not as good as selling tea-leaves eggs" (*gao daodande buru mai chayedande* 搞導彈的不如賣茶葉蛋的). This popular saying testified to the widespread "leaving the socialist work-unit and entering the business world" (*xiahai* 下海) sentiment in 1980s and 1990s China. Then what is the relationship between the old petty bourgeoisie and the (big) bourgeoisie? Understandably, the old petty bourgeoisie would like to climb up the social ladder and become the (national) bourgeoisie. The old petty bourgeoisie is interested in expanding its business and obtaining more control of capital and means of production. It is possible that individual members of the old petty bourgeoisie may rise to become the private bourgeoisie. Nevertheless, due to the demand of scientific knowledge and technological skills in the global financial economy, it is unlikely for the old petty bourgeoisie to become the reserve army of the (big) bourgeoisie. The old petty bourgeoisie cannot become the dominant subject of Chinese history in the context of global capitalism. Critical of the monopoly of the transnational and national bourgeoisies, the old petty bourgeoisie may demand the party-state to intervene in the market so that small- and medium-sized enterprises can survive amid fierce competitions with big enterprises.

During their conversation, Wang Chaohua brings up "the American middle-income class who buy cars and houses." By this she refers to the white-collar, professional-managerial class or, in short, the middle class. Unlike the bourgeoisie, the new petty bourgeoisie does not own capital or have direct control over the means of production. The new petty bourgeoisie is part of the salaried class. It sells its labor power in the market in exchange for wages. In this sense, the new petty bourgeoisie is similar to the working class. In fact, it is the working class. However, unlike the industrialized working class, the new petty bourgeoisie does not perform manual and physical labor but mental and intellectual labor. In the context of postsocialist and neoliberal China, the new petty bourgeoisie encompasses the white-collar and professional-managerial class. This social actor boldly entered the social scene in the 1990s. After Deng Xiaoping, in 1992, had traveled to southern China to give his neoliberal blessings to the country, the new petty bourgeoisie rapidly expanded. After the PRC had become an official member of the World Trade Organization (WTO) in 2001, the new petty bourgeoisie promptly flourished.[23]

Then, what is the relationship between the new petty bourgeoisie and the (big) bourgeoisie? Indeed, the new petty bourgeoisie is not a stable, self-determining, and autonomous class but a class fraction whose existence is structurally dependent on the bureaucratic bourgeoisie and private bourgeoisie (including the transnational and national bourgeoisies). This explains why the new petty bourgeoisie is a weak and unstable social formation. If the party-state makes any drastic changes to the country's economic, political, and social policies, such as inflating the prices of residential real estate or changing the exchange rates of the currencies, the new petty bourgeoisie will noticeably reduce in size. If transnational capital withdraws from China, the new petty bourgeoisie is also going to shrink considerably. (Indeed, this was already the case for the Japanese middle class since Japan's economic recession beginning from 1991. The sociological theorization of the downward sliding society [*xialiu shehui* 下流社會] and M-shape society in the Japanese academy already testifies to this fact.) In short, the new petty bourgeoisie realizes its historicity in times of crisis.

In her book *Fast Cars, Clean Bodies: Decolonization and the Reordering of French Culture* (1995), cultural critic Kristin Ross argues that the new French professional-managerial class can be interpreted as an allegory of the class-specific, racial, and national politics of post–World War II France. On the class level, the professional-managerial class, or the *jeune cadre* in Jacques Tati's films, has a limited extent of power. This class fraction manages labor while also being an employee. On the racial and national levels, the new professional-managerial class symbolizes the changing geopolitical configurations that confronted France. While dominating Algeria, France was dominated by the United States. Although Ross primarily deals with the French *jeune cadre*, her argument can creatively be deployed to describe how the Chinese new petty bourgeoisie reveals tensions within and without China. To be sure, the Chinese new petty bourgeoisie manages labor and enjoys some of the privileges of the boss while still being an employee punching a time clock. Both dominating and dominated, a technician and victim of the process of capital accumulation, its position is laden with tensions. Indeed, the Chinese new petty bourgeoisie can also be interpreted as representing China's changing class hierarchy and political economy. Its role as a dominated agent of capitalistic domination mirrors the class and national situations of postsocialist and neoliberal China. From the class perspective, the Chinese new petty bourgeoisie resembles a comprador class in the sense that it helps the bureaucratic and private bourgeoisies to exploit the working class for profit. From the national perspective, China is beginning to compete with the United States and Europe for natural resources in Africa (e.g., China has been competing for oil in Sudan, Algeria, Angola, and Nigeria during the past decades.) Exploiting the working class in its own country and the developing world and entering in close collaboration with the most advanced and wealthy nations in the context of global capitalism, the contradiction of China's modernization and globalization can be located in the mediating role of the Chinese new petty bourgeoisie.

However, the structural dependency of the Chinese new petty bourgeoisie as a symbol of China is only one part of the contradiction. The other side of the contradiction is that China is becoming more powerful. In terms of geopolitical economy, China is structurally dependent on the United States but at the same time is gaining power over the United States. In his essay "China's Rise in Global Economy" (2009), political economist Raymond Lotta writes:

> The dynamics of China's rise is complex and contradictory, characterized by both dependency and growing economic strength. China is dependent on foreign capital and foreign markets. But China has also emerged as world economic power, a center of world manufacturing. It has accumulated vast foreign reserves, and gained considerable financial leverage—increasingly

over the dollar. It is more aggressively seeking markets in the third world and exporting capital beyond its borders. Stepping back, what seems to be guiding the Chinese ruling class is a long-term, strategic, and competitive orientation to diversify and fortify a domestically rotted industrial base, to extend the country's international economic and financial reach, and to strengthen military capabilities but to do so without provoking direct show-downs with US imperialism.[24]

While Lotta presents a compelling political-economic analysis of U.S.-China transnationalism, a cultural studies response to this contradiction is needed.

THE PETTY-BOURGEOIS CULTURE

There is a cultural, subjective, and ideological dimension of the Chinese new petty bourgeoisie. This can be observed in contemporary Chinese literary critic Li Tuo's (李陀) preface (2010) to the reprint of Bei Dao's (北島) novel *Waves* (*Bo dong* 波動) (1981, 2010). In this preface, Li Tuo makes three points concerning the new petty bourgeoisie, or what he calls the "*xin xiaozi*" (新小資), in China.[25] First, the recent emergence of the Chinese middle class (*zhongchan jieji* 中產階級) or middle stratum (*zhongjian jieceng* 中間階層) should be evaluated as part of the historical genealogy of the Chinese petty bourgeoisie. Second, the new petty bourgeoisie, as opposed to the old petty bourgeoisie, has already secured cultural hegemony in twenty-first-century China. Third, the new petty bourgeoisie is uninterested in such metanar-ratives as revolution and politics; instead, they have turned serious mean-ings into disposable commodities for a cheap laugh (*gaoxiao* 搞笑).[26] Li Tuo's preface has inspired intellectual conversations within the Chinese academy. While some commentators discuss the differences between the old and new petty bourgeoisies, other critics debate whether the new petty-bourgeois sensibility has genuinely become the hegemonic force in 2000s China. Engaging with Li Tuo and his interlocutors, I emphasize the fate of the new petty bourgeoisie. In the second decade of the twenty-first cen-tury, the new petty bourgeoisie has devolved to become what Chinese slang calls the 屌絲 (*diaosi*), which literally refers to pubic hair around a penis. The *diaosi* connotes losers who are economically impoverished. In contrast with the Chinese middle class that owns apartments and cars (*youfang youche* 有房有車), the *diaosi* have achieved almost nothing in their lives. They have mediocre jobs and have no apartments or cars.

In the preface, Li Tuo examines the old petty bourgeoisie and its sensibility in the context of socialist and revolutionary China. (According to my observation, Li Tuo's old petty bourgeoisie is different from the old petty bourgeoisie I mentioned earlier in this introduction. His old petty bourgeoisie refers to the intellectual, rather than the shopkeeper or owner of a small business.) In the preface's fourth part, Li Tuo focuses on the literary representation of Xiaoling (肖凌) as a member of the old petty bourgeoisie during the Cultural Revolution. According to Li Tuo, Xiaoling consumes and indulges in Western culture, such as *Moonlight Sonata*, Federico Garcia Lorca's poetry, white dress, and red tea and wine. Moreover, she is filled with nihilism. In the preface's fifth part Li Tuo turns to the new petty bourgeoisie in the context of postsocialist and neoliberal China. According to him, the recent emergence of the Chinese middle class or middle stratum should be evaluated as part of the historical genealogy of the Chinese petty bourgeoisie.

> The Western society generally agrees that after WWII, the "new middle class" is constituted by the salaried class. Meanwhile, in China, there is a consensus that the middle class should have an apartment and a car; and those who have an apartment and a car also belong to the salaried class. Thus, why can't we consider the middle class as the petty bourgeoisie in contemporary China? According to the theories of social class, the petty bourgeoisie refers to the shopkeepers, merchants, or peasants. While the new middle class in the West has already come into being, and while the new middle class in China has just been produced, shouldn't we revisit the concept of the petty bourgeoisie? Can't we regard the urbanized middle class as a newly formed petty bourgeoisie? Can't we consider the middle-class society as the petty-bourgeois society within the context of globalization?[27]

Second, Li Tuo suggests that this new petty bourgeoisie has already secured cultural hegemony in early twenty-first-century China.

> China's "economic reforms" produce not only a group of millionaires, rich businessmen, and rich bureaucrats, but also a group of petty-bourgeois elites. The latter occupies leading positions in the cultural sphere. These include editors of magazines and newspapers, producers of commercial films and

popular music, producers of advertisements and online videos, people in charge of internet webpages, cultural entrepreneurs and industry planners and executors, writers of new media, as well as teachers and scholars in schools, colleges, and educational institutions. In short, the petty bourgeoisie has already secured all the important positions in the cultural domain. This leads to a very unique situation. On the one hand, the state and capitals are very powerful; they try to lead cultural production in contemporary Chinese society. Through policy adjustment and capital investment, they try to change the direction of culture. But on the other hand, since cultural production is controlled or managed by the petty bourgeoisie, cultural hegemony is ultimately located in the hands of the petty bourgeoisie.[28]

Third, Li Tuo compares the old petty bourgeoisie with the new petty bourgeoisie, which emerged in China in the 1990s and onward. According to him, the old petty bourgeoisie, such as Xiaoling, is idealistic; she is serious about seeking meanings. Her nihilism is a result of her inability to locate meanings in life. In contrast, the new petty bourgeoisie is indifferent to such metanarratives as revolution and politics. To them, these serious meanings can be turned into products of consumption. These commodities are only intended for a cheap laugh. "The new petty bourgeoisie has an obvious characteristic, which is to turn meanings into games, taste, consumption. For the new petty bourgeoisie, these meanings are for a cheap laugh. These meanings have become deteriorated and devalued. They are just intended for entertainment."[29] Li Tuo suggests that the way in which the new petty bourgeoisie has destabilized and deconstructed meanings coincides with the logic of global capitalism in China. To illustrate the complicity between this class fraction and capital, he gives three examples. The first example concerns internet gaming. The new petty bourgeoisie turns such subject matters as love and war into signs, games, and fun. The second example deals with the production, circulation, and consumption of gossip through cell phones, computers, and the internet. The third example has to do with the culture of lies (*Dahua wenhua* 大話文化) in the 1990s and the recent popularity of "little freshness" (*xiao qingxin* 小清新). According to Li Tuo, the new petty-bourgeois culture is meaninglessness; it is just for fun. He concludes:

We can use "for a cheap laugh" (*gaoxiao*) to describe and generalize the characteristic of this new culture. We can even say that this attitude has become the essential quality of this culture. In contrast, Xiaoling's nihilism looks absolutely absurd and ridiculous to them. Why are you so serious? Stupid![30]

Li Tuo's preface has inspired intellectual discussions concerning the Chinese petty bourgeoisie in the Chinese academy. The Chinese-language journal *Southern Literary Forum* (*Nanfang Wentan* 南方文壇) devoted part of its first issue of 2013 to the topic "The New Petty Bourgeoisie and Cultural Hegemony" (*xinxiaozi yu wenhua lingdaoquan* 新小資與文化領導權). For instance, cultural critic Mao Jian (毛尖) responds to Li Tuo's third point. She suggests that the petty-bourgeois culture is pretentious (*zhuang B* 裝 B) rather than funny. She mentions: "I do not think 'just for a cheap laugh' is the essence of the new petty bourgeoisie. I think it is more accurate to describe the logic of their cultural productions as being pretentious (*zhuang B*)."[31] In his article "The Age of the Petty Bourgeoisie Is Dead" (*Siqule de xiaozi shidai* 死去了的小資時代) (2013), cultural critic Yang Qingxiang (楊慶祥) responds to Li Tuo's third point by highlighting the difference between the old and new petty bourgeoisies. According to Yang, the old petty bourgeoisie, such as Xiaoling in Bei Dao's novel, has historical consciousness. The symbols of this old petty bourgeoisie, such as Western classical music or modern poetry, also have concrete historical referents. This old petty bourgeoisie has a political subjectivity. Even when it presents itself as being antipolitical (e.g., nihilism), it is still political. In contrast, Yang continues, the new petty bourgeoisie, such as the "beauty writers" in the new millennium, is ahistorical and depoliticized. The young writers such as Wei Hui (衛慧) and Anni Baobei (安妮寶貝) deliberately present the idea of baby in their literary works: while Wei Hui wrote her controversial novel *Shanghai Baby*, "baby" is part of the pen name of Anni Baobei (Baby). The symbols of this new petty bourgeoisie, such as their "baby-ness," are only intended for consumption. They do not signify any historical depth, political ambition, or revolutionary horizon. In my interpretation, this new petty-bourgeois culture exemplifies the postmodern condition of the loss of historicity (rather than the loss of history as such) in the context of global capitalism.

Adding to Yang's example, I bring the reader's attention to the new petty bourgeoisie's full-fledged assertion of middle-class taste through consumption in the late 1990s and 2000s.[32] In fact, the new petty bourgeoisie's favorite film directors and literary writers also include Hong Kong film director Wong Kar-wai (Wang Jiawei 王家衛) (b. 1958) and Chinese/Chinese American writer Eileen Chang (Zhang Ailing 張愛玲) (1920–1995). In fact, Wong's, Chang's, and Anni Baobei's works feature sensuous objects such as fashion and food, sentiment and the body, and the global city in Asia. For instance, Wong Kar-wai's beautiful film *In the Mood for Love* (*Huangyang nianhua* 花樣年華) (2001) centers on the Shanghai *qipao*, forbidden love between married couples, and colonial Hong Kong (and, indirectly, semicolonial Shanghai). Chang has written about fashion in "A Chronicle of Changing Clothes" (*Gengyiji* 更衣記) (1943). She has also expressed the sentiment of desolation (*beiliang* 悲涼) in wartime Shanghai and Hong Kong. Meanwhile, Anni Baobei, in her fiction, describes the taste of Häagen-Dazs ice cream, café latte, cappuccino, and tiramisu and the feeling of melancholy in globalizing Shanghai. These cultural commodities, bodies, and sentiments express the gendered and sexualized sentiments of the new petty bourgeoisie. From these works, one can also sense the connection between consumption and the loss of sense of history or memory in global capitalism.

In his essay, Yang also responds to Li Tuo's second point, which is that the new petty bourgeoisie has already secured cultural hegemony in China. Considering Li Tuo's claim too optimistic, Yang argues that the new petty bourgeoisie does not have the necessary economic capital or political power to control or change the established social and cultural order. Rather, this class fraction merely consumes; it can only passively follow or belatedly respond to the cultural productions that have already been prepared for them. Contrary to Li Tuo, Yang thinks the new petty bourgeoisie has limited cultural agency. In his essay "The Proletarianization of the New Petty Bourgeoisie and the Question of Cultural Hegemony" (*Xin xiaozide dicenghua yu wenhua lingdaoquan wenti* 新小資的"底層"化與文化領導權問題) (2013), cultural critic Li Yunlei (李雲雷) has made a similar remark. He argues that with the exception of its elite segment, the new petty bourgeoisie has very restricted cultural power. According to him, the consumerist ideas of owning an apartment and a car and of having a fashionable, refined, sophisticated, and individualistic lifestyle are not the ideology of the new petty bourgeoisie. Rather, these ideas are the culture of the economically wealthy, successful individuals (*chenggong renshi* 成功人士), including the private entrepreneurs and (big) bourgeoisie. Li Yunlei maintains that the new petty bourgeoisie has not yet constructed its own distinctive values and ways of life that can be shared by other classes or groups.

I agree with Yang and Li Yunlei. I add to their observations by quoting Walter Benjamin's comment regarding the petty bourgeoisie during his time. In a footnote in the second version of his famous essay "The Work of Art in the Age of Its Technological Reproducibility" (1937), Benjamin suggests that in Germany the petty bourgeoisie is a mass rather than a class. Also, the petty-bourgeois culture is reactive rather than affirmative. Governed by the logic of mass psychology, the petty-bourgeois culture is unmediated. In contrast, the proletariat is a class; its consciousness is affirmative and mediated. Benjamin writes:

> The petty bourgeoisie is not a class; it is in fact only a mass. And the greater the pressure acting on it between the two antagonistic classes of the bourgeoisie and the proletariat, the more compact it becomes. In *this* mass the emotional element described in mass psychology is indeed a determining factor. But for that very reason this compact mass forms the antithesis of the proletarian cadre, which obeys a collective *ratio*. In the petty-bourgeois mass, the reactive moment described in mass psychology is indeed a determining factor. But precisely for that reason this compact mass with its unmediated reactions forms the antithesis of the proletarian cadre, whose actions are mediated by a task, however momentarily. Demonstrations by the compact mass thus always have a panicked quality—whether they give vent to war fever, hatred of Jews, or the instinct for self-preservation.[33]

Inspired by Benjamin's remark, I suggest that the Chinese petty bourgeoisie is also a reactive mass, rather than a self-affirming class. Rather than asserting its values, it belatedly reacts to the culture of (big) bourgeoisie. This idea intersects with Li Yunlei's idea that the Chinese petty bourgeoisie does not have its own values yet.

In his book *Mythologies* (1972), Roland Barthes proposes that during the Cold War era, the French national identity is a "neither/nor" social formation. According to him, France was neither the United States nor the Soviet Union, neither capitalism nor communism, and neither individualism nor collectivism.[34] Barthes's idea can also be used to articulate the negative impulse in the construction of the Chinese petty bourgeoisie's subjectivity. The latter is neither the bourgeoisie nor the proletariat. Its subjectivity or identity is constituted through a process of disidentification rather than identification. It disidentifies from what it is not (e.g., the proletariat) in order to be or become what it is (i.e., the petty bourgeoisie).[35]

In addition, Li Yunlei examines Li Tuo's second point from two other perspectives—namely, class analysis and ideological critique. Concerning class analysis, Li Yunlei perceptively points out the objective fact that most of the new petty bourgeoisie is becoming economically proletarianized in China today. Similar to the so-called ant tribes (*yizu* 蟻族) and laboring bees (*gongfeng* 工蜂), many of them have slid to the bottom of the society and are struggling to make a living. Their lives are unstable, insecure, and precarious. In this sense, the new petty bourgeoisie has not secured any hegemony in China. Adding to Li Yunlei's analysis, the social discussion regarding "dwelling narrowness" (*woju* 蝸居), inspired by the Chinese TV drama with the same title in 2009, also testifies to the fact that the new petty bourgeoisie is becoming proletarianized. Contemporary Chinese society can be a downward sliding society (*xialiu shehui* 下流社會). In fact, many university-educated and hardworking individuals cannot afford to buy an apartment. Li Yunlei adds that the proletarianized new petty bourgeoisie should realize that its economic position is not very different from that of the working class. The new petty bourgeoisie can discover its commonality with the working class and learn from their culture. Furthermore, Li Yunlei provides an ideological critique of the new petty bourgeoisie. Due to the new petty bourgeoisie's structural dependence on the party-state and capitals, it is extremely difficult for this class fraction to achieve success simply through aspirational dreams, personal struggle, and hard work. He also provides a critique of their ideals of humanism, humanitarianism, and love. However, according to Li Yunlei, because the new petty bourgeoisie can turn elite cultures into commodities and signs of consumption, it can be a useful intermediary for the elite and mass/popular cultures. Although this class fraction does not actively produce culture, it can communicate and transmit cultural symbols.

裝 (ZHUANG)

Given the advantages and disadvantages of using the terms "middle-class cultures" and "new petty-bourgeois cultures/sensibilities" to name my object of study, I use the concept of 裝 (*zhuang*) to explore the complexly mediated relationships between cultural productions and social class. By working with and thinking through 裝, one can better grasp the desire, fantasy, and imagination of the Chinese middle class and new petty bourgeoisie. One can appreciate their sentiment, sensibility, and disposition.

Indeed, 裝 has multiple meanings. First of all, 裝 refers to fashion, clothes, garment, fabric, and textile. 裝 can be combined with the word 服 (*fu*) to indicate clothes (*fuzhuang* 服裝) and with the word 時 (*shi*), meaning time, to refer to fashion (*shizhuang* 時裝). During the socialist period, Chinese people wore the Mao suit (*zhongshanzhuang* 中山裝). During the Cultural Revolution, the most popular piece of clothing was the military uniform (*junzhuang* 軍裝). In 1961 Mao Zedong wrote a poem titled "To the Female Soldiers" (*Wei nüminbing tizhao* 為女民兵題照) to glorify the female military soldiers. According to him, they do not like the red dress but prefer the military uniform (*bu'ai hongzhuang ai wuzhuang* 不愛紅裝愛武裝).[36] During the economic reforms period, Chinese people were encouraged to wear different kinds of clothing. Men wore men's clothing (*nanzhuang* 男裝), women wore women's clothing (*nüzhuang* 女裝), and children wore children's clothing (*tongzhuang* 童裝). New clothes were called 新裝 (*xinzhuang*). A one-piece suit was called a 套裝 (*taozhuang*). Formal and elaborate clothing were called 盛裝 (*shengzhuang*). And the list goes on.

In this book, I examine the representations of a wide variety of 裝 in contemporary Chinese films. Concerning the 1960s, I examine Xie Tieli's film *Never Forget* (1964). I focus on proletarian factory worker Ding Shaochun's (丁少純) desire for a high-quality suit (*liaozifu* 料子服). To make money to purchase this suit, Ding shoots wild birds in his spare time. Because his leisure activity has badly interfered with his work performance, Ding has allegedly forgotten about class struggle and socialist revolution. His father needs to teach him about the importance of "never forget class struggle" even within the socialist context. Regarding the 1980s, I turn to Huang Zumo's film *Romance on Lu Mountain* (1980). I attend to Chinese American character Zhou Yun (周筠) and her appearance in more than forty fashionable outfits during her travels to Lu Mountain. Her fashion presentations are visually attractive, appealing, and provocative. They anticipate the success of China's socialist modernizations. Seen in this way, China's economic reforms and opening up resemble a fashion show. Moving to the 2000s, I discuss Xu Jinglei's film *Go! Lala Go!* (2010). In this fashion film, white-collar worker Du Lala (杜拉拉) and the other ladies in the office appear in more than one hundred fashionable outfits in the course of the narrative. The office of DB, a top American company in China, has been turned into a catwalk. Switching gears from the middle class to the working class, I note that the Chinese migrant factory workers also desire the fashion commodities that they themselves produce. In Ho Chao-ti's documentary film *My Fancy High Heels* (2010), teenage girl Little Boo (Xiao Budian 小不點) desires the expensive high heels that she makes while working in a shoe factory in Guangdong, China. In *Iron Moon* (2015), a documentary film directed by Qin Xiaoyu and Wu Feiyue, female migrant worker Wu Xia (鄔霞) fantasizes about the sundresses (*diaodaiqun* 吊帶裙) that she helps to produce. I inquire what the high-quality suit, high heels, sundresses, and other fashion commodities reveal about history, class formation, social structure, and political economy.

Second, 裝 is concerned with making, fashioning, composing, constructing, forming, and producing. This is evident in such words as *zhuangzai* (裝載), which means to pack, load, and carry; *zhuangxie* (裝卸), which means to load and unload; *zhuangzhi* (裝置), which means installation; and *anzhuang* (安裝), which means to install. Taken together, they mean packing, installing, stuffing inside, carrying, and constituting the core. Importantly, 裝 as fashion and clothes can help construct the Chinese middle-class and new petty-bourgeois subjectivities. Also, 裝 has the connotation of improvement, development, advancement, and progress. This can be seen in such words as *baozhuang* (包裝), which means packaging; *zhuangshi* (裝飾), which means decoration, adornment, ornament; and *zhuangxiu* (裝修), which means renovation. 裝 exemplifies a desire for upward mobility and individual betterment. It is about fantasy and imagination.

In this book, I attend to how fashion helps constitute the Chinese middle-class and new petty-bourgeois subjectivities as well as their imaginaries. In the socialist film *Never Forget*, the factory worker Ding tries on a high-quality suit. Looking at himself in the mirror, he momentarily imagines that he resembles a state engineer or technician. Ding is not satisfied with simply being a proletarian worker; he desires to be someone whose occupational status is higher than his. This explains why he imitates the fashion of the socialist middle class and new petty bourgeoisie. In the 1980s the discourse of fashion and consumption has changed. Rather than being regarded as detrimental to class struggle and social revolution, as was the case during the most intense period of the Cultural Revolution in the mid- and late

1960s, fashion and consumption have become the living proof of the success of socialist modernization and development. In *Romance on Lu Mountain*, by showcasing Zhou in more than forty fashionable outfits, the film director imagines and envisions the achievements of China's economic reforms. Precisely because China's opening up is successful, Chinese people can enjoy a higher standard of living and dress in a more sophisticated manner. In the 2000s, fashion and consumption are connected to the formation of the Chinese middle class and new petty bourgeoisie. This is the case in *Go! Lala Go!*, marketed as the first fashion film in globalizing China. In this commercial film populated with product placement, the petty-bourgeois and later middle-class Du is dedicated to her work in the American company in China. She also appears in numerous brand-name fashionable outfits. By doing so, she fantasizes about belonging to the Chinese and cosmopolitan middle classes. Meanwhile, the Chinese migrant factory workers also desire the fashion commodities, such as high heels and sundresses. These objects enable them to dream about a different "I" not burdened with poverty, hardship, and separation from family. In short, the culture of 裝 is productive. It molds the subject.

Third, 裝 can mean to pose, simulate, pretend, fake, feign, fabricate, mask, conceal, disguise, deceive, and lie. This can be observed in such words as 裝扮 (*zhuangban*), 裝作 (*zhuangzuo*), 假裝 (*jiazhuang*), 偽裝 (*weizhuang*), 裝模作樣 (*zhuangmo zuoyang*), and 裝腔作勢 (*zhuangqiang zuoshi*). 裝 is about faking and making up. It is about ideology in the sense of falsehood. (However, 裝 is also about desire and fantasy. 裝 can be interpreted as what critical and cultural theorist Fredric Jameson calls the dialectic of ideology and utopian impulse in mass culture.[37]) For this third meaning of 裝, my example comes from Jia Zhangke's documentary film *Useless* (2007), a transmedial dialogue with Chinese fashion designer Ma Ke. Ma's ready-to-wear fashion line is called Exception (Liwai 例外) (1996–); it is sold in boutiques and department stores in major Chinese cities, such as Guangzhou. Her fashion exhibit *Useless* (2007) is showcased in museums and art galleries in France and England. In her *Useless* fashion exhibit, Ma meditates on the handmade object, the industrialized mass-produced commodity, fashion as ready-to-wear, and fashion as art. To infuse her *Useless* fashion exhibit with emotion, memory, and history, Ma buries the clothes that she designed under earth for some time. When the garments are excavated, she thinks they will be imbued with the imprint of the time and space of their soil. However, the nature on her clothes is not natural but naturalized; it is fabricated and contrived. The way in which she tries to create story for her clothing object is fake. Her work can be slightly pretentious (装).

I note the slippage between the second meaning of 装 (making) and the third meaning of 装 (making up). It is easy for the making to become the making up, and vice versa. To be sure, Zhou in *Romance on Lu Mountain* and Du in *Go! Lala Go!* are modern and fashionable women; they resemble the petty bourgeoisie and the middle class, respectively. However, they can also be regarded as too modern, too fashionable, trying too hard, and therefore fake. In fact, unnatural or unrealistic representation is also a form of 装. As I have mentioned, Zhou appears in more than forty fashionable outfits in *Romance on Lu Mountain*. Oddly, she wears her high heels to climb up Lu Mountain. Equally strangely, at the bottom of the mountain, she appears in one outfit. In the middle of the mountain, she appears in another outfit. On the top of the mountain, she appears in a third outfit. There is something over the top and, indeed, 装 about her fashion presentations. In *Go! Lala Go!*, Du's fashion presentations are excessive and overdone. Miraculously, she can appear in one outfit in one room. When she enters another room, she can appear in another outfit. When she has a meeting in a third room, she can appear in a third outfit. This undercuts the realism of the film. These conspicuous displays reveal a nouveau riche mentality. This "trying too hard" behavior is 装.

This brings me to the argument that 装 also concerns storytelling, fictionalizing, narrativizing, and the process of making an artifice. In this book, I investigate the forms of fiction films (e.g., family melodrama and romantic comedy), documentary films, popular fiction, and fashion shows. For example, in her fashion exhibit *Useless*, Ma tells an interesting story about the handmade object, the industrialized mass-produced commodity (the fashion line Exception), and her fashion exhibit (*Useless*). Jia creates a documentary film *Useless* to dialogue with Ma concerning her antifashion and anticonsumption idea. Producing a documentary film that looks like a fiction film, Jia invites the viewer to reconsider the connection between real and fake. To Jia, this 装, understood as "fictional," "fake," and "false," is productive of thinking. Thinking with Ma and Jia and engaging with the theoretical genealogy of Western Marxism, I in turn produce cultural criticism, which is another kind of 装 because this book is also a narrative.

Fourth, 裝 is about labor. Many Chinese words associated with 裝 concern labor and work, including *baozhuang* (包裝), *zhuangshi* (裝飾), *zhuangxiu* (裝修), *zhuangzai* (裝載), *zhuangxie* (裝卸), *zhuangzhi* (裝置), and *anzhuang* (安裝). Indeed, labor and work are an important motif in this book. Several characters, such as the factory worker Ding in *Never Forget*, the migrant factory worker Little Boo in *My Fancy High Heels*, and the migrant factory worker Wu in *Iron Moon*, engage in manual and physical labor. Other characters take part in mental and intellectual work. These include intellectuals Zhou and her boyfriend Geng Hua (耿樺) in *Romance on Lu Mountain*, white-collar office worker Du in *Go! Lala Go!*, fashion designer Ma in *Useless*, and fashion designer Sena Yang in *My Fancy High Heels*. I also include the types of labor that are either invisible or not usually regarded as labor. These include falling in love and maintaining a relationship (which is a lot of work), studying, traveling, making art, shopping, and "accidentally" or "unintentionally" showing off the brand-name fashion logos to the people around oneself. In other words, the characters in this book are actively working and producing. They debate, document, and fabulate the many kinds of 裝 of contemporary China.

CHAPTER SUMMARIES

The first part of this book (chapter 1) stages a commodity chain of fashion involving production, consumption, and disposal. The second part (chapters 2–4) focuses on the representations of fashion and consumption in Chinese cinema in the 1960s (the socialist period), the 1980s (the economic reforms period), and the 2000s (the globalization period). The third part (chapters 5–6) turns to the undersides of consumption, particularly production and migrant labor as well as disposal and waste.

Chapter 1 presents an aspiring Chinese fashion designer Ma Ke and her fashion exhibit *Useless* (2007). Ma intends to draw attention to the loss of the emotional bond between the maker and the user of clothes in the age of industrialized mass production and consumption. To help fashion recover this lost memory, Ma buries her apparel under dirt for a period of time. When the garment is unearthed, she reasons, it will find itself imbued with the imprint of the time and space of its soil. Presented at Paris Fashion Week in February 2007, Ma's fashion exhibit *Useless* was intended to be a critique of consumer culture. My analysis then turns to Jia Zhangke's documentary film *Useless* (2007), a transmedial dialogue with Ma's fashion exhibit *Useless*. What characterizes the *Useless* documentary is its tripartite structure. Contrary to the second part of the documentary, which focuses on Ma's middle-class fashion, the first part features a group of laborers in a garment factory in China's Guangdong Province. These workers produce Ma's first fashion line, Exception. Linking consumption to production, the director emphasizes the fact that Ma's fashion is manufactured by the Chinese factory workers. The third part of the documentary turns to the working class in China's Shanxi Province. With the rise of the market economy, the local tailors cannot compete with factories and department stores. To make a living, some tailors have to work as coal miners; thus, their expertise is rendered useless. In this chapter, I argue that Jia's documentary engagement with Ma's fashion is double-edged: although he embraces some parts of *Useless*, he critiques other parts of her design. I demonstrate how the director brings a new level of visual complexity to the designer's anticonsumption gesture through the use of montage.

By using Jia's documentary *Useless* as an anchor (hence the title of my book), the following five chapters mimic the tripartite structure of the documentary: chapters 2–4, on consumption, resemble the second part of the film; chapter 5, on production and labor, the first part; and chapter 6, on waste, the third part. More specifically, chapters 2–4 attend to the stories about fashion and consumption in selected Chinese films. Considering these narratives as a socially symbolic act, I explore what Fredric Jameson calls the political unconscious of the text—namely, the unprecedented historical, social, and political-economic transformations of contemporary China.[38]

Focusing on the Maoist period, chapter 2 engages with Xie Tieli's film *Never Forget* (1964) to investigate the socialist politics of clothes, leisure, and consumption. Similar to the dress in Zhao Ming's (趙明) film *The Young Generation* (*Nianqing de yidai* 年青的一代) (1965) and the nylon socks in Wang Ping (王蘋) and Ge Xin's (葛鑫) film *Sentinels Under the Neon Lights* (*Nihong dengxia de shaobing* 霓虹燈下的哨兵) (1964), the high-quality suit in *Never Forget* is not represented negatively but ambivalently. Such a portrayal can be interpreted as a symptom of the profound contradictions that confront Chinese socialist modernity at the dawn of the Great Proletarian Cultural Revolution (1966–1976). The representational form condenses and allegorizes the tensions between production and consumption, between work and leisure, and between political revolution and economic construction. In addition, my analysis reconsiders the theoretical discussions concerning the repression and the sublimation of the libidinal by the political during the revolutionary period.

Moving from the socialist to the postsocialist eras, chapter 3 engages with Huang Zumo's film *Romance on Lu Mountain* (1980) to explore the consumption of romantic love (including the first representation of the kiss in PRC cinema), fashionable clothes, and petty-bourgeois sensibility. Similar to the red dress in Qi Xingjia's (齊興家) film *Red Dress Is in Fashion (Jieshang liuxing hongqunzi* 街上流行紅裙子) (1984) and the red shirt in Lu Xiaoya's (陸小雅) film *The Girl in Red (Hongyi shaonü* 紅衣少女) (1985), the depiction of the female character and her fashion in Huang's film can be regarded as a signifying site where the changing relationship between the libidinal and the political from the Cultural Revolution to the post–Cultural Revolution periods are staged and dramatized. I also present the fashion shows, magazines, and television melodramas that accentuate the rise of this fashion consciousness. Taken together, I contend that the desublimation of love, the refetishization of gender, and the rearticulation of ethnicity and culture are ultimately a political process: the politicized culture of revolution is replaced by the ideology of economic modernization. Moreover, I participate in the feminist discussions concerning fashion, femininity, and the economic reforms. I confront this revisionist argument by showing its contradictions and limitations.

Moving from the postsocialist to the globalization periods, chapter 4 focuses on the culture of the Chinese middle class in the 2000s and early 2010s. I engage with Li Ke's workplace novel *Chronicle of Du Lala's Promotion* (2007) to discuss the cultures of the Chinese middle class: aspirational dream, hard work, personal struggle, upward mobility, and success. (According to the novel's marketing strategy, "Du Lala's story is worthier for emulation than Bill Gates's story!" It is a Chinese version of the American dream.) I also examine the representations of fashion, consumption, and product placement in Xu Jinglei's commercial film *Go! Lala Go!* (2010), an adaptation of Li's popular novel. Regarding fashion as the main character (this film was marketed as the first fashion film in globalizing China), I explain how the commodities look at the viewer as much as the other way around. I illustrate how the state and commercial cultures collaborate to construct the new Chinese middle-class subject. This chapter contributes to the current scholarship about the Chinese middle class and culture by arguing that it is through the consumption of popular and media cultures that the middle-class subjectivities are constructed and the middle-class ideologies are transmitted. Resembling self-help books, these cultural productions teach the Chinese readers and viewers to recognize the symbols of the middle class, acculturate them to look at the world through a middle-class perspective, and instruct them to act and perform in a distinctively middle-class manner. They also teach them how to distinguish themselves from other social groups, such as the nouveau riche who own economic capital but not cultural capital.

Extending the analysis from consumption to production and labor, chapter 5 examines Chinese migrant factory workers as an underside of consumption. By engaging with recent documentary films such as Ho Chaoti's *My Fancy High Heels* (2010), Qin Xiaoyu and Wu Feiyue's *Iron Moon* (2017), and David Redmon's *Mardi Gras: Made in China* (2005), I analyze the depictions of the production of fashion commodities in Chinese factories and the labor disciplines that accompany these processes. What intrigues me is that the female workers desire the very commodities they themselves produce. What does it mean for them to dream about fashion and consumption? What can one learn from their desires, fantasies, and imaginations? In the existing literature, scholars have analyzed this issue by focusing on the tensions between production and consumption, and between temporality and spatiality. I contribute to their analyses by dwelling on the tension between utopian impulse and what Lauren Berlant calls cruel optimism. Although these consumerist desires do not fundamentally challenge the unequal relations of production, they express the workers' collective political unconsciousness and provide raw materials for building an alternative world. In other words, consumption can also be productive. Nevertheless, these aspirational attachments can also be an obstacle to the workers' flourishing, hence cruel optimism. Through documentary films, ethnographic writings, and cultural theories, I inquire how a transmedial and interdisciplinary engagement with the migrant factory workers can offer a different vision for conceptualizing Chinese consumer culture.

Furthering the analysis to disposal and waste, chapter 6 attends to garbage as another underside of consumption. I ask how the representations of rubbish and the scavengers in Wang Jiuliang's documentary *Beijing*

Besieged by Waste (*Laji weicheng* 垃圾圍城) (2010) can be treated as a productive site for political thinking. With reference to the psychoanalytical theories of Sigmund Freud, Julia Kristeva, and Fredric Jameson, I approach the figuration of rubbish from three different angles—as the return of the repressed in the form of the uncanny, as the abject, and as the dialectic of ideology and utopian impulse. I also invoke Walter Benjamin's writings about history to contemplate how the temporality of garbage can provide an alternative method to revisit the discourse of economic modernization and development.

Chapter One

DIRTY FASHION

Ma Ke's Fashion Exhibit *Useless* (2007), Jia Zhangke's Documentary Film *Useless* (2007), and Cognitive Mapping

Imagine we are resting comfortably in a glamorous and luxurious Louis Vuitton (LV) flagship store in Chengdu, the capital of Sichuan Province in southwest China. Everything is clean, shiny, and polished. Soft-sounding music is playing in the background. Dressed in Lacoste polos, wearing Christian Louboutin shoes, and carrying LV handbags, a group of Chinese middle-class women are sipping cocktails and eating hors d'oeuvres in a leisurely manner. Some of them are sitting on a comfortable sofa and have begun to discuss the brand-name fashion commodities they just purchased. They seem very enthusiastic about them.

ANNOUNCEMENT: For those ladies who have joined the "Friends of LV," please proceed to the second floor.

VOICE 1 (IN AN ANNOYING VOICE): Look at this! This is such a cheapie! Show me something more refined! Show me a distinctive brand!

VOICE 2: Prada?

VOICE 1: Prada? I just mentioned Prada . . .

VOICE 2: Prada's designs are so philosophical!

VOICE 3: It's more suitable for Europeans.

VOICE 4: What about for young men?

VOICE 2: Paul Smith is good too. It's an English brand. Their cotton shirts are very comfortable.

VOICE 5: Lacoste has the best colors, I think.

VOICE 2: Since most of the products sold in China are mass-produced in China, they have low quality. They don't feel right.

This exchange is one of the memorable scenes in Jia Zhangke's (賈樟柯) documentary film *Useless* (*Wuyong* 無用) (2007), a transmedial dialogue with Ma Ke's (馬可) fashion exhibit *Useless* (*Wuyong* 無用) (2007). The reader may laugh at the somewhat comical conversation among the Chinese middle-class consumers. However, their conversation reflects the problem of conspicuous consumption in the context of contemporary China. In an interview with film critic Tony Rayns, Jia remarks:

> In recent years, "fashion" has become a buzzword in China. The nouveau-riche class is crazy about brand-name commodities, such as Louis Vuitton, Armani, and Prada. But many people buy them because they are famous and expensive, not because they appreciate their designs. Many young people spend way beyond their means to buy these brand-name commodities. This suggests that [in China] wealth has become the most important—maybe the only—index to judge the worth of a human being.[1]

Without question, fashion consumption has become a symbol of class hierarchies and social distinctions in China today.[2] According to Jia, the conspicuous consumption of brand-name commodities has become so prevalent that what one wears, what one carries, what one uses, what one consumes, and what one owns have become the only indication of one's social value. They have become the only criterion for judging the price of a human being.

This chapter engages with contemporary Chinese media cultures—fashion and documentary film—to address consumer culture in China. I am interested in how contemporary Chinese artists such as Ma and Jia appropriate the forms of fashion and documentary film, respectively, to reflect upon the socioeconomic and cultural aspects of Chinese consumer culture. In this chapter, I examine Ma's fashion exhibit *Useless* (2007) and Jia's documentary film *Useless* (2007). By engaging with Marxist cultural criticism, I think alongside Ma and Jia and comment on their ideas. To track the dialectic of uselessness, this chapter is divided into three parts. The first part introduces aspiring Chinese fashion designer Ma Ke—whose name in

Chinese pinyin, interestingly, is spelled the same as the English word "make." Indeed, "to make" is "to fabricate," which is precisely what a fashion designer does. My emphasis is on her fashion exhibit, *Useless*.[3] Presented at Paris Fashion Week in February 2007, Ma's *Useless* was intended to be a critique of modern consumer culture. Her artwork aims to draw attention to the loss of the emotional bond between the maker and the user of clothes in the age of industrialized mass production and consumption. To help fashion recover the loss of this memory in industrialized modernity, Ma buries her garment under dirt for a period of time. When the garment is unearthed, she reasons, it will find itself imbued with the imprint of the time and space of the soil. The second part of the chapter engages with Jia's documentary film *Useless* (2007), which won the Orizzonti (Horizons) award for best documentary at the Venice Film Festival in 2007. My purpose is to show that Jia's engagement with Ma's fashion exhibit is double-edged: although the director embraces some parts of Ma's *Useless*, he critiques other parts of her design. In particular, I argue that the director introduces a new level of complexity to Ma's antifashion and anticonsumption gesture through the use of montage. The last part of the chapter suggests that Jia's documentary film *Useless* can be interpreted as an exercise in what critical and cultural theorist Fredric Jameson calls cognitive mapping, an attempt to capture the complexly mediated relationships between cultural representational forms (e.g., fashion and documentary film) and social totality within the context of global capitalism in China.

MA KE'S FASHION EXHIBIT *USELESS* (2007)

Clothes can cover us. Clothes can convey feelings. Clothes can carry with them stories. An outer layer in close contact with our skin, clothes can also have memories.[4]

Ma is one of the few internationally acclaimed fashion designers from mainland China. Born in Changchun in Jilin Province, China in 1971, she graduated from Suzhou Institute of Silk Textile Technology in 1992. Then Ma attended the Central Saint Martins College of Art in London to receive specialized training in women's wear. After earning her fashion diploma in 1996, she returned to China to establish a business company in the late 1990s. This company, overseen by Ma herself and her partner, Mao Jihong

(毛繼鴻), is called MixMind (Zhuangtai 狀態). (While the Chinese char-acters 狀態 mean form or state, interestingly, they were translated as "MixMind" in English.) Frustrated with the excess of mass-produced commodities that looked strikingly identical and boring to her, Ma felt that creativity and originality were seriously lacking in the Chinese fashion world. She asked: "Does clothing really have to be so shallow or superfi-cial?" This question prompted her to design something completely differ-ent or, in her own words, something exceptional to the norm, hence the birth of her first fashion line, Exception (Liwai 例外), in 1996.[5] According to Ma, exceptionality is what defines her fashion brand Exception.[6] As ready-to-wear, Exception is sold in boutiques and department stores in major Chinese cities, such as Guangzhou. It caters to the demands of the rising Chinese middle-class consumers.

The launch of Exception brought Ma commercial success, enabling her to design for the sake of artistic creativity rather than profit. In the mid-to-late 2000s, Ma embarked on a purportedly noncommercial fashion exhibit called *Useless*, or more precisely, *Useless/The Earth* (*Wuyong/Tudi* 無用/土地). According to Ma, *Useless* is art. Unlike Exception, which is ready-to-wear, *Useless* is haute couture.[7] *Useless* is unique and cannot be easily cop-ied or purchased in boutiques or department stores. (I will explain more about the content and the form of the *Useless* exhibit below.) Without question, *Useless* is couture, but it can be regarded as other art forms as well. For example, the makeup artist of the *Useless* fashion exhibit, Ste-phane Marais, once remarked: "When I was putting on makeup for the fashion models, I felt I was doing sculpture!"[8] *Useless* also resembles instal-lation art or performance art. For instance, the fashion show's lighting specialist, Thierry Dreyfus, once exclaimed: "This is not a fashion show. I was designing lighting for an installation art!"[9] In other words, there is a transmedial impulse in Ma's fashion exhibit. Transcending the boundary of fashion to become something else, the *Useless* exhibit resembles a per-formance in a theater, a sculpture in an exhibition, or an art installation in a museum or art gallery. The boundary between fashion and other art forms is fluid and blurred.

The Western fashion world seemed to endorse Ma's design. In their enthusiastic responses to Ma's fashion exhibit, the journalists in *Le Monde* called Ma an "anti-fashion fashion designer."[10] The French and Chinese media also praised the "anti-fashion" and "anti-consumption" dimensions of her work.[11] Because Ma incorporated useless and discarded objects in her *Useless* creation—for example, she recycled a paint-covered sheet to make a dress, an old tarpaulin to make an oversized coat, and a paint-splashed, ripped, and ragged piece of cloth to create something distinctive—Ma's design was also labeled by the media as an example of "eco-fashion," "promoting sustainable environment development."[12] In recognition of her achievement and contribution to the fashion industry, Ma was invited to present *Useless* in Paris Fashion Week in February 2007, a prestigious honor for a Chinese fashion designer.[13] Subsequently, Ma was invited to display her *Useless* exhibit in the Joyce Gallery in Paris's Palais-Royal from March to April 2007. She was also invited to showcase *Useless* in the Fashion in Motion series in London's Victoria and Albert Museum in 2008. Together with the designs of other Chinese artists, such as Zhang Da and Wang Yiyang, Ma's *Useless* was featured in the *China Design Now* exhibition at London's Victoria and Albert Museum from March to July 2008.[14] In 2008 Ma's company became a guest member of France's Chambre Syndicale de la Haute Couture.[15] Indeed, the success of *Useless* helped establish Ma's reputation as a creative artist, rather than simply a commercial designer. However, the economic capital that Ma earned from Exception enabled her to design her *Useless* fashion exhibit; in addition, the cultural and symbolic capital that Ma accumulated as an artist may eventually be converted into economic capital and help with the sale of Exception. In fact, the interplay between economic capital and cultural capital is already evident in that Ma's recent design for China's First Lady, Peng Liyuan (彭麗媛), boosted the sale of Exception.

At this point, the reader may be very curious about Ma's fashion exhibit. What exactly is *Useless*? What does it look like? Why is it called *Useless*? How useless is it? How can it be a reflection of consumer culture? In the second part of Jia's documentary film *Useless*, Ma presents her fashion idea in the following manner:

> Objects made by hands convey emotions. What I mean is that making things by hand is a long and laborious process. So, handmade objects contain emotional elements that are quite different from mass-produced commodities. According to a line in a traditional Chinese poem: "the mother stitches [to make clothes] for her traveling son" (慈母手中線, 游子身上衣). That's the kind of emotion I am talking about. It's never there in industrialized production.

It's easy to see why. With industrialized production, there is no link between the maker and the user. You don't know who made your clothes. In a materialistic society, handmade objects will obviously never be popular. They go against the principles of business. Handmade objects last longer. People use them continuously. Precisely because they take longer to make, because the maker invests so much in them, even when such things get broken, they are unlikely to be thrown away. . . . . But, if we buy a disposable cup, we will use it once and throw it away. There will be no stories to tell about it. It's essentially lifeless.

Ma's fashion idea is so provocative that it warrants a closer scrutiny. Her narrative engages with the handmade object, the industrialized mass-produced commodity, and *Useless*. Let us examine them one by one. The first point is the handmade object. According to Ma, the close and intimate relationship between the maker and the user of the handmade object can be evoked by a line in the famous Tang Dynasty poem: "The mother stitches to make clothes for her traveling son." This poetic line conjures a scene in which the mother takes the time and effort to make clothes for her son because he has to travel far away. This is a good example of what Ma means by the emotional connection between the mother and her son, and how their relationship is mediated by the clothes that she makes for him. The handmade object is a special and meaningful object, carrying with it the affective investment of the mother in her son. Because maternal love is imbued in its making, the garment is a sentimental object. Because time goes into the making of it, the object embodies a unique story. Because it has histories and memories, the handmade object is less likely to be abandoned. In her narrative, Ma offers another example to further elaborate the connection between the handmade object and storytelling. She invites the viewer to imagine a particular scene involving the grandfather, the father, and the son. In Jia's documentary, Ma explains: "A simple household object might be handed down from the grandfather, or maybe he made it by himself, and then he handed it to his son [the father]. And the father used it, he would explain to his son where it came from. The whole process of life infuses the object. It has its own story. It becomes a conversation piece." Ma notes that such an object tends to have a longer life span. If the object is worn out, it will be repaired, reused, and recycled. It will not be thrown away reflexively.[16]

Ma's second point refers to the mass-produced commodity in the context of industrialization.[17] The manufacturing process involves two primary actors: the producer of the commodity (the factory worker) and the consumer of the commodity. Jia articulates the issue that Ma raises poetically: "The assembly line has cut off our emotions." Undoubtedly, the producer and the consumer are not connected in any personal ways. Their emotional bond is simply nonexistent. The factory worker does not know the consumer; the consumer does not know the factory worker. Their relationship is one of disconnection or, in Marxist parlance, alienation. (However, it should be noted that Marx's emphasis is on the producer whereas Ma's focus is on the consumer. Certainly, Marx's understanding of alienation is more multidimensional. While Ma attends to how consumers are alienated from producers, Marx also investigates how producers are alienated from the product of their labor [i.e., the commodity], from their own labor, from themselves, from their fellow producers, and from their humanity or "species-being."[18]) Due to the nonexistence of a relationship between consumers and producers, continues Ma, the mass-produced commodity does not embody any stories, histories, and memories. It does not remember. Thus, if the commodity breaks and wears out, it is more likely to be discarded. It will not be reused or recycled. Similar to the disposable cup, Ma says, the mass-produced commodity is essentially lifeless.

Simply put: Ma believes that the handmade object is good and that the mass-produced commodity is bad. Rebelling against the lack of emotional connection between the consumer and the producer, Ma designed *Useless*. Indeed, Ma's fashion ideas can be compared with the cultural theory that Walter Benjamin presents in his famous essay "The Work of Art in the Age of Mechanical Reproduction" (1936). The story embodied in the handmade object can be analogized to what Benjamin calls the "aura" of artwork (e.g., painting) and the meanings associated with it, such as uniqueness, originality, authenticity, tradition, authority, and ritualism. Along the same line of thought, the loss of history and memory in the industrialized mass-produced commodity can be compared to Benjamin's idea of the withering or liquidation of the artwork's aura following the modern invention of mechanical reproduction. However, contrary to Benjamin, who celebrates the progressive and revolutionary potentials of mechanically reproduced arts (e.g., film and photography), Ma would like to return to the premodern era when "the mother stitches to make clothes for her traveling son."

Her *Useless* fashion exhibit intends to recreate the affective connection between individuals or generations before the arrival of modernity and industrialization. In other words, Ma is nostalgic and retrospective. She embraces the old and rejects the new. Opposing the mass-produced commodity, she cherishes the handmade object, or, in the language of Benjamin, she prefers "auratic art" rather than "mechanically reproduced art." It is in this sense that Ma's fashion was "antifashion" (understood as "anti-new"), anticonsumption, and I would add, antimodern.

In the discussion above, I have attempted to explain the content of Ma's fashion exhibit. However, what about its form? Indeed, the form of *Useless* is intimately related to its content. A crucial aspect of Ma's fashion exhibit is the emphasis on craftsmanship. *Useless* is handmade. Rather than being produced by sewing machines, *Useless* is sewn by female laborers working on handlooms in Ma's workshop in China.[19] This process is shown in the second part of Jia's documentary. Without question, the choice of making clothes with one's hands—and the choice of not using electric machines to produce the garment—is significant. It is part and parcel of Ma's fashion idea. The fashion designer intends to refabricate the situation in which "the mother stitches to make clothes for her traveling son," or the situation in which the object is passed from the grandfather to the father to the son. *Useless* attempts to reclaim the affective bond between individuals before the rise of market capitalism and its mode of technology.[20]

Moreover, Ma's fashion exhibit is natural and organic, as opposed to mechanical or artificial. Embracing the interactions between human beings and nature, Ma invites nature to perform part of the design. In Jia's documentary, Ma explains her ideas concerning fashion, nature, and history:

> Objects that have stories behind them are attractive. A few years back, I thought about making some clothes and burying them, leaving them to change through time. I was wondering if I could interact with nature by surrendering some control of the effect so that nature could do part of the designing. I'd just start by creating the basics and initiating the idea, leaving the rest to nature. So, when the fashion was dug up, I felt it would be imbued with the time and space in which it was buried, not to mention the traces of its history. I think that objects do carry memories.

To resist the loss of the emotional connection between the maker and the user of the object and to help the garment regain its lost memory, interestingly, Ma buries the fashion that she designed under soil for a period of time. When the fashion material is unearthed, she reasons, it will find itself imbued with the imprint of the time and space of the soil. The dirt will then endow the fashion object with a sense of history and memory, turning it from a garment that forgets to a garment that remembers. This is the meaning of dirt on Ma's fashion on a micro level. On a macro level, the dirt functions to challenge bourgeois temporality. Having no teleological destination, dirt disrupts and intervenes in the capitalistic narrative of progress, development, and modernization. Contrary to the glittery surfaces and shiny reflections of the LV and Prada advertisements, which can be interpreted as metaphors of speed, consumption, and disposability, in Jia's documentary, the dirt on Ma's fashion exhibit represents slowness, duration, permanence, and history. Disrupting the rush toward the future, the dirt attempts to stop, decelerate, and defer the capitalistic narrative of progress and modernization.

Indeed, the manner in which Ma presented her fashion exhibit is distinct. For example, in terms of venue, Ma did not present *Useless* in a high-end or luxurious hotel, or in a glamorous exhibition hall in a business convention center. Instead, she presented *Useless* in a school gymnasium in Paris's suburbs. Later, the fashion exhibit was shown in London's Victoria and Albert Museum. If fashion is about the new and the museum is about the old, then Ma's choice of presenting her work in a museum is integral to her antifashion (understood as anti-new) idea. In addition, rather than hiring professional models, Ma used amateur models in her fashion show. Compared with professional models and celebrities, the amateur models looked more natural, human, and down-to-*earth*. This resemblance can be related to the dirt motif in *Useless*. What is also striking is that there were no runways. Rather than asking the models to saunter down catwalks to display the clothes, Ma instructed her models to stand on tall, illuminated boxes. This arrangement is integral to her antifashion idea. If the ephemeral presentation of clothes on a catwalk expresses speed, efficiency, fast consumption, disposability, and waste in the age of mass production and consumption, then the way that Ma presented her fashion exhibit emphasizes permanence, preservation, and longevity. Moreover, the seating arrangement of Ma's fashion show is special. In a conventional fashion show, the most important people, such as the patrons and sponsors, are invited to sit in the front row so that they can see and be seen. However, Ma's fashion show challenged this form of power dynamic. Audience members were encouraged to stand up, leave their seats, walk down the stairs, and walk around the fashion models to appreciate her artwork. In this way, the conventional power structure is critiqued and the hierarchical relationship between the audience and the fashion exhibit is reversed and turned upside down.[21]

JIA ZHANGKE'S DOCUMENTARY FILM
WUYONG (USELESS) (2007)

To dialogue with Ma's fashion exhibit, Jia made the documentary *Useless* (2007). Judging from this documentary's content and form, I argue that Jia's engagement with Ma's fashion exhibit is double-edged: although the director embraces some parts of the *Useless* fashion exhibit, he is critical of other parts of her design. To explore the director's critique, one needs to be familiarized with the documentary. *Useless* comprises three major components. Presented in an observational style (with no voiceovers or interviews), the first part of the documentary features a group of manual laborers working in a garment factory in the city of Zhuhai in Guangdong Province, China. These workers produce Ma's first fashion line, Exception (ready-to-wear). Three dimensions of their lived experience are featured: the factory where they work, the dining hall where they eat, and the clinic where they receive treatments from the doctor when they are sick. To be sure, the representations of the migrant factory workers are a continuation of the director's long-standing interest in the subalterns and underprivileged groups in China's economic reforms. The genealogy of this interest can be traced back to the director's portrayal of the urban wanderers in his first fiction film *Xiaowu* (*Xiaowu* 小武, 1997), the socialist cultural performers in *Platform* (*Zhantai* 站台, 2000), the abandoned youths in *Unknown Pleasures* (*Renxiaoyao* 任逍遥, 2002), the migrant workers in *The World* (*Shijie* 世界, 2004), the poor and those who were displaced by the Three Gorges Dam project in *Still Life* (*Sanxia Haoren* 三峡好人, 2006), the sex workers in Bangkok, Thailand, in *Dong* (*Dong* 東, 2006), and the factory workers laid off from the state-owned enterprise in *24 City* (*Ershisichengji* 二十四城記, 2008). Similar to the other documentary films about fashion, such as David

Redmon's *Mardi Gras: Made in China* (2005), Micha X. Peled's *China Blue* (2005), Lixin Fan's (范立欣) *Last Train Home* (*Guitu lieche* 歸途列車, 2009), and Ho Chao-ti's (He Zhaoti 賀照緹) *My Fancy High Heels* (*Wo'ai gaogenxie* 我愛高跟鞋, 2010), Jia explicitly links consumption to production. In *Useless*, the director emphasizes that Ma's first fashion line, Exception, is produced by the factory workers in southern China. The factory workers should therefore be regarded as the historical conditions of possibility and the fields and forces of production of Ma's fashion. Whereas the first part of the documentary focuses on Ma's Exception, the second part features Ma's fashion narrative and her fashion exhibit in Paris in 2007. (Her ideas have already been articulated in the previous section.)

Focusing on clothes as everyday necessities, the third part of Jia's *Useless* turns to the lives of working-class individuals in Fenyang in Shanxi Province, China. With the rise of the market economy, the local tailors in Shanxi cannot compete with factories and department stores in more developed parts of the country. In a memorable scene in Jia's *Useless*, a tailor-turned–coal miner explains to the interviewer (who, one may presume, is the director himself) that, excluding the cost of labor, it costs him forty yuan to buy the necessary materials to make a suit. However, the department store sells the finished suit for only thirty yuan. It is simply impossible for the local tailors to compete with factories equipped with advanced technologies and with department stores furnished with competitive marketing strategies. To make a living, some local tailors have to relinquish their jobs and work as coal miners instead.[22] To that extent, the tailors are the underside of the mass-manufactured suit. Their expertise is rendered useless by the factories and department stores. The third part of Jia's *Useless* tells a story of how the petty bourgeoisie is unable to compete with the big bourgeoisie in competitive market economy.

Montage as Ideology Critique

The dirt in France is to be put onto the faces. The dirt in Shanxi is to be breathed into the lungs.

—JIA

Jia's documentary is an ideological critique of Ma's fashion exhibit. To resist mass production, consumption, and commodification, Ma attempts to endow her *Useless* fashion exhibit with stories, histories, and memories. However, has she succeeded in recovering the emotional connection between the producer and the consumer? I am not certain that she has achieved this purpose. According to the second part of the documentary, which presents Ma's fashion exhibit, there is no evidence that the visitors to Ma's fashion exhibit in France or England, after appreciating the *Useless* exhibit, are drawn to the Chinese laborers working in Ma's studio in China. As we see from the responses in the media (e.g., *Le Monde*), Ma's *Useless* exhibit invites the audience to get to know the designer herself but not the Chinese workers. The latter's labor is rendered invisible. Ma's *Useless* exhibit does not bring the Chinese workers closer to the European viewers either. In other words, Ma has not fulfilled the mission she set out to achieve in the first place. While Ma's *Useless* fashion exhibit has not undone the alienation of the audience from the workers, has she managed to rebuild such lost connections through the Exception commodity? Again, I am not certain that she has. According to the first part of the documentary, there is simply no interaction between the producers and the consumers of Ma's Exception. In the production process, the factory workers do not encounter the consumers; in the consumption process, the consumers do not become acquainted with the laborers either. There is no emotional connection between them. If we use the logic of Ma's *Useless* exhibit to examine her Exception collection, it is logical to conclude that Exception, similar to the disposable cup, is also essentially lifeless. Nevertheless, the task of connecting disparate groups of people is ultimately fulfilled by the director Jia. By juxtaposing the fashion exhibit viewers with the factory workers within the documentary, Jia re-presents and re-creates the linkages between the producer and the consumer. Through the image, the director attempts to de-alienate, de-differentiate, and relate the consumer to the producer.

Furthermore, Jia's documentary enables one to see that some of the claims that Ma makes may not be entirely true. According to the fashion designer, the emotional relationship between the maker and the user is present in the handmade object. Interesting stories about the object can be told. Owing to the memories that it embodies, the handmade object is typically preserved for a longer period of time. However, with the emergence of industrialized mass production and consumption of commodities, such affective experience is unavoidably lost. Ma insists that the mass-produced commodity does not carry any histories or memories. However, is this actually the case? In the third part of Jia's *Useless*, the workers, such as the coal miners, do endow meanings in, and create stories for, the mass-produced commodities. Take, for instance, the director's interview with the working-class couple who works as coal miners.

INTERVIEWER: Where did you buy the clothes you're wearing?
WIFE: In Fenyang.
INTERVIEWER: Why do you like them?
[The couple looks embarrassed but happy.]
HUSBAND: Actually, I chose them for her. She wanted a suit. So, she went to the Jiadeli Superstore and looked at some suits. That's a woman's suit. A three-piece suit. At that time, she did not know much about fashion, but she thought that the suits looked good. Anyhow, she saw lots of advertisements on TV. She realized that she already had everything except the suit. So, I chose one for her.

The husband, formerly a tailor, has purchased a pink suit for his wife in the department store. His wife is very fond of the pink suit simply because her husband chose it for her. (Ironically, this couple does not seem to be bothered by the fact that the husband, who used to work as a tailor, did not make the pink suit for her.) This scene can be interpreted as the agency of the consumer: the working-class couple adopts the pink suit and creates stories—in this case, the story of love—for the mass-produced commodity.

Indeed, the middle-class individuals also create stories for their commodities. In the second part of the documentary, Ma notes that the commodity, such as the disposable cup, does not embody any stories. Then Jia makes an abrupt cut to show the façade of a Louis Vuitton flagship store in China. This cut seems to suggest that the Louis Vuitton handbag, which is a branded commodity, can be compared to the disposable cup. If we follow Ma's *Useless* logic, then the Louis Vuitton handbag must not embody any stories because it is also mass-produced. It must therefore be essentially lifeless. However, the Chinese middle-class consumers, particularly the female "friends of Louis Vuitton," are genuinely passionate about their Louis Vuitton handbags. The director presents an interesting scene in which a group of Chinese middle-class women, dressed in fashionable clothes, discuss the brand-name products that they have purchased. One of them, in an annoying voice, announces that she likes Louis Vuitton. Another customer likes Paul Smith because their shirts are comfortable. Another one expresses her preference for Prada because "Prada is very philosophical!" In fact, by making such a claim, the consumer is actively creating a story—in this case, the philosophical story about the aesthetic object—for the mass-produced commodity. Indeed, branding is a form of storytelling. In effect, all of these personal choices are stories created by the middle-class consumers that end up endowing meanings to the (brand-name) mass-produced commodities.

I further suggest that even Ma herself is participating in this process of storytelling. This is especially true when she presents the reasoning behind her first fashion line Exception.

MA: Back then, there were no Chinese brands. The Chinese manufacturing industry was labor-intensive. Although China was the world's largest fashion exporter, there was not a single Chinese fashion brand. Nobody thought of us [the Chinese] as being creative. I thought it was really sad and shameful. I felt I had a duty to do something about it.

Dissatisfied with the fact that China can only be a labor-intensive and export-oriented factory-nation that produces cheap and low-quality clothes for Western consumption ("made in China"), Ma aspires to establish a fashion brand for China ("designed in China"). She would like Chinese fashion to be recognized by the international fashion world. This is the meaning par excellence that Ma creates for Exception as a brand-name mass-produced commodity. Although Ma says that the mass-produced commodity does not embody any stories, she is actively producing one herself.

Jia's documentary shows that the individuals create stories for their clothing commodities: the working-class coal miners craft the love story for the pink suit, the middle-class consumers construct the philosophical story for their Prada handbags, and the designer, Ma, invents the story of national origin for her fashion design.[23] Importantly, the behaviors of these groups of people work together to refute Ma's claim that the mass-produced commodities do not have any stories. In fact, whether an object embodies stories has less to do with whether it is handmade or mass-produced but more to do with how people use this object. In fact, it is the embeddedness of the object in concrete historical situations that is the source of the object's story. This idea can be further confirmed if we return to the point that Ma makes regarding the handmade object and storytelling. According to Ma, stories are created when the object is handed down from the grandfather to the father to the son. However, Ma does not explain where exactly the stories originate. Do the stories come from the handmade quality of the object? Or do they come from the transferability of the object from one individual or generation to another? In the latter, the object does not necessarily have to be handmade; it can be mass-produced. Although Ma's first example ("the mother stitches to make clothes for her traveling son") illustrates the idea that the handmade object can embody histories and memories, her second example ("the object is handed down from the grandfather to the father to the son") does not specify whether the object is handmade or mass-produced. She notes in passing that "*maybe* it is made by the grandfather" (my emphasis). However, maybe it is not; maybe it is mass-produced. Indeed, stories can continue to be told about the mass-produced commodity when it is handed down from the grandfather to the father to the son, or when it is chosen and purchased by the husband for his wife. When the mass-produced commodity is used and appropriated in concrete historical situations, memories are fashioned. The incoherence of Ma's fashion narrative reveals that contrary to what she proclaims, there is no simple causal relationship between the handmade object and storytelling.

Moreover, Ma claims that because no stories can be told about the mass-produced commodities, they are disposable. They are less likely to be reused or recycled. However, is this actually the case? The third part of the documentary renders visible the desire on the part of the working-class individuals to prolong the lifespan of their commodities. Many of them attempt to preserve their clothes so that they can last longer. Some of the clothes have been worn for such a long time that they have become thoroughly worn out. This can be seen from the clothes hanging outside the house of the coal-mining couple and the clothes hanging inside the coal miners' bathing areas. The color and texture show that these clothes have been worn and washed many times. Moreover, by the end of the documentary, the working-class individuals, such as the man in the red vest, the wife in the coal-mining couple, and the middle-aged woman, bring their clothes to the local tailors to have them mended. In other words, at odds with Ma's claim that the mass-produced commodities are readily disposable, the clothing commodities tend to be repaired, preserved, and ultimately healed by the hands of the working class.

Importantly, Jia uses montage to reveal the double standard of Ma's narrative. To illustrate Jia's ideological critique of Ma's fashion exhibit, I direct the reader to the representation of the coal miners in *Useless*. Indeed, why does the director include the coal miners in his documentary about fashion and consumption? In the third part of *Useless*, Jia focuses on the lived experience of the coal miners. Their uniforms are covered with dirt, and their faces and bodies are also blackened with coal. When one juxtaposes this scene with the scene in which Ma's fashion models are covered with dirt, one can realize that the coal miners are dirty due to the nature of their work whereas the fashion models are made to look dirty. The fashion models' uncleanliness is artificial. In the second part of the documentary, Jia shows the work that goes into the making of the fashion exhibit. During preparation, Ma is meticulous about the type of dirt to be used for her fashion exhibit. In response to her assistant who has just shown her a sample of dirt, Ma comments: "The mud won't do. It's too damp. We need earth, not this type of fine earth. It should be like the sample that we sent in earlier." Ma does not want to use just any type of dirt but a particular type of dirt for her fashion exhibit. Indeed, the same also holds true for the lighting effect. In her conversation with Mao Jihong about the color of the light boxes, Ma notes: "That color paper won't do. . . . It's too yellow!" Ma does not want to use just any type of light but a particular type of light for her fashion exhibit. Ultimately, the nature in her *Useless* design is not natural but naturalized, controlled, and contrived.

The montage of the fashion models and the coal miners is a powerful revelation. It allows one to see that the dirty coal miners, who have just exited the coal mines, should be regarded as fashionable as—or even more fashionable than—Ma's fashion models. If we use Ma's logic to view the world, the dirty coal miners should be regarded as the perfect incarnations of her fashion idea. They, too, must be seen as a new type of fashion model. They, too, perfectly express Ma's *Useless* idea. The dirt on the coal miners' clothes suggests the material conditions of coal mining. What is fascinating about Jia's documentary film is that the director has thoroughly defamiliarized Ma's idea and pushed her claim to such an extreme that the idea may appear uncanny and unbelievable to Ma herself. What is equally interesting is that Ma herself does not recognize it.

However, will Ma acknowledge the fact that the poor coal miners are fashionable? In the transitional scene between the second and third parts of the documentary, Ma is shown driving a van from the city to the countryside. Visiting poor, remote, and underdeveloped parts of the country, Ma says, is similar to the recovery of memory for a person who has lost consciousness. (Indeed, her narrative sounds slightly condescending. It resembles the claim made by some nineteenth-century and early twentieth-century European imperialists who claimed that their colonial experience in Asia, Africa, and the Middle East allowed them to revisit the childhood or primitive stage of human civilizations.) There is little evidence that Ma will joyfully embrace the idea that these dirty coal miners are fashionable. Given the fact that Ma considers the countryside to be backward, it is unlikely that she will use her idea to judge the coal miners and conclude that they are fashionable through and through. Jia's inclusion of the coal miners reveals Ma's double standard.

Ironically, when we examine this phenomenon from the perspective of the working class, the coal miners seriously consider their clothes and bodies to be dirty. They do not think there is anything artistic or philosophical about their dirty uniforms. After a day of hard work, what they want is to take a shower to get rid of the dirt.[24] According to the coal-mining couple, what is fashionable for them is what they see in commercials or advertisements. The wife says that she would like to buy a three-piece suit because she has seen one on television. Indeed, the working-class couple's understanding of fashion is quite different from Ma's. Thanks to Jia's montage, such an ironic mismatch can be interpreted as the ideology of Ma's fashion idea. Reflecting on how the industrialized mass production and consumption of clothing commodities has radically transformed human interactions and sociality, Ma aestheticizes and romanticizes dirt to be able to offer a diagnosis of modern consumer society. Ironically, however, the coal miners, who should actually be considered a perfect example of Ma's fashion idea, do not idealize how dirt can potentially disrupt capitalistic and bourgeois temporality. For the tailors and coal miners, dirt is just dirt; it has to be removed after a day of hard work.[25]

DOCUMENTARY AS COGNITIVE MAPPING

Now, we can turn to the cultural criticism of Jia's films. In his essay "Market Socialism and Its Discontent" (2013), cultural critic Xudong Zhang comments on Jia's oeuvre in this way:

> The breaking of the ideological totality at the end of the 1980s and the intensified disintegration of the "reform consensus" throughout the 1990s finally resulted in a fragmentation of Chinese society in every dimension and domain such that a "discovery" of reality could no longer meaningfully envisage a new unifying totality. Rather, a search for "reality" must start with a cognitive mapping of the contradictory multiplicity of realities.... Jia Zhangke's work can be understood most effectively in this context as a cinematic discursive invention.[26]

Zhang suggests that Jia's early films, such as *Xiaowu* (1997), *Platform* (2000), and *Unknown Pleasures* (2002), can be understood as an attempt to cognitively map the convoluted realities of postsocialist China in cinematic terms. Here Zhang is appropriating Fredric Jameson's concept of cognitive mapping, a theoretical device for capturing the complex mediations between the global capitalistic system (late capitalism) and its dominant cultural and ideological expression (postmodernism).[27] The concept of cognitive mapping aspires to link representational forms to the otherwise unrepresentable social totality. According to Zhang, the representation of the county-level city (*xiancheng* 縣城) ("the site of a county, governing townships but in turn governed by districts or district-level cities") in Jia's films can be interpreted as a formal perspective or position to visualize the disappearance of an old reality and the emergence of multiple new realities. What characterizes the Chinese *xiancheng*, Zhang explains, is its liminality: "between rural and urban, between industrial and agricultural, between 'state' and 'non-state,' between high culture and low culture, xiancheng becomes a meeting place of all current or anachronistic forces."[28] The *xiancheng* is a location where "all the failings and compromises of socialist industrialization, of postsocialist reforms, and even of the sweeping market forces" and indeed "different modes of production or consumption" are rendered visible.[29] Although I mostly agree with Zhang's analysis, I think his argument concerning the Chinese *xiancheng* can only explain Jia's early films, at most up to *The World* (2004). However, his observation is unequipped to capture the variety and multiplicity of Jia's works in the mid- and late 2000s, such as his fiction film *Still Life* (2006) and, importantly, his documentary films, such as *Dong* (2006), *Useless* (2007), *24 City* (2008), and *I Wish I Knew* (2010), in which he experiments with the representations of fiction and reality. Maintaining that Jia's works in the mid- and late 2000s can also be regarded as examples of what Jameson calls cognitive mapping, I suggest that the director's use of the block structure (*bankuai* 板块) is another formal strategy Jia deploys to scan and map the social totality. I illustrate this point by referencing *Useless*.

In an interview with film reviewer Tony Rayns, when asked about the significance of the tripartite structure of his documentary *Useless*, Jia explains how this new representational form enables him to grasp the otherwise unrepresentable global capitalistic totality in China. He says:

> Since making *The World*, I have become more interested in using the block structure to represent more than one group of characters or more than one setting. *Dong*, for example, brings together two Asian cities that are very far apart: Fengjie in the Three Gorges area of China's Sichuan Province and Bangkok in Thailand. In *Still Life*, I tell two unrelated stories that take place in the same town. As I grow older, I experience life's complexity and diversity, and it seems difficult to represent these characteristics through a conventional linear narrative, such as a 90-minute story of one man and one woman in a relationship. These days it is no longer unusual to travel, to meet a wide variety of people, and to experience different kinds of relationship. Our sense of the world changes as we travel and cross-reference different realities and lives. Obviously, low-cost air travel, satellite TV, and the internet all contribute to this changing sense of the world. In most parts of China, it is already the case that most people no longer only know the immediate reality around them.[30]

Extending the formal experimentation in his hometown trilogy, which showcases a particular group of individuals within a fixed particular locale (*xiancheng*) in Shanxi Province, Jia's following film, *The World*, traces the dialectic of mobility and immobility of a cohort of young migrant workers in the World Park—an allegorical figuration of the world—in Beijing. However, beginning in the mid-2000s the director begins to adopt a different representational approach in his documentary films. For example, in *Dong*, Jia uses a bipartite structure to trace the footsteps of contemporary Chinese painter Liu Xiaodong (劉小東). Liu is shown painting two groups of individuals in two geographical locations: the male migrant workers in the Three Gorges Dam area in China and the female sex workers in Bangkok, Thailand. Similar to the alienation of the consumer from the producer in Jia's *Useless*, the Chinese migrant workers and the Thai sex workers have never encountered each other. What connects these two groups of people is Liu's painting—and, we can add, Jia's documentary about Liu's artwork. In *Useless*, Jia uses a similar structural technique—a tripartite structure—to feature different groups of people located in different geographical regions: the factory workers in Guangdong (China), the fashion models in Paris (France), and the coal miners in Shanxi (China). Although these groups of people do not know one another, the director insists on their intimate socioeconomic relationships and gestures to what lies between these global, regional, national, and local realities. The director notes the importance of grasping these invisible connections. He says: "In fact, we are all [economically] related. The tailors in Shanxi are related to the migrant workers in Guangdong. We are all related in this [economic] chain. Regardless of which stratum [or class] you are in, which profession you are in, in reality, we are all related." To demonstrate how these disparate groups of people are connected within the same economic chain, Jia says:

> In the documentary, I show that Ma Ke created her *Wu Yong* [*Useless*] label to protest against the industrialization of garment making on a mass scale. In Shanxi, garment workshops in remote areas are dying out because they cannot compete with the garment factories in Guangzhou. By showing the Guangzhou factories, the fashion show in Paris, and the small tailor's shop in Shanxi in the same documentary, I hope to build a more complex and revealing picture.[31]

Importantly, the director notes the necessity of grasping the complex economic and social relationships among seemingly incompatible and contradictory realities through cultural and ideological interventions. In the first and second parts of *Useless*, Jia presents the factory workers and the fashion models (as workers). Both groups of individuals work to produce Ma's fashion design—the factory workers labor to produce the ready-to-wear

Exception line, and the fashion models labor to wear and show off the *Useless* exhibit. In the first and third parts of the documentary, the director shows the class competition in the market economy. In many ways, the inability of the local tailors in Shanxi to compete with the large-scale factories and department stores in Guangdong is the story of how the petty bourgeoisie (e.g., the shopkeeper) is unable to compete with the big bourgeoisie (e.g., transnational business company) in market capitalism. Indeed, it may be no coincidence that the tailors in Shanxi have to work as coal miners after they have lost their original jobs. The coal that they mine may serve as energy resources for the operation of the factories in Guangdong. Furthermore, it is possible that after the local tailors in Shanxi have lost their jobs, some of them have to move to work in the factories in Guangdong. If so, then the local tailors have been doubly exploited. Indeed, the three parts of this documentary are closely intertwined. If, according to Zhang, the cinematic representations of the Chinese *xiancheng* in Jia's early works capture the liminality of the urban and the rural, the industrial and the agricultural, the socialist past and the postsocialist present, then I argue that the director's use of the block structure in his documentary films in the mid- and late 2000s arrests the historical contradictions of global capitalism in China on a more transnational scale. Indeed, Jia's *Useless* visualizes what lies between the local and the global, between the national, the regional, and the transnational. Also, it maps what lies between extraction (coal mining), production, design, and consumption. Furthermore, it scans what lies between fashion as ready-to-wear (Exception), as fashion exhibit (*Useless*), and as everyday necessity (the coal miners' clothes). What Jia has achieved is to relate, connect, de-alienate, and de-differentiate these seemingly fragmented, incoherent, and contradictory realities. In addition, he shows the viewer what lies between them. Jia's *Useless* is an exercise in cognitive mapping precisely because this documentary provides a vantage point for telling a more totalizing story of global capitalism in China within the transnational context.

Chapter Two

THE HIGH-QUALITY SUIT, CLASS STRUGGLE, AND CULTURAL REVOLUTION

The Politics of Consumption in Xie Tieli's Film *Never Forget* (1964)

I begin this chapter with a story about class struggle on trouser legs. This story concerns the consumption of a pair of tight-fitting trousers before the dawn of the Great Proletarian Cultural Revolution (1966–1976). On May 17, 1964, a woman went to Gao Mei boutique on Nanjing West Road, Shanghai. She asked to buy a pair of narrow and tight-fitting trousers. This kind of trousers is sometimes called chicken-wing trousers. Because the trouser legs become narrower from the knees downward, they resemble the shape of chicken wings. (The opposite kind is called bell-bottom trousers, in which the trouser legs become wider from the knees downward. Since they have the shape of a broom typically used for house cleaning, they are sometimes called floor-sweeping trousers or simply floor sweepers.) However, the salesperson turned down the customer's request, replying that "if we re-adjust the trousers to satisfy your request, then your trousers will cling closely to your backside and the trouser legs will become very narrow. This kind of strange-looking outfit (*qizhuang yifu* 奇裝異服) will not be welcome in our socialist economy. We cannot make commodities that will disturb social morality." Angry to hear this, the customer replied: "I am not happy about this. You have not satisfied my request. I don't understand why you can turn this down. As long as you can provide what I have got in mind, I am happy to pay for the trousers." She even asked the salesperson to explain how clothes can be linked to social class and ideology. "How is it possible that the tight-fitting trousers can be imbued with bourgeois thinking? How can this kind of clothing have negative influence on social morality?" Then the two women fought.[1]

Later a staff member in the store wrote to *Liberation Daily* newspaper to inquire what could have been done about this incident. After receiving the letter, the editorial board suggested that the readers have a public discussion about this incident. The editorial board asked how one should treat strange-looking outfits within the Chinese socialist context. Many readers wrote to participate in this discussion. Within four months, *Liberation Daily* received close to 1,700 letters. Eventually, on November 14, 1964, the Department of Propaganda published an article in *People's Daily* newspaper to conclude this debate. According to this article:

> What one wears is supposed to be a small thing in life. But it is also a reflection of the perspective and taste of different classes. Based on the discussion of the masses, a conclusion can be drawn: what one wears cannot be separated from what one thinks. Some people think that strange-looking clothes are pretty, while some think that they are ugly. The difference in opinions can be attributed to the fact that they belong to different classes, share different worldviews, and lead different lifestyles, hence the difference in perspectives and tastes. A number of readers wrote to *Liberation Daily* to point out the fact that the strange-looking clothes are the products of capitalism. From the perspective of the lazy and exploitative class and the kind of hooligans who do not have proper jobs, the strange-looking clothes are suitable for their sex-driven, decadent, and licentious lifestyles. In contrast, the laboring people enjoy economical, comfortable, convenient, and thrifty clothes.[2]

Rather than pursuing class analysis and ideological critique in a serious manner, the Department of Propaganda concluded this debate with a moralistic tone: members of the bourgeoisie enjoy decadent lifestyles and like to wear strange-looking outfits such as chicken-wing trousers or floor sweepers. In contrast, members of the proletariat value frugality and practicality and like to wear more basic, practical, and functional clothes.

Fashionable clothes, such as bell-bottom trousers, high-heel shoes, long hair, lipstick, and makeup, were radically critiqued during the most turbulent years of the Cultural Revolution. Fashion was evaluated by some individuals as an expression of petty-bourgeois sensibility; it could also be linked to counterrevolution or revisionism. While the Department of Propaganda concluded that what one wears mirrors one's social class and its cultural taste, what is missing is how they have arrived at this decision. What made the socialist government conclude in this way? One is not told, but it is worthwhile to ask what one can draw from this story. How do clothes reflect social class and ideology? How is the wearing of fashionable clothes or strange-looking outfits an expression of bourgeois thought and counterrevolutionary behavior? Moreover, what is the politics of fashion and consumption within the context of Chinese socialist modernity?

This chapter engages with Xie Tieli's (謝鐵驪) film *Never Forget* (*Qianwan buyao wangji* 千萬不要忘記) (1964) to investigate the socialist politics of clothes, leisure, and consumption. Adapted from a theater play, this film is part of the socialist education campaign that promoted Mao Zedong's (毛澤東) political slogan "never forget class struggle" (*Qianwan buyao wangji jieji douzheng* 千萬不要忘記階級鬥爭). The narrative of *Never Forget* concerns a young factory worker, Ding Shaochun (丁少純), and his desire for a high-quality suit (*liaozifu* 料子服). To save enough money to buy this suit, he shoots wild birds in his spare time and his mother-in-law sells them on his behalf. However, these leisure activities have interfered with Ding Shaochun's work performance to such an extent that his behavior may have brought disastrous consequences to the supply of electricity in his town. By the end of the film, Ding Shaochun is schooled by his father.

In this chapter I engage with Fredric Jameson's theory of the political unconscious to analyze second-world cultures. Rejecting the claim that consumption is simply denied or forbidden during the socialist and revolutionary period, I explain that the depiction of the high-quality suit in *Never Forget* is not negative but ambivalent. Furthermore, I argue that such a portrayal is not a mirror reflection of Chinese socialist reality; instead, it is a symptomatic expression of the profound contradictions that confronted Chinese socialist modernity at the dawn of the Cultural Revolution. Interestingly, this representational form-as-symptom reveals the contradictions between production and consumption, between work and leisure, between manual labor and intellectual labor, and between the country and the city. Ultimately, these contradictions point to the uneasy balance between revolution and construction after the founding of the PRC.

They also store secret information regarding the Sino–Soviet split (due to Soviet revisionism) and the struggle between PRC-led socialism and U.S.-led capitalism during the Cold War.

My work dialogues with the existing scholarships in Chinese cultural studies. First, I maintain the importance of engaging with contradictions—historical, social, and political-economic—in cultural critique. In addition, while Tina Mai Chen, Tang Xiaobing (唐小兵), and Cai Xiang (蔡翔) have provided insightful analyses of Chinese socialist literatures and arts, I bring Jameson's critical theory to systematize their discussions and interrogate their ideas. Second, I bring another set of discussions regarding love, gender, and sexuality in the socialist context to the existing dialogue. Conversing with Meng Yue (孟悦), Ban Wang, Jason McGrath, and Jianmei Liu, I inquire how the discourse of fashion and consumption can be explained by the repression or the sublimation of the libidinal by the political. I argue that fashion and consumption, similar to love, gender, and sexuality, cannot easily be sublimated by revolutionary politics. Instead, they coexist with revolutionary politics during what cultural critic Zhuoyi Wang, in his periodization of revolutionary Chinese cinema, calls the First Hundred Flowers period (1956–1958) and the Second Hundred Flowers period (1961–1964). My work provides a theoretically informed framework to analyze socialist cultures and society.

Here I present this chapter's organization so that my reader will never forget my research. In "Clothing and Film Histories," I engage with the historical accounts of Antonia Finnane and Zhuoyi Wang and provide a brief overview of Chinese socialist clothing and cinema cultures. In "To Buy or Not to Buy?," I present *Never Forget* as a cautionary tale of the danger of fashion, leisure, and consumption within the context of Chinese socialist modernity. In addition, I engage with Cai Xiang who, in his book *Revolution and Its Narratives: China's Socialist Literary and Cultural Imaginaries, 1949–1966* (2016), provocatively proposes that Chinese socialism produces its own middle class or, more accurately, its own new petty bourgeoisie.[3] His view problematizes conventional understanding regarding capitalism, socialism, and the middle class. In "The Politics of Socialist Consumption," I perform a critical reading of *Never Forget*. I argue that the narrative's form maps, scans, and identifies the symptoms of otherwise imperceptible contradictions that confronted Chinese socialist modernity in the early and mid-1960s. Furthermore, in "Repression or Sublimation," I engage with

Marxist, feminist, and psychoanalytical critiques and revisit the complex mediations between the libidinal (i.e., love, gender, and sexuality) and the political (i.e., revolutionary politics) in Chinese socialist cultures. I examine the intellectual exchanges among Meng (repression), Ban Wang (sublimation), McGrath (sublimation), and Liu (the problems of sublimation). While Liu focuses on socialist fiction, I contribute by introducing several socialist films that showcase fashion and consumption in the mid-1950s and in the mid-1960s.

CLOTHING AND FILM HISTORIES

To explain the socialist politics of clothes and consumption, let me describe what was regarded as suitable and appropriate to wear during the socialist era. In her book *Changing Clothes in China: Fashion, History, Nation* (2008), Antonia Finnane provides an overview of the historical development of Chinese clothing from the late imperial to the economic reforms periods. In the chapter "The New Look in the New China," she suggests that in the 1950s, the cadre suit was a desirable outfit for Chinese people. This suit signified progressive thinking, simplicity of lifestyle, frugality, and practicality. Male comrades would like to wear Sun Yat-sen suits (中山裝), whereas female comrades would like to wear Lenin suits (列寧裝). From her description, I realize that Chinese men and women did not dress in exactly the same way during the Maoist period. Furthermore, the fact that femininity was not pronounced in women's clothing does not necessarily mean that it was repressed or rejected at that time. Finnane also analyzes the artist Yu Feng's (郁風) dress reforms campaign in 1955, which can be regarded as a Hundred Flowers Campaign on the clothed body. Although this reform was short-lived, it saw the blossoming of various experimentations with fashions, styles, and gender presentations. In the subsequent chapter "Dressed to Kill in the Cultural Revolution," Finnane suggests that during the stormiest years of the Cultural Revolution, the most favored piece of clothing was the military uniform. On the surface, Chinese people appeared to dress in similar ways; however, what differentiated the people were the details of their clothes. From her account, I realize that individualities were not completely erased during the socialist era. Instead, they were either unpronounced or were rechanneled to other sites. Finnane also analyzes the dress reforms that Jiang Qing (江青), Mao Zedong's wife, supervised in the 1970s. These dress reform campaigns can be regarded as Chinese socialism's creative attempts to design clothes not governed by the logics of capitalistic commodification and patriarchal voyeurism.[4]

The military uniform was a desirable piece of clothing for Chinese men and women in the late 1960s. Indeed, soldiers in the People's Liberation Army (PLA) were figures that people emulated. They would wear military uniforms with loose-fitting trousers. They would also carry thick belts on their waists and carry bags imprinted with such slogans as "Serve the People" or "The Red Army is Not Afraid of the Long March." They might also wear "liberation shoes." This type of outfit was the most sought after. Practical and functional, this kind of outfit is convenient for labor. However, what about the bourgeoisie? What kind of outfit would they be wearing? During the most turbulent years of the Cultural Revolution, strange-looking outfits were radically critiqued as an expression of petty-bourgeois sensibility. Personal taste and lifestyle were sometimes linked to counterrevolution. In their book *Personal Voices: Chinese Women in the 1980s* (1988), Emily Honig and Gail Hershatter explain: "With the onset of the Cultural Revolution, everyone began to wear army-style green as a sign of revolutionary zeal . . . A woman's coiffure was thought to indicate her politics, and groups of Red Guards chopped off the braids of women on the street, accusing them of politically incorrect attitudes. In such an environment, interest in fashion and adornment was regarded as bourgeois and counter-revolutionary."[5]

In addition, curiously enough, different kinds of clothes were assigned a class label by the most "radical" fractions of the Red Guards. The Western suit was bourgeois or capitalistic, the Chinese *qipao* feudalistic, and, due to the Sino–Soviet split, the Soviet-style *bulaji* dress revisionist. It is unclear how these Red Guards could rationalize the political-economic, social, and cultural ideologies of clothing.[6]

Film further depicts the complexity of Chinese socialist cultures. In his book *Chinese Cinema: Culture and Politics since 1949* (1987), Paul Clark offers an early overview of Chinese cinema during the socialist period.[7] He distinguishes between the Yan'an tradition and the Shanghai tradition and explains how they influenced socialist filmmaking. Clark's effort has recently been updated by Zhuoyi Wang, who, in *Revolutionary Cycles in Chinese Cinema, 1951–1979* (2014), provides a nuanced, meticulous, and complex picture of the conflicts and balances of power in Maoist revolutionary campaigns and cinematic productions.[8] Specifically, Zhuoyi Wang examines how scriptwriters, directors, party authorities and bureaucrats, cultural critics, audiences, and other social actors contested and negotiated the meanings of films produced during the Maoist era. Diverging from conventional periodization that divides the socialist period into the seventeen-years period (1949–1966) and the Cultural Revolution period (1966–1976), he breaks up the socialist era into five distinctive phases as a new way to historicize Chinese socialist cinema. The first phase is called the Nationalization period (1951–1955) because film industry and studios were nationalized soon after the PRC had been founded. Zhuoyi Wang analyzes how film artists, such as Sun Yu (孫瑜) and Zheng Junli (鄭君里), and Chinese Communist Party (CCP) authorities took part in the production and reception of the politically contentious films *The Life of Wu Xun* (*Wuxun zhuan* 武訓傳) (1951) and *Song Jingshi* (宋景詩) (1957). The second phase, called the First Hundred Flowers period, was short-lived. It began with the Hundred Flowers Campaign in 1956 and ended with the Anti-Rightist Campaign in 1957 and the Campaign to Wrench Out White Flags in 1958. Engaging with Guo Wei's (郭維) film *Blooming Flowers and the Full Moon* (*Huahao yueyuan* 花好月圓) (1958), an adaptation of Zhao Shuli's (趙樹理) novel *Sanlian Village* (*Sanliwan* 三里灣) (1955), Zhuoyi Wang explains how this film epitomizes the uneasy tension between political agenda and commercial appeals. He also explores Lü Ban's (呂班) satirical comedies (*fengcixing xiju* 諷刺性喜劇), particularly *The Unfinished Comedies* (*Meiyou wancheng de xiju* 沒有完成的喜劇) (1957), that ridicule bureaucratic corruption and party-line didacticism. For this film, Zhuoyi Wang tells us, the director was labeled a rightist and got into trouble. The third phase took place during the Great Leap Forward period (1958–1961). Zhuoyi Wang engages with Zheng Junli's film *Nie Er* (*Nie'er* 聶耳) (1959), a biography of the composer of PRC's national anthem, to illustrate the flourishing of the combination of revolutionary realism and revolutionary romanticism (as opposed to the Soviet-styled socialist realism). For the fourth phase, which Zhuoyi Wang calls the Second Hundred Flowers period (1961–1964), the author explores the revival of star cultures and a particular kind of comedy called praising comedies (*gesongxing xiju* 歌頌性喜劇).[9] The fifth phase, which lasted from 1964 to the Cultural Revolution, witnesses the intense politicization of cultural productions and everyday life. Zhuoyi Wang calls the pendulum swings from propaganda/education to entertainment and back the revolutionary cycles in

Chinese cinema. Thanks to this periodization, I locate the filmic representations of fashion and consumption in the First Hundred Flowers and the Second Hundred Flowers periods. In what follows, I focus on the film *Never Forget*, which came out in 1964.

TO BUY OR NOT TO BUY?

Xie's film *Never Forget* is an adaptation of a play. The play, written by Cong Shen (叢深), was originally called *Wish You Good Health* (*Zhuni jiankang* 祝你健康) (1963). Later Cong modified some parts of the play, and the revised version was renamed *Never Forget* (*Qianwan buyao wangji* 千萬不要忘記). The filmic adaptation of this revised play was directed by Xie, who had just finished the film *Early Spring in February* (*Zaochun eryue* 早春二月) (1963). The latter was radically critiqued and presented as a negative example during the Cultural Revolution.[10] To be sure, *Never Forget* is a cultural elaboration of political propaganda. Never Forget—or, more precisely, "Never Forget Class Struggle" (千萬不要忘記階級鬥爭)—was a slogan of intense socialist mobilizations and revolutions in the 1960s. This film explained Mao's emphasis on continuous class struggle and permanent revolution after the initial success of socialism.[11] The regime was worried that China's young generation would be hit by sugar-coated bullets (*tangyi paodan* 糖衣炮彈): bourgeois and revisionist lifestyles were imagined as materialistic, individualistic, decadent, and detrimental to socialist revolution.

Never Forget is a cautionary tale of the danger of fashion and consumption within the context of Chinese socialist modernity. The protagonist is a young, innocent, and politically confused man called Ding Shaochun. He is subjected to the influence of two opposing sides: the proletarian side and the petty-bourgeois side. On the one hand, the proletarian side is represented by the Ding family, whose members include father, Ding Haikuan (丁海寬); mother, Ding Mu (Mother Ding) (丁母); son, Ding Shaochun; daughter, Ding Shaozhen (丁少真); and grandfather, Ding Yeye (Grandfather Ding) (丁爺爺). Added to the list is a model factory worker, Ji Youliang (季友良), a good friend of Ding Shaochun. In fact, the family name Ding (丁) connotes the political affiliation of this proletarian family. The word 丁 (*ding*) has the same pronunciation as 釘 (*ding*), as in screws and nails (*luosi ding* 螺絲釘). Because *Never Forget* came out in 1964, there are good reasons to believe that the family name evokes the nationwide Learn from

Comrade Lei Feng (向雷鋒同志學習) campaign in 1963. Born in 1940, Lei Feng (雷鋒) was an orphan. After the Japanese imperialists had killed his father, and after his mother had committed suicide as a result of the sexual harassment that she had suffered at the hands of the landlord's son, members of the CCP raised him as their child. Later, Lei joined the PLA and became a member of the CCP. Through diligent study of Chairman Mao's works, he led a life of frugality, eschewed selfishness, and fully dedicated himself to communist revolution and the people. In *The Diary of Lei Feng* (1962), Lei expresses his aspiration to become "a revolutionary screw that never rusts." He writes:

> A man's usefulness to the revolutionary cause is like a screw in a machine. It is only by the many, many interconnected and fixed screws that the machine can move freely, increasing its enormous work power. Though a screw is small, its use is beyond estimation. I am willing to be a screw. The screw needs to be maintained and cleaned in order to avoid rusting. The thought of a human being is the same. It needs to be constantly checked or else it will have problems.[12]

Unfortunately, Lei died at the age of twenty-two. In 1963 Mao initiated the Learn from Comrade Lei Feng campaign. China's youth was encouraged to follow Lei's example and become a socialist new person.[13] Later, the campaign evolved to become the Learn from the People's Liberation Army campaign. In *Never Forget*, members of the Ding family are devoted to socialist revolution and construction. They are useful screws of the socialist machine.

On the other hand, the petty-bourgeois side is represented by the Yao family, whose members include the money-minded mother, Yao Mu (Mother Yao) (姚母) and her daughter, Yao Yujuan (姚玉娟). These two families are related because Yao Yujuan is married to Ding Shaochun. Again, the family name, Yao, is telling: the word 姚 (*yao*) has the same pronunciation as 妖 (*yao*), which means evil spirits (妖精) or wicked monsters (妖怪). It can also be pronounced as 搖 (*yao*), which means to shake or destabilize. Nicknamed as family tutor, Mother Yao teaches Ding Shaochun to give into petty-bourgeois, individualistic, and materialistic temptations. Because Mother Yao used to work as a shopkeeper, she symbolizes the survival of the old petty bourgeoisie in the new socialist society. This class fraction is believed to be able to weaken and undermine the young generation's commitment to socialist revolution. Here the gendered representation of negative characters deserves attention. The petty-bourgeois figure is a woman. Similar to the Adam and Eve story in the book of Genesis, it is Mother Yao (like the snake) that causes the downfall of Ding Shaochun (like Adam). It is also his wife Yao Yujuan (like Eve) who encourages him to buy a high-quality suit (like the forbidden fruit) and facilitates his demise. From the socialist government's perspective, heterosexual marriage, family, and kinship, which lie outside of the state's radar, can be sites of concern.

In *Never Forget*, Ding Shaochun and Yao Yujuan are fascinated with smart-looking clothes. In the beginning of the film, Ding Shaochun has borrowed a leather jacket from a performance group. Looking at himself in the mirror, he feels gratified. Then he asks his wife and his mother-in-law whether he looks like an engineer. Similarly, in the beginning of the play, when Mother Yao sees Ding Shaochun in a leather jacket, she compliments him for looking like a technician. Then his wife brings in a high-quality suit that she has borrowed from Doctor Xu in the clinic. Ding Shaochun tries it on, and Mother Yao commends him for looking like a senior engineer. In both cases, the engineer that Mother Yao has in mind is Shao Yongbin (邵永斌), the husband of Yao Yujuan's second sister. Working as an engineer in the Department of Water and Electricity, Shao is part of the new professional-managerial class, or the new petty bourgeoisie, in the newly established socialist state. Because members of this group earn more than the average factory workers, they have extra money to buy nicer clothes and can dress in a fancier manner. However, how is Shao dressed? In the beginning of *Never Forget*, Mother Yao tells Ding Shaochun how impressed she is with Shao's outlook. She says: "Your brother-in-law is an engineer. Look at what he wore! That day, we saw him off at the airport. He was wearing a Western-style suit that cost as much as 200 yuan (or more). He was also wearing a high-quality suit and a pair of leather shoes. They were all foreign imports!"[14] In the beginning of the story, Ding Shaochun tries to imitate the clothing style of someone whose job is more respectable than his and whose social status is higher than his. Through imitation, he has the fantasy that he can be like Shao. However, he does not have enough money to buy these clothes.

In his book *Revolution and Its Narratives*, Cai explains how Ding Shaochun's imitation of Shao's outlook reveals a larger social problem:

It is without question that socialism produced its own bureaucratic class, a factor directly related to the outbreak of the Cultural Revolution. At the same time, *socialism also produced its own middle class or middle social level. This social level mainly consists of factory managers, experts, and technicians* [my emphasis]. The city became the major space in which they existed. As such, they were part of the so-called three big differences (*san da chabie*) identified by Mao (between workers and peasants, between city and countryside, and between mental and manual labor). Because of the existence of these differences, due to which the new urban middle level was able to enjoy a relatively comfortable life and working environment, this social level in turn became the object of envy and imitation (in pursuit of social status). Hence, we have Lin Yusheng in *The Young Generation* and his insistence on staying in the city, and we have in *Never Forget* Ding Shaochun's taste in imitating an engineer.[15]

In his book *Distinction* (1984), Pierre Bourdieu argues that the dominant taste of a society is the taste of the ruling class. In *Revolution and Its Narratives*, Cai challenges Bourdieu's argument by highlighting the fact that in Cong's play—and, one can add, in Xie's film—Ding Shaochun does not imitate the taste of the proletariat that is the ruling class of Chinese socialist modernity. He does not imitate the taste of Mother Yao who is a former shopkeeper, or the old petty bourgeoisie either. Instead he imitates Shao, who is a state engineer or technician. Shao belongs to the new professional-managerial class, or the new petty bourgeoisie, in the Chinese socialist state. According to Cai, this new petty bourgeoisie should not be considered a residue of the old society plagued by feudalism, imperialism, and bureaucratic capitalism; instead, it is a new and emergent social formation in the newly established socialist setting. In other words, the new professional-managerial class, or the new petty bourgeoisie, is an internal product of Chinese socialist modernity: it is actively produced by the new socialist state rather than being abolished by it. Cai's provocation—namely, that Chinese socialism produces its own middle class—challenges one's conventional understanding of the relationship among the middle class, capitalism, and socialism. He proposes the idea of the socialist middle class. Moreover, Cai is observant to point out that the figure of socialist new petty bourgeoisie has not been satisfactorily handled in *Never Forget*. After this new social actor has been introduced, the issues surrounding its emergence are prematurely foreclosed. The problem concerning the socialist new petty bourgeoisie is downplayed by the playwright and, I add, by the director. In the later part of the narrative, Cong depicts Shao in his humble proletarian outfit: "Mother Yao went outside, opened the door, and saw someone in a uniform carrying a distinctive travel bag. [Shao] appeared to be ungroomed and scruffy."[16] This is also true in the film. In *Never Forget*, the problematic figuration of the socialist new petty bourgeoisie is abruptly solved rather than being discussed and interrogated.

Back to the narrative: Later, Ding Shaochun and Yao Yujuan are informed that Shao will come to visit. One day, when the couple is shopping in a department store, they discover a high-quality suit that looks really nice. However, it costs as much as 148 yuan. It is too expensive for them. Nevertheless, the business-minded Mother Yao offers them a solution. She turns Ding Shaochun's interest in bird shooting into a business and helps him sell the birds in the market. Later she manages to collect enough money to help his son-in-law buy the high-quality suit. Because Ding Shaochun spends a lot of time shooting wild birds, he makes numerous mistakes at work, and each mistake is more serious than the previous one. In the beginning, Ding Shaochun yawns at work, which is discovered by his father. Because he spends too much time shopping in the department store, he arrives at his work late. He has also become more careless and absent-minded. For example, he forgets to close the machine's electrical door. Because of this mistake, the production is interrupted. To go bird hunting, he leaves work early twice: the first time he has to go back home to pick up the equipment and other necessities, and the second time he has to catch a train. Both times he has not obtained his supervisor's approval to leave work early. Worst of all, because he does everything in a hurry, he has carelessly dropped his key into the machine. This mistake can bring disastrous consequences to the supply of electricity in his town. He also becomes so engrossed with shooting birds that he misses the train to go back home. Because he misses work, Ding Haikuan and Ji have to take Ding Shaochun's shift in the factory. It is clear that Ding Shaochun's hobby has adversely impacted his work performance. In the end, Ding Haikuan lectures his son and Mother Yao:

Mother Yao, it is fine to dress beautifully. What I am worried is that the person who is wearing the clothes is getting less beautiful! It's similar to the goods that you used to sell. You focused on the packaging but what was inside was all rotten pears! [Then Haikuan turns to Shaochun.] Shaochun, the question is not what you wear or what you eat. The question is what you think, what you desire, and what you aspire toward! My child! In this world, there are thousands and millions of people who do not have proper clothes to wear! If you are only looking for personal satisfaction and material fulfillment, then you will forget to open the machine door, forget to go to work, forget socialist construction, and forget world revolution![17]

Despite this, Mother Yao does not keep Ding Haikuan's warning in mind. To return the money that she has borrowed from Daliu (大劉), Mother Yao asks Ding Shaochun to go bird shooting again so that she can sell more birds. This is the third time that she has asked Ding Shaochun to go bird hunting. Upon hearing this, Ding Haikuan becomes absolutely furious. As he is afraid that Ding Shaochun will end up selling the thoughts and feelings of the working class, he explicitly expresses his concerns: "Child! My child! Have you forgotten who you really are? Your grandfather is a peasant. Your father is a worker and a communist party member. You used to wear a red neckerchief and belong to the communist youth organization! You are a member of the proletariat! Now, you are selling this and that, and eventually, you will sell all the thoughts and feelings of the proletariat away!"[18]

Mother Yao feels so embarrassed that she plans to leave. However, Ding Haikuan asks her to stay. Then he lectures the whole family about the importance of continuous class struggle in the context of socialism. According to him, the forces of the old society are still resilient, and bourgeois ideology may resurface at any moment.[19] Ding Haikuan explains:

Do you think once you have sent your mother away, then you will be safe? No! Your thinking is far too simple. This is not a question of your mother alone. This is the inertia of the old society. There are many people who are similar to your mother and they are everywhere! It is hard to notice that they have already harmed your ideological health. . . . The Party would like you to become the heirs of the proletarian class. But they would like you to become the heirs of the bourgeois class. This is class struggle! This kind of class struggle does not come with the sound of gunfire or cannon. They creep into our lives when we are talking and laughing. This kind of class struggle cannot be detected easily! This kind of class struggle is also easily forgotten. Never, never forget![20]

The message of this film is obvious: "Never forget class struggle" even after the initial success of socialism!

THE POLITICS OF SOCIALIST CONSUMPTION

In his essay "The Formation of the Theme of *Never Forget*" (<千萬不要忘記>主題的形成), the playwright Cong explains how he formulates the story:

One night, my roommate (who currently works as a branch secretary) and I had a conversation. There are twenty-four hours in a day. The factory workers work for eight hours, and even if there are extra meetings, one works for, at most, ten hours. The workers spend the rest of their time outside the factory and are exposed to different kinds of people and ideas. It is difficult to determine what kind of education they receive at home. It is difficult to know who their relatives and friends are. When we are not promoting socialist education, others may spread bourgeois ideologies to them. It is true that what the workers have learned in the factory can be undone at home. The branch secretary kept saying: "the impact of the family cannot be underestimated!"[21]

Cong perceptively points out the problem of time management in the context of socialist modernity. (In fact, time management is also a problem of capitalist modernity because it involves the reproduction of labor.) There are twenty-four hours in a day. If eight hours are dedicated to sleep and rest, eight hours are devoted to production and work, then the remaining eight hours can be devoted to leisure, consumption, and the family. However, how should the latter eight hours be organized in Chinese socialist modernity? What should socialist everyday life look like? What should socialist consumption be like?

In *Never Forget*, the primary source of conflict—namely, Ding Shaochun's desire for high-quality suit and his involvement in leisure activities—has to do with consumption and spare time. When he shoots wild birds, he does it outside the space and time of the factory. When he purchases the high-quality suit, he does it outside the space and time of production and labor. In this sense, the film expresses the socialist regime's anxiety toward consumption or, more accurately, excessive consumption and overconsumption. However, how is consumption represented in this film? Judging from Ding Haikuan's angry reactions, it appears that the socialist attitude toward consumption is strictly negative: consumption should be condemned. However, careful study of Ding Haikuan's speech makes it clear that his view toward consumption is, in fact, ambivalent. He does not explicitly endorse or disapprove Ding Shaochun's consumption; rather, he expresses his view in the form of "I do not object to it, but. . . ."

From Ding Haikuan's perspective, the most important tasks in his agenda are production and revolution, not consumption. In the filmic narrative, he does not oppose Ding Shaochun's leisure activities in an explicit manner. He warns his son: "I don't object to the fact that you shoot wild birds. Just be careful not to get addicted to it."[22] In other words, as long as it does not interfere with Ding Shaochun's work performance, and as long as Ding Shaochun does not become addicted to it, Ding Haikuan has no objection to his son's hobbies. Moreover, Ding Haikuan has never disapproved of his junior colleague, Daliu, from shooting wild birds in his spare time, nor has he warned his colleague not to go bird shooting with his son. He has never stopped his daughter, Ding Shaozhen, from watching football game with Ji either. Interestingly, Ding Haikuan has never explicitly objected his son's wearing the high-quality suit. He exclaims: "Shaochun! The question is not what you wear and what you eat. The question is what you are thinking, what you desire, and what you aspire toward!" On a different occasion, he says: "It's fine to dress smartly. I am just afraid that the person who wears the clothes is becoming less beautiful!"

I go further to assert that Ding Haikuan *implicitly* endorses consumption in the new socialist society. This can be observed at the end of the play when he lectures his son:

> A high-quality uniform, this is a good thing. It's better than the piece of clothing that I am wearing. It's also better than synthetic materials. This is something that the laboring people dare not imagine to have. Now, you dare to have it, and some people can also own it. This is a good thing. This is the result of revolution and construction! There will be one day when everyone in China and everyone in the world can wear the best kind of clothing! But now, thousands and millions of people do not even have the worst kind of clothing to wear![23]

Ding Haikuan regards the high-quality suit as "a good thing," and the desire to buy and wear it is "a very good thing." The socialist authority implicitly approves consumption in the new society. In his essay "The Formation of the Theme of *Never Forget*," Cong explains how he rewrote the play. In the original version, he portrayed the purchase of the high-quality suit in a negative manner. Later he was advised to rewrite some parts of the play and depict consumption in a more neutral way. He explains: "In the first draft of the play, the representation of the high-quality suit was one-dimensional. It gave people an impression that we oppose the wearing of the high-quality suit. Then some leaders and comrades pointed out the problem to me. I rewrote the play accordingly. In the final version, the description of this particular scene was very different."[24] Indeed, there is no reason for Chinese socialist modernity to oppose material abundance or a prosperous life. This should be one of the purposes of socialist revolutions and constructions.

In *Never Forget*, four different kinds of clothes are featured. The first kind is the piece of gunnysack cloth (*madaipian* 麻袋片). Too poor to buy a decent piece of clothing, Grandfather Ding can only use a piece of gunnysack cloth to cover his body during imperialism and feudalism. This is certainly not an option for clothing Chinese people after the revolution. The second kind is the clothes that the proletarian characters wear in socialist China. The clothes that Ding Haikuan and Ji wear in their everyday lives are simple, functional, and practical. The third kind is the red sweater that Ding Shaozhen wears when she goes to see the soccer game with Ji. What distinguishes the third kind is that the red sweater, a gift from Ding Shaozhen's parents, is slightly more fashionable than ordinary clothing. Ding Haikuan says to his daughter: "Now all the young people in the factory have got one [the red sweater] already. You should probably get one too." The red sweater is fashionable and popular among the factory workers. From this line, I see that Ding Haikuan endorses a mild and reasonable degree of fashion during the socialist period.[25] It is therefore incorrect to say that fashion and consumption are completely rejected or denied during the socialist period. The fourth kind is the high-quality suit that Ding Shaochun has bought in the department store. This suit is made of excellent materials and is aesthetically pleasing.

The portrayal of these four different kinds of clothes resonates with Mao's idea. In his famous speech *Yan'an Talks on Literature and Art* (在延安文藝

座談會上的講話) (1942), Mao articulates the dialectic of popularization (*puji* 普及) and raising standard (*tigao* 提高) regarding arts and literature. In the beginning of his talk, Mao asks a question: "Whom does one serve?" His answer is that one should first serve the proletariat, including the workers, peasants, and soldiers. The working class is the primary audience of arts and literature produced by socialist cultural workers. Then Mao poses another question: "How should one serve?" While he offers two options, namely, popularization or raising standard, which one should be the priority? Mao emphasizes that in the 1940s, the most urgent task should be popularization, that is, to make arts and literature widely available to people.[26]

Although Mao deals primarily with arts and literature, his idea can be creatively adopted to articulate the socialist order of things, including consumption. Indeed, one can relate Mao's idea to *Never Forget*. According to this logic, clothes should be produced first and foremost for the proletariat and the people, not for individuals in a privileged class. The most urgent task is popularization—that is, to make clothes widely available to everyone. However, this goal has yet to be completely actualized in the new socialist society. Ding Haikuan exclaims: "But now, thousands and millions of people do not even have the worst kind of clothes to wear!" The objective is to offer Chinese people the most basic and functional kind of clothes. The dialectic evolves: the change in quantity will lead to the change in quality, and popularization will lead to the demand of a higher standard. Once the most basic and functional kind of clothes has been widely democratized, then Chinese people can strive to wear clothes made of better-quality materials, such as the red sweater that Ding Shaozhen wears. Once the standard has been raised, then, through a dialectical turn, the task of popularization can begin. After the red sweater has been widely adopted, then Chinese people can aspire to wear the high-quality suit that Ding Shaochun has purchased in the department store. The long-term goal is that high-quality clothes are available to everyone.

In *Never Forget*, although Ding Haikuan authorizes consumption in the new socialist society, he presents his endorsement with some reservations. He says: "yes, but. . . ." Even though he acknowledges the appeal of the high-quality suit, he emphasizes that it is not something to be desired in the present but something to be achieved in the future. Such a yearning is immediately postponed. In *Revolution and Its Narratives*, Cai makes a similar point regarding the deferral of desire in *Never Forget*. He writes: "In this ideologically clear speech, interestingly enough, the fact that the [high-quality suit] still dominates the ruling taste is tacitly accepted, even if it is being postponed to the future."[27]

The narrative begins with Ding Shaochun's desire for a high-quality suit and ends with Ding Haikuan's serious warnings about the dangers of fashion and consumption. He lectures his son: "If you are only thinking about the high-quality suit, if you are only thinking about shooting a few more wild birds, then you will forget closing the electrical door, you will forget going to work, you will forget the fact that our country is making progress, and you will forget world revolution!"

Two scenarios are presented. In the first scenario, Ding Shaochun buys the high-quality suit, shoots wild birds, and makes mistakes that can bring disastrous consequences to the supply of electricity in his hometown. In the second scenario, Ding Haikuan works all the time, not only in the factory, but also at home. His home is an extension of his workplace. During dinner, he still discusses work with his family. Similarly, Ji works very hard the entire day. Sometimes he discusses work with Ding Haikuan even after dinner is over. He spends all his energy on work and sacrifices his personal time to do scientific experiments for the factory. However, Ji does not have any hobbies outside his workplace. Contrary to Ding Shaochun who works and shoots wild birds, Ji spends most of his time in the factory. Preoccupied with work, Ding Haikuan and Ji do not consume and do not cause any troubles.[28] In his Chinese-language essay "The Historical Meaning of *Never Forget*—The Anxiety of Everyday Life and Modernity" (《千萬不要忘記》的歷史意義—關於日常生活的焦慮及其現代性), Tang Xiaobing remarks that the characterizations of Ding Haikuan and Ji suppress the distinctions between production and consumption, between work and leisure, between factory and home, between the public and the private, and between the collective and the individual.[29] In *Never Forget*, the socialist new persons seem uninterested in leisure and consumption.

While these two scenarios are extreme, *Never Forget* does not attempt to imagine a third scenario that can simultaneously accommodate production and consumption. In my analysis, there is simply no logical connection between the desire to own a high-quality suit and shoot wild birds in one's spare time, on the one hand, and the consequences of (1) forgetting to close the machine door, (2) missing work, (3) forgetting the fact that one's country is still in the early stage of development, and (4) forgetting world revolution, on the other hand. The fact that Ding Shaochun desires to wear smart-looking clothes should not necessarily lead to the conclusion that it will be detrimental to his work performance. In fact, it is possible for him to wear the high-quality suit, arrive at work on time, and perform his duties in a responsible manner. Similarly, the fact that Ding Shaochun enjoys shooting birds should not inevitably mean that he will become less committed to class struggle, nation building, and world revolution. In fact, he can enjoy bird shooting while serving as a politically committed revolutionary. However, in *Never Forget*, this "work hard and play hard" attitude is not offered as an option.

Nevertheless, rather than consider the lack of the third option to be a mirror reflection of the socialist attitude toward consumption, I argue that this is a symptom of the larger problems that confronted Chinese socialist modernity in the mid-1960s. My inspiration comes from Fredric Jameson's critical theory. In his groundbreaking book *The Political Unconscious: Narrative as a Socially Symbolic Act* (1981), Jameson constructs a theoretical model to interpret the politics of European literary productions, such as the novels of Balzac, George Gissing, and Joseph Conrad. In the chapter "On Interpretation: Literature as a Socially Symbolic Act," Jameson explains that his theory consists of three related levels. The first level concerns historical contexts and events. By history, he means the chronicle-like sequence of happenings in time. The second level attends to social classes and groups. The third level focuses on the economic mode of production. For the third level, he devises the concept of ideology of form to decipher the latent content embedded in the text. For Jameson, form is sediment content; the form carries with it latent ideological messages that are not the same as the manifest messages. Jameson explains: "[Formal] specification and description can, in a given . . . text, be transformed into the detection of a host of distinct [formal] messages—some of them objectified survivals from older modes of cultural production, some anticipatory, but all together projecting a formal conjuncture through which the 'conjuncture' of coexisting modes of production at a given historical moment can be detected and allegorically articulated."[30]

Extending this interpretative model to second-world cultural productions, I argue that selected Chinese socialist texts, including propaganda films, can also be analyzed as allegories. Delving into the symptoms of representational forms, I reveal the contradictions of Chinese socialist modernity in the early and mid-1960s. I also map how coexisting modes of production have been inscribed into and permeated within these socialist texts.

I argue that the narrative concerning the consumption of clothes and leisure in *Never Forget* maps, scans, and identifies the symptoms of the profound contradictions that confronted Chinese socialist modernity in the early and mid-1960s. These contradictions can be demonstrated on the three levels that Jameson outlines in *The Political Unconscious*. Concerning the first level on the historical, I have focused on Chinese socialist clothing and film histories in the first part of this chapter. Regarding the second level on the social, I have attended to social relations and class hierarchies, proletarian consciousness, and bourgeois ideology in the second part of this chapter. Considering the third level on the political-economic, I engage with the representational form to interrogate the struggle between socialist modernity and capitalist modernity (including revisionism) during the Cold War. In short, Chinese socialist texts have their political unconscious; the narrative form of *Never Forget* surprisingly reveals otherwise imperceptible worlds.

I maintain the importance of thinking through contradictions when analyzing Chinese socialist cultures. In what follows, I converse with scholars Zhang Yiwu (張頤武), Tina Mai Chen, Tang Xiaobing, and Cai Xiang, who have examined Chinese socialist cultures. In his blog entry "The Temptation of Fashion" (時尚的誘惑) on May 29, 2007, Zhang points out the contradiction of fashion and consumption within the context of Chinese socialist modernity. Analyzing socialist classics such as *Never Forget* (1964) and *Sentinels Under the Neon Lights* (*Nihong dengxia de shaobing* 霓虹燈下的哨兵) (1964), he points out:

> On the one hand, fashion is regarded as a dangerous temptation. It is regarded as one way through which the bourgeoisie may invade the socialist body. In

order to have a good and communist future, fashion has to be repressed. But on the other hand, fashion is also regarded as one goal to be achieved in the future. Fashion does not have to be something far-fetched. It is something that everyone can enjoy. It is not that this goal cannot be achieved at all. It is only on the condition that everyone is given the chance to appreciate this kind of life that one can really enjoy fashion. . . . The socialist planned economy affirms the legitimacy of fashion, but at the same time, fashion is denied and is relegated as something to be achieved in the future.[31]

Zhang confirms my analysis concerning the representation of fashion in *Never Forget*: it is simultaneously affirmed and denied.

In her article "Proletarian White and Working Bodies in Mao's China" (2003), Tina Mai Chen also engages with contradiction to examine the richness and complexity of Chinese socialist cultures. Going further, she argues that in Chinese socialist iconography, the proletarian working body dressed in white reveals "the difficult relationship between proletarianization and modernization."[32] According to Chen, this iconography presents the proletariat—an alliance of worker, peasant, and soldier—as healthy, fit, strong, and muscular. While the workers roll up their sleeves and bare their arms, the peasants push their trousers above their knees and exhibit their calves. In contrast, the skilled workers and technicians cover their bodies with white shirts and uniforms.[33] Their white shirts and uniforms signify professionalization, modernization, and technical expertise. The educated youths, who have migrated to the countryside to contribute to socialist construction, often wear white and short-sleeved shirts while working in the fields. While the white shirts denote their professional knowledge and technical expertise, the short sleeves suggest that their physical bodies need to be tempered by manual labor so that their bodies can match their knowledge and expertise. Chen also explains how white aprons, caps, sleeve covers, and laboratory coats donned by the skilled workers in textile and manufacturing industries symbolize science, technology, and rationalization. These pictorial examples lead her to argue that the proletarian white and working bodies condense the contradiction of "proletarian politics and modernization goals."[34]

Chen's argument concerning proletarianization and socialist modernization echoes Mao's idea regarding the dialectical operation of popularization and raising standard. It is also useful to analyze *Never Forget*.

Indeed, the clothes that Ding Haikuan and Ji wear in their everyday lives are an example of proletarianization; meanwhile, the high-quality suit that Ding Shaochun has purchased and the Western suit that the engineer Shao wore when Mother Yao saw him off at the airport are examples of socialist modernization. Referring to the scene in which Ding Shaochun tries on the leather jacket at home and the scene in which he tries on the high-quality suit in the department store, Cai would say that it is the proletarian character's imitation of the new petty bourgeoisie produced by the new socialist party-state. However, Chen would regard the smartly dressed Ding Shaochun as an example of the "proletarian white (professional) and working body." Similar to the socialist state technician or engineer, this figure embodies the contradiction of proletarianization (proletarian work) and socialist modernization (the high-quality suit). Concerning the scene in which the engineer Shao appears in humble proletarian clothes when he meets the Ding family members in the later part of *Never Forget*, Cai would suggest that the problem of the socialist new petty bourgeoisie has been brought up but is prematurely foreclosed and insufficiently addressed. However, Chen would maintain that this figure is also an example of the "proletarian and white working body." Similar to the educated youth in the countryside, the figuration of Shao expresses the contradiction of proletarianization (clothes) and socialist modernization (middle-class occupation).

Similar to Chen, Tang Xiaobing delves into contradiction to dissect the richness and complexity of Chinese socialist culture. In "The Historical Meaning of *Never Forget*—The Anxiety of Everyday Life and Modernity," Tang analyzes Cong's play and suggests that it symptomatically reveals the contradiction that confronts Chinese socialism with regards to *industrialized* modernity: "This play has fully captured the contradictory imaginations of an age toward industrialized modernity. It has expressed a strong desire for modernity but at the same time it refuses and resists it."[35] In my interpretation of Tang's essay, the contradiction is as follows: on the one hand, the socialist government desires and embraces the productivity and efficiency of industrialized modernity; but on the other hand, the socialist administration is worried about the problems brought by the industrialized modernity. Tang calls this reaction "anxiety of everyday life."

Thinking with Tang, I suggest that the emergence of industrialized modernity results in the breaking up of traditional organization of time and space, resulting in the separations between work time and leisure time and between the factory and home. The socialist government attempts to overcome this crisis by erasing the divisions between production and consumption and between labor and leisure. This can be observed in the father figure, Ding Haikuan, and the socialist new person, Ji, who work all the time and do not take time off. This can also be detected in Ding Haikuan's critique of Ding Shaochun for having forgotten about class struggle as Ding Shaochun's hobbies have badly affected his work performance.

The arrival of industrialized modernity also involves the dissolution of traditional social structures. Contrary to the petty-bourgeois Mother Yao, who embraces commodity exchange, the old-fashioned Ding Haikuan seems to prefer social relations, hierarchies, and values in agricultural society because the latter appears to be more natural, organic, wholesome, and un-alienated to him. Traditional family relation comprising grandparents, parents, and children is the social organization that he cherishes. (However, such a familial arrangement can be patriarchal because the power resides in men.) From the characterization of Ding Haikuan, one can detect a nostalgia to return to earlier times characterized by strong communal bonds, respect for the authority, and reciprocal relations.

Building on Tang's observation, I argue that *Never Forget* condenses what Marxist cultural critic Raymond Williams, in his book *Marxism and Literature* (1977), calls the residual, the dominant, and the emergent of the modes of production.[36] I contend that the form of *Never Forget* abbreviates the feudalistic and agricultural as the residual survival of an older mode of production, the socialist (and its Cold War counterpart, the capitalist) and industrial as the dominant mode of production, and the utopian and communist as an anticipation of a newer mode of production that has yet to fully actualize. In fact, the conjunctures of the feudalistic as the residual, the socialist (and the capitalist) as the dominant, and the communist as the emergent are exactly what Jameson calls the political unconscious.

Responding to the dissolution of traditional conceptions of time, space, and social relations, the socialist leadership attempts to erase the spatial and temporal divisions of work and leisure. However, rather than regarding modernity as a site of political contestation—that is, to argue that socialism can be as modern as, or perhaps more modern than, capitalism—the socialist regime can only manage its "anxiety of everyday life" by repressing and displacing its anxiety to its external enemies. Tang explains:

> The historical meaning of *Never Forget* is that it has displaced and repressed the root of the problem, and because of this, it has recorded the collective anxiety of its historical period. If *Wish You Healthy* [the earlier title of the play] expresses the desire of overcoming modernity, *Never Forget* [the final title of the play and the film] symptomatically expresses the avoidance of answering the question. It has externalized its internal anxiety onto the other—"bourgeois quagmire/slime-pit," "disease/virus," and "class enemy" etc.[37]

In my observation, Tang tries to think dialectically. He does not consider the "anxiety of everyday life" in industrialized modernity to be a flaw of Chinese socialism. Rather, he suggests that what is bad about the text is actually what is good about it. What is bad about the text is that it has displaced and repressed the root of the problem. What is good about the text is that it has recorded the collective anxiety of its historical period. Building on this understanding, I explain how repression and displacement function in *Never Forget*.[38]

To be sure, repression and displacement are at work in *Never Forget*. In the first scenario, characters such as Ding Haikuan and Ji reveal the repression of the divisions between production and consumption, between work time and leisure time, and between factory and home. The socialist regime also displaces its "anxiety of everyday life" to its external others—namely, the bourgeoisie (an empty signifier) and the old petty bourgeoisie (Mother Yao). Here I note that the use of bourgeoisie in *Never Forget* is unclear. This term can refer to the remnants of the bourgeoisie formed during the pre-liberation era and continued during the New Democracy period. It may signify specific class interests, ideological positions, and political attitudes. It can also denote the new bureaucratic and ruling class formed within the CCP since the founding of the PRC.[39] In *Never Forget*, the playwright Cong and film director Xie do not specify what they really mean by the bourgeoisie. In the second scenario, as Cai suggests, the most problematic figure in *Never Forget* is the socialist engineer Shao (the new petty bourgeoisie), rather than Ding Shaochun (the proletariat) or Mother Yao (the old petty bourgeoisie). Although Shao is brought up, his class position and cultural taste are insufficiently interrogated. The new petty bourgeoisie is repressed, and the blame is shifted, or displaced, to Mother Yao, who is thought to have had a bad influence on the young generation.

While Tang focuses on the contradictions of industrialized modernity, Cai Xiang goes one step further to highlight the contradiction of *socialist* industrialized modernity, or simply socialist modernity. By doing so, Cai emphasizes that socialism is as modern and industrialized as capitalism. Such a conceptualization enables him to argue that the issues registered in *Never Forget* are the products of socialist, rather than capitalist, modernity. In his book *Revolution and Its Narratives* (2016), Cai draws attention to the dialectic of revolution and construction after the founding of the PRC. According to him, in the 1950s, Chinese people were willing to engage in revolutions because they desired to build a materially abundant, prosperous, and utopian society. However, in the 1960s, as they had already begun to enjoy the benefits created by the success of revolutions in the previous decade, their willingness to further the revolutions diminished. Cai writes: "On the one hand, [the goal of] revolution lies in the construction of a materially well-off society. On the other hand, this materially well-off society may also destroy the revolution itself or at least cause it to stop."[40]

Cai then focuses on socialist construction in the 1960s. Specifically, he considers distribution and consumption to be central issues of socialist construction. Because distribution and construction challenged and threatened to dissolve the polity, the socialist government initiated and promoted the Cultural Revolution (1966–1976) to solve these problems. Targeting the unequal distribution of resources between state cadres and masses, the Cultural Revolution radically critiqued the "capitalist roaders" (*zou zipai* 走資派) within the CCP. The revolution also intended to solve the problem of consumption within the context of socialist modernity. What is truly provocative about Cai's argument is that he considers consumption a problem of socialism rather than a problem of capitalism. Similar to how he suggests that socialism creates its own middle class, Cai thinks that socialism also creates its own consumption. According to him, Ding Shaochun's purchase of high-quality suit and his shooting of wild birds should be regarded as an internal problem of socialism. These activities are created by socialist modernity as such; they are not the result of being influenced by capitalist revival or bourgeois revisionism. Moving further, Cai argues that socialist modernity creates consumption as much as it creates production; moreover, socialist modernity produces desire, leisure, lifestyle, and everyday life as much as it produces labor. Thus, Cai's provocation animates another contradiction in Chinese socialist modernity in the 1960s. On the one hand, socialism produces consumption and desire; but on the other hand, consumption and desire, as products of socialism, produce the crisis of socialism.

Here I compare Cai's argument with Tang's argument to observe their specificities. In his essay "The Historical Meaning of *Never Forget*," Tang discusses the spatial, temporal, and social fragmentations within the context of *industrialized* modernity. In particular, he explains how industrialized modernity produces the divisions between work space and leisure space and between work time and leisure time. In *Revolution and Its Narratives*, Cai agrees with Tang and further underscores how *socialist* industrialized modernity also produces the divisions between production and consumption and between the collective and the individual. Cai stresses that socialist modernity produces its own mode of consumption and individualness. Arguing against the understanding that socialist modernity focuses on production at the expense of consumption, Cai insists that socialist modernity creates consumption as much as it creates production. Opposing the view that socialist modernity emphasizes the collective at the detriment of the individual, Cai maintains that socialist modernity produces the individual as much as it produces the collective.[41] According to Cai's evaluation, socialist modernity also manufactures its own mode of cultural taste, lifestyle, and everyday life.

According to Tang, the socialist regime responds to the crisis of spatial, temporal, and social fragmentations by erasing the divisions between work time and leisure time and between the factory and home. In Cai's analysis, the socialist government reacts to the problem of consumption by mobilizing the political discourse of class struggles and continuous revolutions ("never forget class struggle"). This way, the socialist authority imagines, the separation between the collective and the individual can be canceled and the individual can be safely subsumed under the collective. Cai thinks that this solution is highly problematic because the root of the problem is cultural rather than political or economic. He writes: "When socialism was unable to offer a unique and good lifestyle and relied on power to turn conflicts between [different] tastes (lifestyle) into political ones (in terms of class struggle), in effect a kind of anxiety was manifested."

Cai continues:

> Even though the proletarian class had absolute political and economic power in the socialist state, in the cultural domain, especially in terms of everyday life, it did not acquire absolute power. Because of that, it had to resort to political and collective or communal narrative forms to reexamine the existing cultural order. So long as the reexamination is about the existing world order, it is bound to be political. This particular situation regarding the narratives of the time indicates the awkward position occupied by proletarian literature in China's socialist period: politically strong while culturally weak. What cultural conflicts existed were aided by the political power that ironically prevented cultural politics from being further carried out. The deeper difficulty about this awkward position still has to do with the question of how socialism deals with the class differences and individual desires that it itself produces.[42]

According to Cai, in the first half of the 1960s, while the socialist government managed to achieve political and economic powers, it had yet to obtain cultural hegemony, especially in the realm of everyday life. The socialist authority could only clumsily resort to political order to reorganize cultural life. This tactic is problematic. The Cultural Revolution in the second half of the 1960s was then initiated and mobilized to refashion the socialist order of things, such as consumption, leisure, and everyday life.

Inspired by Cai's scholarship, I conclude that the ambivalent representation of high-quality suit in *Never Forget* and what Tang calls "anxiety of everyday life" in the context of socialist industrialized modernity are symptomatic expressions of the historical contradiction that confronted Chinese socialism on the eve of the Cultural Revolution. The contradiction is that in the 1960s, socialist China had already achieved the control over politics and economy, but the regime had yet to obtain hegemony over culture and everyday life. When one examines Chinese socialist modernity in this manner, the Cultural Revolution is not only a radical critique of the bureaucratic bourgeoisie or capitalist roaders within the CCP but also a serious attempt for the socialist regime to overcome the contradiction ("strong in terms of politics and weak in terms of culture") and regain cultural power and ideological supremacy.

REPRESSION OR SUBLIMATION

Now I turn to another set of scholarly conversations to enrich my analysis. Tackling cultural critiques from Marxist, feminist, and psychoanalytical perspectives, this set of dialogues involve Meng Yue, Ban Wang, Jason McGrath, and Jianmei Liu. Although these cultural critics do not focus on *Never Forget*, their works regarding love, gender, and sexuality, on the one hand, and revolutionary politics, on the other hand, can be creatively adapted to explain my view toward fashion, leisure, and consumption in the context of socialist China.

Meng provides the language of repression to articulate the socialist politics of gender and sexuality. Her analysis enables one to see that fashion, consumption, and leisure are repressed in *Never Forget*. In her Chinese-language article "*White-Haired Girl* and the Historical Complexities of Yan'an Literature" (《白毛女》與「延安文學」的歷史複雜性) (1993), Meng engages with the evolution of Chinese socialist classic *White-Haired Girl*— from the folk opera through the film to the ballet—to explain how socialist politics works with and accommodates local cultures and customs. She demonstrates that the folk opera staged in Yan'an in 1945 can be considered a combination of popular and folk culture (e.g., the folktale), May Fourth new culture, and political culture of the newly established authority in the liberated areas. The folk opera embodies the tensions between popular culture and high culture, between the country and the city, between tradition and modernity, and between China and the West. Traditional aesthetics, ethical principles, and community practices also contribute to the folk opera's political message.[43]

Then Meng turns to the film directed by Wang Bin (王濱) and Shui Hua (水華) in 1950. She emphasizes how the love story between female peasant Xi'er (喜兒) and male peasant Dachun (大春) serves as the theme. Indeed, it is their love that legitimizes the politicized socialist discourse.[44] Shifting gears to the ballet in 1966, Meng underscores how the socialist discourse of class struggle and revolution is prominently emphasized, and how gender, sexuality, and the body (e.g., rape, pregnancy, and birth) are strategically erased.[45] For instance, in the ballet, Xi'er's father, Yang Bailao (楊白勞), is filled with the spirit of revolt. The landlord, Huang Shiren (黃世仁), abducts Yang's daughter, and Yang fights against him until his death. Moreover, by the end of the ballet, Xi'er joins the revolutionary army and devotes herself to the CCP's mission. From these adjustments, one can observe the gradual politicization of culture during the socialist period; it reaches a peak during the Cultural Revolution. In her English-language essay "Female Images and National Myth" (1993), Meng further explains how gendered subjectivity is suppressed and eliminated. On the one hand, she writes, "the state's political discourse translated itself through women into the private context of desire, love, marriage, divorce, and familial relations, and on the other, it turned woman into an agent politicizing desire, love, family relations by delimiting and repressing sexuality, self, and all private emotions."[46] According to her, what emerges in this process is not only the becoming visible of the absolute authority of the CCP but also the de-gendering or de-sexualization of the individual.

Whereas Meng suggests that love, gender, and sexuality are repressed in Chinese socialist cultures, Ban Wang argues that they are sublimated by revolutionary politics. Following Ban Wang's acute analysis, one can say that fashion, consumption, and leisure are sublimated in *Never Forget*. In the chapter "Desire and Pleasure in Revolutionary Cinema" in his book *The Sublime Figure of History: Aesthetics and Politics in Twentieth-Century China* (1997), Ban Wang argues that Chinese socialist cultures in the seventeen years (1949–1966) do not repress sexual libidos or psychic energies but instead sublimate and convert these erotic impulses to revolutionary passions.[47] His notion comes from Herbert Marcuse's idea of non-repressive sublimation. Commenting on Meng's critique of socialist patriarchy, Ban Wang wonders why socialist cultures have such strong emotional appeals and imaginative impacts to the audience. Engaging with Cui Wei's (崔嵬) film *Song of Youth* (*Qingchun zhige* 青春之歌) (1959), Wang explains that intellectual woman Lin Daojing (林道靜) is not repressed and replaced by the communist collective; rather, she is reborn in and through the multitude. The feeling of being in and belonging to a collective is joyful, pleasurable, and, in the language of Slavoj Žižek, enjoyable. (Žižek says that one can enjoy politics, including one's nation, class, and race.[48]) In addition, examining Zheng Junli's film *Nie Er* (*Nie'er* 聶耳) (1959), Ban Wang suggests that the romantic love and desire between the composer of Chinese national anthem, Nie Er, and his lover-cum-revolutionary mentor, Zheng Leidian, is not denied; instead it is assimilated by and rechanneled for revolutionary politics. Interestingly, Ban Wang argues that communist cultures are sexually charged: these cultures are attractive because they incorporate rather than reject sexuality (here, sexuality should not be narrowly defined as genital sex). According to Ban Wang, the relationship between sexuality and communist politics should be the reverse of what is commonly perceived: it is that sexuality exists in the guise of politics, not that politics appropriates sexuality for its purpose. It is sexuality that has been politicized (political sexuality), not that politics has been sexualized (sexual politics).[49] In Ban Wang's analysis, communist politics can also assume an aesthetic and a libidinal dimension; it, too, can be enjoyed as art.

Inspired by Ban Wang's argument regarding sexual sublimation, Jason McGrath focuses on the impact of Hollywood cinema on Chinese revolutionary cinema. In his article "Communists Have More Fun!" (2009), McGrath examines Xie Jin's (謝晉) film *The Red Detachment of Women* (*Hongse niangzijun* 紅色娘子軍) (1961), Cui Wei's film *Song of Youth* (*Qingchun zhige* 青春之歌) (1959), and two other films in order to trace the changing relationship between the libidinal and the political in the second half of twentieth-century China. Following Ban Wang's thinking concerning sublimation, McGrath suggests that the love between the characters, such as the romantic feeling between Wu Qionghua (吳瓊花) (female) and Hong Changqing (洪常青) (male) in *The Red Detachment of Women*, and that between Lin Daojing (林道靜) (female) and Lu Jiachuan (盧嘉川) (male) in *Song of Youth*, are sublimated by and rechanneled to revolutionary politics. McGrath goes further to point out how "trans-narrational sublimation" operates in these socialist films. By this, he draws attention to how generic conventions of classical Hollywood romance are appropriated and deployed in Chinese revolutionary films. For example, narrative conventions such as mise-en-scène, editing (e.g., shot/reverse shot), close-up, framing, and nonverbal performance cues are preserved in Chinese revolutionary films. However, rather than signaling the romance between the characters, these devices are now resignified with new political meanings. For instance, in *The Red Detachment of Women*, while the visual narrative implies that Wu is in love with Hong and that Hong is likely to reciprocate, the manifest content focuses on how the communist comradeship between them is growing stronger. Meanwhile, in a particular scene in *Song of Youth*, while Lin and Jiang Hua (江華) are rowing a boat together, the visual cues show that

Jiang is proposing to Lin, and Lin is moved to tears. However, the manifest content turns out to center on revolutionary politics: Jiang is telling Lin that her application to become a CCP member has been accepted. She is so over-joyed that she cries. Taken together, McGrath considers that such "generic residua" facilitate sublimation and re-signify for the revolutionary cause.

I am interested in thinking with Ban Wang and McGrath. Certainly, one can positively look at the sublimation of the libidinal by the political and argue that this process produces visual pleasures and enhances political identifications. However, I think the opposite can also be true: visual plea-sures do not necessarily lead to political identifications. It is possible that the viewers do not respond to or identify with the revolutionary message; instead, they may subscribe to what the conventional narratives and formal styles (e.g., Hollywood conventions, Shanghai traditions) originally signify. This is evidenced in the documentary film *Yang Ban Xi: The 8 Model Works* (*Yangbanxi* 樣板戲) (2005), which presents the eight model operas produced during the Cultural Revolution period. In this film, one male interviewee recalls how he was sexually aroused by the female dancers' bodies when he watched the ballet *The Red Detachment of Women* when he was young. This anecdote shows that he was more interested in the ballet dancers' bodies than the ballet's political message. Such nonidentification is also illustrated in Carma Hinton's documentary film *Morning Sun* (*Bajiu dianzhong de tai-yang* 八九點鐘的太陽) (2003), which focuses on the political, social, and cul-tural dimensions of the Cultural Revolution. In this film, one male inter-viewee recollects how he was sexually attracted to the female spy in the espionage film *Intrepid Hero* (*Yingxiong Hudan* 英雄虎膽) (1958) directed by Yan Jizhou (嚴寄洲) and Hao Guang (郝光). Played by Chinese actress Wang Xiaotang (王曉棠), this spy dances rumba in a feminine and seduc-tive manner. Rather than focusing on the film's political message, this male viewer delves into what he is not supposed to concentrate on: the eroticized female body. A third example can be found in Zhuoyi Wang's book *Revolu-tionary Cycles in Chinese Cinema, 1951–1979*. In one chapter, he analyzes the Chinese students' responses to Xie Tieli's film *Early Spring in February* (*Zaochun eryue* 早春二月) (1963). According to the socialist authority, this film should be viewed as a negative example (*fanmian jiaocai* 反面教材). Although the students were instructed to critique the petty-bourgeois sen-sibility of this film (e.g., the intellectuals lack political commitment), some students enjoyed this film so much that they imitated the flirtatious and playful interactions between the male and female characters onscreen.

Indeed, these are the moments when sublimation is not successful: it either does not happen or does not properly function.

The problem of sublimation is also taken up by Jianmei Liu in her book *Revolution Plus Love* (2003). In the chapter "Love Cannot Be Forgotten," she engages with the PRC's seventeen-years literature and comments on Meng's thesis of repression and Ban Wang's thesis of sublimation. According to Liu's consideration, Meng's argument can have the advantage of deconstructing the CCP's discourse of women's liberation and gender equality; however, it does not explain why communist ideology could arouse pleasure and a sense of romance for its audience.[50] Wang's proposition, Liu continues, can explain why communist culture can have a strong emotional appeal to the mass audience; nevertheless, it has yet to properly articulate the ambiguity of gender.[51] Regarding Meng's and Wang's theses as two sides of the same coin, Liu concludes that "Meng Yue's reading shows too much of the repressive side of the dominant power, whereas Wang Ban [i.e., Ban Wang] portrays the political power's transformation of personal sexual love and libidinal implication too positively and romantically."[52] While I suspect that Liu is more inclined to endorse Ban Wang's analysis, her idea complicates the debates by emphasizing the complexity and fluidity of gender in the negotiations between revolution and love. In addition to questioning whether love, gender, and sexuality are subordinated to the political discourse of class, the political party, and the nation, Liu inquires whether there are literary cases in which the gendered discourse of love cannot be easily channeled to the revolutionary cause. Analyzing a range of fiction written during the seventeen years, such as Xiao Yemu's (蕭也牧) *Between Me and My Wife* (*Women fufu zhijian* 我們夫婦之間) (1949), Deng Youmei's (鄧友梅) *On the Cliff* (*Zai xuanya shang* 在懸崖上) (1956), Lu Ling's (路翎) *Battle of the Lowlands* (*Wadishang de zhanyi* 窪地上的戰役) (1954), Ouyang Shan's (歐陽山) *Three-Family Lane* (*Sanjiaxiang* 三家巷) (1959), and Zong Pu's (宗璞) *Red Beans* (*Hongdou* 紅豆) (1957), Liu argues that there are instances when love cannot be elevated and sublimated by revolutionary politics. In some cases, love can exist harmoniously with politics; in other cases, love is postponed and insufficiently handled by the end of the stories.

In the above, Meng, Ban Wang, McGrath, and Liu have expressed their opinions concerning love and politics during the socialist period. Meng thinks that gender was subordinated, repressed, and co-opted by the socialist discourse of class, the CCP, and the nation. In dialogue, Ban Wang argues that personal sexual love was sublimated and rechanneled to political passions and revolutionary goals. Following Ban Wang's line of thought, McGrath points out how the "trans-narrational sublimation" works in Chinese revolutionary cinema. Meanwhile, Liu analyzes socialist fiction and argues that love, gender, and sexuality cannot be easily repressed or completely sublimated by political power. Indeed, their ideas can be deployed to describe and explain the relationship between the libidinal and the political in *Never Forget*. Inspired by Meng's proposal, I suggest that fashion, leisure, and consumption are repressed by revolutionary politics. (Because Tang briefly mentions repression and displacement in his essay, he would probably agree with Meng's idea regarding repression.) Following Ban Wang, I also suggest that the discourse of fashion, consumption, and leisure is sublimated and rechanneled for the revolutionary cause. Meanwhile, Liu's work enables me to suggest that fashion, leisure, and consumption cannot easily be sublimated by revolutionary politics; they can coexist with revolutions.

While I agree that Meng's repression thesis and Ban Wang's sublimation thesis are two sides of the same coin, I need to explain how one can reconcile the conflict between sublimation (Ban Wang) and incomplete sublimation (Liu). Here, I bring Zhuoyi Wang's periodization of Chinese revolutionary cinema back to the discussion. In his book mentioned earlier in this chapter, Zhuoyi Wang calls the pendulum swings from propaganda/education to entertainment and back "revolutionary cycles in Chinese cinema." Following his periodization, I propose that fashion, consumption, and leisure were more likely to be repressed or sublimated by socialist and revolutionary politics during the Nationalization period (1951–1955), the Great Leap Forward period (1958–1961), and the Cultural Revolution period (from 1964 to the 1970s). Meanwhile, narratives concerning fashion, consumption, and leisure were more likely to appear during the First Hundred Flowers period (1956–1958) and the Second Hundred Flowers period (1961–1964). In the latter two periods, the libidinal refuses to be entirely repressed or sublimated; instead, during these more ideologically relaxed periods, the libidinal exists side by side with revolutionary politics.

While Liu focuses on socialist fiction, I further contribute to the existing discussions by introducing several socialist films that feature love, fashion, and consumption during the First Hundred Flowers and Second Hundred Flowers periods. In the mid-1950s, love, fashion, and consumption appear in Chinese cinema; it seems that they are not entirely repressed or sublimated by revolutionary politics. Films such as *So Passionate* (*Ruci duoqing* 如此多情) (1956), *Shanghai Girls* (*Shanghai guniang* 上海姑娘) (1958), and *The Nurse's Diary* (*Hushi riji* 護士日記) (1957) present the petty bourgeoisie, such as intellectuals and professional-managerial class, and their sensibilities. These films tend to delve into love, especially unrequited love and love triangles. The female characters are often beautiful, feminine, attractive and fashionable. For instance, in Fang Ying's (方熒) film *So Passionate*, the polyamorous character Fu Ping (傅萍) tries to manage four love relationships at the same time. Desiring to climb up the social ladder, she dates a university student, a film studio worker, a junior cadre, and a senior cadre who has already been engaged to another woman. These couples date in a park, in a department store, in a movie theater, and in other spaces of leisure and consumption. In one scene, while boating on a lake and enjoying the romantic atmosphere, Fu confesses her love to the state employee, whom she has mistaken as the senior cadre. When the sexually assertive Fu tries to kiss the state cadre on his cheek, the boat immediately rocks. The viewer may wonder whether this is a metaphor of sexual encounter. In several scenes, Fu appears in *qipaos* and high heels. The film *So Passionate* does not focus on revolutionary politics.

In Cheng Yin's (成蔭) film *Shanghai Girls*, the character Bai Mei (白玫) is a soft, feminine, attractive, and fun-loving young woman from Shanghai. After graduating from university, she becomes a technician/engineer and works at a construction site far away from Shanghai. Her high and professional standard at work has earned her the respect of the young, good-looking male technician, Lu Ye (陸野). Although Lu and Bai fancy each other, neither of them has the courage to express their feelings to the other person. Unfortunately, their romance cannot develop. In this film, Bai is quite fashionable: she has curly, wave-like hairstyle (大波浪頭) and wears an overcoat and a scarf. She is also good at dancing.[53] The film *Shanghai Girls* does not emphasize revolutionary politics. (However, during the Great Leap Forward, this film was criticized because the intellectuals onscreen had not been properly remodeled by the workers and the CCP.[54])

Meanwhile, in Tao Jin's (陶金) film *The Nurse's Diary*, the character Jian Suhua (簡素華) is a nurse working at the frontier. In a local clinic, she works alongside a medical doctor and another nurse. However, during work time, the doctor and the other nurse openly flirt with each other. They even hug and cuddle. When they think Jian is not around, they also "kiss" for less than half a second. Although Jian works at the remote frontier, the viewer may assume that Jian should dress in a frugal and practical manner. However, Jian appears in around twenty-four beautiful outfits in the film. Dissatisfied with the extravagant presentation of clothes, one critic complained that Jian appears as a "fashion show model" and that this film showcases an "aesthetics of waste."[55]

In the early and mid-1960s, Chinese socialist films were sprinkled with stories concerning the dangers of fashion and consumption. The tone was critical: fashion and consumption were imagined as dangerous, bringing disastrous consequences to class struggle, socialist revolution, and nation building. This socialist anxiety of everyday life can be detected in Xie Tieli's film *Never Forget* (1964). This discomfort can also be perceived in Zhao Ming's (趙明) film *The Young Generation* (*Nianqing de yidai* 年青的一代) (1965). In this film the recent college graduate Lin Yusheng (林育生) purchases a dress (*lianyiqun* 連衣裙) for his girlfriend, enjoys reading literature and listening to music, and is unwilling to return to the faraway Qinghai Province to contribute to socialist revolution and construction. He is later schooled by his father, who represents the perspective of the CCP.[56] (I will analyze *The Young Generation* in the final section of this chapter.) The connection between fashion consumption and ideological regression can also be noticed in Fu Chaowu's (傅超武) film *Family Problems* (*Jiating wenti* 家庭問題) (1964).[57] The latter focuses on the worker Du Fumin (杜福民), who has just completed professional training in college. Since he thinks the hat his father has bought for him is too old-fashioned and does not match with his newly cut "airplane hairstyle," he desires to have a more stylish hat. Moreover, he is dissatisfied with his elder brother for spoiling his shirt. According to Du, "the workers' hands are too coarse." From his reaction, it is clear that Du looks down on the factory workers and loathes manual labor. Du is eventually educated by his father.

The relationship between fashion consumption and ideological deterioration is also expressed in Wang Ping (王蘋) and Ge Xin's (葛鑫) film *Sentinels Under the Neon Lights* (*Nihong dengxia de shaobing* 霓虹燈下的哨兵) (1964).[58] In this film, the PLA solider Chen Xi (陳喜) is allured to commercial cultures on Nanjing Road in Shanghai. He desires new nylon socks (*nilong wazi* 尼龍襪子) advertised in the department store and abandons his old and coarse socks made of cloth (*cubu wazi* 粗布襪子 or *laobu wazi* 老布 襪子). This act shows that he has deserted proletarian frugality and begun to embrace bourgeois extravagance.[59] In addition, he looks down on his coworker and behaves indifferently toward his wife, who travels from the countryside to visit him. Because Chen Xi has lost vigilance to political reactionaries, he needs to be educated by the senior soldiers in the PLA. From the high-quality suit in *Never Forget* to the dress in *The Young Generation*, and from the hat in *Family Problems* to the nylon socks in *Sentinels*, the filmic narratives concerning fashion and consumption are a crucial site of political debates and ideological contestations.[60] These stories propagate Mao's idea of class struggle even after the success of revolutions.

DRESS (連衣裙) AND REVOLUTION

I conclude by briefly discussing the film *The Young Generation* (*Nianqing de yidai* 年青的一代) (1965).[61] Similar to *Never Forget*, *The Young Generation* is a cautionary tale of the danger of fashion, leisure, and the city within the context of Chinese socialist modernity. The protagonist of the film is a politically immature student, Lin Yusheng. Resembling Ding Shaochun in *Never Forget*, Lin Yusheng is subjected to the influence of two opposite sides: the proletarian side and the "bourgeois" side. On the one hand, the proletarian side is represented by the Lin family, whose members include father, Lin Jian (林堅); mother, Xia Shujuan (夏淑娟); son, Lin Yusheng; daughter, Lin Lan (林嵐); and Lin Yusheng's girlfriend, Xia Qianru (夏倩如). Added to the list is Xiao Jiye (肖繼業), who, similar to Ji in *Never Forget*, is a socialist new person. Xiao Jiye was brought up by Grandmother Xiao (肖奶奶) who is also a revolutionary. On the other hand, the "bourgeois" side is epitomized by Lin Yusheng's friend, Little Wu (小吳), who is described as someone who "[doesn't] obey his assignment," "uses his family's money to show off their wealth," and "doesn't earn his own living."[62] Little Wu is depicted as a negative character in the new socialist society. Because he does not physically appear in the story (in fact, one gets to know him through the conversations between Lin Yusheng and the other characters), one can infer that bourgeois influence is invisible and can unexpectedly creep into the characters' lives. Such a representation is telling of Chinese socialism's anxiety: human sociality such as friendship, which lies outside of the censor of the state and its repressive and ideological apparatuses, can be a site of concern for socialist power and governmentality. Intimacy is imagined as a dangerous interface where capitalism and revisionism may return and counterattack the socialist polity.

Lin Yusheng, Xiao Jiye, and Xia Qianru are students of geology. After graduating from college, armed with passion to contribute to socialist construction, Lin Yusheng, Xiao Jiye, and their fellow students volunteered to travel to the remote, barren land of Qinghai to research and explore ore deposits. Because Lin Yusheng has arthritis in his leg, he needs to return to Shanghai to seek medical treatment. However, unlike Xiao Jiye, who is deeply committed to the collective, Lin Yusheng does not want to return to the frontier. Instead, he desires to stay in Shanghai because city life is more comfortable. He would like to find an administrative or research position in Shanghai. He also asks his girlfriend, Xia Qianru, who has planned to join the exploration team in Qinghai upon graduation, to stay with him. Preferring intellectual labor to manual labor, Lin Yusheng also encourages his sister, Lin Lan, to attend a film school rather than an agricultural college. To him, an ideal life is one that maintains a healthy balance between work and leisure in the city. He persuades his girlfriend in this way: "Just imagine how great it'd be if they kept you in Shanghai! During the day we'd go to work together, and at night we'd come home, listen to some music like *Carmen* and *La Traviata*, read novels or poetry, or see movies. On Sundays we'd go to the park or find some friends to chat with. . . . Of course, we'd have to do a good job, and we'd have to make some contributions to our field."[63] Indeed, Lin Yusheng's view of happiness is drastically different from Xiao Jiye's view. In the beginning of *The Young Generation*, Lin Yusheng is busy preparing for a birthday party for his girlfriend. He has bought two bottles of wine, some candy, and, with Little Wu's recommendation, a dress for his girlfriend.[64] According to the narrative, the dress is an "exotic foreign thing" (*yangli yangqi de dongxi* 洋裡洋氣的東西) and "an export item."[65] Similar to the high-quality suit in *Never Forget*, the dress marks Lin Yusheng's reluctance to contribute to class struggle and socialist revolution.

The climactic moment centers on the debates about happiness (*xingfu* 幸福) in socialism. The father figure, Lin Jian, sets the tone of the discussion. He explains to his daughter, Lin Lan: "For a true revolutionary, happiness and struggle are inseparable. . . . There is no greater happiness than for a young person to be able to take part in today's class struggle and social-ist construction, to contribute his or her share to the work for the Party and for the people."⁶⁶ Then Xiao Jiye and Lin Yusheng engage in a heated argument about happiness in socialism. Similar to Lin Jian, Xiao Jiye insists that happiness should be tied to contributing to the collective, the broad masses, the people, the CCP, and the nation. Although Lin Yusheng under-stands this because he grew up in a revolutionary family, he maintains that the purpose of revolution is to bring prosperity and comfort to one's life. He asks: "We do intend to make our lives better, more comfortable, to make our lives richer and more varied. Why is everyone working so hard? Isn't it just to make life better and happier?"⁶⁷ Lin Yusheng admits the importance of individual happiness as well. He reasons: "If we do feel some interest in our own happiness, well, so what? We work and we labor like anybody else. We neither go around robbing and plundering, nor do we exploit or interfere with others; we just spend our days according to our own wishes and our own ideals."⁶⁸ However, rather than thinking with Lin Yush-eng concerning the possibility of individual happiness against the back-drop of collective struggle, Xiao Jiye harshly condemns Lin Yusheng for "[hiding] away in [his] petty, individual world, satisfied with [his] medio-cre trivial existence."⁶⁹ He seriously warns Lin Yusheng: "the danger is that you are not thinking of the revolution anymore!"⁷⁰ He urges Lin Yusheng to overcome his petty-bourgeois thinking and individualism and "commit [himself] wholeheartedly to the magnificent work of building socialism."⁷¹

In fact, Lin Yusheng's arthritis is not as serious as he claims it to be. He has forged a medical note to exaggerate his illness, which turns out to be Little Wu's idea. It is later discovered by Xiao Jiye. Meanwhile, Xiao Jiye has some real medical problems with his leg to such an extent that it may have to be amputated. However, Xiao Jiye remains fully committed to revolu-tionary struggle and insists on going back to Qinghai to continue his polit-ical mission. More melodramas abound: It turns out that Lin Jian and Xia Shujuan are not Lin Yusheng's biological parents. Twenty-four years prior to the story, Lin Yusheng's biological parents had been captured, impris-oned, and eventually executed by the Guomindang (Nationalist) officers due to their involvement in labor movements. Before she was killed, Lin Yusheng's biological mother had left a note to Lin Yusheng, reminding him that "you [Lin Yusheng] must never forget the world that still harbors our class enemies! You must struggle for the sacred ideals of communism!"⁷²

In the end, Lin Jian lectures the young generation: "Yusheng, it wasn't easy for the proletariat to obtain power! The imperialists and reactionaries are just dreaming of a chance to get their wish to oppose the revolution and restore the old order by using you young people. Son, you've got to be careful!"[73] Similar to *Never Forget,* the political message of *The Young Generation* is obvious: Never forget class struggle even within the context of socialism. In the end, the young people including Lin Yusheng set out to faraway places, such as Qinghai, Xinjiang, and Tibet, to contribute to the magnificent project of building socialism.

The Young Generation condenses the issues that I have discussed in the third part of this chapter. This film also inquires how the socialist everyday life (e.g., clothes, consumption, and leisure) can look. *Never Forget* is interested in whether there is a place for buying a high-quality suit and shooting wild birds while engaging in production. Similarly, *The Young Generation* wonders whether it is permissible to buy a dress, organize a birthday party, listen to classical music, read literature, watch movies, and stay in the city while contributing to socialist construction. In both films, the responses from the socialist administration are ambivalent. On the one hand, the government quietly affirms the legitimacy of a materially prosperous life. There is no point for Chinese socialist modernity to oppose the high-quality suit, the dress, leisure, and, indeed, a materially abundant life. However, on the other hand, the socialist management rejects these commodities, fearing them as a possible interface where the bourgeoisie may counterattack the socialist body.

I maintain that contradiction is a privileged method to analyze Chinese socialist cultures. In 1942 Mao Zedong delivered the famous "Talks at the Yan'an Forum on Literature and Art." His discussion of the dialectic of popularization and raising standard can be deployed to comprehend the socialist's attitude toward clothes, consumption, and leisure. In addition, Zhang Yiwu, Tina Mai Chen, Tang Xiaobing, and Cai Xiang also delve into contradictions when analyzing Chinese socialist cultures and arts. According to Zhang, fashion was both affirmed and denied during the socialist period. In her research, Chen detects "the contradiction of proletarianization and modernization" in the figuration of "proletarian white working body" in socialist iconography. In *The Young Generation,* Xiao Jiye and Lin Yusheng wear white shirts and work in a faraway site where mineral deposits can be found. They are also "proletarian white working bodies." The same is also true for Xia Qianru, who wears the dress that Lin Yusheng has bought for her. These figures reveal the contradiction of proletarianization and modernization, which, in Mao's perspective, can be conceptualized as the contradiction of popularization and raising standard. Borrowing from Tang, *The Young Generation* expresses the socialist regime's contradictory attitude—affirmation and disavowal—toward *industrialized* modernity. On the one hand, the socialist government desires and endorses the material benefits of industrialized modernity; on the other hand, it is fearful of the divisions of time, space, and social relations created by the industrialized modernity. To solve these problems, the socialist regime attempts to repress its "anxiety of everyday life" and displace it toward an external other. In *The Young Generation*, this negative other is the "bourgeois" character, Little Wu, who has a profound influence on Lin Yusheng. In the narrative, the proletarian characters Lin Jian and Xiao Jiye only produce but do not consume. When Lin Yusheng is discovered to consume, he is radically criticized for having forgotten about class struggle and socialist revolution. Going further, *The Young Generation* reveals the contradiction of *socialist* industrialized modernity. Borrowing from Cai, this film visualizes the fact that socialism produces its own consumption, leisure, and everyday life as much as it produces production. Regarding Xiao Jiye's passionate debate with Lin Yusheng concerning the possibility of happiness in socialism, the discourse of class struggle and continuous revolution has been clumsily mobilized to conquer the ideological domain. To genuinely tackle socialist consumption, a cultural discourse of socialist everyday life should be meticulously constructed and elaborated. This way the socialist regime can regain cultural hegemony and secures people's consent.

Chapter Three

"MAO'S CHILDREN ARE WEARING FASHION!"

Romantic Love, Fashion Consumption, and Modernization Politics in Huang Zumo's Film *Romance on Lu Mountain* (1980)

To celebrate the thirtieth anniversary of the People's Republic of China's (PRC) economic reforms and opening up (*gaige kaifang* 改革開放), China Photographers Association published a photo album titled *China's Thirty Years* (*Jianzheng: gaige kaifang sanshinian* 見證:改革開放三十年) (2009). According to the entry "A Fashion Comeback" (*Fushi* 服飾):

> The Cultural Revolution was a dark time for fashion in China. People were forced to abolish "antiquated" concepts, culture and dress, and anything associated with "the bourgeoisie." As a result, people wore neither traditional Chinese costumes nor Western-style suits, and China became renowned for its uniform dress code of blue or green "Mao suits." Those who wore jewelry or make-up faced serious consequences. The Mao suit—fashion from sturdy blue serge—and green army uniforms were the only attire available to most of the population for decades until the end of the Cultural Revolution. Dress in China underwent a drastic change after the turbulence. In 1979, French designer Pierre Cardin staged a fashion show in Beijing, and his bold and futuristic designs excited Chinese audiences, most of whom were still wearing simple cotton-padded jackets. China's youth rediscovered the joy of dressing up as a result of Deng's "open-door" policy, and modern fashions began to reappear on the streets. Today, China's young are among the most

fashion conscious in the world and the cities' clothes shops are jam-packed at weekends with customers eager to dress to impress.[1]

During the past forty years, the story of unprecedented political-economic, social, and cultural transformations of the PRC has often been told from a revisionist perspective. According to this revisionist narrative, the Great Proletarian Cultural Revolution (1966–1976) denied human nature, suppressed Chinese people's natural desires, and created abnormal political passions in them. In contrast, the economic reforms liberated the Chinese people from the shackles of continuous revolution, class struggle, and ideological critique. The result was that they could embrace their true humanities and express their innermost desires. Closely examining the rhetoric of this narrative, this revisionist argument is presented in the form of binary oppositions: the Cultural Revolution versus the economic reforms, Chinese socialism versus socialism with Chinese characteristics, sameness versus difference, homogeneity versus heterogeneity, and uniformity versus multiplicity. According to the revisionist logic, Chinese socialism, or more accurately, Maoist socialism, a repressive power and governmentality, promoted sameness at the expense of difference.[2]

A common example that the revisionist critics cite to strengthen their argument is the clothes that the Chinese people wore then and now. According to these revisionist critics, during the Cultural Revolution, the Chinese people had to wear proletarian uniforms. The colors of their outfits—blue, green, white, and gray—were boring, dull, and monotonous. Thus, the Chinese people were turned into identical beings and could not express their personalities.[3] However, during the economic reforms, the Chinese people were encouraged to wear colorful clothes and express their individualities. The government made it clear that the people's standard of living, including the clothes that they wore in their everyday lives, had to be improved; their clothing styles could also be diversified. In the 1980s, re-dressing signifies redress: re-dressing the Chinese population means redressing a past political mistake.

This revisionist argument was also widely disseminated through the films sponsored by the reform-minded government. For example, Bao Zhi-fang's (鮑芝芳) film *Black Dragonfly* (*Hei qingting* 黑蜻蜓) (1984) celebrates fashion and socialist modernization. Focusing on the new profession of fashion modeling, this film features a scene in which Zhou Zhou (周舟) (a film director) tells his wife (a singer), his daughter (a fashion model), and two of his friends (one is an aspiring fashion designer and the other is an actor-turned-fashion-model) that he is going to make a film about the richness of life.[4] He says:

> Fashion should be rich and colorful. After the third plenum [i.e., Third Plenum of the Eleventh Central Committee Congress of the Chinese Communist Party in December 1978], people dare to pursue beauty. . . . During those ten years of turmoil [i.e., the Cultural Revolution (1966–1976)], people were imprisoned in the world of blue and gray. They could not see the world of changing colors. . . . Monotonous colors cannot represent our China. I . . . desire the richness of life and aspire to bring beauty and life together forever!

In *Black Dragonfly*, fashion is strategically deployed to critique the Cultural Revolution and to celebrate the economic reforms.

To unpack the ideology of this revisionist narrative, this chapter examines the fashion discourse in China in the late 1970s and early 1980s. By the fashion discourse, I refer to the fashion films, fashion shows, fashion magazines, and feminist debates concerning fashion and gender. I argue that during the economic reforms, fashion was mobilized to prove the success of socialist modernization and development; it was presented as a living proof of the rising standard of living for the Chinese people. Such a depiction is in stark contrast with the negative portrayal of fashion in the mid- and late 1960s. During the most turbulent years of the Cultural Revolution, fashionable outfits such as bell-bottomed trousers, high-heeled shoes, lipstick, and makeup were radically critiqued. They were regarded as being detrimental to class struggle and socialist revolution.[5] In fact, the reversal of judgment toward fashion and consumption from the 1960s to the 1980s has a theoretical implication. In the first volume of *The History of Sexuality*, Michel Foucault suggests that "sexuality . . . [is] . . . an especially dense transfer point for relations of power."[6] Appropriating Foucault's observation, I argue that romantic love, fashionable clothes, and gender presentations are a dense transfer point for relations of socialist power and

governmentality. They constitute a signifying site where the changing relationships between the libidinal and the political from the Cultural Revolution to the post–Cultural Revolution periods are dramatized, negotiated,
and worked out.

To stage my argument, I organize this chapter in five parts. In "Romantic Love, First Kiss, and Fashion," I focus on Huang Zumo's (黃祖模) film
Romance on Lu Mountain (*Lushanlian* 廬山戀) (1980). I explore the depiction of romantic love (including the first representation of a kiss in PRC cinema), fashionable clothes, and petty-bourgeois sensibility (*xiaozi qingdiao*
小資情調). Viewing this film as a passionate love story between Chinese
American woman Zhou Yun (周筠) and Chinese man Geng Hua (耿樺), I
feature how the romantic love, including the dizzying sensations of the first
kiss, is imagined and visualized onscreen. I also explain how Zhou Yun is
presented in more than forty outfits and appears as a fashion model or icon
to Chinese viewers. *Romance on Lu Mountain* marks the gradual (re-)emer-
gence of fashion consciousness in 1980s China. In "The Fashion Discourse
in Early 1980s China," I introduce the other fashion films, fashion shows,
fashion magazines, and television melodramas that accentuate the rise of
this fashion consciousness. I present French fashion designer Pierre Cardin's visit to China in 1979. I also suggest that China's socialist modernization resembles a fashion show. In addition, I introduce two more fashion
films—namely, *Red Dress Is in Fashion* (*Jieshang liuxing hongqunzi* 街上流
行紅裙子) (1984), directed by Qi Xingjia (齊興家), and *The Girl in Red* (*Hongyi shaonü* 紅衣少女) (1985), directed by Lu Xiaoya (陸小雅). These films also
feature fashion and consumption in interesting ways. To enrich my discussion, I engage with cultural theorist Rey Chow's discussion of fetishism,
gender representations, and Chinese cinema. Inspired by Chow's idea, I
interpret *Romance on Lu Mountain* as a refetishization of the screen image
of women in contemporary Chinese cinema. However, I add to her discussion Chineseness as ethnicity and culture, so that her argument can
accommodate *Romance on Lu Mountain* and the other 1980s fashion films.
In "From Revolution to Modernization," I emphasize that the de-repression
or de-sublimation of love, the refetishization of gender, and the articula-
tion of ethnicity and culture are, in fact, an intensely political process: the
culture of political revolution is replaced by the ideology of economic
modernization. This shift illustrates what culture critic Wang Hui (汪暉)

calls depoliticized politics (*Qu zhengzhihua de zhengzhi* 去政治化的政治).[7] The farewell to political revolution is not apolitical but political through and through.

Furthermore, I juxtapose the filmic representations of gender, love, and fashion with Chinese feminist debates. In "The Revisionist Narrative and Its Discontents," I participate in the feminist discussions concerning fashion, femininity, and gendered consciousness during the economic reforms period. According to the revisionist critics, the ways in which Chinese people dressed during the Maoist era indicate the fact that socialism promoted sameness at the expense of difference. The colors of their proletarian uniforms—blue, green, white, and gray—were dull and monotonous. Because Chinese women had to wear proletarian clothes, Maoism denied their natural femininities, turning them into masculinized or genderless beings. However, China's economic reforms encouraged the Chinese people to wear colorful outfits and express their personalities through fashion and makeup. The Chinese women were encouraged to express their natural femininities and regain their consciousness as gendered beings. In this part, I confront this revisionist argument by showing its contradictions and limitations. I argue that the historical reality regarding fashion and gender subjectivity is more complex than what the revisionist critics claim. In addition, their feminist politics is conservative and backward-looking because it denies the Chinese women other possibilities of expressing and performing their genders.

In the academic study of 1980s Chinese cultures, scholars have engaged with critical and cultural theories to debate the aesthetics and politics of post-Mao cultural productions. For example, in *Chinese Modernism in the Era of Reforms* (1997), Xudong Zhang provides an overview of Chinese intellectual, literary, and cinematic discourses. In *High Culture Fever* (1996), Jing Wang delves into the aesthetics, politics, and ideology of Deng Xiaoping's China. She examines the debates over socialist alienation and Marxist humanism in 1983, culture fever in 1985, the TV series *River Elegy* (*Heshang* 河殤) in 1988, the problem of subjectivity, and the propositions of pseudomodernism and postmodernism. In *Primitive Passions* (1995), Rey Chow engages with the theories of poststructuralism, postmodernism, and postcolonialism to analyze the cinema of the fifth generation of directors, Zhang Yimou (張藝謀) and Chen Kaige (陳凱歌). In *Occidentalism* (1995), Xiaomei Chen examines the cross-cultural exchanges of Chinese and Western dramas. She also discusses how the Chinese artists used the Western other to critique the Chinese self. The list goes on. Whereas these scholars have focused on the avant-garde and experimental cultures, such as fiction, poetry, film, and drama, I contribute to the existing discussions by focusing on popular cultures, particularly fashion films, in the first half of 1980s China. In *Postsocialist Cinema in Post-Mao China* (2004), Chris Berry engages with scar films (*shanghen dianying* 傷痕電影) to reflect on the trauma of the Cultural Revolution. In dialogue, I analyze the films that celebrate China's socialist modernization. In *Masculinity Besieged?* (2000), Xueping Zhong explores the relationship between male subjectivity and modernity in the Chinese fiction written in the late twentieth century. In exchange, I focus on femininity as an ideology of economic reforms. My work shows how gender is fundamentally constitutive of the radical trans-formation of the PRC in the 1980s.

ROMANTIC LOVE, FIRST KISS, AND FASHION

Contrary to the images of heroic proletarian characters actively engaged in class struggle and national liberation in the Cultural Revolution litera-ture, film, and model operas, Huang's film *Romance on Lu Mountain* feels soft and feminine. This film features the romantic encounters between a Chinese Romeo and a Chinese American Juliet (minus the tragic ending) after the end of the Cultural Revolution. Indeed, this film is replete with petty-bourgeois sensibility not only because the main characters are intellectuals and belong to the petty bourgeoisie but also because the content indulges in "trivial" matters such as the first kiss, forbidden love, and fashion presentations.

Romance on Lu Mountain focuses on the love between Zhou Yun and Geng Hua amid China's changing political landscape. Zhou Yun is a young, feminine, attractive, and fashionable Chinese American woman. Although she grew up in the United States, she identifies with her Chinese roots. Since the diplomatic ties between the United States and China had been reestab-lished after President Richard Nixon's visit to the PRC in 1972, overseas Chi-nese were welcome to return to China to help reconstruct the nation. This is why Zhou Yun has an opportunity to visit China, a country in which she has never set foot. Her father, Zhou Zhenwu (周振武), was a military com-mander in the Nationalist Party (KMT). After the end of the civil war in

1949, he fled to the United States. While living in the United States, he remains passionate about traditional Chinese culture and history. Due to political reasons, Zhou Zhenwu cannot return to the PRC. Because her father is fond of Lu Mountain in the northern part of Jiangxi Province, China, Zhou Yun decides to visit this scenic mountain. It is on this occasion that she meets Geng Hua.[8]

Geng Hua, whom Zhou Yun nicknames "Confucius" (*Kongfuzi* 孔夫子), is a young, good-looking, and forward-looking Chinese man. He loves to read, draw, and learn English. His name is telling: *geng* (耿) means honest and dedicated, and *hua* (樺) refers to China. Geng Hua is patriotic and loves his country. He has great ambitions to contribute to China's modernization. Geng Hua's father, Geng Feng (耿烽), was a military commander in the Chinese Communist Party (CCP) and has been wrongly labeled as a rightist during the Cultural Revolution. Because Mother Geng is sick, Geng Hua brings her to Lu Mountain to rest so that she can recover sooner. In his spare time Geng Hua tours around this scenic mountain and meets Zhou Yun. They become friends and hang out together. Because Geng Hua is reported to have become acquainted with a Chinese American woman (the undertone is that she may be a spy from the United States), he has been asked to talk with the CCP members. Upon realizing this, Zhou Yun is thoroughly devastated. She has no choice but to leave Geng Hua immediately, otherwise she will bring more troubles to him. Sadly, their intense romantic encounter has come to an end. The first part of the story ends with their separation.

The second part of the film begins five years later—that is, after the end of the Cultural Revolution. Zhou Yun has another opportunity to visit Lu Mountain. Nostalgic for her experience, she asks around about Geng Hua. At that time Geng Hua has become a graduate student in architecture at Tsinghua University, a prestigious institution in China for studying science and technology. Coincidentally, Geng Hua has returned to Lu Mountain to attend an academic conference. Zhou Yun and Geng Hua finally manage to see each other. This time they fall in love passionately. In the end, they decide to get married. However, Geng Hua needs to obtain approval from his parents, and Zhou Yun sends a telegram to her parents. Another melodramatic moment arrives: it turns out that Geng Hua's father and Zhou Yun's father have known each other for decades. They had served in the army together when they were young. However, one day, on Lu Mountain, Geng Feng and Zhou Zhenwu decided to part ways because they held opposite political views. Zhou Zhenwu remained a firm believer of the KMT, whereas Geng Feng, perceptively enough, joined the CCP. By the end of the civil war, the KMT was defeated and Zhou Zhenwu fled to the United States. In his telegram reply, Zhou Zhenwu tells Zhou Yun the truth, emphasizing that it is unlikely for Geng Feng to agree to her marriage with Geng Hua. Completely shattered, Zhou Yun decides to leave China the following day. When she is about to leave the hotel, Geng Hua's parents have come to deliver good news to her. They have decided to allow Geng Hua to marry Zhou Yun. In the end, their marriage is not only the union of Geng's family and Zhou's family but also the coming together of the CCP and the KMT in the name of love, patriotism, and traditional Chinese culture. Romantic love, combined with the love for the nation and its cultural heritage, can be a powerful force that reconciles political conflicts.

In the Chinese TV program called *Narrating the Past Events of Cinema,* actor Guo Kaimin (郭凱敏), who played Geng Hua in the film, characterizes *Romance on Lu Mountain* as a film about the natural scenery (*fengguang pian* 風光片) of Lu Mountain, a film about romantic love (*aiqing pian* 愛情片), and a film about fashion (*fuzhuang pian* 服裝片). In what follows, I analyze this film from these three angles. Indeed, the viewer of this film can appreciate the beautiful landscape of Lu Mountain. Resembling a travel guide or a landscape painting, *Romance on Lu Mountain* presents many picturesque attractions, such as the White Deer Cave Academy (白鹿洞書院), Flower Path (花徑), Imperial Pavilion (御碑亭), Immortals Cavern (仙人洞), Laojun Temple (老君廟), Dragon Head Cliff (龍首岩), Water Fall (瀑布), Yuezhao songlin (月照松林), Botanical Garden (植物園), Longgou Lake (龍溝湖), East Grove Temple (東林寺), Wisdom Well (聰明泉), The Protector of Buddhist Doctrines (護法烈士), Shenlong yuekong (神龍躍空), Guanyin Bridge (觀音橋), and Jade Cliff (玉淵). This film also resembles a wall calendar that presents Lu Mountain's spectacular and scenic landscapes in four seasons.

The viewer can also enjoy the passionate love story. To feel how striking this romance was in the early 1980s, one should note the background against which the love story surfaced. In fact, romantic love was substantially critiqued during the most intense period of the Cultural Revolution. In the late 1960s and early 1970s, Chinese literature, films, ballets, and model operas were mostly concerned with such subjects as class struggle, revolutionary politics, and national liberation. Themes focusing on romantic love, especially those that do not directly intersect with revolutionary politics, were rarely found. When love appeared in the narrative, it was often repressed, subsumed, transferred, or sublimated. Other times it was rechanneled to the proletariat and the masses or redirected to the CCP or the nation. However, this situation began to change after the end of the Cultural Revolution. In literature, titles with the word love began to emerge. Examples include notable fictions such as Zhang Jie's (張潔) *Love Must Not Be Forgotten* (*Aishi buneng wangjide* 愛是不能忘記的) (1979), Zhang Kang-kang's (張抗抗) *The Right to Love* (*Aide quanli* 愛的權利) (1979), and Liu Xin-wu's (劉心武) "The Place of Love" (*Aiqing de weizhi* 愛情的位置) (1979). The reemergence of love after the end of the Cultural Revolution has been documented by Kam Louie in the chapter "Love Stories: The Meaning of Love and Marriage in China, 1978–1981" in his book *Between Fact and Fiction* (1989).

The recuperation of love is also evident in film. In his book *Postsocialist Cinema in Post-Mao China* (2004), Chris Berry meticulously counts the number of films that presented romantic love after the end of the Cultural Revolution. According to his statistics, in 1976 and 1977, zero out of fifteen Chinese films featured love; in 1978, two out of eleven Chinese films presented love; in 1979, five out of fourteen Chinese films showcased love; in 1980, sixteen out of twenty-three Chinese films displayed love; and in 1981, fifteen out of eighteen Chinese films exhibited love. In my research Zhang Qi (張其) and Li Yalin's (李亞林) film *The Corner Forgotten by Love* (*Bei aiqing yiwang de jiaoluo* 被愛情遺忘的角落) (1981) went further to hint at sex.

In the Chinese TV program *Narrating the Past Events of Cinema*, Guo speaks of how love was cinematically constructed in the 1970s and early 1980s:

> Slow motion had already appeared at that time. The formula is this: you chase and I run. Once you see the characters running, it is a hint that they are already in love. Then you will see an empty shot. You will also see a shot in which they throw their clothes and shoes up in the air. When they run toward each other, there will be a cut. Afterward, you will see the couple embrace each other. This was the cinematic convention at that time. (My translation)

This pattern is exactly what happens in the beginning of the second part of *Romance on Lu Mountain*. Chris Berry describes the reunion of Zhou Yun and Geng Hua at Longgou Lake on Lu Mountain:

When Zhou and Geng meet again after five years, they first spot each other from different sides of a lake. The camera cuts back and forth between them as they call out each other's names and race down to the lake, Zhou moving rightwards, and Geng leftwards. In one shot, the frame is even split into three columns, Zhou and Geng running towards each other in each of the side panels, and the lake in the central one. When they reach the lakeside, items of clothing are shown flying into the air, although the following shots reveal that they are not stripped completely. They then dive in and race to embrace in the center of the lake.[9]

Eventually, Geng Hua and Zhou Yun are passionately reunited in the water. In the following scene Zhou Yun dries her hair after a shower and asks Geng Hua whether he would like to smoke a cigarette. It is tempting to interpret these scenes as a metaphor for sex (e.g., taking off their clothes and shoes, jumping into the lake [i.e., the bed], swimming [i.e., sex], showering, and smoking afterward). This film shows how romantic love was imagined and constructed in Chinese cinema in the late 1970s and early 1980s.

Importantly, *Romance on Lu Mountain* is the first film to present a kiss in the PRC cinema. By a kiss, I mean a peck on the cheek. In the Chinese TV program *Narrating the Past Events of Cinema*, Guo explains the cinematic formula of love between a man and a woman: "The common practice is to show them hold hands. If a director shows them hug, it is already very daring!" However, the director of *Romance on Lu Mountain* does more than this. Huang shows the open-minded Chinese American Zhou Yun giving Geng Hua a peck on his cheek. "Confucius" has gained a kiss.

The presentation of this kiss was provocative in late 1970s and early 1980s China. In 1979 the Chinese film magazine *Mass Cinema* (*Dazhong dianying* 大眾電影) used the poster of British film *The Slipper and the Rose: The Story of Cinderella* (水晶鞋和玫瑰花) (1976) as the back cover of its publication. The cover features a passionate kiss between Cinderella and the prince. This image unsettled Chinese reader Wen Yingjie (問英傑), from Xinjiang Province, China. Wen wrote an angry letter to the editorial board to express his dissatisfaction. He complains:

I have not watched *The Slipper and the Rose: The Story of Cinderella*, so I cannot tell if the film is a fragrant flower or a poisonous weed. . . . Chairman Mao has taught us to appropriate Western ideas for Chinese use. Do you think the most important and urgent task in socialist China is a hug and a kiss? What is your intention of prominently displaying a kiss? What are you trying to advertise? Do you think we need this kind of propaganda to promote the mission of Chinese Communist Party? Do you think nine hundred millions of Chinese people need this kind of inspiration to launch the new Long March? . . . What are you trying to show to the young people in our country? Do you have any conscience for the people and nation? Comrades, don't think that Western fart necessarily smells more fragrant! (My translation)

From Wen's angry letter, one can sense what the political and cultural climate was like in the late 1970s.

Indeed, the peck that Zhou Yun gives on Geng Hua's cheek was provocative. However, how is this kiss portrayed onscreen? In one scene Zhou Yun and Geng Hua are appreciating the landscape at Jade Cliff. While Geng Hua is looking at the scenery, Zhou Yun, consumed by her infatuation with Geng Hua, secretly looks at him. This gaze is gendered: while the man focuses on the world, the woman, seized by passion, admires him. The viewer looks at Zhou Yun looking at Geng Hua.

ZHOU YUN: Geng Hua! Geng Hua!
[And then she turns around and lies down on the grass.]
ZHOU YUN (*SHE WHISPERS*): Confucius, can't you be a little more aggressive?
GENG HUA: What did you say?
[Then he turns around and realizes that Zhou Yun is lying on the grass waiting to be kissed.]
GENG HUA (*WITH HESITATION*): I am . . . I am . . . [Then Zhou Yun gets up and quickly gives Geng Hua a peck on his cheek.]
GENG HUA (*EMBARRASSINGLY*): Other people can see it!
ZHOU YUN: Let them see it! Confucius! Nobody is around, just the two of us. These two birds are laughing at us!

While *Romance on Lu Mountain* is, in the history of PRC cinema, the first film to feature a kiss (or, more accurately, a peck on the cheek), how exactly is it constructed in cinematic language? Immediately after Zhou Yun has given Geng Hua a peck on his cheek, Geng Hua appears bewildered and disoriented. We see a close-up shot of Geng Hua's eyes from

Zhou Yun's perspective. Next the film gives a shot/reverse shot from Geng Hua's perspective, followed by a close-up of Zhou Yun's face. The composition begins with a crisp image that suddenly becomes gauzy and unfocused before returning to its original clarity. Afterward, the camera moves in circles that mimic Geng Hua's dizziness. The same sequence is repeated. In the end the viewer can see the couple from a third-person perspective. Although this sequence seems a bit mechanical by today's standard, the cinematic language suggests a clear message: they are deeply in love.

How did Chinese viewers respond to this film? In the Chinese TV program *The History of Cinema: The Female Star Who Presented the First Kiss in New China—Zhang Yu*, a member of the audience recalled how he or she reacted to the film when the film was first shown in China in 1980. "When the male character and the female character kiss onscreen, what I could hear in the theater was aiya! When I turned around to look at what had happened, everyone had their mouths wide open and their eyes covered with their hands."

Journalist Bryan Johnson also made a similar remark in *The Globe and Mail* newspaper. In his review of *Romance on Lu Mountain* on November 7, 1980, Johnson wrote:

> When the timid Chinese boy [Geng Hua] evades her [Zhou Yun's] advances, Miss Zhang [Zhou Yun's role is played by Chinese actress Zhang Yu] lies on her back, sweatered bosom thrust skyward, and tells the local hero to be "more aggressive." The boyfriend gulps in surprise. The camera pans lovingly over Miss Zhang's Lushan-like profile. And eyeglasses in the audience begin to mist over from the steam generated in the theater. By Chinese standards, this is very, very hot stuff.[10]

In fact, contemporary Chinese popular film and media cultures teach the young generation how to express themselves. The Chinese viewers learned to express their emotions by imitating what the actresses and actors perform onscreen. They learned how to fall in love, kiss, and express their romantic feelings.

In fact, when the viewer is watching *Romance on Lu Mountain*, they are simultaneously watching two narratives. The first narrative centers on the love story and the first kiss. The second narrative, which is semiautonomous from the first one, focuses on fashion. Indeed, Geng Hua and Zhou Yun appear as fashion models and icons for Chinese viewers. In this film Geng Hua wears a white shirt and, at another point, a blue shirt with an undershirt beneath it. He also wears a pair of loose-fitting military trousers. His shoes, made of cloth, are fashionable too. He carries a military bag. Interestingly, romantic love improves Geng Hua's fashion taste. After he has fallen in love, Geng Hua begins to dress more fashionably.

Undoubtedly, the most striking feature of this film is Zhou Yun's fashion presentations. From bell-bottomed trousers to toad-eyed sunglasses (*hama jing* 蛤蟆鏡) or panda-eyed sunglasses (*xiongmao jing* 熊貓鏡), and from super-short skirts to high heels, Zhou Yun is a fashion model to Chinese viewers, appearing in more than forty outfits in the film. It is common for Chinese film critics to compare this film with Hong Kong director Wong Kar-wai's (*Wang Jiawei* 王家衛) beautiful and stylish film *In the Mood for Love* (*Huayang nianhua* 花樣年華) (2000). In Wong's film, the character Su Lizhen (or Mrs. Chan), played by famous Hong Kong actress Maggie Cheung (*Zhang Manyu* 張曼玉), appears in more than twenty beautiful Chinese *qipaos*. If *In the Mood for Love* is fondly remembered as the film of Chinese *qipao*, *Romance on Lu Mountain* can certainly be appreciated as China's fashion film in the 1980s. Compared with an ordinary Chinese woman who, in the early 1980s, only had several outfits in her everyday life, Zhou Yun's outfits were very appealing. In the Chinese TV program mentioned above, Guo draws attention to the visual impact of Zhou Yun's clothes when the film was first shown in mainland China:

> For Zhang Yu [the actress who performed the role of Zhou Yun], she brings fashion from the West, and her clothes are very fashionable. Why do people remember the clothes that the actress wears in *Romance on Lu Mountain*? It's because the visual impact, especially in terms of colors, is so big. At that time, we did not have bell-bottomed trousers. We did not have super-short skirts. By super-short skirts, I mean the kind of skirts that just cover the knees. Her dress—sometimes it is as short as this and sometimes it is as short as that—it is full of varieties! Do you think the audience can handle this easily? No, they can't.[11]

In particular, Guo points out how striking Zhou Yun's super-short skirt was. "In terms of the length, the dress should be somewhere between the calf and the ankle. If the calf was revealed, this was already a bit too much. If the thigh was revealed, this was just scandalous!"

In this film, Zhou Yun's thighs are revealed at least twice. In the waterfall scene, Zhou Yun appears in a super-short skirt while sitting on a rock. Her feet are immersed in the water. Then she asks Geng Hua to come closer to her. However, Geng Hua, who is Confucian enough to maintain strict boundaries between man and woman, is too embarrassed to do so. However, this young Confucius eventually succumbs to her seduction. In another scene, while having a swim at the lake, Zhou Yun appears in her swimsuit, thus revealing her thighs. Geng Hua, in his swimming trunks, also has his thighs exposed. Against the conservative background, such sexualized fashion and bodily presentations, including how Zhou Yun's bell-bottoms cling so closely to her backside that one can see the curve of it, were quite alluring and bewildering. The reception of this film was mixed. Contrary to the older generation who might not be impressed with Zhou Yun's fashion presentations, the younger generation was fond of it.[12] Some young viewers even brought their tailors to the film theater so that their tailors could see what their customers desired. In short, *Romance on Lu Mountain* taught the young Chinese generation how to love, kiss, and dress, or be suitably modern in the beginning of China's economic reforms.

THE FASHION DISCOURSE IN EARLY 1980S CHINA

The fashion presentation in *Romance on Lu Mountain* is only part of the larger fashion discourse in China in the first half of the 1980s. One can observe the rise of this fashion consciousness in fashion shows, fashion magazines, other fashion films, and television melodramas. In this part, I briefly present world-renowned French fashion designer Pierre Cardin's visit to Beijing and Shanghai in 1979.

A photograph in Situ Beichen (司徒北辰) and Li Zhao's (李兆) article "Pierre Cardin: A 'Crazy Man' from France" (*Pi'er kadan: cong faguo lai de fengzi* 皮爾·卡丹: 從法國來的'瘋子') in *China News Weekly* (*Zhongguo xinwen zhoukan* 中國新聞週刊) features Cardin's encounter with a group of

Chinese female factory workers.[13] On the left is a group of young workers in their work uniforms. With the exception of their shoes, these workers' clothes are quite similar to one another; the color of their uniforms is
also plain. On the right is Cardin. His shoes match his suit (including
jacket and trousers). Underneath his suit, he wears a shirt and a tie; he also
has a pocket square. Judging from the action of Cardin and the workers, it
is as if they were engaging in a tug-of-war. This tug-of-war can be creatively interpreted as a confrontation between, on the one hand, Chinese
socialist and proletarian culture and, on the other hand, French capitalistic and bourgeois culture. This tug-of-war can also be perceived as a struggle between manual labor (e.g., factory work) and intellectual/mental labor
(e.g., fashion design), between sameness and difference, between the collective and the individual, between political revolution and economic
modernization. Similar to the passionate ways in which female fans express
their love for their male idol/singer/actor/film star, this scene features how
the young people are attracted to fashion and consumption in the beginning of China's opening up.

That year Cardin also brought twelve fashion models, including eight
from Europe and four from Asia, to China. He presented his fashion shows
at the Beijing Ethnic Cultural Palace (*Beijing minzu wenhuagong* 北京民族
文化宮) and another venue in Shanghai. In fact, Cardin's presentation was
not called a fashion show (*shizhuang biaoyan* 時裝表演); rather, it was called
a clothing observation event (*fuzhuang guangmo hui* 服裝觀摩會). To
further tone down possible controversy of this special event, the entrance
to this performance was restricted. Only professionals in clothing industries and governmental officials were invited.

During this clothing observation event, the fashion models showed off
the fashionable outfits that Cardin had designed. Each outfit had its own
distinctive flair. Indeed, the colorful clothes presented onstage constituted
a huge contrast with the drab-colored uniforms that the Chinese audience
wore. According to the article "Paris Fashions Go to Peking [Beijing] with
Cardin's Couture, a Great Leap Sexward" in *Time* magazine on February 12,
1979, "The [Pierre Cardin] collection . . . ranges from garments with thigh-
high slits and see-through torsos to dresses and coats with overstuffed
'pagoda' shoulders and gold kimono jackets worn over tight silk pants."
Such fashion presentations were quite foreign and unfamiliar to the Chinese audience who grew up during the Cultural Revolution. The fashions

designed by Cardin emphasized women's femininities and highlighted their sex appeal. Cardin's fashions were almost the opposite to the Mao suits or Sun Yat-sen uniforms that downplayed gender and sexual differences. The author of the *Time* magazine article describes the "sexless" or, in my opinion, gender neutral clothes that Chinese people wore in the late 1970s and early 1980s. The author writes: "Sex is not something they talk about openly in China. Nor do they dress with it in mind. The country's slim, trim women wear no perfume, jewelry, nail polish, or shadow on their almond eyes; for the most part, they march around in the same austere white shirts, shapeless blue pants and sandals as the men folk."

While watching this clothing observation event, the Chinese audience could appreciate the fact that men and women wore different types of clothes in other countries. The author of the *Time* magazine article considered Cardin's fashion show in China to be a "Great Leap Sexward."[14] (I will comment on this [Orientalist] revisionist narrative in "The Revisionist Narrative and Its Discontents" later.)

In an episode titled "Catwalk" (*Tianqiao* 天橋) in the Chinese TV program *Phenomenon 1980* (*Xianxiang 1980* 現象 1980), *Xinhuashe* (新華社) journalist Li Anding (李安定), who had attended Cardin's fashion show, recalls how Cardin's presentation was drastically different from Chinese shows. He says: "Cardin's show was closer to everyday life and was more relaxed. It was very different from the kind of performances, such as singing and dancing, that we were used to seeing. The Chinese performances were more rehearsed." In addition, Li explains the climactic moment of Cardin's fashion show: "A beautiful woman [fashion model] with blond hair walked toward the audience and then she stopped. Out of impulse she opened the buttons of her outfit. The result was stunning: It is as if a big wave had come toward the audience. Many viewers moved their bodies backward immediately."[15]

In fact, Xu Wenyuan (徐文淵), who later became one of the leaders of the Shanghai Fashion Performance Team (*Shanghai shizhuang biaoyandui* 上海時裝表演隊) in 1980, also made a similar observation. Recounting her experience of watching Cardin's clothing exhibition event, she says,

Most of the fashions that he [Cardin] designed were more Westernized in that the chest and the back were revealed. When the models were doing the catwalk, the audience was very quiet. I had a strong impression of one outfit. One of the models had a very good body shape. When she walked to the catwalk's center, she allowed the outer layer of her clothes to fall down. You could see her chest and her back! It was unimaginable in our society at that time. Some of the male comrades lowered their heads and dared not look at her![16]

Similar to the clothes that Cardin brought to China, the French designer himself is a spectacle to the Chinese viewers. In a memorable photograph, Cardin is walking in the middle of a street in Beijing. He is wearing a Western suit, a scarf, an overcoat, and a pair of leather shoes. The clothes that Cardin wears are unique and distinctive to the Chinese viewers. In terms of cut, his suit seems more tight-fitting and clings closer to his body. In contrast, the Chinese men are wearing the Mao suits and their outfits are more loose-fitting. It is true that Cardin's fashion models show off Cardin's designs and perform this French art to the Chinese viewers. However, in my interpretation, Cardin himself is also a fashion model for the Chinese people. Conversely, the Chinese people are also fashion models for Cardin because the Mao suits can be an exotic object to Cardin himself. In 1979 the major streets of Beijing and Shanghai became catwalks. Thanks to the success of these fashion observation events in 1979, Cardin was invited to Beijing to present another fashion show in 1981. His brand became well-known in China beginning in the 1980s.

Cardin's visit prompted the Shanghai Clothing Company (上海服裝總公司) to set up the first clothing performance team in China in 1980. The first Chinese fashion magazine, *Fashion* (時裝), was launched in the same year. It should be noted that the title of this magazine is *Fashion* (*shizhuang* 時裝) rather than *Clothing* (*fuzhuang* 服裝). Judging from the title, one can already sense the (re)emergence of a fashion consciousness in early 1980s China. Similar to the fashion films and the fashion show, *Fashion* magazine functioned as an ideological state apparatus of China's economic modernization. According to the article "Liberate Thinking; Be Bold and Innovative" in *Fashion* (1983), Liu Fang (流芳) writes:

Since the Third Plenum of the Eleventh Central Committee Congress of the Chinese Communist Party, Chinese people's standard of living has been improved, their thinking continues to be liberated, and their demand for clothing has been rapidly rising. . . . Everyone loves beauty. The attention to clothing presentation is an expression of one's desire for beauty. However, during the fashion reforms, many people expressed concerns. They were afraid to be labeled as wearing "strange-looking outfits." . . . Nobody has ever proposed a scientific standard to measure "strangeness." Because one had not been exposed to it or had not become used to it, something could appear as strange. . . . History has proved that clothing must change. Clothing closely intersects with social reforms. . . . Today, we should have a better understanding of the definition of "strangeness." We should not label certain kinds of clothing "strange-looking" too easily. Of course, we are not promoting "strange-looking" outfits either. Clothes should be good-looking, embody good taste, and suit one's physical body so that one can work and act easily. The fashion designed by the most famous fashion designers in the world, or the fashion presented in the fashion shows in Paris, may not become fashion trends. Only those outfits adopted by the majority of the Chinese people should be preferred. Our goals are to remove the obstacles, encourage free thinking, support the designers and consumers to try out new ideas, and promote the design and export of our country. . . . We have the conditions to create something new for our nation and generation and contribute to the development of world fashion.[17]

In fact, imported television programs from the United States and Japan, in addition to those from Hong Kong and Taiwan, also played an active role in animating this fashion consciousness during the economic reforms period. For example, in 1980 David Moessinger and Virgil W. Vogel's TV series *The Man from Atlantis* (大西洋底來的人) (1977) was introduced to China. After this American TV series was broadcast, the main character, Mark Harris (麥克.哈克斯戴), played by actor Patrick Duffy, immediately became a hero in China. The sunglasses that Harris wears in the TV series became popular among the young Chinese generation. While the sunglasses were called Mark Harris sunglasses, they were also called panda-eyed sunglasses or toad-eyed sunglasses in China. In addition, in 1982 the Japanese TV melodrama *Red Suspicion* (*Chide yihuo* 赤い疑惑/赤的疑惑) (1975–1976) was introduced to China. When this Japanese TV series was first broadcast in China, it was called *Red Suspicion* (*Xueyi* 血疑). The main characters—Ohshima Sachiko (大島幸子), played by actress Momoe

Yamaguchi (山口百惠), and Sagara Mitsuo (相良光夫), played by actor Tomokazu Miura (三浦友和), immediately became the darlings of the Chinese audience. While some female viewers mimicked Sachiko's haircut (幸子頭), others imitated how she dressed in the TV melodrama, resulting in the creation of Sachiko shirts (幸子衫).[18] As the loose sleeves of these shirts resemble bats' wings, these shirts were also called bat-sleeved shirts (蝙蝠袖襯衣). Some male viewers also imitated how Mitsuo dressed onscreen, hence the creation of Mitsuo shirts (光夫衫) in China. This Japanese TV melodrama also helped create a fashion consciousness in 1980s China.

Red Dress Is in Fashion (1984)

Two films, Qi Xingjia's *Red Dress Is in Fashion* (1984) and Lu Xiaoya's *The Girl in Red* (1985), depict fashion and consumption in the mid-1980s. The main character of *Red Dress Is in Fashion*, Tao Xinger (陶星兒), is a young, kind, beautiful, and diligent garment factory worker in Shanghai. Due to her responsibility and commitment at work, she has earned the title of model laborer (*laodong mofan/laomo* 勞動模範/勞模). In the beginning Tao does not have much interest in fashion. She dresses in plain colors, mostly white and sometimes dark or blue. Her lack of curiosity of fashion is sharply contrasted with A Xiang (阿香), a coworker from the countryside. To prove that she is not a country bumpkin, A Xiang purposely buys clothes made of foreign, especially American, materials and clothes imported from Hong Kong. To overcompensate, A Xiang dresses in a hyper-urban manner. One day, Tao discovers a red dress in A Xiang's factory locker. Tao is curious about this dress and wonders how she would look in it. Meanwhile, A Xiang is looking for her red dress in the locker room.

A XIANG: Where is my red dress?
TAO: It's here!
A XIANG: Here you are. Let me see! Why don't you wear it so that I can have a look at it?
[Then Tao tries it on.]
A XIANG: Pull this up a little bit.
[A Xiang helps Tao make minor adjustments to the outfit.]

A XIANG: Loosen your hair.

[Tao follows A Xiang's suggestion.]

A XIANG: It's good. Let me see. Oh my goodness! I am so jealous!

[Tao looks embarrassed. She uses her hands to cover her face.]

A XIANG: Let me see!

TAO: It's too revealing! It's too revealing!

A XIANG: It's like this dress has been tailor-made for you! Look at your figure. So
   Venice!

TAO: Venice? Venus!

A XIANG: Yes! Yes! Yes! Venus!

[Then the two girls laughed.]

A XIANG: Come! Come! Come! I can guarantee you are going to lead the fashion
   trend. Fashion models in this world are in trouble!

TAO: Do you think I can wear this dress?

A XIANG: Why not? I can lend this to you. Come! Turn around! Good! Tomorrow,
   we can go to the "dress exhibition/competition" in the park together!

Later, Tao, A Xiang, and the other factory girls go to a local park to join
the dress exhibition/competition (*zhanqun* 展裙/斬裙/戰裙), an informal
fashion show. The film sequence presents the meticulous labor that goes into
the production of feminine beauty. In this sequence the factory girls are
busy putting on makeup, coloring their eyebrows and eyelashes, using hair-
spray to stylize their hair, twisting their hair, using lipstick, combing their
hair, wearing earrings, cleaning their faces, and so on. These activities are
shown in close-up, emphasizing each character's individuality. The use of
shallow depth of field further enhances this effect. While the background
and foreground are fuzzy, the viewer's gaze is directed to how this beautiful look is laboriously achieved. Indeed, beauty takes work.

The story reaches a climax when the girls present their fashions in the
dress exhibition/competition. In sisterhood, they walk hand-in-hand across
the park and present themselves in a confident and elegant manner. This
attracts attention from many onlookers. Then Tao is encouraged by her
coworkers to do the catwalk on her own. When Tao walks and shows off
her red dress, the tempo of the music dramatically slows down, and her walk
is featured in slow motion. Indeed, Tao is young, beautiful, and feminine.
The way in which she gently shakes her head to show off her long, smooth
hair resembles what a star does in a shampoo commercial on television.

Later, more shots of her red dress are presented. The viewer is led to focus on the changes of the shape of Tao's dress thanks to her elegant movement. The red dress brings out the gentility, refinement, and femininity of Tao as a woman. It makes her even more charming, attractive, and desirable. The shot/reverse shot shows the viewers' reactions. From their facial expressions, it is evident that some men enjoy looking at Tao and her red dress. Tao also enjoys the pleasure of being looked at. She is definitely the winner of this dress competition. Living up to her name, Xinger, which means little star, Tao becomes the little star of this contest. The factory girls spend the rest of the day in the park enjoying sublime happiness. This experience helps Tao gain more confidence in expressing herself through fashion. By the end of the film, the model factory worker is finally liberated: no longer imprisoned by old and conservative (understood as revolutionary) values, Tao realizes that she can be a model factory worker and be feminine and beautiful at the same time. In a conversation with her close friend, when asked whether she prefers to be a model factory worker or participate in a beauty contest, Tao expresses that she desires both. In the economic reforms, the model factory worker does not have to choose either production or consumption. It is perfectly fine for her to desire fashion and to dress beautifully.

The Girl in Red (1985)

Lu Xiaoya's film *The Girl in Red* (1985) is an adaptation of Tie Ning's (鐵凝) story "The Red Shirt That Does Not Have Buttons" (*Meiyou niukou de hongchenshan* 沒有紐扣的紅襯衫) (1984). The main character is An Ran (安然), who is characterized by her red shirt in school. An Ran is a good student and a decent person. Not only does she have good grades in school, she also helps others and treats them with kindness and respect. Unlike the class monitor, Zhu Wenjuan (祝文娟), who is slightly selfish and protective of herself, An Ran is willing to be friends and spend time with her fellow students who are not as academically successful as she is. She invites her classmate Mi Xiaoling (米曉玲), who has to drop out of school because of family issues, to her home for dinner. She also visits Mi at her workplace to see if she has settled down in her new position. One day she bikes with her male classmates, who cheat a peasant. However, An Ran returns the money to the peasant. An Ran's classmate Liu Donghu (劉東虎) respects An Ran for doing this. An Ran's elder sister, An Jing (安靜), works as an editor in a publishing house. To help An Ran secure the "Three Excellences Student" (*sanhao xuesheng* 三好學生) title, which refers to excellence in moral character, academic achievement, and healthy body, An Jing tries to bribe An Ran's teacher, Wei Wan (韋婉), who was An Jing's primary school classmate. An Jing helps publish Wei's low-quality poem. She also gives her film tickets as a gift. In return, the insecure and corrupted Wei gently manipulates her students' opinions and helps elect An Ran for the "Three Excellences Student" honor. In this story An Ran and An Jing have different personalities. An Ran is earnest, sincere, and honest. She speaks the truth and has a sense of integrity and justice, including in situations when her righteousness may not help her secure an advantageous position. Although An Jing is also a kind person, she is more calculating and manipulative. She knows how to read other people's minds and please them so that they can help her obtain what she desires. Their differences can be observed in their reactions toward people's comments concerning An Ran's red shirt, which stands out from her fellow students' school uniforms.

AN JING: When can you learn to be more mature?

AN RAN: Sister, what happened to you today?

AN JING: I hope you can be more down-to-earth.

AN RAN: What happened to me?

AN JING: You'd better not wear that red shirt.

AN RAN: How strange! Didn't you buy it for me? Everyone said I look nice in this red shirt. Because you have said this, I am going to wear it for another three days. Let's celebrate after the exams.

AN JING: Don't wear this. People in school have made comments on your red shirt.

AN RAN: How strange! Why should they comment on my clothes?

AN JING: Don't you need to be evaluated for the "Three Excellences Student" title?

AN RAN: I will wear the red shirt on the day when my fellow students vote.

AN JING: Don't wear it because it stands out!

An Ran insists on wearing the red shirt. Due to her personality and behavior, she earns the respect of her classmates. In contrast, her parents and elder sister may not be as admirable as she. For example, her father has a weak and passive personality, and her mother has made several unwise decisions in life. Similar to the teacher Wei, An Jing turns out to be a bit controlling and corrupted. The class monitor Zhu is not the best role model either, as she is not brave enough to stand up for correctness, justice, and moral righteousness. However, An Ran is not afraid to express herself and look at the world through her own perspective. She does not see any contradiction between, on the one hand, wearing the red shirt and expressing her individuality in an honest manner and, on the other hand, being a good student and belonging to the class collective. The film *The Girl in Red* shows that a good person can also express a healthy dose of individuality.

From the revolutionary period in the mid-1960s to the economic reforms period in the mid-1980s, the filmic representations of the model characters and their relationship to consumption have drastically changed. In the mid-1960s the model characters work all the time; they are simply uninterested in clothes, leisure, and consumption. Meanwhile, the problematic characters consume and make mistakes. This is prominently illustrated in Xie Tieli's film *Never Forget* (1964), discussed in the previous chapter. In this film, the socialist authority figure Ding Haikuan and the model factory worker Ji Youliang devote all their time to work. Dedicated to socialist production, Ding Haikuan and Ji do not consume or have any hobbies outside of the factory. In comparison, the proletarian worker Ding Shaochun purchases a high-quality suit, shoots wild birds, and has allegedly forgotten about class struggle. He needs to be educated by his father about the importance of "never forget class struggle." The connection between fashion consumption and ideological deterioration is also articulated in Zhao Ming's film *The Young Generation* (1965), also discussed in the previous chapter. In this film narrative, the socialist authority figure Lin Jian and the model laborer Xiao Jiye are thoroughly committed to socialist construction. Whereas Xiao Jiye embraces physical hardship in faraway Qinghai and is indifferent to consumption, leisure, and city life, the college graduate Lin Yusheng indulges in petty-bourgeois activities such as listening to music, reading literature, and watching movies. He has also bought a dress for his girlfriend and organized a birthday party. However, it turns out that Lin Yusheng has forged a medical note and exaggerated his illness, hoping that he can stay in Shanghai rather than go back to Qinghai. In the end, Lin Yusheng is schooled by his father about the danger of bourgeois revisionism.

However, in the films in the early and mid-1980s, the model characters, while continuing to work hard, have begun to show more interest in fashion, leisure, and consumption. They do not see contradiction between, on the one hand, production and labor and, on the other hand, consumption and leisure. In *Romance on Lu Mountain*, the Chinese American woman Zhou Yun appears in more than forty fashionable outfits and vows to contribute to China's modernization by working as an architect. In *Red Dress Is in Fashion*, the model factory worker Tao Xinger, while performing her duties in a diligent, attentive, and responsible manner, desires to wear the red dress and express her femininity. In *The Girl in Red*, the "Three Excellences Student" An Ran is not concerned with the fact that her red shirt stands out from her fellow students in school. She also insists that the older generation (e.g., her parents, elder sister, and teacher) can make mistakes and may not be entirely correct. These examples register a new ideology of China's economic reforms: the new subjects of China's socialist modernization can consume and be beautifully dressed.

REFETISHIZATION OF THE SCREEN IMAGE OF WOMEN IN 1980S CHINESE CINEMA

In furthering the discussions concerning the (re-)emergence of romantic love and fashion consciousness in early 1980s China, Rey Chow's work on gender and contemporary Chinese cinema can be useful. In her essay "Fetish Power Unbound" (2013), Chow engages with Karl Marx's theory of commodity fetishism, Sigmund Freud's theory of fetishism, and Laura Mulvey's feminist film theory to propose a small history of women in Chinese cinema. Beginning with Wu Yonggang's (吳永剛) film *The Goddess* (*Shennü* 神女) (1934), Chow suggests that the figure of sex worker complicates Marx's idea of commodity fetishism in the sense that the sex worker is both a producer and a commodity. In addition, the sex worker can be analyzed through Freud's theory of fetishism: she can be interpreted as a repository of sexual desires that modern civilization must repress and displace somewhere else. Then Chow introduces another layer to her analysis: the actress/female film star. Focusing on actress Ruan Lingyu (阮玲玉) in the context of Republican China, Chow highlights a curious disjuncture between the gendered representations of the character and of the actress: "*socially debased subject matters or characters [are represented] in a cultural form whose effects tend to be spectacular and glamorous"* (original emphasis).[19]

Chow argues that the commodification and fetishization of screen images of women is evident in Chinese cinema in the 1930s and 1940s, particularly in Shanghai. Chow also suggests that Chinese socialist cinema, such as Wang Bin (王濱) and Shui Hua's (水華) film *White-Haired Girl (Baimaonü* 白毛女) (1950) and Xie Jin's (謝晉) film *Red Detachment of Women (Hongse niangzijun* 紅色娘子軍) (1961) are distinctive in the sense that they feature Chinese women as heroic and determined subjects (rather than objects or commodities). According to Chow, Chinese socialist films presented de-fetishized and de-commodified screen images of women. Extending her analysis to the economic reforms period, Chow explains how screen images of Chinese women became refetishized and recommodified in Zhang Yimou's (張藝謀) films in the late 1980s and early 1990s. This role was played by Chinese actress Gong Li (鞏俐) in Zhang's early films, including *Red Sorghum (Hong gaoliang* 紅高粱) (1987), *Ju Dou (Judou* 菊豆) (1990), and *Raise the Red Lantern (Dahong denglong gaogaogua* 大紅 燈籠高高掛) (1991).[20] In the end, Chow highlights the transmedial movement or *"medially migratory dimension of fetishized femininity"* from film to ubiquitous advertisements of commodities in everyday life, hence fetish power unbound. She concludes her essay by posing a provocative question: "Do our conventional deconstructions of phallocentric, orientalist, and heterosexist gazes still suffice as viable modes of critical intervention?"[21]

According to Chow, "Zhang [Yimou]'s success . . . consists in his rediscovery and reanimation of the conventions of fetishism that had been evident in early Chinese film-making and fully developed in Taiwan and Hong Kong cinema of the postwar eras, but that were temporarily suspended and censured under communist orthodoxy."[22] Thinking with Chow, I am not certain whether one has to wait until Zhang Yimou's early works (*Red Sorghum* came out in 1987) to detect the symptoms of the refetishization and recommodification of screen images of women in China's economic reforms. In fact, such a refetishization and recommodification had already begun with *Romance on Lu Mountain* in 1980. In this film the character Zhou Yun, played by actress Zhang Yu, appears in more than forty fashionable outfits. Her outfits are modern, Westernized, and feminine. Some of them, including her super-short skirts and swimsuit, are so sexy to the extent that one can see her thighs. One also sees close-ups of her face and the first onscreen presentation of a kiss—or, more accurately, a peck on the face—in the history of PRC cinema. Although my observation does not invalidate Chow's argument because her focus is on the transnational circulation of Chinese cinema, I argue that *Romance on Lu Mountain* has already displayed concrete evidence of the refetishization and recommodification of screen image of women within the national context.

While Chow has provided insightful analyses concerning gender, sexuality, and contemporary Chinese cinema, her discussion in this particular essay is not sufficiently equipped to analyze the complexity of *Romance on Lu Mountain*. What is missing is an active engagement with Chineseness as ethnicity and culture. In my analysis, gender is a structuring principle of this film. However, gender cannot effectively function on its own. It needs to work in conjunction with Chineseness as ethnicity and culture to make the film's ideology intellectually convincing, aesthetically attractive, emotionally appealing, or, in short, "interpellatable."

The ideological message of *Romance on Lu Mountain* is as follows: the PRC should embrace economic modernization and development and abandon political revolution and ideological battles. As a principle, the integrity of the Chinese nation cannot be violated or compromised. To implant this ideology into the film, first, the Cultural Revolution and the economic reforms should be presented as opposite political discourses. If the Cultural Revolution films present production and revolution, then the *Romance on Lu Mountain* film can feature consumption, leisure, and enjoyment. These political discourses can also be gendered. If the Cultural Revolution films emphasize the masculinized or degendered portrayals of women, then the *Romance on Lu Mountain* film can offer a boy-meets-girl love story. Indeed, gendered depictions can be creatively reworked to signify the modernization discourse of romantic love, the first kiss, and fashionable clothes.

When constructing the narrative, the woman character must be a foreigner bringing modernization to the PRC. If so, where must she come from? Must she come from Japan, the United States, Taiwan, Hong Kong, or other developed nations? Let's consider the first option. Given the history of Japanese imperialism in China in the first half of the twentieth century, depicting the female character as a Japanese woman is not an ideal choice. For the second option, if the love is between a white American woman and a Chinese man, then the film has to show their conversations in English. If their conversations are in Chinese, the story needs to explain how this white American woman learns to speak Mandarin and why she loves traditional Chinese culture and history. In addition, the issue of ethnic and cultural nationalism cannot be brought up. For the third option, if the film features the love between a Taiwanese woman and a mainland Chinese man, then the story seems to acknowledge that the KMT-controlled Taiwan is more modern and economically developed than the CCP-controlled mainland China. This may lead the viewer to have an impression that capitalism is better than socialism, or that Taiwan is better than the PRC. The question of national integrity will also surface. For the fourth option, if the film showcases the love between a Hong Kong woman and a mainland Chinese man, then the story appears to endorse the idea that this British colony is more prosperous than mainland China. This may lead the viewer to believe that British imperialism is better than Chinese socialism. The above four options are not viable.

However, if the story depicts the love between a Chinese American woman (Zhou Yun) and a Chinese man (Geng Hua), then the question of Chineseness as ethnic and cultural nationalism can be legitimately deployed to reconcile the conflict between political revolution and economic modernization. In fact, the figuration of Chinese American woman can simultaneously signify the advantages and disadvantages of a foreign modernity coming to China. Cultural hybridity allows room for political ambiguity and strategic maneuvering. Zhou Yun's fashion can simultaneously be used to promote socialist modernization (due to her Chineseness) and to condemn capitalistic excess and moral decadence (due to her Americanness). In his essay "The Absent American," cultural critic Michael Berry suggests that "the identity of the Chinese American opens a window through which the figure can be ambiguously both American while culturally, ethnically, and ethically Chinese."[23] This ethnicity-centered observation, when combined with a gendered perspective, can explain the politics of economic modernization in this film.

I further suggest that the characterization of Zhou Yun as a Chinese American woman is, in fact, a Chinese fantasy. Because Zhou Yun grew up in the United States, she is imagined to have a direct personality and to be assertive in pursuing the man in whom she is interested. She is also thought not to be embarrassed to give Geng Hua a peck on his cheek. Indeed, the passionate reunion between Geng Hua and Zhou Yun at the lake (for example, the couple runs toward each other, throws their clothes and shoes up in the air, jumps into the lake, swims across the lake, and finally embraces each other in the water) is also a fantasy not likely to happen in everyday life. Because Zhou Yun comes from the United States, she is imagined to be fashionably dressed: she appears in more than forty outfits in the film. However, there is something excessive about the number of outfits in which she appears during her visit to Lu Mountain. One starts to wonder what this over-the-top modernity may connote. While it is possible for her to dress fashionably when she travels overseas, why does she bring so many outfits (including high heels) to hike and climb up Lu Mountain? Even if she can somehow fit more than forty outfits in her small suitcase, and even if there is enough space for her to store her fashions in the hotel room (which, the viewer can see, is actually small), how is it possible that within the same day, she can appear in one outfit at the bottom of the mountain, a second outfit while climbing up the mountain, and a third outfit on the top of the mountain? The representation of Zhou Yun in all of the fashionable outfits undercuts the realism of the story. Meanwhile, while she was born in the United States and has never been to China before, the film narrative has yet to explain why and how Zhou Yun can manage to speak Mandarin perfectly. Similarly, the film narrative has not adequately clarified why and how Zhou Yun learns to identify with traditional Chinese culture and history. Why does she not identify with American or Asian American culture and history? These questions lead me to suspect that this Chinese American character is, actually, an invention of Chinese mind. The characterization of Zhou Yun is a Chinese projection of a Chinese American woman. In other words, the construction of this Chinese American character is self-referential: it reveals more about China and its fantasy of economic modernization than about the reality of American or Chinese American life.

FROM REVOLUTION TO MODERNIZATION

In the second part of *Romance on Lu Mountain*, after Geng Hua and Zhou Yun have drunk some water from Wisdom Well, they come across a strange-looking sculpture.

GENG HUA: What kind of god is this?
ZHOU YUN: The god of love!
GENG HUA: The god of love does not exist [on Lu Mountain]!

ZHOU YUN: Then what kind of god do you think it is?

GENG HUA: Oh! It's written here. It is the Protector of Buddhist Doctrines.

ZHOU YUN: In my opinion, this is the Protector of Love.

GENG HUA: The Protector of Love?

ZHOU YUN: Yes!

GENG HUA: No! It's written here. It is the Protector of Buddhist Doctrines.

ZHOU YUN: You! You have drunk the Wisdom Water in vain!

GENG HUA: Yes?

ZHOU YUN: To us, he may be the Protector of Love!

GENG HUA: Oh! (Then he laughed loudly.)

Geng Hua is correct: the sculpture is called the Protector of Buddhist Doctrines (*hufa lishi* 護法力士). While the word *fa* (法) means law or doctrine—and, by extension, politics—it is reasonable to call it the protector of politics. However, Zhou Yun insists on specifying the sculpture as the protector of love (*hu'ai lishi* 護愛力士). In my interpretation, her renaming depoliticizes the sculpture. Such a resignification condenses the changing ideologies of the PRC: from a revolutionary government that prioritizes politicization (the protector of politics) to one that emphasizes depoliticization (the protector of love). The latter is connected to the farewell to revolution and the welcoming of economic development.

In the above, I have presented *Romance on Lu Mountain* as a passionate love story between Geng Hua and Zhou Yun. However, if we expand our interpretive horizon to include the parents of Geng Hua and Zhou Yun in our analysis, this film can be read as a political family melodrama. Indeed, the different characters symbolize different political forces. The father, Geng Feng, is a CCP military commander. Wearing a Mao suit, Geng Feng is the personification of socialist and revolutionary China. He is shocked to realize that Geng Hua would like to marry the daughter of his former political opponent Zhou Zhenwu. However, after serious considerations, Geng Feng finally changes his mind and allows his son to marry Zhou Yun. By the end of the film, he says to his future daughter-in-law:

Child, forgive me. For young people like you, some problems are easy to solve. But for those of us who have fought in battles with hatred for half of our lives, it is not as easy as reading newspapers or singing a song. We have to think about it and struggle with it. But we are good old people. We will be enlightened. Write a letter to your father. Tell him that to actualize the motherland's project of four modernizations, we need the unification of our country and the solidarity of Chinese people. Geng Feng welcomes him to return to China.

Thus, this film can be analyzed as a story about the growing up and education of Geng Feng (rather than Geng Hua). In contrast to Geng Hua and Zhou Yun, who remain passionately in love with each other throughout this film, Geng Feng is the only character who has changed and matured. His decision to allow his son to marry the daughter of his former political opponent allegorizes the radical transformation of socialist China after the end of the Cultural Revolution.

If Geng Feng is the personification of socialist and revolutionary China, then Geng Hua is the embodiment of China in the age of economic reforms. Seen this way, *Romance on Lu Mountain* is more concerned with the changing relationship between father and son and, by extension, the evolution of the PRC from socialism to postsocialism. The clue to Geng Hua being the symbol of postsocialist China can be found in the Flower Path scene. In the woods, Geng Hua practices speaking the English phrase "I love my motherland. I love the morning of my motherland" several times. Zhou Yun, hiding behind the trees, corrects his pronunciation. In fact, when one carefully listens to Geng Hua's pronunciation, the way he pronounces love is somewhere between love and learn. Certainly, Geng Hua is learning how to love. He is learning how to love Zhou Yun. He is also learning how to love his motherland. Rather than uttering this phrase in Chinese, Geng Hua says it in English, another symbol of modernization. In retrospect, the fact that Geng Hua gives the old phrase (*wo'ai zuguo* 我愛祖國) a new expression (I love my motherland) can be compared with what political leader Deng Xiaoping did with Chinese socialism. In the 1980s Deng gave the old phrase (Chinese socialism) a new interpretation (socialism with Chinese characteristics) and connected it with economic modernization and development.

Zhou Zhenwu was a military commander in the KMT. After his defeat in the civil war, he fled to the United States and settled there. He can be considered a figuration of capitalism. If he symbolizes the old type of capitalism, then his daughter, Zhou Yun, personifies a new stage of capitalism—namely, global capitalism—and its cultural logic, postmodernism. Her assertive, even aggressive personality resembles the predatory nature of transnational capital. Her fashionable presentations also correlate with the image economy in global capitalism.

However, what about Mother Geng? In the second half of the story, after Geng Hua has informed his parents that he would like to marry Zhou Yun, Geng Feng and Mother Geng have a serious conversation. While getting impatient, Geng Hua knocks on the door, and it is Mother Geng who opens the door and answers his call. By the end of their discussion, it is Mother Geng who again opens the door to tell Geng Hua that his father would like to talk to him. In other words, Mother Geng mediates the interaction between Geng Feng (socialist China) and Geng Hua (postsocialist China) and indirectly allows Geng Hua to marry Zhou Yun (global capitalism and postmodernism). What does Mother Geng stand for? The answer, once again, can be found in the Flower Path scenes. In the woods, Geng Hua practices speaking the English phrase "I love my motherland" several times. He identifies with his motherland. Then Mother Geng calls him: "Geng Hua! Geng Hua!" and he replies to her immediately. "Mother! I am coming!" Mother Geng is a symbol of the motherland. Geng Hua's response to his mother's call is also his response to the interpellation from his motherland. This call hails him as a patriotic subject. Accompanied with the images of wild geese flying toward their homeland, the two lyrical songs "Fly Toward the Homeland from Far Away" (飛向遠方的故鄉) and "Oh! Homeland!" (啊, 故鄉) further reinforce the desire for the motherland. Chinese intellectuals are called upon by their motherland to participate in socialist modernizations.[24]

While Mother Geng is the personification of the motherland, what kind of China does she represent? In my analysis, she symbolizes premodern and traditional Chinese culture. Such an interpretation can be confirmed by the fact that she was ill during the Cultural Revolution, and Geng Hua brought her to Lu Mountain to rest. The "four olds" (sijiu 四舊)—old customs, old cultures, old habits, and old ideas—were radically critiqued during the Cultural Revolution. The Anti-Confucius campaign (pikong yundong 批孔運動), which emerged alongside the Anti–Lin Biao campaign (pilin yundong 批林運動) in the early 1970s, also testified to this. Importantly, the Lu Mountain presented onscreen is primarily concerned with premodern and traditional Chinese culture and history. It is shown from the perspectives of

Dongjin (東晉) Dynasty poet Tao Yuanming (陶淵明) (365–427), Tang (唐) Dynasty poets Li Bai (李白) (701–762) and Bai Juyi (白居易) (772–846), Song (宋) Dynasty poets Lu You (陸游) (1125–1210), Su Dongpo / Su Shi (蘇東坡/蘇軾) (1037–1101), and Zhu Xi (朱熹) (1130–1200). In addition, before Zhou Yun visits Lu Mountain, her father has explained to her the legends of Zhu Xi on Zhenliu Stone and of Bai Juyi in the Flower Path. During their tour, Geng Hua lectures Zhou Yun on the history of Imperial Pavilion: the architecture was built by Ming (明) Dynasty emperor Zhu Yuanzhang (朱元璋) in commemoration of his friendship with monk Zhou Dian (周顚). Geng Hua also details the history of the ancient bridge built a thousand years ago. Furthermore, after they have swum in the lake, Geng Hua recites a traditional Chinese poem to Zhou Yun while both of them are still in their swimming outfits.

The Lu Mountain presented onscreen is not only a traditional and premodern version of the mountain but also a depoliticized one. It is completely detached from the history of Chinese socialist revolutions. In fact, what is not represented onscreen is as important as, or perhaps more important than, what is represented onscreen. Notably, what is not mentioned is the politicized version of Lu Mountain: the culture and history of modern and revolutionary China. Certainly, Lu Mountain is inseparable from the culture, history, and politics of revolutionary China. It is the place where Zhou Enlai (周恩來) and Chiang Kai-shek (*Jiang Jieshi* 蔣介石) met in the summer of 1933 to negotiate the formation of an alliance between the Communists and the Nationalists so they could cooperate to resist the expansion of Japanese imperialism in China. It is also the place where the famous Lu Mountain conferences (廬山會議) were held. The first Lu Mountain conference, held in July and August 1959, witnessed the fall of Peng Dehuai (彭德懷) from political power. The second Lu Mountain conference was held in August 1961. The third Lu Mountain conference in August 1970 saw the fall of Lin Biao (林彪) and Chen Boda (陳伯達) (former editor of *Red Flag*) from political power. Although Lu Mountain is an important location for Chinese revolutionary politics, such politicized descriptions are purposely omitted in this film. Such a repression is deeply ideological. In his essay "The Absent American," Michael Berry argues that "the primary function of Lushan's historical, cultural, and national objectification is not so much to serve as a handy tourist film, but to consciously neutralize or nullify the impact of America."[25] Adding to his interpretation, I argue that the primary function of the depoliticized representations of Lu Mountain is to consciously neutralize or nullify the impact of the politicized depictions of the mountain. Depoliticization is an ideology of China's economic reforms and opening up.

THE REVISIONIST NARRATIVE AND ITS DISCONTENTS

During the past forty years the story of the unprecedented transformations of the PRC has been told from the revisionist perspective. According to this narrative, the Cultural Revolution repressed Chinese people's humanity, which was later liberated by the economic reforms. This revisionist narrative is often told in terms of fashion and gender presentations. According to the revisionist critics, the fact that Maoist socialism promoted sameness can be observed in how the Chinese people dressed at that time. The colors of their uniforms—blue, green, white, and gray—were dull and monotonous. Furthermore, because Chinese women had to wear proletarian clothes, Maoist socialism denied their femininities, turning them into masculine or genderless beings. However, the revisionist critics continue, the reform-minded government promoted difference. During the economic reforms, the Chinese people were encouraged to wear colorful outfits and express their personalities and individualities. The Chinese women could also express their femininities through fashion and makeup and regain their consciousness as gendered beings.[26] In this part, I confront this revisionist argument by showing its limitations. First, I argue that the historical reality concerning fashion and gender subjectivity is more complex than what the revisionist critics claim: the revolutionary period is not as repressive as what they present it to be; meanwhile, the economic reforms era is not as emancipatory as what they imagine it to be. (However, I do not necessarily mean that the revolutionary period is entirely emancipatory, nor do I imply that the economic reforms era is completely repressive.) Second, I argue that the gender politics of the revisionist critics is conservative because it denies the Chinese women other possibilities of expressing and performing their genders and identities.

According to the revisionist critics, China's socialism repressed gender and fashion presentations, resulting in masculinized sameness; in contrast, difference and femininity were promoted by the reform-minded government. This can be observed in Canadian Broadcasting Corporation's TV documentary *China's Sexual Revolution* (2007). In the beginning of this documentary, the narrator declares: "[Chinese socialism] turned couples into comrades, not lovers, and cloaked men and women into the same asexual Mao suit." This is a typical narrative of the revisionist story. Then the viewer is introduced to the perspectives of two diasporic Chinese women, Zha Jianying (查建英) and Kan Yue-sai (*Jin Yuxi* 靳羽西). The latter brought cosmetics to China in the 1980s. Kan, the narrator tells the viewer, is a very successful businesswoman. In China she has "the fame of Oprah and Martha Stewart combined."

ZHA JIANYING: [During the Cultural Revolution] women were turned into men. Everyone was dressed alike, men and women. The fashion statement back then was that you can all become brothers and sisters. The only way women could show a bit of their figure was by sewing in their blue uniform so that they could have a waistline.[27] . . . The Red Guards went on the street and cut everybody's long hair and that's a very blatant way of trying to make everyone the same.
KAN YUE-SAI: They [Chinese women] dressed like men. Women dressed like men. No color. No makeup. The hairdo was only one kind of hairdo. Basically, no style. Nobody was wearing anything provocative. Nobody was going to prominently display their lips.

Zha and Kan suggest that gender and fashion expressions were denied during the socialist period. Their revisionist viewpoints are shared by mainland Chinese feminist critic Li Yinhe (李銀河). In her conversation with feminist critic Harriet Evans, Li commented on socialist China's gender politics:

In China, from the 1950s to 1960s until the end of the Cultural Revolution, the atmosphere was that men and women were the same. Women had to do what men did. Women demanded gender equality and the blurring of gender boundaries. At least this is how it was promoted in mainstream culture. For example, women had to work in the mines. Women worked on the railways. These were men's jobs in the past. At that time, women used to cover all their feminine characteristics. No women put on makeup. The clothes they wore did not show any secondary sexual characteristics. The way women dressed was the way men dressed. They tried not to highlight any gender differences. This was the tendency of the first thirty years of the PRC. In the early 1980s—that is, the beginning of the economic reforms—the display of gender differences was becoming increasingly obvious. Some women put on makeup. Some women wore clothes that exposed their bodies' secondary sexual characteristics. Some women went back home and became housewives. . . . After the 1980s Chinese women displayed a tendency of going back to their traditional gendered roles. They also displayed a tendency of emphasizing gender differences. This is how the question of sex and gender evolved in China historically.[28]

According to such revisionist critics as Zha, Kan, and Li, Maoist socialism erased gender, even murdered gender (*xingbie mousha* 性别谋杀). Since the Chinese women were asked to wear working-class uniforms, Maoist socialism suppressed their femininities and turned them into genderless beings. (According to this logic, the socialist regime also emasculated Chinese men and prevented them from expressing their true masculine selves.) In contrast, the economic reforms emancipated the Chinese women and helped them recover their lost womanhood. No longer required to wear masculine or unisex clothing, they could wear dresses and makeup and express their femininities. (Similarly, the Chinese men were also empowered to become real men and act out their masculine selves.) The modernization of China is presented as a developmentalist project of recovering essentialized and normative gender.

To problematize this revisionist argument, I engage with the keywords of their progress narrative—namely, "gender sameness," "gender repression," "gender difference," and "gender liberation." I structure my critique of their argument by asking four questions. First, is the revolutionary period really characterized by the erasure of gender and the celebration of gender sameness? Second, does the celebration of gender sameness in the revolutionary period necessarily result in gender repression? Third, is the economic reforms period characterized by the celebration of gender difference? Fourth, does the celebration of gender difference in the economic reforms period necessarily equal gender liberation? I argue that the answers to these questions are all negative.

First, according to the revisionist critics, because the Chinese women were asked to wear proletarian clothing during the revolutionary period, their femininities were erased and a masculinized version of gender sameness was promoted. However, was this really the case? Although these critics are correct to say that gender was not emphasized or pronounced in

131

"MAO'S CHILDREN ARE WEARING FASHION!"

women's clothing, it is, historically speaking, inaccurate to say that wom-
en's femininities were completely eliminated. When one looks at the Chinese sources, such as the photographs in the Chinese Cultural Revolution
Research website (*Zhongguo wenge yanjiu wang* 中國文革研究網), Chinese
men and women did dress in slightly different ways during the revolutionary period. When one looks at the non-Chinese sources, such as Michelangelo Antonioni's documentary film *Chung Kuo Cina* (1972), which
chronicles the lives of Chinese people in the early 1970s, there were still
signs of difference on women's clothes. Compared with men's shirts, wom-
en's shirts have different colors and patterns (e.g., check shirts and plaid
shirts). In addition, the collars of the outer layers of women's clothes were
wider. Women also had different hairstyles. My observation is confirmed
by Evans, who has researched Chinese feminism in the twentieth century.
In her conversation with Li Yinhe, Evans says:

> You [Li Yinhe] mentioned that men and women were the same from the
> 1950s to the 1960s. I cannot fully agree with you. On the surface, the ways in
> which men and women dressed were similar. But when you pay close
> attention to the photographs taken at that time, you can see that there were
> feminine patterns on women's clothes, and also, some women had braided
> hair. Women's images, including the representations of women in the offi-
> cial propaganda, did display signs of femininities. This is related to what I
> have been researching on. If you look at some of the women's magazines pub-
> lished during the socialist period, such as *Women of China, China Youth
> Daily*, and the like, these publications were concerned with the issues relat-
> ing to sex and gender. The topics included sex education, puberty, physical
> development, and many other things. True, the quantity was limited, but at
> least they were there. Through these materials, it is clear that gender differ-
> ences were indeed present [during the socialist and revolutionary period.][29]

In her book *Chinese Fashion: From Mao to Now* (2009), Juanjuan Wu makes
a similar observation concerning the socialist and revolutionary period:

> Although both men and women wore plain clothes in the same drab colors
> and the same square, simple cuts, minor details in women's and men's wear
> did exist that, to some extent, served to differentiate the sexes in Chinese
> eyes. For instance, to a casual observer a woman's dual-purpose jacket looked

very much like a man's Mao-suit jacket, but it differed in the type and number of pockets and in the number of buttons.[30]

Wu explains the difference between the Mao suit worn by men and the dual-purpose jacket (*liangyongshan* 兩用衫) worn by women. For men, alongside the military attire (*junzhuang* 軍裝), the most fashionable clothes were the three old styles (*laosanzhuang* 老三裝) and three old colors (*laosanse* 老三色). The three old styles refer to the Mao suit, formerly called the Sun Yat-sen suit (*zhongshanzhuang* 中山裝); youth jacket (*qingnian-zhuang* 青年裝); and causal army jacket (*junbianzhuang* 軍便裝). The three old colors refer to subdued blue, white, and gray. In addition, olive green, the color of the military uniform, was also popular. For women, the most common outfits were the plain, dual-purpose jacket and traditional-styled jacket. Interestingly, the number of pockets and buttons indicates gender. For men, the Mao suit had five buttons on the front closure, one button on each of the four front patch-pocket flaps, and three buttons on each sleeve.[31] For women, although the dual-purpose jacket resembled the Mao jacket in color and silhouette, it had four (rather than five) buttons and two (rather than four) rectangular, flapless front patch pockets.[32] These minor differences work like labels: they indicate either men or women.[33] Wu also says that a modest degree of fashion presentation was permitted during the socialist period. For women, an accepted way of being fashionable was to wear the inner shirt's patterned collar on the outside of the plain jacket. Different styles of scarves were also regarded as fashionable accessories.[34] Since there were signs of difference, albeit minor ones, on women's clothes, it is not entirely historically accurate to claim that femininities or gender differences were completely erased, even murdered, during the socialist and revolutionary periods.

Second, according to the revisionist critics, because the Chinese women were asked to wear masculinized or genderless clothing, gender difference was repressed during the socialist period. Rather than endorsing their terms—gender repression, gender erasure, and the murdering of gender—I suggest that it is more productive to use gender neutrality or androgyny to describe the gender politics of the socialist and revolutionary period.[35] Rather than looking at the negative aspects, I think we can look at the positive aspects of gender neutrality or androgyny. Indeed, what kinds of new gender possibilities were available to the Chinese women when they were not expected to perform their femininities or gender differences? What could they gain, and how were they inspired and empowered when they were permitted to cross gender (without being male identified)? What kinds of gender options were open to them when they could act as what Xiaomei Chen calls "manly women?"[36] To pose the question in a slightly different way is to inquire what kinds of gender options are foreclosed by the revisionist categories of gender repression and gender erasure.

Third, according to the revisionist critics, during the economic reforms period, Chinese women were free to wear feminine clothing, and gender difference was recovered. However, the revisionist critics' idea of femininity, such as Kan's idea, closely intersects with commercialized consumer culture. (Kan introduced makeup to 1980s China.) The kinds of femininity not directly associated with consumption are not included. In my opinion, the revisionist critics' idea of gender difference is limiting because it is not different enough. Going further, the revisionist critics deny Chinese women other ways of being feminine because they only celebrate one kind of femininity—the consumerist kind—at the expense of other kinds of femininity. While the revisionist critics claim that revolutionary politics results in gender erasure, paradoxically, their version of gender politics turns out to be another form of gender erasure.

Fourth, the revisionist critics presented the opportunities to wear feminine clothes in the economic reforms period as gender liberation. However, to what extent is it gender liberation? What kinds of gender possibilities are excluded and foreclosed? Underlying their progress narrative is the assumption that the Chinese women must necessarily dress in a feminine way to be liberated. However, why must they dress in a feminine way? Why must they perform in a feminine way to be liberated? Why can't they dress in a masculine way and be liberated? In a gender utopia, the women should be able to dress and behave in a masculine way, in a feminine way, both, or neither. For example, if they desire, they should feel free to dress and behave in a masculine way in the morning, in a feminine way in the afternoon, in an androgynous way in the evening, and in a genderless manner after midnight. They should be able to change their gender preference the next day. In a gender utopia, men should feel free to dress and act in whatever gender they prefer too. In other words, when the revisionist critics assume that in order to be liberated, the Chinese women should dress in a feminine way (rather than in a masculinized or genderless manner), they have already recuperated and rehearsed the very object and relationship that they critique in the first place. Ultimately, their version of gender difference can be potentially oppressive, especially to some lesbians, transgender individuals, or women who enjoy acting in a masculine way. Their feminist politics turns out to be a gender determinism that denies women other ways of expressing or performing their genders. Intending to critique gender erasure in the socialist and revolutionary period, the revisionist critics' version of gender difference turns out to be gender erasure in disguise.[37]

To end this chapter I return to the film *Romance on Lu Mountain* and the images associated with this mountain. In his poem "Written on the Wall of West Forest Temple" (*Tixilinbi* 題西林壁), the Tang Dynasty poet Su Dongpo writes about the Lu Mountain:

横看成嶺側成峰，　Sideways a mountain range, vertically a peak.
遠近高低各不同。　Far-near, soaring-crouching, never the same.
不識廬山真面目，　No way to know Lushan's true face
只緣身在此山中。　When you're in the middle of this mountain!

I read Su's famous poem by using poststructuralist methodology. Su sets up several binary oppositions: profile view versus side view, far versus near, high versus low, appearance versus reality, and inside versus outside. The last two lines—"No way to know Lushan's [Lu Mountain's] true face / when you're in the middle of this mountain!"—can be interpreted as his deconstructionist move. The opposition between appearance and reality turns out to be a false problem because this opposition has always already been embedded in another reality. Deploying this poststructuralist reading of Su's poem to analyze *Romance on Lu Mountain*, I suggest that in the early 1980s, one could not clearly see the reality of *Romance on Lu Mountain* because one was embedded in another reality—namely, the economic reforms. It is only after one has moved beyond this reality that one can begin to observe its historical embeddedness. In short, *Romance on Lu Mountain* signals an unprecedented transformation of the PRC in the early 1980s: the emergence of a depoliticized ideology of economic modernization after the end of the Cultural Revolution.

Chapter Four

IMAG(IN)ING THE CHINESE MIDDLE-CLASS CULTURE

White-Collar Work, Romantic Love, and Fashion Consumption

I begin by referencing two scenes in two Chinese commercial films about love and consumption. The first image comes from the romantic comedy *Love Is Not Blind* (*Shilian sanshisan tian* 失戀三十三天) (2011) directed by Teng Huatao (滕華濤). In this film wedding planner Huang Xiaoxian (黃小仙) is extremely upset because her boyfriend, Lu Ran (陸然), has cheated on her by having an affair with her best friend. She realizes that romantic love can disappear any time. While preparing for her client's wedding ceremony, Huang converses with Wei Yiran (魏依然), a "tall, rich, and handsome" (*gaofushuai* 高富帥) man engaged to Li Ke (李可) (this Li Ke, a character in *Love Is Not Blind*, is different from Li Ke, the author of *Chronicle of Du Lala's Promotion*). Coming from Henan Province, China, Li speaks Mandarin with a fake Taiwanese accent. She likes to act like a teenage girl and be cute. Huang secretly asks Wei why he has chosen to marry Li.

HUANG: You are a good-looking man and have a good career. You have so many choices. I don't know who you will eventually choose, but it should not be like Li Ke. Of course, you are not an exception. I've met many couples like you and her. Many great guys date girls who always talk about Louis Vuitton (LV) and Prada (張口 LV, 閉口 Prada). This girl will most likely tell you that the limit you set on her credit card indicates how much you love her. Why?

WEI: The answer is quite simple. Two words: Save troubles. Simply put, we want to find wives who can stay with us even when love fades away. Can you accept it? But Li Ke can. For her, LV is an everyday necessity and love is a luxury (LV 是生活必需品,愛情是奢侈品). But for women like you, love is an everyday necessity and LV is a luxury (愛情是生活必需品, LV 是奢侈品). The LV company will not suddenly go bankrupt, but love can end in any minute.

The second scene comes from Guo Jingming's (郭敬明) commercial film *Tiny Times* (*Xiaoshidai* 小時代) (2013), which chronicles the lives of several high school and college students in cosmopolitan Shanghai. In one scene a wealthy young man, Gu Yuan (顧源), expresses his love for his girlfriend, Gu Li (顧里), despite the fact that his parents oppose their relationship (partly because Gu Li does not come from a wealthy family). Gu Yuan emphasizes that his love for Gu Li is pure and genuine.

GU YUAN: I like you [Gu Li], not because you've had a driver since you were little, and not because you have designer bags, and definitely not because you gave me expensive boots. Even if you didn't have a cent, I would still like you.
GU LI: Let me tell you: love without materialism is just a pile of sand (沒有物質的愛情只是一盤散沙)! . . . You have read too much Shakespeare!

In these two commercial films, the young Chinese women prefer fashion, materialism, and money to love. What do these scenes reveal about the aspiring Chinese middle-class consumers and how they make sense of the world? How do these films help reflect or construct the Chinese middle class?

In the previous two chapters, I engage with *Never Forget* (1964) and *Romance on Lu Mountain* (1980) to investigate the representations of fashion and consumption in Chinese cinema in the 1960s and 1980s, respectively. Contributing to the scholarship on socialist cultures, I argue that during the seventeen-years period (1949–1966), fashion and consumption are not represented negatively but ambivalently. Such a depiction is not a mirror reflection of the socialist reality; instead it is a symptomatic expression of the profound contradictions that confronted Chinese socialism at the dawn of the Cultural Revolution. In addition, I suggest that during this seventeen-years period, fashion and consumption, similar to love, gender, and sexuality, are either repressed and subsumed by, or sublimated and rechanneled to, revolutionary politics. Turning to China's economic reforms and opening up, I contend that fashion and consumption, similar to the screen image of women in Chinese cinema, become refetishized as objects of desire. Ultimately, I propose that in the new era, the de-repression and de-sublimation of romantic love, the refetishization of fashion and gender, and the rearticulation of ethnicity and culture are ultimately a political process. They closely intersect with, on the one hand, the regime's decision to withdraw from class struggle, ideological battle, and political revolution and, on the other hand, the regime's desire to embrace economic modernization and development.

In this chapter, I focus on the culture of the Chinese middle class, with an emphasis on the representations of white-collar work, romantic love, and fashion consumption in Chinese media and popular culture in the late 2000s and early 2010s. I contribute to the current scholarship about the Chinese middle class and culture by arguing that it is through the consumption of popular and media cultures that the middle-class subjectivities are constructed and the middle-class ideologies are transmitted. Resembling self-help books, these cultural productions teach the Chinese readers and viewers to recognize the symbols of the middle class, acculturate them to look at the world through a middle-class perspective, and instruct them to act and perform in a distinctively middle-class manner. They also teach them how to distinguish themselves from the other social groups, such as the nouveau riche who own economic capital but not cultural capital.

This chapter is organized in three parts. In the first part, I engage with Li Ke's (李可) popular workplace novel *Chronicle of Du Lala's Promotion* (*Dulala shengzhiji* 杜拉拉升職記) (2007). I discuss the cultures of the Chinese middle class: an aspirational dream, hard work, personal struggle, upward mobility, and career success. According to the novel's marketing strategy, "Du Lala's story is worthier for emulation than Bill Gates's story!" It is a Chinese version of the American dream. It is also a Chinese dream. Indeed, this popular workplace novel serves as a guidebook or an instructional manual for the *xiaozi* (petty bourgeoisie 小資), or the aspiring Chinese middle class. The latter can learn what it is like to work in an American company in China. In the first part, I suggest that the Chinese middle-class subject is not an autonomous or independent class but a class fraction whose existence is structurally shaped and overdetermined by the party-state and the transnational and national capitals. To decenter the "I"-ness of the Chinese middle class, I turn to Jacques Lacan's theory of the mirror stage and to Louis Althusser's concept of interpellation. I use these critical concepts to explain how contemporary Chinese popular and media cultures help constitute the Chinese middle-class subjectivity. In the second part, I turn to Xu Jinglei's (徐靜蕾) commercial film *Go! Lala Go!* (*Dulala shengzhiji* 杜拉拉升職記) (2010), an adaptation of Li's workplace novel. This film was marketed as one of the first fashion films in globalizing China. I examine the representations of fashion, consumption, and product placement in this film. I approach *Go! Lala Go!* from two angles: Focusing on the content, I present it as a romantic love story. Focusing on the form, I suggest that the main character is fashion (rather than Du Lala); the film also appears as a fashion show to the viewer. The fashion commodities look at the viewers as much as the viewers look at the commodities. Taken together, I illustrate how the party-state, capital, and their ideological apparatuses collaborate to construct the new Chinese middle-class subject in the context of globalizing China. In the third part, I focus on class, gender, and fashion and trace the changing relation between the subject and the object from the socialist to the postsocialist and globalization periods.

WHITE-COLLAR WORK: A STORY OF UPWARD MOBILITY

Beginning in the mid- and late 2000s, the Chinese cultural scene was populated with workplace novels (*zhichang wenxue* 職場文學), self-help books, and guidebooks of success studies (*chenggongxue* 成功學). Members of the aspiring Chinese middle class tried to find inspirations from workplace fiction such as Wang Qiang's (王强) novel *Circles and Traps* (*Quanzi quantao* 圈子圈套) (2006), Fu Yao's (付遙) novel *Win or Lose* (*Shuying* 輸贏) (2006), Li Ke's novel *Chronicle of Du Lala's Promotion* (2007), and Cui Manli's (崔曼莉) novel *Floating and Sinking* (*Fuchen* 浮沈) (2008), to name a few.[1] One of the most well-known novels is Li Ke's *Chronicle of Du Lala's Promotion*, which follows white-collar worker Du Lala (杜拉拉) as she advances her career in an American company in twenty-first-century China. When this novel came out, it immediately became a bestseller and was so successful that it had three sequels, which were published in 2009, 2010, and 2011. This series sold more than five million copies in China. The success of the Du Lala story is also evident in its adaptation to other media forms, including a live theater drama (2009), a film (2010), a TV drama (2010), and an internet series (2012). Further adaptations of this story flourished, including the film *Go! Lala Go! 2* (*Dulala zhuihunqi* 杜拉拉追婚記) (2015) and the TV drama *Still Lala* (*Woshi Dulala* 我是杜拉拉) (2016), and others.[2] The success of the four novels reinforced the box office of the films and TV dramas; likewise, the popularity of the films and TV dramas boosted the sales of the novels. The marketing of the original Du Lala novel is notable. According to the book cover, it is "a must-read workplace and training novel for Chinese white collars" (中國白領必讀的職場修煉小說). It reveals "the workplace experience of office ladies in the world's top 500 companies" (白領麗人500強職場心得) and offers "survival wisdom for those working in foreign companies!" (揭示外企生存智慧的更值得參考!). Interestingly, "Du Lala's story is worthier for reference than Bill Gates's story" (她的故事, 比比爾蓋茨的更加值得參考). Certainly, this story helps construct the emerging Chinese middle class in the first and second decades of the twenty-first century. It anticipates what the Chinese government calls the Chinese dream and, I add, the American dream in China.

Chronicle of Du Lala's Promotion tells the story of how Du, a Chinese white-collar worker in her twenties, climbs up a career ladder within an American company in China called DB. Although Du does not come from a rich family or have any social connections that can help her secure a good job, she receives a good education. Through diligent work and personal struggle, she manages to receive promotions and salary raises.[3] In the beginning of the narrative, when she arrives at DB, she is immediately informed by her coworker of DB's hierarchy. In this company, she is told, the *xiaozi* (petty bourgeoisie 小資) occupies the lowest rank, which is followed by the manager, which is then followed by the director. Meanwhile, the president occupies the highest position. In addition, one's income and position in the company inform the choices of one's consumption:

> Those below the rank of manager are called *xiaozi* (petty bourgeoisie), which is the same thing as being poor; usually they go to the office by public transportation because they have a mortgage to pay off. Those with the rank of manager are the middle class: they don't need to get a loan to purchase their first house and typically drive a Bora if they are first-level . . . and a Passat if they are second-level. . . . Those with the rank of director are the

bourgeoisie; they own more than one apartment, which is normally located in a prime area of town, or a villa, and can freely pick a company car or buy a sedan with the company benefits. . . . The vice president and president are the rich; they have a butler and a door keeper at home, the company provides them with a personal driver and they fly first class when they go on a business trip.[4]

In the beginning Du works as a sales assistant and earns as little as 4,000 yuan per month. After accumulating some work experience, she becomes an administrator and earns 6,825 yuan per month. Admirably, Du has single-handedly handled the renovation of the offices before the global CEO arrives. However, her contribution has not been sufficiently recognized by her boss. Du tries to adopt a new strategy, which is to become more confident and assertive. She also tries to communicate with her supervisor more frequently and to familiarize him with the progress and challenges of her work. These tactics enable Du to earn the respect of her boss, and he comes to see her contribution to the company more clearly. Du is then promoted to the position of a manager and her salary is further increased. In addition, Du has learned to present a professional image of herself to her coworkers and her clients. The narrative attends to the bodily movements and gestures, or what French sociology theorist Pierre Bourdieu calls habitus, of professionals at DB. The successful white-collar workers are described as having upright postures; confident eye contact, voice, and diction; and firm handshakes. When they work, they have super-high energy and look like triathlon champions. Even though many of them have to work overtime in the evening, they appear to have full energy the next day at work.[5] While not working, the male managers run and work out in the gym, and the female managers visit the beauty salon.[6] Du has thus adopted and internalized this professional image and learned to present herself as a professional. By the end of the story, Du works as a director of human resources and earns close to 10,000 yuan per month, at only thirty years old.

The novel chronicles Du's upward mobility within the American company in China. It describes how she manages to transform herself from a *xiaozi* (petty bourgeoisie) to a professional middle class. (Crudely speaking, in China, the middle class is defined as someone who owns an apartment and a car [*youfang youche* 有房有車].) However, by the end of the novel, Du does not rise to the level of the company's president or director.

This is largely because the representation of the Chinese dream in *Chronicle of Du Lala's Promotion* is gendered. Certainly, Du is industrious, successful, and productive. However, she is not too successful to the extent that her work may threaten the masculinist authorities of the state and capital. This is especially true when one compares Xu's film *Go! Lala Go!*, an adaptation of Li's novel, with Peter Chan's (Chen Kexin 陳可辛) film *American Dreams in China* (*Zhongguo hehuoren* 中國合伙人) (2013). In Chan's film, the male characters eventually become successful entrepreneurs and the company's CEOs. In contrast, in Xu's film, the young, hard-working, and ambitious Du is preoccupied with gendered and sexualized matters such as romance, consumption, marriage, and family. She is distracted by romantic love and fashion consumption. In another film, *Go! Lala Go! 2* (杜拉拉追婚記), Du gets married. The success of Du does not directly challenge patriarchy or heteronormativity. It does not initiate social change.

By the end of the novel, Du has a conversation with a new acquaintance on an airplane. She says to him: "Middle-class life is exhausting. Middle-class people don't have family backgrounds or social connections. They need to work very hard in order to succeed. How can the middle class be truly free?"[7] Her acquaintance replies: "Precisely because the middle-class life is so tiring that they desire freedom. Precisely because they work diligently and are successful in their careers that they can achieve financial freedom earlier than others, and therefore realize their dream of being really free."[8] According to Du, being middle-class is fatiguing; moreover, one cannot really be free unless one has achieved economic security.

The narrative emphasizes the rational operation of the American company. As well as depicting Du's assertive business strategy, diligent work, and responsible attitude, the novel meticulously details how DB functions. Its business operations are presented as impersonal, objective, transparent, fair, and predictable; the causes and effects are clearly articulated. In this company, Du has acquired useful business principles and tips. For example, everyone in the company must follow the SOP (standard operating procedures) so that subjective judgments can be prevented. It is advisable to analyze business problems through the STAR formula, which stands for situation, task, action, and result, and through the SWOT formula, which refers to strengths, weaknesses, opportunities, and threats.[9] When setting business objectives, it is best to adhere to the SMART principle—namely, that the outcome should be specific, measurable, attainable, relevant, and time-binding. When requesting financial support and manpower from one's boss, one should be prepared to answer questions about the budget, whether it follows the company's existing policies, the advantages of engaging in this project, the disadvantages of not engaging in this project, and the expected deliverable outcomes. The employees will also be subjected to a 360-degree assessment, which means that the assessment will be done by three groups of people: one whose status is higher than, another one whose status is equal to, and a third whose status is lower than the employee in the company. The client will also do the evaluation. By reading this novel, the reader can learn more about how business operates in an American company in China.

The novel also delves into the tension between the company's standardized operations and interpersonal issues at the workplace. The narrator emphasizes the causal relationship between the input and the outcome. For instance, the American boss says to Du several times, "you deserve it!" (in English). What he means is that she deserves to be promoted and have her salary raised as a result of her excellent work performance. In English, "you deserve it" can simultaneously have two opposite meanings. The first one has a positive meaning: *Shizhi minggui* (實至名歸) means that one deserves it because one has worked hard for it. However, "you deserve it" can also have a negative connotation: *Zuiyou yingde/huogai/baoying* (罪有應得/活該/報應) means that one deserves to be punished (e.g., receive demotion or lose one's job) because one's work does not meet the minimum expectations. These formulas give the reader an impression that the operations in this American company are fair, reasonable, and objective. The rest of story is devoted to office politics because subjective judgments and personnel issues cannot be completely avoided in everyday reality. For example, to circumvent competitions, Du chooses to hire someone who is good enough but not outstanding and who has a nice personality but is not ambitious to desire career advancement. This way, the new hire will not compete with her.

Focusing on the relationship between individual action and institutional framework, the narrative makes clear that Du's hard work pays off precisely because she works in a top American company, not a Chinese one. It is in this supposedly fair system that she can flourish. However, I think the novel has not gone far enough to acknowledge the fact that Du's upward mobility is overdetermined by other structural forces. In fact, her rising middle-class position is fundamentally shaped by China's economic reforms, in addition to the influx of global, regional, and national capitals into neoliberal China since the 1980s and 1990s. Such deterritorialized movements of capitals are also supported and facilitated by the party-state, local governments, and their ideological apparatuses. If global and regional capitals withdrew from China, the number of the Chinese middle class would definitely diminish. If the Chinese government changed its policies, the size of the Chinese middle class would certainly shrink. While it is undeniable that Du has some limited individual agency and she works for her own career success, it is crucial to recognize that the Chinese middle class is not a completely autonomous and self-determining subject. Rather, it is a petty-bourgeois class fraction structurally dependent on these economic, political, and social forces. To further explain the over-determination of the Chinese middle class as an unstable class fraction, I engage with two critical concepts in critical and cultural theories—namely, Jacques Lacan's idea of the mirror stage and Louis Althusser's idea of inter-pellation. These concepts serve to decenter the "I"-ness of the Chinese middle-class subject.

The Mirror Stage

The tradition of theorizing ideology in Western Marxism is profoundly use-ful to articulate the complex mediations among cultural productions, social formations, and political economy. The critical concept of mirror stage proposed by French psychoanalyst Jacques Lacan can be deployed to relate culture to class subjectivity. In his essay "The Mirror Stage as Formative of the 'I' Function as Revealed in Psychoanalytic Experience" (1949), Lacan explains how the ego is formed in childhood development. According to him, unlike chimpanzee babies who show little interest in their own mirror reflection, human babies (between six and eighteen months old) look at themselves in front of a mirror and are fascinated with their own image. While human infants used to see themselves as fragmented parts, this is the first time that they see themselves as a distinct whole. This process of looking at oneself in front of the mirror contributes to the for-mation of the "I" as an identity. However, human infants cannot distinguish between their real selves and the mirror image of themselves. In seeing themselves in front of a mirror, human infants recognize or, more precisely, misrecognize the alienated image of themselves as their real selves. For Lacan, this moment of self-recognition and self-identification is also the moment of the misrecognition and misidentification of the self. Moreover, the fundamental gap between the subject and its image can never be bridged. Lacan writes: "The important point is that this form [of the subject in the mirror stage] fixed the instance of the ego, well before any social determination, in a line of fiction that is forever irreducible for the individual himself—or rather that will rejoin the subject's evolution in asymptomatic by which as an ego he must resolve his discordance with his own reality."[10] According to Fredric Jameson's explanation of Lacan's work, "the words '*dans une ligne de fiction*' . . . underscore the psychic function of narrative and fantasy in the attempts of the subject to reintegrate his or her alienated image."[11] The mirror stage is part of the imaginary, Lacan tells us.

In the above, I have presented Lacan's theory of the mirror stage in the form of chronology. Before this mirror stage the human infant, in its primordial, polymorphous autoerotic state, sees its body in fragmented parts ("bits and pieces"). After this phase it sees the totalizing image of itself from the outside. In her book *Reading Lacan* (1987), Jane Gallop points out the problem of origin and asserts that "the temporality of 'The Mirror Stage' is alien to the logic of chronology."[12] In actuality, the mirror stage itself is both an anticipation and a retroaction; these two processes are intertwined.[13] Gallop writes: "the self is constituted through anticipating what it will become, and then this anticipatory model is used for gauging what was before."[14] Gallop explains that "the time of the *Ecrits* is a future perfect."[15] Whereas Gallop focuses on the temporality of the mirror stage and how Lacan stages his idea, I highlight the visuality of the formation of the "I"— that is, the image construction of the subjectivity of the emerging Chinese middle class through popular and media cultures.

The nonchronological mechanism of the mirror stage helps illustrate how the Chinese popular and media cultures contribute to the constitution of the subjectivity of the "I" of Chinese middle class. To be sure, the emerging Chinese middle class is still in its infant stage and early development. The Chinese middle class does not yet have its own language, discourse, or what Lacan calls the symbolic to articulate their distinctive experience. In this sense the Chinese middle class can be analogized to the human infant. The popular workplace novel, such as *Chronicle of Du Lala's Promotion*, resembles the mirror through which the readers-as-infants can recognize themselves and learn to see themselves as a coherent subject. Before this reading experience, readers may only be able to see themselves as fragmented parts. For instance, they may see that they value higher education as an opportunity for upward mobility, or that they would like to improve their English skills. They may see that they would like to work in a transnational company, preferably an American company, or that they enjoy fashion and consumption. They may also dream of being successful in their lives. However, the novel-as-mirror enables the readers-as-infants to see themselves, for the very first time, as coherent, professional, white-collar, and middle-class subjects. (The idea of the "middle class" might be foreign to many Chinese people in the mid-2000s.) *Xiaozi* readers may learn to regard the image of the aspiring middle-class character, namely, Du, as their real identity ("this is me!"), which is a moment of self-recognition and self-identification. They may also mimic Du's professional behaviors and strategies.[16] However, according to Lacan, the moment of recognition is also the moment of misrecognition. The image of the successful, white-collar professional is ultimately an image externalized, objectified, and alienated from readers. In fact, there is no Du Lala in reality. She is a fictional construct. She is an idea. The images, imaginations, fantasy, picture thinking, and dreams associated with her belong to the imaginary as opposed to the symbolic or the Real.

In his Chinese-language essay "The Myth of Half a Face" (*Banzhanglian de shenhua* 半張臉的神話) (1998) in the edited volume *Enveloped in the New Ideology: Cultural and Literary Analysis in the Nineties* (*Zai xinyishi xingtai de longzhaoxia: 90 niandai de wenhua he wenxue fenxi* 在新意識形態的籠罩下:90年代的文化和文學分析) (2000), cultural critic Wang Xiaoming (王曉明) analyzes the ubiquitous images of successful individuals (*chenggong renshi* 成功人士) and nouveau riche (*xinfuren* 新富人) in 1990s Chinese popular and media cultures. At the turn of the new millennium, Wang points out, the successful entrepreneurs have replaced the proletarian heroes and petty-bourgeois intellectuals to become the models for Chinese people. The latter desires these entrepreneurs' career achievements, money, and lifestyles. Examining the glamorous depictions of these successful people and nouveau riche in contemporary Chinese popular cultures, Wang concludes that one can only see "the portrait of half of their face" (*banzhanglian de xiaoxiang* 半張臉的肖像), whereas the other half of their face is not visible to the viewer.[17] Even for the visible part, Wang continues, the image is often unclear and ambiguous.[18] Wang writes: "Because the portrait of half of their face is hidden, the other half of the face visible to us becomes unclear. The ambiguous image can attract those who do not belong to the 'nouveau riche' stratum and lead them to misrecognize the image that they see as their own portrait."[19] What is fascinating about Wang's essay is the language of visuality that he uses to stage his argument. Indeed, there are striking similarities between Wang's argument and Lacan's theory of the mirror stage. Both of them focus on visuality, or how the visual image helps construct the subjectivity or identity of the individual. For Lacan, infants see the mirror image of themselves; it is this mirror image that constitutes the self-identity of the infant. For Wang, it is the image that the masses observe in the popular and media cultures that hail the masses' identity as potential successful individuals and members of the nouveau riche and, for my purpose here, the middle class. In my Lacanian interpretation, popular and media cultures resemble a mirror through which the readers-as-infants can recognize themselves and learn to regard themselves, for the first time, as coherent and wholesome middle-class subjects. Before this reading or viewing experience, the readers-as-infants or viewers-as-infants can only see themselves as fragmented parts. Both Lacan and Wang emphasize recognition—or, more accurately, misrecognition—as an important mechanism of subjectivity formation. For Lacan, infants, in their imaginary stage, misrecognize their reflected images as their real selves. For Wang, the masses may imagine and fantasize the images that they see as their potential selves. Nevertheless, these images are ultimately objectified and fictionalized reflections. They are externalized and alienated from the aspiring Chinese middle-class readers and viewers.

What distinguishes Wang's analysis from Lacan's theory is that the image that Wang articulates is only half of the face, whereas Lacan focuses on the complete mirror reflection. Whereas one can assume that the mirror image that Lacan discusses is clear (at least he does not mention the vagueness of the reflected image), Wang emphasizes how the image of the successful Chinese individuals is ambiguous. In his essay, Wang examines the lack of clarity of the first half of the image and the invisibility of the second half of the image. Relating the image to political economy, Wang suggests that the wealth of the successful people and nouveau riche should be attributed to governmental and business corruptions. He underlines the dirty complicity between power and money. He writes: "I am inclined to understand the myth of the success of these individuals as ideology. Deep down, I can see clearly the direct and indirect operations of politics and business power. In many ways, they are the product of these operations."[20]

While Wang points out the fact that the successful individuals and nouveau riche are produced by the joint collaboration between the party-state and the capital at the expense of the working class, his argument can be appropriated to analyze the media representations of the Chinese middle class. Inspired by Wang's assertion, I argue that one can only see half of the image of the Chinese middle class in *Chronicle of Du Lala's Promotion*. The first half of the image is visible but ambiguous; meanwhile, the second half of the image is invisible to the reader and viewer. The first half of Du's image is visible because the narrative presents her career success as a consequence of her diligent work, personal struggle, and individual action, in addition to the institution in which she works. The second half of Du's image is invisible because the narrative does not account for the way in which Du's subjective agency is, in fact, largely shaped by, dependent on, and overdetermined by structural forces such as political economy. The second half of her image is indiscernible also because the narrative has repressed social class and history as the conditions of possibility of the formation of the Chinese middle class. In his essay, Wang highlights how the discourse of successful individuals and nouveau riche prevents one from analyzing the working class and the workers laid off by state-owned enterprises during China's neoliberal experiments. In fact, a similar argument about the Chinese middle class can be made. In the late 1970s and early 1980s liberal-minded Chinese intellectuals desired science and technology, democracy and freedom, literature and arts as well as economic prosperity and material abundance. These wishes constituted the ideologies of China's economic reforms. However, in the 2000s these longings have been silenced, foreclosed, and rendered invisible in the discourse of the Chinese middle class. What remains is the desire for job promotion and consumption.

Interpellation

Louis Althusser's theorization of ideology is also useful to explain how the middle-class culture conjures the middle-class subjectivity. In his essay "Marxism and Humanism" (1965) in his book *For Marx*, Althusser discusses ideology as "a system (with its own logic and rigor) of representations (images, myths, ideas, or concepts, depending on the case) endowed with a historical existence and role within a given society."[21] He contrasts ideology with science: the former has a practico-social function whereas the latter has a theoretical and knowledge function.[22] Because ideology is a system governed by rules, Althusser thinks that we are all within ideology and nobody is outside of it. We inhabit the system of representations. We also obey the rules governing the system without realizing that what we believe to be our choice is, in fact, an obedience to these rules. The latter is unconscious and feels obvious and commonsensical to us. Althusser explains the unconscious nature of ideology in this way:

> Ideology is indeed a system of representations, but in the majority of cases these representations have nothing to do with "consciousness": they are usually images and occasionally concepts, but it is above all as structures that they impose on the vast majority of men, not via their "consciousness." They are perceived-accepted-suffered cultural objects and they act functionally on men via a process that escapes them. Men "live" their ideologies . . . "not at all as a form of consciousness, but as an object of their world"—as their "world" itself.[23]

In Althusser's essay "Ideology and Ideological State Apparatus (Notes Towards an Investigation)" (1969) in his book *Lenin and Philosophy, and Other Essays*, he expands and reformulates his understanding of ideology and further emphasizes its material dimension. Going beyond the traditional conception of ideology as consciousness, he focuses on the institutionalization of ideology. He makes the distinction between, on the one hand, the repressive state apparatus (e.g., the police, the army, the prison) that works through force and violence, and on the other hand, the ideological state apparatus (e.g., religion, education, media) that works through persuasion and consent. In this essay Althusser makes three points. First, "ideology has no history" and, similar to the unconscious, it is transhistorical.[24] Second, "ideology is a 'representation' of the imaginary relationship of individuals to their Real conditions of existence."[25] Related to this point, "ideology has a material existence."[26] Third, "ideology interpellates individuals as subjects."[27]

Central to Althusser's theorization is the concept of interpellation. According to him, interpellation refers to the process whereby an individual is called upon and recruited to become a subject. The example that he provides is the call of the policeman. When the policeman says "Hey, you!" and when one turns around to respond to his call, this is a moment of successful interpellation.[28] This example concerns the visual (the scene) and the audio ("Hey, you!"): interpellation is a specular or mirroring process whereby ideology hails the individual as a subject, who recognizes himself (or herself) in the image of the dominant ideological Subject. This in turn enables the mutual recognition of the subject and the Subject and finally the subject's self-recognition. According to Althusser, ideological interpellation persuades individuals to occupy a subject position that has already been prepared for them. Individuals are encouraged to see themselves from that particular position, and in this process they forget their original positions. In this sense, ideological interpellation transforms the individual into the subject. In addition, the subject is subjected to the Subject. Subjected beings are the ones who freely accept their submission and submit themselves to the higher authority (e.g., the police). For example, commercial advertisements can be regarded as ideological interpellation. The commercial advertisements recruit individuals. They invite them to identity with the image of the consumer subject (or with the image of other consumer subjects who purchase the same commodity). They transform the individuals so they regard themselves as the subjects of consumption (rather than the subjects of production and labor). Such a recognition is also a misrecognition. The consumer subjects may believe that they are self-determining and are free to choose the commodities that they desire in the market. However, they may not be cognizant of the fact that they have already been produced by the discourse of consumption. What the consumers choose has already been chosen for them in advance. Their "free" choices turn out not to be completely free. Althusser's concept of interpellation can be deployed to discuss how the state and capitals call into being the subjectivity of the emerging Chinese middle class.

Similar to Gallop, who is careful about the temporality of the mirror stage, Althusser is cautious with the temporality of interpellation. Althusser clarifies that so far, he has presented his narrative "in the form of a sequence, with a before and an after, and thus in the form of temporal succession."[29] However, according to Althusser, "in reality these things happen without any succession" because "ideology has always already interpellated individuals as subjects."[30] The individuals have always already been interpellated by ideology as subjects not only because the subject position preexists them in the institutions, apparatuses, and practices that make them subjects but also because they must have already been subjects to undertake the act of recognizing the fact that they are recognized. In his book *Althusser and His Contemporaries* (2013), Warren Montag points out that "interpellation begins . . . with the subject's recognizing himself in order then to be recognized by the other, constituting himself within himself as subject in order to be able then to recognize the recognition that the other extends to him."[31] Montag's acute observation enables one to see the subject's recognition of self-recognition.

While Althusser focuses on successful and complete interpellation, it appears that his theory does not provide sufficient analytical tools to entertain the possibility of incomplete interpellation. In his article "Beyond Interpellation" (1993), Mladen Dolar gestures to psychoanalytical remainder and discusses how the subject cannot be fully interpellated. Dolar writes: "In short, the subject is precisely the failure to become the subject— the psychoanalytical subject is the failure to become an Althusserian one."[32] Echoing Dolar's explanation, I add that Althusser's theory is not sufficiently equipped to deal with the possibilities of failed interpellation (i.e., the interpellation does not happen: the policeman calls "Hey, you!" but nobody turns back) and misinterpellation (i.e., ideology has interpellated the wrong individuals into subjects: the policeman calls "Hey, you!" but the wrong person turns back).

Despite its potential problems, Althusser's idea of interpellation can still be made useful to theorize how Chinese popular and media cultures try to conjure and call into being the Chinese middle-class subject. According to Althusser, interpellation refers to the process whereby individuals are called upon and recruited to become a subject. When the policeman says "Hey, you [i.e., Du Lala]!" and then when one turns around to respond to his call, this is a moment of successful interpellation. Interpellation is a specular process whereby ideology hails individuals as subjects, who recognize themselves in the image of the dominant ideological Subject (e.g., Du Lala). This in turn enables the mutual recognition of the subject and the Subject and finally the subject's self-recognition. The reader of the novel may recognize himself (or herself) as an aspiring Chinese middle-class subject. According to Montag, "interpellation begins . . . with the subject's recognizing himself in order then to be recognized by the other, constituting himself within himself as subject in order to be able then to recognize the recognition that the other extends to him."[33] In other words, the successfully hailed reader must already have had some ideas of the Chinese middle class before reading the workplace novel *Chronicle of Du Lala's Promotion*. This is a necessary condition for the successful interpellation to take place. Then, upon hearing the voice "Hey, you!," readers recognize themselves and submit to the summon. "This is me! I am [like] Du Lala!," or "Here I am! I also aspire to become the Chinese middle class!" These individuals may also share their thoughts and feelings in websites, blogs, and social media. The confessional stories in the media evidence cases of successful interpellation.

Althusser's theory also includes the figure of policeman. But who is the policeman in the Du Lala discourse? I have suggested that although the Chinese middle-class subject such as Du Lala has some limited individual agency, its mobility is fundamentally shaped and overdetermined by the party-state, the national and the transnational capitals, and their ideological apparatuses. The party-state and the capital are the Althusserian policeman.

Let's take a closer look at the summon of the party-state-as-policeman. In modern Chinese literary and cultural studies, scholars have discussed *Chronicle of Du Lala's Promotion* and related the Du Lala phenomenon to the formation of the Chinese middle class in the context of globalizing China.[34] For example, in his article "*Chronicle of Du Lala's Promotion*: Exemplary Literature, the Middle Class, and the Socialist Market" (2016), cultural critic Marco Fumian argues that the novel is not simply a commercial product that portrays the upward mobility of Du as a female white-collar professional but also "serves the function of educating its [Chinese] readers in the dominant ideological values and goals promoted by the Communist Party in this [neoliberal] period, which are precisely those necessary to the construction of the 'socialist market economy.'"[35]

Thus, according to Fumian, Du can be regarded as an exemplary figure worthy of emulation. In fact, Fumian's observation confirms my argument concerning the politics of the Du Lala narrative construction. Both Fumian and I are interested in the larger structural forces that contribute to the successful story of the Chinese white-collar workers. While Fumian attends to the role of the state in educating and, I add, in interpellating the reader, I am interested in the role of transnational and national capitals and their reliance on the ideological apparatuses to spread their ideologies and concretize their hegemonies. In addition, Fumian delves into what Althusser calls the ideological state apparatus, a term that Fumian himself does not use in his article. To be sure, the novel can be considered an ideological state apparatus that aims to transmit and concretize the ideology of the state to the reader; it is a major melody (*zhuxuanlü* 主旋律) literary work in the late 2000s and early 2010s.

Moreover, Fumian shows that *Chronicle of Du Lala's Promotion* is not an isolated literary phenomenon. In fact, it is part and parcel of the larger political, intellectual, and cultural discourse surrounding the emergence of the Chinese middle class. To illustrate this point, Fumian cites the CCP's strategic plan to "enlarge the size of the middle-income group" in 2002.[36] He also quotes the work of Lu Xueyi (陸學藝), who published an important book concerning the social stratification of the Chinese society in 2002.[37] He also references Zhou Xiaohong (周曉虹), who published an influential report of the Chinese middle class in 2005.[38] According to Fumian, the dissemination of the ideologies of the middle class can also be observed in contemporary Chinese popular and media cultures. Similar to *Chronicle of Du Lala's Promotion*, other workplace novels (職場小說), officialdom novels (官場小說), motivational novels (勵志小說), the literature of success studies (成功學), and self-help books propagate the neoliberal values of individual enterprise, commodity ownership, self-care, and personal responsibility (rather than relying on the welfare state for support). In short, the Du Lala novel coincides with the Chinese state's policies in engineering the Chinese middle class in the first decades of the twenty-first century.[39] Concerning the role of the transnational and national capitals-as-policeman, the Chinese readers can also be consumers of brand-name commodities. The commodities are prominently displayed in the filmic adaptation of the novel.

ROMANTIC LOVE AND FASHION CONSUMPTION

The novel *Chronicle of Du Lala's Promotion* was so successful that it was adapted into a film. The latter, *Go! Lala Go!* (2010), was directed by Xu Jinglei. Xu herself also plays the character Du Lala in the film. Similar to the novel, the film tells the story of Du's upward mobility and career success. However, unlike the novel, this film emphasizes the love triangle among Du, her colleague Wang Wei (王偉), whose English name is David, and another colleague called Rose. Originally, David and Rose were boyfriend and girlfriend. After they broke up, Wang became involved with Du. However, Du did not know of Wang's previous relationship with Rose until much later; meanwhile, Rose intends to repair her relationship with Wang but does not know that Wang is already dating someone else. In *Go! Lala Go!*, all the office ladies working in this American company, including Du, Rose, Helen, Eva, and Maggie, appear in very fashionable outfits. To the viewer, this film appears as a fashion show, and the office resembles a catwalk.

This film focuses on Du's career advancement and romantic relationship.[40] When the twenty-seven-year-old Du arrives at this top American company, she works as a secretary and makes 3,000 yuan per month. Her senior colleague, Rose, needs to have surgery, so the responsibility of overseeing the company's renovation is delegated to Du. In this process Du becomes acquainted with Wang, the director of regional sales department, and they develop romantic feelings for each other. Thanks to her excellent job with the company's renovation, Du is promoted to the rank of executive secretary and makes 3,500 yuan per month. Later, during the company's retreat in Pattaya, Thailand (this retreat is absent from the novel), Du and Wang have a passionate one-night encounter. In the film, Beijing and Pattaya are presented as polar opposites: while Beijing is characterized by the business district (e.g., Yintai Center [銀泰中心]), tall office buildings, glitzy surfaces, crowded spaces, and busy and overtime work, Pattaya is depicted as a tourist paradise where one can relax, enjoy the beach, party, play, and have a good time.[41] If the company makes it clear that romantic relationships between colleagues are strictly prohibited, then one can momentarily break the rule and have causal sex in Pattaya. This is exactly what happens to Du and Wang.

After coming back to Beijing, Du continues to work diligently and is further promoted at work. At the age of twenty-nine, she makes 6,000 yuan per month. She becomes the secretary of the director of regional sales, which means she works as Wang's secretary. In addition, she becomes Wang's girlfriend, but they cannot make their relationship public. Later, Du becomes more successful at work and is further promoted. As a supervisor of human resources, she makes 12,000 yuan per month. In her new position, Du's first assignment is to fire her colleague and good friend Helen because it has been discovered that Helen has been having an amorous relationship with her senior colleague Li Wenhua. Meanwhile, Wang's mother in the United States—who believes Wang and Rose are still together—is sick; Wang does not want to disappoint his mother, causing her to get sicker, so he brings Rose to visit her. Their traveling together is later discovered by Du, who is so upset that she goes out shopping—even buying an expensive Mazda car![42] Later, at the company's party, Du is so jealous of Wang's previous relationship with Rose that she decides to break up with him. Later, for various reasons, Rose and Wang resign from DB while Du stays in this company. Two years later, Du is further promoted and becomes the manager of human resources. At the age of thirty-three, she makes 25,000 yuan per month and becomes a member of the Chinese middle class. However, she is not genuinely happy because she misses Wang. In the end, with a happy coincidence, Du and Wang each happen to travel to Pattaya again, and they run into each other. The ending of this romantic comedy is typical: they are finally together.

When one focuses on the film's content, the main character is Du. This story concerns her white-collar work and especially her romantic relationship with Wang. However, when one focuses on the film's form, the main characters turn out to be the actresses and film stars and, more importantly, fashion. The latter is semiautonomous from the white-collar work and the romantic relationship. Du's role is played by Xu, who has been hailed as one of the four major actresses in mainland China in the 2000s. She has also directed noncommercial films before directing *Go! Lala Go!* Meanwhile, Rose's role is performed by Hong Kong actress and singer Karen Mok (Mo Wenwei 莫文蔚), and David Wang's role is played by Taiwanese American actor and singer Stanley Huang (Huang Lixing 黃立行). Because Mok and Huang are diasporic and Westernized Chinese, their presence enhances the international sensibility of this Chinese film. When the viewer watches *Go!*

Lala Go!, many of them can recognize Xu, Mok, and Huang. This can be confirmed in such film review websites as Douban (豆瓣). For instance, when discussing *Go! Lala Go!*, some of the reviewers refer to the character Xu (the actress) rather than Du (the character). Some of them call her Old Xu (Lao Xu 老徐) as if they already knew her in person or were close to her. They relate Xu's directing of *Go! Lala Go!* to her earlier films. They also compare her acting in this film with her performances in the other works, such as the Chinese TV drama *Cherish Our Love Forever* (*Jiang aiqing jinxing daodi* 將愛情進行到底) (1998) and its adaptation into film, *Eternal Moment* (*Jiang aiqing jinxing daodi* 將愛情進行到底) (2010). When the viewer watches *Go! Lala Go!*, they not only see the characters but also see the actresses and film stars in their fashionable outfits.

Notably, the viewer can appreciate the fashions onscreen. Whereas the novel downplays Du's attire and only makes passing remarks on her Nike casual wear and LV handbag, the film prominently emphasizes the fashionable outfits that Du wears to work at the American company in China.[43] Indeed, the upgrading of Du's wardrobe parallels her salary increase and career success. In the beginning of the film, Du wears ordinary clothes. However, as Du becomes more successful and professional, she appears more fashionable to the viewer. Eventually, similar to Rose, Helen, Eva, and the other office ladies in the company, Du appears in highly fashionable outfits and wears expensive watches and jewelry.[44] To the film viewer, these characters resemble fashion models, and the office has been turned into a catwalk. In fact, the production team for *Go! Lala Go!* hired Patricia Field, who had designed costumes for such films as *The Devil Wears Prada* (2006), *Sex and the City* (2008), and *Sex and the City 2* (2010), to be the fashion consultant of *Go! Lala Go!* The fashionable outfits selected by this Oscar-nominated costume designer enhances the American and cosmopolitan sensibilities of this Chinese fashion film. The result is that the female characters appear in dazzling dresses every two or three minutes onscreen.

Given that the film's content focuses on the characters and that the film's form emphasizes the actresses and film stars in their fashionable outfits, how should we describe their relationships? In her short essay "A Chronicle of Changing Clothes" (*Gengyiji* 更衣記) (1943), famous Chinese writer Eileen Chang (Zhang Ailing 張愛玲) describes the connection among clothes, gender, and embodied subjectivity in this way: "The sloping of shoulders, narrow waist, and flat chest of the ideal beauty, who was to be both petite and slender, would disappear under the weight of these layers on layers of clothing. She herself would cease to exist, save as a frame on which clothing could be hung."[45]

Chang's description can be used to visualize the roles of the female characters in Go! Lala Go! While Du, Rose, Helen, and Eva appear in numerous fashionable outfits throughout the film, the primary function of these characters is to show off the beautiful clothes. In this sense, these characters resemble clothes hangers or even mannequins. On the surface, the characters/actresses/film stars appear to wear fashions. However, they are worn by the fashions. If the fashions wear the female characters, then the fashions are the subject whereas the female characters are the object.

This reversal between gendered individual and fashion is complicated by another reversal. While one may assume that the spectators of the film are appreciating the fashionable outfits as commodities, in fact, they have always already been looked at by these commodities. For Lacan's mirror stage, six-month-old infants who look in the mirror have the illusion that they are looking at their own reflected image. In reality, they are looked at or, more precisely, they have always already been looked at by their own reflected image in the mirror. Similarly, when watching the film Go! Lala Go!, the spectators appreciate the fashionable outfits and brand-name commodities. But actually, they have always already been looked at by the commodities. They have always already been looked at by the brand-name logos such as Gucci, Dior, Chloe, and Chanel, and by product placements such as Lenovo and, quite interestingly, Lipton Tea. Product placement is part of the story.[46] Since the planning of this film, the viewer has already been targeted by the commercial advertisements as potential consumers.

Examining Go! Lala Go! more closely, I conclude that this film does not provide an accurate representation of white-collar life in China. To begin with, it is curious that Du can advance her career so unrealistically easily. The film narrative shows that she does not have to work very much or very hard. She does not feel stressed, overwhelmed, or frustrated at work. How does she learn to navigate her career so easily? How does she handle difficulties and challenges at her workplace? What kinds of mistakes has she made, and how does she make improvements? The viewer is not told. In addition, the emphases of the film—namely, successful career, romantic love, and fashion consumption—are not easily achievable at the same time. Logically speaking, the more time Du devotes to her career, the less time she has for finding a partner and for nurturing her love relationship. Conversely, the more time she invests in romance, the less time she has for developing her career. This is also true for family relationships and friendships, which are also laborious. And this is also true for fashion and consumption. Indeed, it takes time and effort to become knowledgeable about different kinds of fashion styles and trends. It is also costly to buy fashionable clothes and makeup. One may wonder how Du can have sufficient money to have such stylish outlooks. One may also wonder where she has space to store all her fashionable outfits in her small apartment in Beijing. Indeed, how is it possible for her to climb up the career ladder so easily, be highly successful at work, have a boyfriend, have a supportive family, and be surrounded by good friends at the same time? Most importantly, how is it possible for her to be completely effortless in achieving all these? Personally, I am curious how she can sit in front of her office desk, eat a lot of chocolate, but have a slim body.

In terms of reception, *Go! Lala Go!* has been criticized for not offering a convincing representation of Chinese middle-class life. In fact, the viewer does not even know what kind of company DB is. What kind of service does DB provide and specialize? What kinds of clients does it serve? Who are its competitors? What makes DB distinctive from its rivals? The viewer is not told. In addition, it is strange that Du and her colleagues do not have to work that much in DB. Instead, they spend most of their time falling in love and presenting themselves in fashionable outfits to one another. To me, what is interesting is that while claiming to be very busy working, Du can appear in several attires and hairstyles within the same day. While she rushes from one meeting to another, she can appear in one fashionable outfit in an office, in a second dress in another office, and then in a third outfit in a different room. Did she bring many outfits to work and get changed between each meeting? Why does she do this? It is also difficult to believe that her limited salary (even after her several raises) can enable her to buy brand-name fashions and an expensive Mazda car, live in a luxurious apartment, and lead a lavish lifestyle. However, despite such unrealistic depictions, I am inclined to see this as a Chinese desire and fantasy. The *xiaozi* (petty bourgeoisie) and aspiring middle class is trying to imagine what it is like to work in a top American company in China.

SHE IS WEARING HER BODY ON HER CLOTHES

In Canadian Broadcasting Corporation TV documentary *China's Sexual Revolution* (2007), the director presents the radical transformations of gender roles and sexual attitudes in China. In one scene a group of female Red Guards, dressed in military uniforms, boldly marches in Beijing's Tiananmen Square. Shouting revolutionary slogans, these Red Guards desire to make a revolution. In another scene a group of female models show off their fashionable outfits on a catwalk. This juxtaposition reveals the changing relationship between the subject and the object from the socialist to the postsocialist periods.

In the first scene the Red Guards, a symbol of proletarian subjectivity actively engaged in socialist production and construction, wear the military uniform. This can be confirmed by Mao Zedong's poem "To the Female Soldiers" (為女民兵題照) (1961).

颯爽英姿五尺槍，　Five-foot rifles, flashing bravely,
曙光初照演兵場。　On the training ground, at the break of the day,
中華兒女多奇志，　How remarkable the spirit of Chinese women,
不愛紅裝愛武裝。　They love the martial dress, not the red dress.[47]

According to this poem, Chinese women reject the red dress and embrace the military clothing (不愛紅裝愛武裝). Here, the red dress refers to bourgeois and feminine clothing. In her essay "Fashions and Feminine Consumption," feminist critic Harriet Evans points out the equalizing politics of the military uniform:

The lines of differentiation in the Mao images were determined by the ideological and political tendencies of the time, and not by the social hierarchies of consumption. In the class terms of the time, they included the rural, the elderly, the uneducated, and the poor, leaving many potential spaces for a gendered and even sexual appeal across the boundaries of difference that operate in today's consumer culture. The accouterments of fashion now displayed to appeal to women's consumer passions exclude everyday gendered identities that are not commercially valued by consumer culture. The rural, the older, the poor, and the disadvantaged are virtually absent from the images that dominate the front covers of women's magazines.[48]

I agree with Evans that the Red Guards and their military uniforms are more democratic and inclusive. On the contrary, what typifies Chinese bourgeois and middle-class women's outfits in the 2000s onward is feminine clothing. Appropriating Mao's poem, one can say that Chinese bourgeois and middle-class women reject the military uniform and embrace the red dress (不愛武裝愛紅裝). This is exactly what is promoted in *Go! Lala Go!* The fashions donned by Du, Rose, Helen, Eva, and Maggie mark hierarchies and differences: they distinguish the wearers from other social groups.

In fact, how the female Red Guards wear the military uniforms during the socialist and revolutionary period is not the same as the way the Chinese women wear the red dress (or fashionable outfit) in the TV documentary *China's Sexual Revolution* and the film *Go! Lala Go!* While the female Red Guards in their military uniforms actively engage in class struggles, productions, and revolutions, the female Red Guards are the subject whereas their military uniforms are the object. However, this subject–object relation is reversed later on. Following Chang, who claims that some women in their outfits resemble clothes hangers, I suggest that the red dress (or fashionable outfit) is the subject whereas the female consumers are the object. It is the clothes that wear the female characters, actresses, film stars, and fashion models. These female consumers are worn by their outfits.

To further explain the changing relationship among the military uniform, the red dress (or fashionable outfit), and gendered subjectivity from the socialist to the post-socialist periods, I borrow from Susan Willis's work. In her book *A Primer for Daily Life* (1991), appropriating Fredric Jameson's idea concerning the dialectic of ideology and utopian impulse in contemporary mass culture, Willis examines U.S. suburban cultures. In the chapter "Work(ing) Out," she compares the woman who uses the machine to work with the woman who uses the machine to work out/exercise. Focusing on work, she argues that the woman who uses the machine to work is the subject whereas the work machine is the object. Turning to workout, she explains that the workout machine is the subject whereas the woman who uses the machine to work out is the object. Willis reasons in this way:

> [The Nautilus workout machine] gives women access to the machine but denies access to production. It requires energy and effort and negates the

experience of labor. It isolates the individual from other women who work out and defines her body as an assemblage of body areas and muscle functions, each requiring a specialized machine and machine function. The nautilus machine and the woman who works out on it is the distorted 1980s equivalent of Rosie the Riveter astride the body of a battleship. As an icon in the popular imagination, the nautilus metamorphoses women's relationship to self and to labor. Nothing is produced but the body itself.[49]

According to Willis, the workout machine is the subject whereas the woman who uses the workout machine to exercise is the object. However, this is only one part of the dialectic. Willis tells the reader the other part: "The woman inside the nautilus machine is the object produced by the machine even while she is at the same time the producer producing herself as the product of the machine."[50] I have already explained the first clause, that "the woman inside the nautilus machine is the object produced by the machine." What interests me is the second clause: "she is at the same time the producer producing herself as the product of the machine." On the surface, the woman who uses the workout machine is the producer or the subject. But ultimately the workout machine is the subject, and she is the object. The woman who exercises is the product of the workout machine. In other words, she is simultaneously the subject and the object, but ultimately the object. This explains why Willis argues that she is "the producer [the subject] producing herself [the object] as the product [the object] of the machine."

Willis provides an intriguing analysis of the difference between the work machine (production) and the workout machine (consumption) in relation to women's subjectivity in the context of U.S. suburban culture. I am interested in connecting her observation to the representations of gender, class, and fashion in *Go! Lala Go!* Inspired by Willis's book, I suggest that the female character such as Du wearing the fashion is the object produced by the fashion even while she is at the same time the producer producing herself as the product of the fashion. The first clause is that "the woman character wearing the fashion is the object produced by the fashion." The fashion is the subject (that is, the main character, if one focuses on the film's form). Meanwhile, the female character who wears the fashion is the object. She is the clothes hanger. However, what interests me is the second clause: "she is at the same time the producer producing herself as the product of the fashion." On the surface, the female character who wears the fashion is the producer and the subject. But in fact, the fashion is the subject whereas she is the object. The female character who wears the fashion is the product of the fashion. The woman who wears the fashion is simultaneously the subject and the object, but ultimately the object. She is "the producer [the subject] producing herself [the object] as the product [the object] of the fashion."

Willis further explains the workings of the dialectic of ideology and uto-pian impulse. She details how the utopian impulse is momentarily expressed but immediately contained.

> In the 19th century, Marx wrote against the worker's alienation. He demon-strated that in selling labor power, the worker was separated both from con-trol over production and from the fruits of labor, the commodities and profits from their sale. The contradiction of the commodity is that it can be absolutely divorced from the worker while at the same time it is the container of the worker's alienated labor.... In such a [capitalistic] system, the uto-pian impulse often finds expression in the very forms that simultaneously articulate its containment. The image of a woman producing herself on the nautilus machine and Cindy Sherman dramatically posing into her self-activated camera are both expressions of women's deep desire to deny alienation. Both articulate the desire to seize control over the production and the commodity. Both demonstrate the utopian desire to be in control, to acti-vate the machine. And they express the highly reified desire to be absorbed into the machine's function. Both express the utopian longing to no longer see one's alienated labor in the commodity, but do so by the dystopian for-mula of making the self into the commodity.[51]

Willis appropriates Marx's insight of the contradiction of the commodity. She points out that "the utopian impulse often finds expression in the very forms that simultaneously articulates its containment." Focusing on Amer-ican popular culture, she argues that the form can be detected in how the women use the workout machine to exercise. This form conjures the image of how women use the work machine to produce and to labor. Appropriat-ing Willis's idea to the scenario of contemporary China's consumer culture, I propose that this form can be detected in how the female characters in the fashion films wear their outfits as commodities. In *Go! Lala Go!*, the female characters' desire for fashion and consumption can be interpreted as the Chinese women's utopian desire to deny different kinds of alienations (e.g., boredom, exhaustion, overtime work, competition), to seize control over production and the commodity, and to control their everyday lives. It also demonstrates their unconscious desire to activate their collective experience of being a subject of (Chinese) history. However, by doing so, they make themselves the very object from which they try to seize control in the first place. This utopian impulse is arrested.[52]

Chapter Five

BETWEEN PRODUCTION AND CONSUMPTION

Chinese Migrant Factory Workers in Documentary Films and Ethnographic Works

In 2010 Taiwanese documentary maker Ho Chao-ti (He Zhaoti 賀照緹) released her documentary film *My Fancy High Heels* (*Wo'ai gaogenxie* 我愛高跟鞋), which focuses on the commodity chain of expensive high heels within the context of the United States and China transnational exchange.[1] In addition to examining the design and consumption of the high-end high heels in the United States, she focuses on their production in the factories in Guangdong, China. She also emphasizes the extraction of raw materials and natural resources at the border of China and Russia. Unforgettably, the director presents the killing of calves whose skins are used to manufacture the high heels.[2] *My Fancy High Heels* features several characters: fashion designer Sena Yang (Korean American), factory owner Ben (Taiwanese), manager Mr. Tian (Chinese), production line supervisor Chunming (Chinese), migrant factory worker Little Boo (Xiao budian 小不點) (Chinese), and anonymous workers in the slaughterhouses. To my mind, the most memorable character is Little Boo from Hunan, China. She has been working in this shoe factory for some time and makes 1,300 yuan (around 196 U.S. dollars) each month. In her spare time she hangs out with her friends who also work in the factory. One day they go shopping together. They want to buy two pairs of the same style of shoes in a local shop. The boisterous Little Boo assertively bargains with the shopkeeper and manages to convince her to give them a discount. Each of the girls ends up paying 28 yuan (around 4 U.S. dollars) for her new purple shoes.

In one scene Little Boo has an intimate conversation with her close friends in their dorm room. She expresses that she really likes the high heels she helps to make in the factory; however, she cannot afford to buy them. Then she asks her friends whether they have had the experience of wearing those fancy high heels, such as "putting them on the floor and trying them on" and "circling a few times before putting them back to their original place." While these girls are getting excited about the possibility of wearing these fancy and expensive high heels, Little Boo makes a secret confession: "One time I secretly put a pair on my feet. I walked all over the place. . . . And then the supervisor Mr. Jin came in and saw me with such beautiful shoes on my feet! He asked me: 'What are you doing?' And I took the shoes off immediately. I wish I could own these shoes and wear them back home. I can only look at them, but I can't own them."

Because she enjoys the company of her close friends, Little Boo naively suggests that they can continue to work in the factory for forty more years. Moreover, she communicates how much she misses her mother, who is in Hunan. As Little Boo desires to reunite with her family, the director temporarily fulfills her dream by creating an animation sequence that presents the reunion of Little Boo and her mother and shows how they happily live in a house together.

In this chapter, focusing on production and labor (rather than on consumption), I examine Chinese migrant factory workers as an underside of Chinese consumer culture in the context of global capitalism. I choose the term migrant factory workers because these individuals are not the factory workers in the Maoist sense but the factory workers who labor under the neoliberal and postsocialist conditions of the joint venture between capital and the state. In addition, many migrant workers work in manufacturing. In her book *Subaltern China: Rural Migrants, Media, and Cultural Practices* (2014), Chinese media and communication studies scholar Wanning Sun presents the major employment areas of Chinese migrant peasant-workers (*nongmingong* 農民工).[3] According to a 2012 survey, they worked in manufacturing (35.7 percent); construction (18.4 percent); domestic and other services (12.2 percent); retail and small businesses (9.8 percent); transport, storage, and postal delivery (6.6 percent); and restaurants and hospitality (5.2 percent).[4] Sun also presents the differences between the factory workers and the construction workers.[5] According to her observation, the factory workers tend to be younger and more educated, whereas the construction workers are mostly male and are "more diverse than other employment groups in terms of life experience and are generally older and less well educated." The factory workers "come to the city not only to boost their incomes but also to experience a different way of life—often with the hope of staying in the city."[6] In contrast, says Sun:

> construction workers generally aim to make as much money as possible to pay off family debts, provide for their children's education or weddings, or build a new house. Contrary to the younger migrant women and men in factories, the construction workers tend to have a greater attachment to the land back home, and some even go back to the village during busy farming periods—especially harvesting—and then return to the city during the offseason.[7]

Also, the "factory workers are paid monthly wages, as agreed in their contracts." "Most construction companies, which do not sign contracts with the workers, do not pay wages on a regular basis. Instead, they make the payment at the end of the year, or when the worker leaves the job. . . . As a result, wage arrears and labor disputes are pandemic within the construction sector in urban China."[8] Sun also points out that,

> in comparison with construction workers, factory workers are subject to a much higher level of discipline within the industrial regime. Industrialization entails putting in place a range of spatial and institutional practices in order to turn "a young and rural body into an industrialized and productive laborer," thereby transforming "lazy and unproductive" laborers' "bodies and minds, behaviors and beliefs, gestures and habits, and attitudes and aptitudes." . . . Factory workers are also the most rights-conscious group, as evidenced by the sporadic, though not uncommon, strikes and other forms of collective action at China's factories.[9]

Sun's distinction reveals the heterogeneity of the migrant workers in China. It uncovers the material conditions of the Chinese migrant factory workers.

In this chapter I examine the visual depictions of the production of fashion commodities in Chinese factories and the labor disciplines that accompany these processes.[10] In particular, I explore the representations of Chinese migrant factory workers who produce the fashion commodities in documentary films and ethnographic reports. These works include David Redmon's *Mardi Gras: Made in China* (2005) (Mardi Gras beads), Lixin Fan's (范立欣) *Last Train Home* (*Guitu lieche* 歸途列車) (2009) (garments and jeans), Ho Chao-ti's *My Fancy High Heels* (2010) (high-end high heels), and Qin Xiaoyu (秦曉宇) and Wu Feiyue's (吳飛躍) *Iron Moon* (*Wode shipian* 我的詩篇) (2015) (down coats and sundresses). Focusing on production, these directors emphasize that the fashion commodities are made by the Chinese migrant factory workers. This is one side of the narrative. The other side of the story, which is not explicitly staged yet is inadvertently presented, is that the workers desire fashion and consumption, a recurring motif in these documentary films. Sometimes, the desired commodities are the very commodities that the migrant factory workers themselves produce. Indeed, what does it mean for the Chinese migrant factory workers, such as Little Boo in *My Fancy High Heels*, to dream about the high-end high heels that she helps to make? How can Marxist and feminist cultural critics respond to their consumerist desires? Should these yearnings be interpreted as ideological false consciousness because they are ultimately constructed and perpetuated by the global capitalistic machine and network that systematically exploits them? Or should they be understood as silent labor protests in that these migrant factory workers attempt to imagine an alternative world uncorrupted by class, gender, and ethnic oppressions? This chapter engages with documentary films, ethnographic reports, and cultural theories to discern the subjectivity of the Chinese migrant factory workers as consumers and as producers. Focusing on consumption, I argue that the Chinese migrant factory workers' desires for the fashion commodities reveal different types of tensions: production versus consumption, temporality versus spatiality, and utopian impulse versus cruel optimism. Turning to production, I suggest that their gendered and ethnicized labor is underwritten by the logics and practices of what

Michel Foucault and Gilles Deleuze, respectively, call disciplinary society and society of control.

The first part of this chapter is called "Migrant Factory Workers as Consumers." I present Qin Xiaoyu and Wu Feiyue's documentary film *Iron Moon*, which explores the lived experience of, and the poetry written by, selected Chinese migrant workers in early twenty-first-century China. The directors feature the female migrant factory worker's desire for fashion and consumption. Similar to how Little Boo fantasizes about the expensive high heels in *My Fancy High Heels*, in *Iron Moon*, Wu Xia (鄔霞) is very interested in wearing sundresses (*diaodaiqun* 吊帶裙) and showing off her feminine figure. What kinds of tensions or contradictions are embodied in the female migrant factory workers' consumerist desires for fashion and commodities? To answer this question, I draw on recent scholarship concerning the Chinese migrant workers in the contexts of global capitalism and neoliberalism, such as Pun Ngai's (*Pan Yi* 潘毅) two books, *Made in China* (2005) and *Migrant Labor in China* (2016); Yan Hairong's (嚴海蓉) book *New Masters, New Servants* (2008); and Wanning Sun's two books, *Maid in China* (2008) and *Subaltern China* (2014).[11] These sociologists, anthropologists, and media and communications studies scholars examine the tensions between production and consumption, and between temporality and spatiality. I participate in their discussions by delving into the psychic interiority of the Chinese migrant factory workers. I engage with Gilles Deleuze's idea of desire as assemblage to contemplate the tension between utopian impulse and what Lauren Berlant calls cruel optimism. On the one hand, these consumerist desires do not fundamentally disturb or challenge the unequal relations of production. However, such fantasies can potentially express the migrant factory workers' political unconsciousness and provide raw materials for building an alternative world uncorrupted by exploitations, oppressions, and injustices. In other words, consumption can also be productive, hence productive consumption. On the other hand, these aspirational attachments can also be an obstacle to the flourishing of the Chinese migrant factory workers, hence cruel optimism.

The second part of this chapter turns to "Migrant Factory Workers as Producers." I analyze David Redmon's documentary film *Mardi Gras: Made in China* (2005), which focuses on the production of Mardi Gras beads in Fujian, China, and their consumption in the Mardi Gras carnivals in New Orleans, Louisiana, the United States.[12] Similar to Marx's critique of commodity fetishism, I demonstrate how consumption is fundamentally linked to production; however, I add gender, sex, ethnicity, culture, and the gaze to the discussions. Moreover, I show how critical and cultural theorists Michael Hardt and Slavoj Žižek propose new ways to connect the producer and the consumer and to overcome their alienations. Furthermore, I inquire how such theoretical concepts as disciplinary society and society of control can be deployed to investigate the power and governmentality that confronted and subjected the Chinese migrant factory workers. To do this, I converse with Gilles Deleuze, who critiques Michel Foucault's idea concerning disciplinary society; with Aihwa Ong, who comments on Michael Hardt and Antonio Negri's idea concerning Empire; and with other interpretive social scientists in China studies.

MIGRANT FACTORY WORKERS AS CONSUMERS

Qin and Wu's documentary film *Iron Moon* presents the lived experience of, and the poetry written by, six worker-poets in twenty-first-century China. The first worker-poet is Jike Ayou (吉克阿優) (b. 1985). He is an ethnic Yi (彝族) poet from the Daliang Mountains, Sichuan. His job is to stuff feathers into down coats in the clothing factories. Since many young Yi people, including himself, have migrated to coastal cities to work, they do not have opportunities to learn their traditions and customs. Jike Ayou regrets that the young Yi generation is gradually losing their ethnic identity and culture. The second worker-poet is Wu Niaoniao / Blackbird (烏鳥鳥) (b. 1981) from Huazhou, Guangdong. He used to work as a forklift driver but is now unemployed. Although he tries to look for work at a transportation and logistics recruitment fair, he does not have luck in securing a job. The third worker-poet is Chen Nianxi (陳年喜) (b. 1970) from Shaanxi. He has been a demolition worker, working with dangerous explosives in coal mines, for more than fifteen years. He lives alone. He misses his wife and his son, who live far away, and his parents, who are very ill. The fourth worker-poet is Wu Xia (b. 1982). In her factory in Guangdong, she irons sundresses. She also has to take care of her sick parents and her two children. During her spare time, she likes to wear sundresses and present her femininity. The fifth worker-poet is Lao Jing / Old Well (老井) (b. 1968). He has worked in the coal mines for twenty-five years. He writes poems to commemorate his fellow coal miners who were killed in a gas explosion in 2014. The last worker-poet is Xu Lizhi (許立志) (1990–2014), a former Foxconn worker who made Apple products. Sadly, on the PRC's National Day in 2014, he jumped off a building and committed suicide in Shenzhen, Guangdong. The English title of this documentary, *Iron Moon*, comes from Xu Lizhi's poem "I Swallowed an Iron Moon."[13]

In the *Iron Moon* documentary, a memorable migrant worker-poet is Wu from Sichuan, China. Wu left her hometown when she was thirteen and has been working in Shenzhen, Guangdong, for nineteen years. In the factory, she irons sundresses before they are shipped to department stores or boutiques for sale. In a factory scene, Wu, in her work uniform, is carefully ironing the sundresses. One sees the physical dimension of her labor. Due to the heat emitted by the hot iron, she is sweating. While the viewer becomes acquainted with her working condition, she recites her own poem "The Sundress" (吊帶裙).

鄔霞：《吊帶裙》 WU XIA, "THE SUNDRESS"

包裝車間燈火通明 The packing area is flooded with light
我手握電熨斗 the iron I am holding
集聚我所有的手溫 collects the warmth of my hands
我要先把吊帶熨平 I want to press the straps flat
掛在你肩上不會勒疼你 so they won't dig into your shoulders when you wear it
然後從腰身開始熨起 and then press up from the waist
多麼可愛的腰身 a lovely waist
可以安放一隻白淨的手 where someone can lay a fine hand
林蔭道上 and on the tree-shaded lane
輕撫一種安靜的愛情 caress a quiet kind of love
最後把裙裾展開 last I'll smooth the dress out
我要把每個皺摺的寬度熨得都相等 to iron the pleats to equal widths
讓你在湖邊 或者草坪上 so you can sit by a lake or on a grassy lawn
等待風吹 and wait for a breeze
像花兒一樣 like a flower
而我要下班了 Soon when I get off work
我要洗一洗汗濕的廠服 I'll wash my sweaty uniform
吊帶裙它將被運出車間 and the sundress will be packed and shipped
走向某個市場某個時尚的店面 to a fashionable store
等待唯一的你 where it will wait just for you

陌生的姑娘 Unknown girl
我愛你 I love you

In this poem, the narrator, "I," is a female factory worker who irons the sundresses. One may presume she is Wu herself. The narrator describes how she meticulously irons the sundresses—from the shoulder straps to the waist, from one pleat to another pleat—so the finished products look pretty. When she is ironing, the narrator / the factory worker / Wu imagines that the "unknown girl," probably the consumer of the sundress, is leisurely sitting by a lake or on a lawn. She also fantasizes that this "unknown girl" is in love, and someone gently puts his hand on her waist. By the end of the poem, the narrator / the factory worker / Wu declares her love for this "unknown girl" and hopes that this "unknown girl" can feel her sentiment. From this enchanting poem, the viewer may wonder who this "unknown girl" is. In the mini documentary associated with *Iron Moon*, Wu expresses that this "unknown girl" can be herself, or more precisely, her imagined self. If so, Wu is not only the migrant factory worker and the poet but also this "unknown girl" who wears the beautiful sundress, sits on the grass or by a lake, enjoys leisure, and is in love. The viewer of the documentary and the reader of her poem are invited to envision a different future that goes beyond the drudgery and boredom of factory work.

In the following scenes, Wu is shown to be taking care of her family while working. She lives with her family in a small apartment in Shenzhen. She has to take care of her parents and her two children. (Her father is suffering from depression and has twice attempted suicide.) Despite her hardship, Wu tries to be optimistic. In one scene, she stands next to her closet and presents her wardrobe in an excited manner. She says:

Sundresses are my favorite! It's now autumn, but I don't want to pack my sundresses away. Sometimes I take them out to look at them. This dress is old and a little ripped, but I still want to keep it. When I get a dress, I feel connected to it. I love my sundresses, so I really cannot throw them away. I bought this [purple] one at the market for 25 yuan [3.77 U.S. dollars]. This [gold and black] one is from a street vendor for just 20 yuan [3 U.S. dollars]. My mom bought it for me. It floats up in the breeze and looks so pretty. We [the factory workers] work overtime every day, and every day we wear the same uniform. It's loose and doesn't show off your figure, let alone your waist. I've always wanted to wear pretty clothes. I had one dress that was just 25 yuan [3.77 U.S. dollars]. Once, when I finished work at 2 or 3 a.m., nobody was in the bathroom. So I put the dress on and climbed down from my bunk. I went down the hallway while everyone was sleeping. I had the dress on and I went into the bathroom. It was dark. There was a window, and I used it as a mirror and twirled around in front of it. Just for those few moments, I could enjoy wearing a dress!

Wu expresses how much she loves her sundresses. Similar to writing poetry, wearing the sundress gives her pleasure. According to the documentary and her poem, Wu is both a producer of sundresses (she irons them before they are distributed for sale) and a consumer of sundresses. Indeed, how can Marxist and feminist cultural critics respond to the fact that this female migrant factory worker is so deeply enchanted with the fashion commodity that she herself helps to produce? How can one comment on the fact that she does not complain about her working conditions—for example, the exploitative factory discipline, the long working hours, the lack of overtime pay, the repetitive tasks that she is ordered to complete, and her feeling of alienation from her fellow workers—and instead confesses that she is enthralled by the world of fashion commodities? What is equally unsettling is that in the following scenes, Wu brings her family to the park bordering Shenzhen and Hong Kong. They happily take pictures with the statue of Deng Xiaoping, who initiated China's neoliberal reforms and opened the country to global capital. She even asks her child to call him Grandfather Deng. In reply, some Marxist and feminist critics might say that her behavior expresses ideological false consciousness because she does not know that her consumerist desire is ultimately constructed and perpetuated by the global capitalistic system that oppresses her. While I am sympathetic toward this view, I find Wu's consumerist desire an interesting problem that demands further analysis.

To answer this question, I turn to the existing scholarship concerning the Chinese migrant workers in the contexts of globalization and neoliberalism. I draw on the works of sociologists Pun Ngai and Eileen Otis, anthropologists Yan Hairong and Lisa Rofel, and media and communications studies scholar Wanning Sun, who have touched upon the Chinese

migrant workers' desire for fashion and commodities in their research projects. In my examination, Pun's and Yan's ethnographic works dwell on the
tension between production and consumption. Meanwhile, Rofel's and
Sun's discussions revolve around temporality and spatiality. I add to their
discussions by contemplating on the tension between utopian impulse and
cruel optimism.

In my interpretation, the first set of scholarly conversations focuses on
the tension between production and consumption. Responding to Wu's
desire for the sundresses in *Iron Moon*, Pun and Yan would argue for the
importance of production. In her article "Subsumption or Consumption?
The Phantom of Consumer Revolution in 'Globalizing' China" (2003), Pun
features the Chinese female migrant factory workers as producers and as
consumers. Arguing against Jean Baudrillard, who claims that consumption has replaced production in the context of postmodernity, Pun insists on
the persistence of production. She maintains that production has been
moved from the West to developing countries such as China. This movement is actively supported by the state and its local apparatuses.[14] She also
discusses how consumption is engineered by the state and is used for governmentality.[15] In her fieldwork in the electronics factories in Shenzhen,
Guangdong, Pun recognizes that the female migrant factory workers are
also interested in fashion and consumption. For example, before they
receive their paychecks, the workers have already begun to discuss what they
intend to buy (e.g., T-shirts, jeans, lipstick, nail polish, and face cream) and
where to go to have fun.[16] According to Pun, they consume in order to ele-
vate their social status; they attempt to reduce the disparity between the
rural and the urban. However, their efforts are not entirely successful
because they still face discrimination and harsh judgment in the cities.

Pun expands her inquiry in her book *Made in China: Women Factory
Workers in a Global Workplace* (2005). In the chapter "Imagining Sex and
Gender in the Workplace," she argues that the Chinese migrant factory
workers are gendered beings. In terms of production, because these workers who come from the rural areas are not naturally obedient and submis-
sive to factory discipline, they need to be trained and remodeled so that they
can become productive subjects for the factory. Gender is actively mobilized as a means of labor control. For example, the male bosses say to the
female migrant workers: "You're a girl, how can you speak to me like this?
Didn't your parents teach you how to be a woman?" "Don't you want to

marry yourself out? Behave yourself, since you're still a young girl." "Don't you know you're a girl? You should treat the work more tenderly. How many times do I have to remind you?" "Look at yourself, like a *nanren po* [butch woman 男人婆]. Can't you learn to be like a woman?"[17] Pun argues that gender is evoked when labor management is at stake. In terms of consumption, the female migrant factory workers desire to become modern and gendered subjects and wish to reduce the discrepancy between themselves and urban dwellers. If they are mocked for having "coarse hands and feet," a symbol of rural backwardness, they try to remedy this by painting their fingernails with shiny colors. If they are ridiculed for having dark skin, they use lotions and creams to lighten their skin. In Pun's observation, rather than individualizing and atomizing the consumers, consumption has the contrary effects of binding the workers into a group.

In addition to Pun, sociologist Eileen Otis also points out how Chinese female migrant workers draw on fashion and consumption to remake their appearance and present themselves as urban citizens. In the chapter "Aspirational Urbanism" in her book *Markets and Bodies: Women, Service Work, and the Making of Inequality in China* (2011), Otis points out how the Chinese migrant service workers adopt urban dress and manners, seek to pass as urban, and try to win the respect of their customers. She writes: "Responding to their own humiliation over stereotypes of rural backwardness, migrant service workers endeavor to conceal their rural origins. They indulge in an urban world of consumption to remake themselves as urban women and socially flee from indictments of rural deficiency. In other words, they seek acceptance in urban worlds through using commodities that signal feminine urban sophistication."[18]

While Otis suggests that the female migrant workers from rural areas desire to become urban, Pun goes one step further and discusses how they are received by urban residents.[19] Pun gives several examples to show that their wishes to become modern, urban, and feminine are unrecognized and unacknowledged by their urban counterparts. Their behaviors also reinforce their rural origins and working-class identities. According to Pun's "Subsumption or Consumption" article, the female migrant factory workers encounter discrimination in such theme parks as Windows of the World and Splendid China in Shenzhen, Guangdong. A man in his mid-forties would like to take pictures in front of the monuments. He calls out to the female migrant factory workers: "Would you please step aside . . .?

Dagongmei! Why don't you get some work done at the factory instead of loafing around!"[20] According to Pun's description, her fellow workers "were stunned by this 'misrecognition.' The man's words 'hailed' them as nothing other than *dagongmei*, as abject subjects who should remain in their factories and not wander into places where they clearly did not belong."[21] In her *Made in China* book, Pun recounts her experience of going shopping with her fellow factory workers in a modern supermarket. Not only did salespersons fail to recognize them as ideal customers, but they also were thought to be potential thieves because a security guard followed them everywhere.[22] Later they went to a café and ordered coffees, lemon teas, and soft drinks. After they had politely returned the drink that had been wrongly brought to their table, the man sitting next to them loudly said to the waiter in Cantonese: "'Their hands have touched the drink. Bring me another one. You don't know how their dirty hands are, those *waishengmei!*' (外省妹)."[23] These examples illustrate the fact that the urban residents refuse to acknowledge and accept the female migrant workers as urban citizens.[24]

In her book *New Masters, New Servants: Migration, Development, and Women Workers in China* (2008), Yan discusses the tension between production and consumption. By drawing on her observation in Anhui Province and in Beijing, China, Yan provides an ethnographic analysis of the rural-to-urban migration of young women serving as domestic workers for urban families in Beijing. She offers a critique of several keywords of China's neoliberal reforms, including "modernity," "modernization," "(self-) development," *suzhi* (素質 human quality), "human capital," and "consumer citizenship." In the chapter "A Mirage of Modernity: Pas de Deux of Consumption and Production," she examines the contradiction of production and consumption in the working-class women's migration to the cities. Yan shows that these *baomu* (保姆)—female migrant domestic workers or nannies—attempt to create respectable images of themselves through fashion and consumption. These workers consciously present urbanized and slightly Westernized (*yangqi* 洋氣) images of themselves to people living in the rural areas, such as those living in their hometowns. However, these workers are selective in telling their stories: they try to erase negative traces of their hardships in the cities. This leads Yan to focus on the disjuncture between, on the one hand, the idealized image—the fantasy of upward mobility, knowledge, freedom, and city life—of the migrant domestic workers and, on the other hand, the difficult reality with which they are confronted while working in the (upper-)middle-class families in Beijing. Moreover, Yan remarks on how the looks of the female migrant workers, who are only contracted to provide domestic labor in the urban households, are also scrutinized by their employers. For example, they are told that they cannot put on too much makeup while at work; they are also criticized for wearing too little makeup and for dressing inappropriately while going out. Yan concludes that these migrant domestic workers are not only a producer but also a commodity consumed for their use-value and personhood.[25] Although these migrant domestic workers can consume in a moderate manner, Yan thinks that they are ultimately constrained by wage and disciplined by labor.[26] Considering consumption as a mirage of modernity, Yan redirects the reader's attention to the workers' production and labor. In her work on the transnational supply-chain factories in China, Lisa Rofel briefly summarizes the viewpoints of Pun and Yan concerning the consumerist desires of the Chinese migrant workers. Rofel writes: "While Yan insists that consumption does not resolve the contradictions that these women face as marginalized workers from the countryside, Pun argues that consumption leads women away from a critique of the conditions of their exploitation."[27]

In my interpretation, the second set of scholarly conversations revolves around temporality and spatiality. Responding to Wu's desire for the sundress in *Iron Moon*, Rofel might inquire how Wu remembers the past, engages with the present, and imagines the future, whereas Wanning Sun might show more interest in how Wu consumes public space rather than the commodity. In the chapter "Temporality-Spatial Migration" in the edited volume *Ghost Protocol: Development and Displacement in Global China* (2016), Rofel analyzes how Chinese people move from the socialist world to the capitalist world from three angles: origin stories, affective engagement with temporality, and transnational encounters.[28] For the origin stories, she examines how individuals in different classes—elite entrepreneurs, government officials, and factory workers—remember the socialist past. According to her fieldwork, she realizes that the elite entrepreneurs totally reject the socialist period and are nostalgic for the pre-socialist past (e.g., the Republican and semicolonial China in the 1930s, when capitalism was temporarily permitted to flourish). Meanwhile, the government officials admit there are problems with the socialist past; however, they retain some sense of the importance of nationalist goals affirmed by socialism. In contrast, the factory workers tend to blur the past with the present; they do not see sharp distinctions between them. Unlike the supporters of the revolutionary era, the factory workers do not embrace the socialist past and condemn the capitalist present; and unlike the capitalists, the factory workers do not reject the socialist past and defend the capitalistic present. According to Rofel, the workers' impression has to do with China's *hukou* (戶口) system, the household registration system that maintains the unequal relationship between the rural and the urban areas from the 1950s to the present. To describe the factory workers' affective engagement with the future, Rofel discusses how the workers are treated as if they were entrepreneurs of their own labors, which means that the relations of production are now resignified with the neoliberal ideologies of self-improvement and entrepreneurship. In terms of transnational encounters, Rofel points out how the factory workers respond to uncertain and ever-changing schedules associated with the export of fashion garments. In fact, this is also true for the migrant factory workers in *My Fancy High Heels* and *Iron Moon*.

In her book *Maid in China*, Wanning Sun discusses the domestic workers in Beijing and Shanghai. Indeed, this book nicely converses with Pun's *Made in China*, which focuses on the female migrant factory workers, and with Yan's book, which focuses on the female migrant domestic workers.[29] Sun points out the difference between her subjects (the nannies, maids, or, in Chinese, *baomu*) and Pun's subjects (the *dagongmei*). According to Sun, the *baomu* tend to be older, married, and have children. In contrast to the *dagongmei*, who are younger and more interested in personal fulfillments, the *baomu* try to make money for their families and children. In addition, unlike the *dagongmei*, who work in factories and live in dorms, the *baomu* have more experience in interacting with urban residents. Because these *baomu* can see the gap between the rich and the poor in the city, they tend to be more realistic in their expectations.[30] Sun's ethnography can also be compared with Rofel's work in that both discuss spatiality: Rofel is more interested in the transnational encounter, whereas Sun focuses on the city. In her analysis, Sun realizes that what is at stake for the *baomu* is less about the consumption of specific objects or commodities and more about their use of public space. The *baomu* are realistic: they understand that even if they had expensive, high-end cell phones, they still would not be able to fully enjoy them because they cannot receive cell phone signals in the buildings' basements. Even if they owned good bikes, these bikes might soon be stolen because they do not have extra space to store them. These observations prompt Sun to go beyond the migrant domestic workers' desires for the commodities, whether fulfilled or frustrated, and to redirect her to focus on their creative use of public space. She argues that the *baomu*'s consumption practices are spatial practices because they are constantly negotiating between, on the one hand, the dominant geography monitored by the state and the market and, on the other hand, the latent geography that they themselves occupy.[31] For instance, the *baomu* visit supermarkets and shopping malls and enjoy browsing and window-shopping, even though they do not intend to buy anything. Because they know that they are not the ideal consumers, they have learned to quietly consume these spaces without drawing attention to their presence. Sun commends their skills in appropriating these public spaces as realistic, practical, and calculating. In her analysis, their opportunistic use of public resources and facilities resembles what Michel de Certeau calls the tactics of the powerless.[32]

In my investigation, the third set of scholarly conversations focuses on the tension between utopian impulse and cruel optimism. Responding to Wu's desire for the sundresses, Gilles Deleuze might call it an assemblage. In Pierre-André Boutang's film *Gilles Deleuze From A to Z* (2011), Deleuze explains his concept of desire.[33] According to him, desire is an aggregate or an assemblage: one does not simply desire a person or an object but a world enveloped in this person or object.[34] In response to interviewer Claire Parnet's inquiry, Deleuze creatively suggests that the "desire for a woman is not so much desire for the woman as for a *paysage*, a landscape, that is enveloped in this woman. Or in desiring an object—a dress, for example—the desire is not for the object, but for the whole context, the aggregate, 'I desire in an aggregate.'" Then Deleuze refers back to drinking (*boire/boisson*) or alcohol. "The desire [is] not just for drink, but for whatever aggregate into which one situates the desire for drinking (with people, in a café, etc.)." In addition, Deleuze thinks that desire is a form of constructivism: to desire is to construct an assemblage that involves the state of things, style, territorialization, and deterritorialization. It is indeed a happy coincidence that Deleuze uses the example of a woman and a dress to explain his concept of desiring in an aggregate. In my interpretation of Deleuze, Wu does not simply desire a sundress but a whole world or a landscape enveloped in the sundress. Through poetry, Wu tries to imagine a different "I" who is not burdened with labor and not stressed with everyday life. She desires an assemblage or an aggregate, a fictional construct of economic sufficiency, material abundance, romantic love, gender expression, leisure, and a prosperous and fulfilling life. In other words, Wu's desire for the sundress is infused with a utopian impulse. Although her desire does not fundamentally disturb or challenge the unequal relations of production, it can be potentially productive of building an alternative world.

Nevertheless, these aspirational attachments can also be what Lauren Berlant calls cruel optimism in that they can prevent the Chinese migrant factory workers from fully prospering. In her book *Cruel Optimism* (2011), Berlant explains her concept in this way: "a relation of cruel optimism exists when something you desire is actually an obstacle to your flourishing."[35] According to Berlant, one projects one's desire onto an object, which magnetizes a cluster of promises, and desires this object to help one move one out of oneself and into the world. This optimistic relation or attachment to the object is not inherently cruel; however, it becomes cruel when the object turns out to impede the aim that brought one to it initially. For Berlant, the object of desire can be the fantasy of a good life—with its promises of job security, upward mobility, middle-class life, social and political equality, romantic life, lively and durable intimacy, and so on. Although abundant evidence reveals that contemporary liberal-capitalistic societies can no longer provide the conditions of possibilities for these potentialities to materialize, one paradoxically returns to the scene of fantasy and imagines that dwelling or sustaining in the object can mean being proximate to the promises embodied in the object. One becomes attached to the object to such an extent that even when the object becomes an obstacle or a threat to one's well-being, one continues to endure in it; sometimes, one can even take pleasure in being damaged by it—hence cruel optimism. In addition, Berlant describes how one, when confronted with the dissolution of the object and the subsequent violence that accompanies it, attempts to make adjustments and survive in crises and sufferings that have become the norm and ordinary in our contemporary world of global capitalism.

In what ways can Little Boo's desire for the expensive high heels in *My Fancy High Heels* and Wu's desire for the sundresses in *Iron Moon* be regarded as cruel optimism? How do these fashion commodities prevent the Chinese migrant factory workers from flourishing? Here I suggest that the object of desire parallels Deleuze's idea of desire as an assemblage. For instance, through fantasizing about the expensive shoes, Little Boo desires a whole new world enveloped in this fashion commodity. She constructs an assemblage of a good life that goes far beyond the scenario of working overtime, feeling exhausted and burned out, and being far away from her mother. Looking at herself in the sundress in front of the mirror, Wu desires an alternative world enclosed in this object. She produces an aggregate of a different world marked by leisure, romantic love, and gender expression. In this sense consumption can be productive in the same way that desire can be constructive. This is one side of the narrative, which Berlant calls the optimistic investment in the object of desire. The other side of the story registers cruelty. In order to secure the object and actualize its promises, one has to work extremely hard and endure the hardship and suffering that accompany the process of achieving the object and its promises. For instance, rather than work eight hours per day, one will have to work fifteen or sixteen hours per day. Because of work, one will have to work far away from one's family, partner, children, and friends. One will have no time to cultivate and nurture relationships with them. Moreover, the more one works, the more one wants to spend; and the more one spends, the more one needs to work. It is difficult to break out of this vicious cycle. Berlant explains that this desire for a good life paradoxically turns out to be "a bad life that wears out the subjects."[36] The entrepreneurial-minded migrant workers can be worn out too.

MIGRANT FACTORY WORKERS AS PRODUCERS

To be sure, the Chinese migrant factory workers consume; but importantly, they produce. To study their roles as producers, I turn to David Redmon's documentary film *Mardi Gras: Made in China*, which focuses on the commodity chain of disposable goods on a global scale. This documentary film focuses on the production, consumption, and to a lesser extent, disposal of Mardi Gras beads. The director presents the lived experience of the Chinese female migrant factory workers who make the beads for the Mardi Gras carnivals. In addition to showing the exploitative working conditions that confront these female migrant factory workers, the director emphasizes the hypocrisy of the national and transnational bourgeoisies and how their businesses are complicit with capitals and the state. The director also features the sexually transgressive behaviors of the consumers in New Orleans, Louisiana. After the carnivals, the beads have served their purpose and become trash. Focusing on the transnational lifecycle of these beads, the director presents how Chinese workers and American consumers are systematically intertwined in the system of global capitalism.

Similar to how Marx provides a critique of commodity fetishism in volume 1 of *Capital*, Redmon focuses on the production of the Mardi Gras beads. Rather than simply focusing on labor, he adds gender, sex, ethnicity, culture, and the gaze to Marx's critique. According to the documentary film, the beads are manufactured and assembled in the Tai Kuen Bead Factory in Fuzhou, Fujian, China. The owner, Roger Wong, is a native of Hong Kong. In the mid-1980s, in response to Deng Xiaoping's economic reforms and opening up policies, Wong moved to the special economic zones in Fujian. He set up a factory, hired workers, made business connections, and traded with the outside world. Successful in his business, Wong has made as much as $1.5 million per year. In the documentary, judging from the architectural design and spatial arrangement of the factory, this factory resembles a prison. According to American entrepreneur Dom Carlone, to whom Wong sells his beads, the factory looks like a concentration camp. In addition to directing the *Mardi Gras* documentary, Redmon published a book, *Beads, Bodies, and Trash: Public Sex, Global Labor, and the Disposability of Mardi Gras* (2014), in which he further elaborates the prison-like or concentration camp–like features of this Mardi Gras beads factory. For example, the compound is surrounded with barbed wire, and the walls reach twelve feet high. To control the factory's population, there is only one entrance/exit, and security guards are positioned at this entrance/exit to monitor who can enter and leave. The layout of this factory maximizes visibility and ensures control over the workers' movements and their access to the outside world.[37]

The factory owner, Wong, attempts to discipline his workers and render them docile and productive subjects. The way this Hong Kong Chinese factory owner oversees his mainland Chinese workers is gendered, ethnicized, and class specific. Factory oversight is concerned with power; it is about having authority to supervise, regulate, and administer laboring bodies. In front of Redmon's camera, Wong tries to present himself as a friendly, easy-going, democratic, and reasonable employer. Rather than wearing a suit and tie, he wears a T-shirt and walks around the factory like an ordinary member of the working collective. At one point, Wong says that he treats his workers as brothers and sisters, but he immediately corrects himself and says that he treats them as workers and friends. In fact, the more he tries to control the production of his own image, or what Laura Mulvey would call his "to-be-looked-at-ness," the more one suspects that he is not what he presents himself to be.[38] To be sure, the director presents Wong in a negative manner. In the documentary narrative, Wong says that he prefers hiring young female workers because they are more docile, subservient, and easier to control. He places very high demands on his workers and expects them to work exceedingly hard and produce as much as they can. For example, Wong installs a chalkboard to record the total weight of beads that the entire factory produces each day. He also keeps a detailed list to keep track of how many pounds of beads each worker manufactures each day. If she manages to produce more than the expected minimum weight, she will receive a 10 percent raise in her salary (but this is unlikely because the minimum weight is already unattainably high). However, if she does not meet the requirement, she will receive a 5 percent deduction of salary. Wong maintains that this method can prevent his workers from taking too many breaks, including washroom breaks, from their work duties. Similar to an authoritative parent, he emphasizes rules and punishments. For instance, he forbids the workers from talking to one another during work. If they are found chatting, they will be fined for one day of salary. If they are discovered not paying sufficient attention to the tasks that they are demanded to complete, more money will be reduced from their paychecks. Nevertheless, Wong insists that he does not treat his workers as slaves or like slaves. Immediately after Wong has said this line, Redmon ridicules him by inserting a scene in which a stuffed animal, when pressed, exclaims "hail to the dictator!" This plush toy is produced in Wong's factory and is intended for sale in the Mardi Gras carnivals.

The viewer is also introduced to the female migrant workers' labor conditions and how they try to overcome their alienation and unhappiness. The viewer's first impression of them is not their faces but their hands. One can see the blisters and burns on their hands and the damage inflicted onto their bodies. The motifs of fragmentation (for example, one is presented with the hand, not the entire body), division of labor, isolation, and alienation are featured. Later the viewer is introduced to the factories where they work, the cafeterias where they eat, and the dorm rooms where they sleep. For example, the eighteen-year-old worker Ga Hong Mei presents her work schedule and reveals that she must work an average of eleven to fourteen hours per day.[39] Eighteen-year-old Lio Lila explains her duties in front of the machine and points out the dangers of operating it. She also comments on her low salary, which is between five hundred and six hundred yuan (seventy-five to ninety U.S. dollars) per month. Sixteen-year-old Qiu Bui shows the repetitive work in which she engages (in the later part of the documentary she brings the film crew back to her hometown during Chinese New Year). The fourth worker adds that sometimes she must work fifteen to sixteen hours per day in order to meet the quota; if she does not meet the minimum requirement, her salary will be reduced. Moreover, their living condition is very crowded. However, the female migrant factory workers try to overcome their alienation by expressing their dreams. Ga Hong Mei thoroughly enjoys dancing with her roommates in their dorm room. She also tries to learn English by listening to cassettes. Lio says that she used to dream of becoming an actress, but she has decided to sacrifice her dream to support her younger brother's education. Qiu is genuinely happy when she is reunited with her family during Chinese New Year. Friendship, sisterhood, and family render lives in this prison-like factory slightly more bearable and livable.

Redmon presents what Michel de Certeau calls tactics, as opposed to strategies, to respond to Wong's exploitation of the workers. In his book *The Practice of Everyday Life* (1984), de Certeau considers strategy the calculation that one makes when one can fully control the variables; in contrast, tactic is the intervention that one makes when one cannot control all the variables.[40] In the documentary film, Redmon's tactic is to feature the inconsistency of the factory owner by juxtaposing what he says with the facts. For example, Wong believes that his factory workers enjoy working in his factory and that after work they are free to pursue their hobbies and interests. According to Wong, they can play tennis, basketball, and football in their spare time. (However, the viewer may wonder when they can have time to play sports if they have to work so many hours each day to meet the required quota. The viewer may also wonder how the workers can afford to buy tennis rackets and hire coaches to teach them to play tennis.) He also says that the workers have friends. Wong is confident that his workers enjoy working in his factory. He even says that he treats them as family and friends. (However, the viewer may wonder whether Wong would punish his family member or fine a friend for not meeting an expected quota at work.) Following Wong's assertions, the director immediately inserts an important scene in which a young female migrant factory worker narrates her experience in organizing a strike to negotiate the workers' pay with the employer. Contrary to Wong's claim, the workers were (and are) so dissatisfied with their working conditions that they stopped working in demand for higher salary. In another instance the caption informs the viewer that the petroleum products, such as polystyrene and polyethylene, generated during the production process are harmful to the human body and its central nervous system. When inhaled, these chemicals may cause cancers. In the next scene Wong claims these chemicals are not toxic or dangerous to the human body, nor do they cause pollution to the environment. Redmon's tactic enables the viewer to realize that Wong offers misleading and inaccurate information in front of the camera.

The narrative then turns to the Mardi Gras carnival in New Orleans. This part of the documentary focuses on the breaking of sexual taboos and prohibitions such as scopophilia, voyeurism, exhibitionism, sex in public, and group sex. In this carnival men and women not only become very drunk but also engage in sexually transgressive behaviors in public. For instance, the women show off their breasts to the men and receive beads, the sexual currency in the carnivals, in return. Some of them perform oral sex on the men and receive beads as compensation for their sexual labors. They may do more than that. While the men take pleasures in looking at the women flashing their breasts, the women enjoy being looked at because they are the center of the voyeurs' attentions.[41] They receive attention capital for their sexual service. In fact, these sexual transgressions can be contrasted with the highly desexualized, even repressive atmosphere of the Chinese factory. Although the young Chinese workers produce highly sexualized toys such as plastic penises, breasts, and vaginas for the American consumers, they themselves are not allowed to express their own sexualities or have sex at all. According to Wong, to prevent the factory from becoming an hourly motel, the factory prohibits the male workers from visiting the female workers in their dorm rooms, and vice versa. They can only see each other on Sundays, and their meetings can only take place outside the factory. It appears that the sexual liberation of American consumers is predicated upon the sexual repression of Chinese producers.

When asked where the beads come from and who makes them, the participants in the Mardi Gras carnivals say either that they do not know or that they do not care. One man says: "I have no idea. I hope it's nothing too bad. But I'm just here on vacation so I don't really care." In fact, some of them know the beads' origins, but they act as if they did not know. This way they do not have to feel guilty about their consumption and can continue to have fun. (Moreover, they know that the Mardi Gras beads are, in fact, worthless. But during the carnivals, they act as if the beads were money and were valuable.) A more interesting answer comes from Ms. Pearl, an elderly hippie, who participates in the festival alongside her daughter April and her grandson Adam. When asked the same question, Ms. Pearl replies that she does not want to know the answer. She explains:

> When I was . . . five years old, they gave me this beautiful box . . . you opened it up and a ballerina stands up and she starts to dance, and it's like ding, ding, beautiful music. . . . [And I asked:] How does that do it? And I pried the back off and I saw this ugly metal rod with little knots and I was just so disappointed. That's all it is. This ugly metal rod with little knots on it? So I don't always ask questions. If you got something that gives you joy, don't question it. Might rub the butterfly off. That stuff off the beautiful wings. It might not be able to fly anymore.

Ms. Pearl prefers fantasy to reality. What she says is a good example of what Slavoj Žižek, in his book *The Sublime Object of Ideology* (1989), calls the ideological fantasy that sustains and structures reality. Ms. Pearl knows very well where the beads come from; however, she acts as if she does not know or does not want to know the answer. In contrast to Marx's theory of ideology ("they do not know it, but they are doing it"), what one observes here is closer to Žižek's critique of cynicism as a form of ideology. In his book *Critique of Cynical Reason* (published in German as *Kritik der zynischen Vernunft* in 1983), Peter Sloterdijk understands ideology as "they know very well what they are doing, but still, they are doing it." Appropriating Sloterdijk's argument, Žižek theorizes ideological fantasy as "they know that, in their activity, they are following an illusion, but still they are doing it."[42] According to Žižek, it is fantasy that sustains reality, not the other way around.

To be sure, alienation is a prominent motif in this documentary film. In the first chapter of volume 1 of *Capital*, Marx presents different kinds of alienation that factory workers experience at their workplace: they are alienated from the commodity that they produce, from their labor, from themselves, from other workers, and from their humanity or "species being." In contrast, Redmon's emphasis is on the alienation of the producer from the consumer, and vice versa. To help the producer and the consumer overcome this alienation, Redmon juxtaposes the Chinese producers with the American consumers. He shows the American partygoers the video footage of how the beads were made in the Chinese factories. He also presents to the Chinese workers the photographs showing what happened to the American partygoers during the Mardi Gras festivals. In addition, he made the *Mardi Gras* documentary to show the transnational lifecycle of the Mardi Gras beads. Despite these efforts, one may ask: What next?

On the one hand, the participants of the Mardi Gras festivals may feel, or may be made to feel, guilty about their beads because the Chinese workers are exploited and paid very little. However, the reasons why the American partygoers desire to join the Mardi Gras carnivals remain unexplored. Moreover, guilt is not a useful or productive political sentiment to initiate social change. On the other hand, while the Chinese workers may find the behaviors of the American partygoers funny and puzzling, how one can help change the Chinese laborers' working conditions remains insufficiently interrogated. The documentary ends with a letter read by a female factory worker who pleads with the boss not to make them work overtime, not to punish them, and to pay them minimum wage.

The special features of the DVD include an interview with Marxist political theorist Michael Hardt. In response to the *Mardi Gras* documentary, he suggests that what the viewer needs to focus on is not only the differences between the Chinese producers and the American consumers but also their commonalities. What needs to be undone is the divisions of labor, whether international, racial/ethnic, or sexual/gendered. According to Hardt, while the workers produce the beads, the consumers also actively produce during the Mardi Gras carnivals, albeit in a different valence. Their creative labors, such as the costumes and the music, that go into the carnival can also be regarded as what I call productive consumption. I concur with Hardt and add that both the Chinese workers and the American consumers belong to the global working class or, one may say, the global multitude created by Empire or transnational capitalism. According to Redmon's book, many of the American participants in the carnivals belong to the working class. Many of his interviewees have boring jobs and do repetitive routines in their everyday lives. They use this carnival (e.g., partying, drinking, and transgressive sex) as an outlet of their depression and lack of meaning and fulfillment in life. Rather than condemning their behaviors as immature, I think it is vital to sympathize/empathize with them and think of ways to create a transnational alliance between the Chinese and American workers. The questions are: How can the unhappy Chinese factory workers identify and connect with the unhappy American consumers who are also producers? What kind of cultural or ideological revolution is needed to awaken, cultivate, and sustain such a global class consciousness that has yet to fully emerge?

In addition, Hardt suggests that the Mardi Gras carnivals can be interpreted as an expression of the refusal of work and a celebration of nonwork. Nevertheless, Marxist theorist Žižek disagrees, arguing that one should not romanticize or idealize carnivals in the context of global capitalism. On the surface, carnivals may serve redemptive, emancipatory, and democratic functions because unequal power relationships can be reversed: the subject can become the object whereas the object can also become the subject. However, such transgressive impulses have already been coopted and contained by the regime of global capitalism, which is evidenced by the fact that many business corporations now sponsor carnivals and parties. In other words, rebellions have already been built and programmed into the machine of global capitalism. In response to Žižek, I take a slightly skeptical position and suggest that individuals may not rebel in exactly the same way that the capitalistic system may anticipate them to rebel. There is still room for contingencies and unexpected outcomes that global capitalism cannot fully control. Social actors can create little cracks, albeit temporarily, within this total system.

To further the discussions about the subjectivity of the Chinese migrant factory workers as producers, I engage with Gilles Deleuze's theoretical concepts of disciplinary society and society of control. In his article "Postscript on the Societies of Control" (1992), Deleuze argues that we are moving away from what Michel Foucault calls disciplinary society toward a new regime of governmentality that Deleuze calls society of control.[43] Whereas the disciplinary society is characterized by enclosure, such as the family, school, barracks, factory, hospital, and prison, the corporation exemplifies the society of control. Deleuze points out the differences between these two modes of power and governmentality: the former is analogical and the latter is numerical.[44] Enclosures are molds and distinct castings; in comparison, controls are a modulation, like a self-deforming cast that will continuously change from one moment to the other.[45] Whereas "in the disciplinary societies one was always starting again . . . in the societies of control one is never finished with anything—the corporation, the educational system, and armed services being metastable states coexisting in one and the same modulation, like a universal system of deformation."[46] Moreover, the disciplinary societies have two poles: individuals are designated by a signature, and their positions within the mass are indicated by a number. In contrast, in the societies of control, the code marks one's access to information.[47] Deleuze provides vivid images to help us imagine the respective differences between the disciplinary society and the society of control: in terms of animal, the animal in enclosure versus the serpent; in terms of sport, the older sports versus surfing; in terms of machine, the machine that involves energy versus the computer.[48] Importantly, Deleuze considers such a transformation an internal mutation within capitalism as such. He explains:

Nineteenth-century capitalism is a capitalism of concentration, for production and for property. It therefore erects the factory as a space of enclosure, the capitalist being the owner of the means of production but also, progressively, the owner of other spaces conceived through analogy (the worker's familial house, the school). As for markets, they are conquered sometimes by specialization, sometimes by colonization, sometimes by lowering the costs of production. But in the present situation, capitalism is no longer involved in production, which it often relegates to the Third World. . . . It's a capitalism of higher-order production. It no longer buys raw materials and no longer sells the finished products: it buys the finished products or assembled parts. What it wants to sell is services and what it wants to buy is stocks. This is no longer a capitalism for production but for the product, which is to say, for being sold or marketed. Thus it is essentially dispersive, and the factory has given way to the corporation. The family, the school, the army, the factory are no longer the distinct analogical spaces that converge toward an owner—state or private power—but coded figures—deformable and transformable—of a single corporation that now has only stockholders.

> The conquests of the market are made by grabbing control and no longer by disciplinary training, by fixing the exchange rate much more than by lowering costs, by transformation of the product more than by specialization of production. . . . Marketing has become the center or the "soul" of the corporation.[49]

For Deleuze, the disciplinary society and the society of control respectively resemble the earlier and later stages of capitalism.[50] However, to what extent can Deleuze's description of the society of control, or what one may call neoliberal governmentality, be made useful to describe and explain the subjection of the Chinese migrant factory workers in the *Mardi Gras* documentary? In my observation, the Chinese migrant factory workers are still enclosed within the Tai Kuen Bead Factory, which is a disciplinary institution. The female migrant factory workers are still disciplined to become docile, subservient, and productive subjects.[51] The question is, where is the society of control in the *Mardi Gras* documentary?

In her work regarding the Chinese migrant domestic workers, anthropologist Yan Hairong argues that how the female migrant workers are recruited in China operates within the logic of neoliberal governmentality.[52] In her article "Neoliberal Governmentality and Neohumanism: Organizing *Suzhi*/Value Flow Through Labor Recruitment Networks" (2003), Yan makes three important claims concerning the discourse of *suzhi* (素質; human quality) in the context of postsocialist China. First, "the emergence of the notion of *suzhi* marks a subsumption of human subjectivity to the discourse of development and is an abstraction and reduction of heterogeneous human subjectivities into a presumed universal equivalence."[53] Second, "*suzhi* is central to the economic production of surplus value extracted from rural migrant workers," and "*suzhi* functions as an intangible operator in the labor contract." Therefore, "*suzhi* facilitates exploitation *and* makes it invisible."[54] Third, "the promotion and deployment of the *suzhi* discourse is central to a neoliberal governmentality that has rearticulated the relationship between the state, market, and subjectivity."[55] According to Yan, the peasants in rural China are constructed and interpellated as having low *suzhi*. They are persuaded that if they work in the city (which is portrayed as an educational institution, like a university), they can eliminate their rustic and backward mindsets and behaviors, improve their *suzhi*, and become modern and civilized human beings. Migration is cast as a project of self-improvement and self-development for, rather than exploitation of, the female migrant workers. Inspired by Yan, I contend that the neoliberal governmentality, or Deleuze's idea of society of control, is already present in how the Chinese female migrant workers are recruited from the countryside to the city. Both the disciplinary society and the society of control *coexist* and *overlap* in the *Mardi Gras* documentary.

The work of anthropologist Aihwa Ong further explains such form of synchronicity. In the chapter "Latitudes, or How Markets Stretch the Bounds of Governmentality" in her book *Neoliberalism as Exception: Mutations in Citizenship and Sovereignty* (2006), Ong provides a situated critique of Michael Hardt and Antonio Negri's two arguments concerning Empire in their book titled *Empire*. First, whereas Hardt and Negri suggest that global capitalism is characterized by "a smooth space of un-coded and deterritorialized flows," Ong argues that the global marketized landscape is "still striated by fluid but highly particularized and coded lateral spaces or latitudes."[56] She gives the examples of Silicon Valley (outside the San Francisco Bay area), Route 128 (outside Boston), and Research Triangle Park (outside Raleigh-Durham, North Carolina) and points out the advantages of these regional hubs. Second, Hardt and Negri maintain that global capitalism has transitioned "from disciplinary society to the society of control." In comparison, by referencing the commodity chains of garments and electronics in the context of Asian America, Ong argues that both modes of power and governmentality *coexist* in this transnational space. Going beyond Yan's analysis, Ong suggests that they are arranged by specific racial and ethnic networks and practices. Considering overseas Chinese business entrepreneurs as agents of the society of control, she suggests that they have the capacities and potentialities—linguistic skills, cultural competencies, local knowledges, and business networks—to respond quickly and with agility to the shifting conditions and requirements of global market demands. Notably, Ong regards ethnic enclaves, families, and factories in Asian America (e.g., Chinatowns) as well as Chinese factories and sweatshops in the Pearl River Delta areas in Guangdong, China, as disciplinary institutions. In these ethnic spaces, which are filled with gendered ideologies, the carceral logic of labor practices is at work; and docile bodies are produced and disciplined.

In the *Mardi Gras* documentary, the Hong Kong businessman Roger Wong can also be considered an agent of neoliberalism or of the society of control. Indeed, Wong is ethnic (Han) Chinese. Coming from Hong Kong, he can speak Cantonese, Mandarin, and English; his language skills are his cultural capital. Moreover, he has business connections with American buyers, such as Dom Carlone, to whom he sells his beads, and with local factories in Fuzhou, Fujian, China. His business networks are his social capital. In other words, Wong has the capacity and potentiality to plug into both the American consumer markets and the Chinese labor markets and to move within these business, ethnic, cultural, and social networks. He can be regarded as what Ong calls a flexible citizen.[57] According to Ong,

> they [the overseas Chinese entrepreneurs] have come to embody the kind of citizenship associated with the society of control, performing the set of attributes that maneuver fluidly and opportunistically in a network of open flows. This regime of control is associated . . . with a set of flexible capacities, assets, and potentialities that can be plugged into parallel worlds of the market and technology. I call such calculated versatility in volatility, and flexible attitude and latitude to manipulate various codes and to exert lateral influence across political domains, "latitudinal citizenship." While latitudinal citizenship is continually monitored, not least by the fluctuating bottom line and unknowable market risks, it is also parasitic on older disciplinary forms.[58]

Redmon has portrayed the factory production in mainland China. The business success of Wong can be said to be built upon the exploitation of gendered labor in his Mardi Gras beads factory in Fujian, an institution of disciplinary society. To follow Ong's logic, the other side of the disciplinary society can be reflected in the exploitations in the ethnic enclaves, families, and factories in Asian America, such as Chinatowns.

Chapter Six

THE PSYCHIC LIFE OF RUBBISH

On Wang Jiuliang's Documentary Film
Beijing Besieged by Waste (2010)

In his famous essay "Theses of the Philosophy of History" (1942), Walter Benjamin offers a new way of interpreting history. Updating the method of historical materialism (which he contrasts with historicism), he invites the reader to leave the mob of conformists and join the army of rebels, to distrust the kind of authoritative analysis that prides itself on objectivity, "to brush history against the grain," "to blast open the continuum of history" (which he considers to be "a sequence of events like the beads of a rosary"), and to scandalize the complicity between history and power.[1] To him, the revision of history is a political undertaking, as it serves an emancipatory purpose—that is, to give the dead an afterlife and to liberate the kinds of voices that have been unfairly repressed and silenced by power. Benjamin remarks: "history is the subject of a structure whose site is not homogeneous, empty time, but time filled by the presence of the now."[2] It is in this particular "now" instance that "time stands still and has come to a stop."[3]

Indeed, Benjamin's notion of history and the past is always present. The sufferings of the past generations continue to seek redemption in the present. And particular moments in the past may flash up as images in a present moment of danger to initiate a revolution and to redeem the dead and the suffering generations of the past.[4] Benjamin calls such an arrested image a constellation, which becomes citable by later generations.[5] For Benjamin, the rewriting of history is a conscious political endeavor for the redemption and happiness of the repressed and subordinated voices.[6] In his imagination, the historical materialist resembles an "angel of history." Endowed with a "weak Messianic power," the angel of history can manipulate and appropriate the present to change the past. Inspired by Paul Klee's painting *Angelus Novus* (1920), Benjamin depicts the angel of history as one caught between the past and the future, between the pile of debris accumulating in front of him and the storm of progress that propels him toward the future. Benjamin writes:

> A Klee painting named "Angelus Novus" shows an angel looking as though he is about to move away from something he is fixed contemplating. His eyes are staring, his mouth is open, his wings are spread. This is how one pictures the angel of history. His face is turned toward the past. Where we perceive a chain of events, he sees one single catastrophe which keeps piling wreckage and hurls it in front of his feet. The angel would like to stay, awaken the dead, and make whole what has been smashed. But a storm is blowing in from Paradise; it has got caught in his wings with such a violence that the angel can no longer close them. The storm irresistibly propels him into the future to which his back is turned, while the pile of debris before him grows skyward. This storm is what we call progress.[7]

In my imagination, contemporary Chinese artist Wang Jiuliang (王久良) resembles Benjamin's angel of history. In his documentary film *Beijing Besieged by Waste* (*Laji weicheng* 垃圾围城) (2010), which can be considered an autoethnography, Wang presents himself taking photographs and shooting footage about garbage in Beijing, China, more than ten times. Similar to Benjamin's angel of history, Wang stands between two seemingly incompatible worlds: in front of him lies a sea of rubbish piling up, whereas behind him is a Beijing cityscape populated with tall residential buildings. As a Chinese angel of history, Wang is situated between the past and the future, between the large pile of wreckage and the unprecedented storm of progress. He is trapped between rubbish dumps and contemporary China's economic modernization and development. However, unlike Benjamin's angel of history, who observes the past generations' sufferings but is too powerless to intervene, this Chinese angel of history uses his digital video (DV) camera to take photographs and to make a documentary film about rubbish surrounding Beijing. By doing so he disturbs and unsettles the progress narrative concerning China's rise on the global stage.

This chapter examines the representation of rubbish and the scavengers in Wang's documentary film *Beijing Besieged by Waste*.[8] It asks how such a visual representation can be regarded as a productive site for political thinking. Deviating from the existing social sciences scholarship that approaches contemporary China's waste from a socioeconomic, data-driven, and quantitative angle, I approach this issue from a perspective informed by cultural studies and theory. By engaging with psychoanalysis, I argue that *Beijing Besieged by Waste* presents a psychic reality of trash; it visualizes the condition of being surrounded, almost engulfed, by garbage. With reference to the theories of Sigmund Freud, Julia Kristeva, and Fredric Jameson, I approach the figuration of rubbish and the scavengers from three perspectives: as the return of the repressed in the form of the uncanny, as the abject, and as the dialectic of ideology and utopian impulse. In addition, I suggest that Wang's documentary film offers a powerful critique of the evolutionary idea of history and progress that the postsocialist party-state and the global, regional, and national capitals deploy to justify their political ideologies and economic interests. I inquire how the depiction of rubbish and the scavengers can provide a different way to revisit China's rise.

WANG JIULIANG AND HIS ARTISTIC WORKS

Born in 1976, Wang is a young, promising, and politically engaged photographer from Shandong, China. Since graduating from the School of Cinema and Television at the Communication University of China, he uses different artistic media, such as photography, documentary film, and visual art, combined with new media and digital technologies, including internet web pages, blogs, Weibo (the Chinese version of Twitter), Global Positioning System, and Google Earth, to tell stories about the underside of China's market reforms. Launching his career in the mid-2000s, Wang's works attempt to capture the residual: in his early works, fascinated with the afterlife of human beings, he captures what remains after life has been completed. In his recent works, interested in the afterlife of commodities, he grasps what is left behind after consumption has ended. His early works, comprising the photographic series *Previous Lives* (2007–8), *Rituals and Souls* (2008), and *Absolute Happiness* (2008), focus on the local conceptions of death and the afterlife in his hometown in Shandong. These photographs were exhibited in the mid- and late 2000s. While photography remains a central interest in his works, Wang has begun to work with other art forms, such as documentary film and installation art, in his more recent productions. In addition to the photographic series *Beijing Besieged by Waste* (2008–2010) and *The Fringes of the City* (2009), for which he earned the Outstanding Artist of the Year (Gold Award) at the 2009 Lianzhou International Photography Festival, he made the documentary *Beijing Besieged by Waste* (2010). This documentary brought the Chinese government's attention, so the Beijing municipal government allocated 10 billion RMB to try to solve the problem of waste. More recently, Wang directed another documentary film, *Plastic China* (*Suliao wangguo* 塑料王國) (2016). These works offer a powerful critique of Chinese consumer culture in the context of globalization.

According to a journalistic report "Rubbish Doesn't Surround the City, but the City Surrounds Rubbish," the director suggests that the drastic transformations that have been taking place in China during the past thirty years can be observed in the changes in Chinese people's attitudes toward consumption. He explains:

> Beginning with the Industrial Revolution, it took 150 years for this kind of consumer culture to be formed in Europe and the U.S. But in China, it only took us thirty years to complete this process. In the space of several years, we departed from a culture that cherished thrift and frugality and entered one that celebrated wild and excessive consumption—as if it were a form of compensation. We need to reflect on this kind of consumer culture.[9]

Wang engages with multiple artistic media—photography, installation art, and documentary film—to evaluate Chinese consumer culture. Indeed, photography remains a central medium in his works. For example, his photographic series *Beijing Besieged by Waste*, together with his documentary of the same title, are primarily concerned with garbage, the repressed underside of Chinese consumer culture. Another photographic series, *The Fringes of the City*, chronicles the lives of the scavengers in Beijing's rubbish dumps. Coming from remote and poor areas of China, such as Sichuan and Henan Provinces, these scavengers do the kind of manual labor that nobody would like to do. In the dumps, they pick up usable leftovers and recycle useful materials from scrapyards. These scavengers live in rubbish-houses, wear rubbish-clothes, and eat rubbish-food. Because their lived experiences are strikingly absent in contemporary Chinese public cultures, the scavengers are also a repressed underside of Chinese consumer culture.[10] While the Chinese filmmaker Jia Zhangke (賈樟柯) empathizes with the Chinese migrant workers and calls himself a "cinematic migrant worker" (*dianying mingong* 電影民工), Wang can also be regarded as a photographic scavenger, a documentary scavenger, or an artistic scavenger.[11] Wang respects and identifies with the scavengers with whom he works.

While Wang's incisive critique of Chinese consumer culture is shown prominently in *Beijing Besieged by Waste* (2010), his evaluation of the aftermath of consumption can also be observed in his installation art. An artistic scavenger, Wang collected disposable commodities in the rubbish dumps. After accumulating numerous abandoned instant coffee packages and disposable hotel slippers, he created two installations, *Fruity Coffee* and *Beijing Hotels*. These works were exhibited at Beijing's Songzhuang Art Center from June 16 to July 20, 2010. These disposable goods were used just once before they were discarded. They had short lifespans, or they were designed to be quickly consumed. Turning the big piles of useless (or useless) rubbish to useful things, Wang recycled these discarded and abandoned materials and exhibited the sea of instant coffee packages and hotel slippers inside and outside the art museum. The result was striking: it was as if the entire art museum was about to be engulfed by the enormous piles of rubbish. His art depicted the condition of being surrounded, enclosed, and overwhelmed by trash. This certainly echoed the theme of his documentary film *Beijing Besieged by Waste*. By turning rubbish into art (i.e., by creating rubbish-art, which is rubbish-but-not-quite and art-but-not-quite), he offered a critical commentary about excessive consumption in contemporary China. The art exhibition was so successful in visualizing excessive packaging that the company that produced these disposable goods sent a letter of complaint to the art museum.

The *Fruity Coffee* and *Beijing Hotel* series were part of Wang's project called *The Supermarket*, a transmedial production involving photography and installation art.[12] This project continued his critique of consumption and waste in China. In an interview, Wang offered a defamiliarizing view concerning the similarities between the supermarkets and the rubbish dumps. He says: "I'd like to show the relationships between rubbish and consumer commodities, between rubbish dumps and supermarkets (both of them can be considered markets), and between the problem of rubbish and the social system. There is a close connection between the excretion (waste) of consumption and people's consumption values."[13]

After collecting disposable commodities, such as packages of instant noodles, in the rubbish dumps, Wang placed them back onto the supermarket's shelves. Then he took pictures of these strange entities that were simultaneously commodities and rubbish: commodities-as-rubbish and rubbish-as-commodities. How should we call these entities that appeared simultaneously familiar and unfamiliar? Wang coined an interesting term: the rubbish's supermarket, which means that there is a supermarket in the rubbish dump. Inspired by his insight, I think the opposite works equally well: the supermarket's rubbish, which means that there is already a rubbish dump in the supermarket. It can be said that when we consume in the supermarket, we are already purchasing rubbish. (We are also consumed by rubbish.) Wang's art shows that there are striking similarities between commodities and rubbish, between supermarkets and rubbish dumps, and, by extension, between consumers and scavengers.

BEIJING BESIEGED BY WASTE (2010)

In an interview in a Chinese TV program called "Traveling with Dreams: *Beijing Besieged by Waste* Photographer Wang Jiuliang," the director explains why he was interested in making a documentary film about trash. He says:

> Before the production of *Beijing Besieged by Waste*, I was making a film about the traditional Chinese concept of ghosts, gods, and beliefs in the afterlife. I was shooting in my hometown for an entire year. That took place in the cemetery. What I needed was a very pure, relatively primitive, and natural environment. I'd like to represent the atmosphere of the ancient times. But in reality, it was hard to find such an environment. What was really annoying was that there was rubbish all over the mountains. This prompted me to ask how a package or a rubbish bag from the U.S. or Germany could arrive at a small village in China.[14]

Wang found that it was not possible to find a place to capture the purity and tranquility that he had hoped to find in his subjects. "Everywhere I went was garbage!" he complained. "In the end, I found myself cleaning up bags after bags of garbage before I could even start taking photographs." This led him to wonder where the garbage came from. After some research, he learned that the plastic bags were used to carry chemical pesticides. Contrary to pesticides in bottles, which could be used for a year, these bags were used only once before they were trashed. The use of plastic bags in agricultural productions prompted him to make a documentary about rubbish. In the beginning, the working title was *A Photographic Investigation of Waste Pollution Around Beijing.*

Wang's method was simple: he rode his motorbike and followed garbage trucks transporting household rubbish to waste management centers. He also followed trucks moving rubbish from transfer stations to incinerators and landfills. Then he studied the visual characteristics of these dumps. To discover where exactly the dumps were located, he used satellite photographs and the Global Positioning System. From 2008 to 2010, he visited 450–500 legal and illegal dumps in Beijing. However, his investigation was not easy. He says:

> People involved in one way or another with the illegal dump sites, in the interest of keeping their trade clandestine, are quite cautious toward outsiders. Because people with cameras on their backs are especially unwelcome, it was impossible to shoot freely at these sites. In fact, I was frequently refused entrance, berated, chased by wolfhounds, or threatened with cooking knives. Several times I was kept hostage and my photographs were deleted from my cameras. In order to photograph these dump sites in detail, I was, therefore, forced to come up with creative solutions. Sometimes I pretended that I was there to repurpose garbage, and looked for opportunities to take pictures when I was granted entrance. More often than not, I engaged in a kind of guerrilla warfare with the guards, quickly shooting pictures and leaving when they were not paying attention. I also looked for commanding heights, such as treetops, or high-voltage electricity poles, where I could take pictures that captured the entirety of a site including its surrounding.[15]

In fact, the DV camera helped to facilitate his social investigation. Contrary to professionalized filmmaking, which involves a group of technical experts carrying large, heavy, and expensive equipment on their shoulders, the DV camera, like a pen, is small, light, easily portable, and relatively inexpensive. Because of its "lightness" and its flexibility, Wang was able to enter and penetrate into the dumps previously inaccessible to outsiders.[16] In addition, the DV camera is useful for amateur filmmakers and documentarians because it does not require much technical knowledge to operate. After the filming was complete, Wang could use his personal computer to edit the footage and produce a documentary.[17]

After visiting a landfill, Wang would mark its location on Google Earth with a yellow sign. After more than a year of hard work, this rubbish detective made a shocking discovery. Based on the distribution of the yellow signs on Google Earth, he concluded that Beijing is literally surrounded by rubbish. This discovery led him to call his documentary *Beijing Besieged by Waste* (*Laji Weicheng* 垃圾圍城). In Chinese, 垃圾 (*laji*) means rubbish, and 圍城 (*weicheng*) means to surround the city. Here the motif of surrounding the city is significant. Whereas students of modern Chinese literature may be thinking of Qian Zhongshu's (錢鐘書) novel *Fortress Besieged* (*Weicheng* 圍城) (1947), students of Chinese Marxism may be thinking of Mao Zedong's (毛澤東) militaristic strategy—namely, the countryside surrounds and overwhelms the city (*nongcun baowei chengshi* 農村包圍城市), a tactic that the political leader proposed after the failed cooperation between the communists and the nationalists in the late 1920s. Also, the documentary's English title is *Beijing Besieged by Waste*, not *Beijing Surrounded by Waste* or *Beijing Enclosed by Waste*. The militaristic overtone emphasizes the tense and antagonistic relationship between rubbish and consumer, and between the dump and its surrounding environment. Similar to Mao's military approach, the rubbish dumps surrounding Beijing can be thought as an armed insurrection. Rubbish is warfare.

The geography of Beijing is divided into six concentric circles: the innermost circle constitutes the first ring. Then it is expanded to become the second through sixth rings. The rubbish dumps, Wang discovered, are mostly located between the fifth and the sixth rings. This is also the place where the majority of the migrant workers reside. Wang calls the enclosure created by these rubbish dumps "the seventh ring of Beijing." Building on the director's description of how Beijing is surrounded and overwhelmed by rubbish, I call the enclosure "the new Great Wall of China." If there is a great firewall (i.e., internet censorship) in the Chinese virtual world, there is a new Great Wall—a rubbish wall—in the real world. In fact, the concept of a rubbish wall is articulated by Chinese cultural critic Wang Min'an (汪民安). In his Chinese-language essay "On Rubbish" (*Lun laji* 論垃圾), Wang Min'an regards rubbish as "corpses of commodities" (*laji de shiti* 垃圾的屍體). In addition to commenting, like Wang Jiuliang, on the similarities between commodities and rubbish, between supermarkets and dumps, and, I add, between consumers and scavengers, Wang Min'an discusses the spatial politics of commodities and rubbish. While it makes sense to see rubbish in areas where commodities accumulate (rubbish is the dead bodies of commodities), Wang Min'an finds it curious that in the urban areas one sees commodities but not so much rubbish, whereas in the rural areas or, more specifically, at the border between the city and the country-side, one does not see so many commodities but more rubbish. He suggests that rubbish creates a border between the urban and rural areas.[18]

Rubbish: The Repressed

To exorcise not in order to chase away the ghosts, but this time to grant them the right . . . to . . . hospitable memory . . . out of a concern for justice.

JACQUES DERRIDA, *SPECTER OF MARX*

Wang's documentary *Beijing Besieged by Waste* chronicles how nature has been scarred, damaged, exploited, and denaturalized in the context of global capitalistic production and consumption. Diverging from contemporary Chinese commercial films (e.g., fashion films), which emphasize the construction of middle-class identity through consumption (i.e., you are what you consume), Wang focuses on rubbish, or what comes after consumption (i.e., you are what you dispose of). In the beginning of the documentary, he presents images of shopping malls and residential districts in Beijing. Then he shows scenes of trucks transporting rubbish away from the residential areas to the refuse transfer stations. It is in these industrial plants that the rubbish is managed and compressed, or, in the language of Freudian psychoanalysis, condensed. While some of the rubbish is processed in the composting plants to make fertilizers, some of it is transported to the incinerators. Some of it is driven to the landfills outside Beijing, or displaced. The rubbish is then buried, concealed, covered up, or repressed. Indeed, there is a psychoanalytical dimension to how rubbish is handled—it is displaced, transferred, channeled, and relocated to a different place out of sight. In contrast to commodities to be displayed and exhibited, rubbish is hidden. Despite this, the rubbish has not fully disappeared.

When I showed Wang's documentary (especially the Google Earth scene, showing Beijing literally surrounded by rubbish) to my friends and colleagues, the most common response I heard was "Holy shit!" In fact, they were perfectly correct to have such a response, not only because it was "holy shit!" to see that Beijing was about to be entirely engulfed by rubbish but also because religion ("holy") and rubbish ("shit") are the prominent motifs in Wang's works. Whereas Wang's early photographic works deal with local beliefs in death and the afterlife, his recent works on rubbish offer a substantial critique of Chinese consumer culture. In one of Wang's web pages, an internet viewer nicknamed Blue Disaster provides an insightful observation to Wang's works. He/she asks the director: "Both your earlier and later works are concerned with things gone and elapsed—rubbish and dead people. So, does rubbish embody a sense of ghostliness?"

The question that Blue Disaster poses points to the possibility of using Wang's early work on death and the afterlife to interpret his later work on Chinese consumer culture and waste. (In fact, it is also possible to use his later work to interpret his early work. For example, how can the Chinese tradition of ancestral offerings, such as the burning of paper clothes, paper houses, paper automobiles, and paper money, be considered consumption?)

To be sure, rubbish embodies a sense of the uncanny in *Beijing Besieged by Waste*. Similar to Sigmund Freud's idea of the uncanny in "The 'Uncanny'" (1919) and Jacques Derrida's idea of hauntology in *Specters of Marx* (1993), there is a sense of ghostliness in rubbish. Indeed, it is possible to appropriate Derrida's idea of the specter to say that rubbish is "neither living nor dead, present nor absent: it spectralizes."[19] Indeed, the haunting of rubbish has to do with the repression of the subject and the possibility of the return of the repressed in the form of the uncanny. In *Beijing Besieged by Waste*, the narrator reminds the viewer that the refuse that one has produced refuses to go away. "Nothing can stop the city from expanding. Nothing can stop the production of rubbish. We move the waste away from the city quickly. We bury it hastily. However, no matter how hard we try to hide it, it has not disappeared. It is still here."

To be sure, the rubbish rendered out of sight has not vanished. It remains. Also, what is repressed is destined to come back. In the natural world, the polluted water, soil, and air will come back to the people living in Beijing. The river carries the rubbish back to the city, and the wind blows the pollutants back to the residents. The motif of the return is also present in the man-made environment. The six-ring highway transport system encircles Beijing. The rubbish ring, or what Wang calls the seventh ring of Beijing, surrounds the city. In the virtual world, the representation of the rubbish ring in yellow signs on Google Earth also emphasizes the horror of eternal return. It seems that there is no way to escape.

In *Beijing Besieged by Waste*, the narrator says: "It's really hard to imagine that the waste that we throw away will somehow come back to us with a new look." In the language of psychoanalysis, the repressed may reappear in some unanticipated form to haunt and even destroy the Chinese consumer subject. In this documentary, the repressed rubbish returns in the form of an animal. The latter appears in a marriage photo and food.

Let us focus on the marriage photo first. In a memorable scene in *Beijing Besieged by Waste*, against the background of Beijing's Wenyu River, which is a wealthy area populated with Western-style golf courses, polo clubs, and luxurious villas, a newly wedded Chinese middle-class couple is taking their marriage photos. This couple is formally dressed: The bridegroom is wearing a tuxedo, and the bride is wearing a wedding gown. They are posing elegantly in front of the camera. While they are immersed in love, a flock of sheep, led by an old herdsman, starts to wander toward them. The animals add to the pastoral and romantic atmosphere. As the bridegroom tries to grab a lamb, the camerawoman immediately takes a snapshot. While this is supposed to be a sweet moment, the couple does not know that they are taking their marriage photos next to a dump. Equally ironically, when the couple takes pictures with these cute and cuddly lambs, they do not realize that these animals have just visited the surrounding landfills. Led by a herdsman who is also a scavenger, these sheep have just eaten rubbish. Some of them have also drunk the water polluted by the dumps. Because they have been eating unhygienic food and drinking contaminated water, these animals are sick and need medical attention.

The marriage photo reveals how rubbish unexpectedly creeps into Chinese people's everyday lives. In fact, the rubbish also comes back to the consumer in the form of food. The beginning of the documentary presents a flock of sheep eating rubbish. The middle part features a herd of cows eating trash. In one scene the director uses close-up to present the cows' udders, reminding us that the milk we drink may come from these deformed udders. The later part presents numerous pigs feeding on swill, the leftovers from the restaurants. The documentary also presents a disturbing scene showing that the oil used in Chinese restaurant cooking may not be entirely hygienic. Some of it has been filtered from the swill. After being boiled, it is reused to feed customers.

MAN (INTERVIEWEE): Now some restaurants filter the oil out of the swill and serve it back to the customers.
WOMAN (INTERVIEWER): That's disgusting! Really?
MAN: Oh, you don't believe me?
WOMAN: I often dine out.
MAN: They just filter and boil it, and then they serve it to the customers.
WOMAN: Do they do it themselves, or do they ask you to do it?
MAN: They don't need us. They just pour the swill into a barrel and then use a bamboo strainer.
WOMAN: Wow! No way! I will not go to restaurants anymore!
MAN: If you don't go, there will always be rich people who will visit the restaurants.

The implications of animals eating rubbish demand our attention. If the animals we consume in our everyday lives eat rubbish, then when we are eating meat, we are also eating rubbish. If the milk we drink is contaminated by rubbish, we are also indirectly consuming rubbish. Wang also shows that the water is badly polluted because dumps have been built along the river. The narrator declares: "this river is a landfill!" and "none of the river flowing through Beijing is clean." Indeed, if the water used to irrigate the crops is contaminated, the vegetables that we consume in our daily lives are also polluted. In fact, several dumps have already been found close to Daxing—Beijing's vegetable basket—in southern Beijing. These examples point to the horror of reality: it is not that the Chinese may live in the apocalypse in the near future but that they are already living in one.

Rubbish: The Abject

When introducing his photograph series *Beijing Besieged by Waste* in a lecture, Wang asked the audience to imagine what their lives would be like if they were the animals in the pictures—the sheep, or pigs, or cows—who were given nothing but rubbish to eat. He asked them to ponder what their lives would be like if they were the plants and vegetables irrigated by dirty water. We can also try to imagine what our lives would be like if we were those scavengers surrounded by rubbish. Many of them worked and lived in the dumps. They claimed these dirty places as homes. According to the narrator, there are as many as two thousand scavengers who live and work in the biggest landfills in Beijing. Some of them live in rubbish-houses, wear rubbish-clothes, and eat rubbish-food.

Here I introduce Julia Kristeva's idea of the abject to enrich my interpretation of the documentary. In her book *Powers of Horror: An Essay on Abjection* (1982), Kristeva explains how the corpse bears upon the formation and the disruption of the viewer's subjectivity. By appropriating the (post-)structuralist principle of binary opposition, Kristeva maintains that the condition that guarantees the existence of the self is the presence of the other. In the beginning of human life, both individually and collectively, the notion of the "I" or the "self" simply does not exist. Instead what we have is a mess of un-nameable desires and instincts. The part that we embrace is called the self, whereas the part that we reject is called the other. The other includes everything that we fear, dislike, loathe, and everything we dream and fantasize about but dare not articulate. The latter includes the desire to hurt, destroy, and behave in ways that are socially intolerable. Kristeva calls the other "the abject." In contrast to Jacques Lacan's idea of "*objet petit a*" (or the object of desire), the abject is situated at a place before we enter the symbolic order. It is located at a place before we enter the narcissistic mirror stage. The abject is therefore associated with our archaic memory—the primitive effort to separate ourselves from the animal. It is also related to the moment when we (as babies) are separated from our mother, when we begin to claim that this is "me" and "the (m)other." In the chapter "Approaching Abjection," Kristeva explains the un-namable and meaningless quality of the abject:

[The abject is a] twisted braid of affects and thoughts . . . [that] does not have, properly speaking, a definable *object*. The abject is not an ob-ject facing me, which I name or imagine. Nor is it an ob-jest, an otherness ceaselessly fleeing in a systematic quest of desire. What is abject is not my correlative, which, providing me with someone or something or something else as support, would allow me to be more or less detached and autonomous. The abject has only one quality of the object—that of being opposed to *I*.[20]

The abject is the ultimate horror of human experience because it is the site where meaning collapses. It is also the locus where human beings are confronted with something one cannot name. Kristeva equates the abject with different kinds of boundaries and ambiguous entities, including food, filth, waste, or dung—the kinds of items that are found on indistinct and unclear borderlines between the self and the other. According to Kristeva, the horror of the abject is "not [the] lack of cleanliness or health that causes abjection but what disturbs identity, system, order[,] [and] what does not respect borders, positions, rules."[21] The abject, a product excluded in the process of constituting the subject, is not external to life but is part of life, or more precisely, is the essence of life. The abject is internal to the subject formation.

The transformation of the abject into the object is another crucial step for our understanding of the formation of the subject in relation to the object. While the abject consists of everything we do not want to be associated with, it does not simply disappear when it is rejected. Instead it is transformed by the subject into what Kristeva calls the "signifiable object." Compared with the abject, the signifiable object is a different kind of other as it is the condition for the stable formation of the self. Kristeva appropriates the idea that the meaning of an item has to be constructed through its structural difference from another item. "I expel *myself*, I spit *myself*, I abject *myself* within the same motion through which 'I' claim to establish *myself*. . . . It is thus that *they* see that 'I' am in the process of becoming an other at the expense of my own death. During that course in which 'I' become, I give birth to myself amid the violence of sobs, of vomit."[22]

In Kristeva's analysis, the object is originally located within the subject. The object comes into being by means of the self-loathing or self-rejection of the subject. The object has always already been part of the subject, but it is only in retrospect that we can say that is the case. In fact, one cannot even say that the process begins with the rejection of the abject from within the boundary of the subject because the existence of the subject does not precede the process but rather emerges as the product at the end of the process. It is only in retrospect when one views the process from the perspective of the subject (which has already come into existence) that one can observe that the process starts with the rejection of the abject from within the boundary of the subject. At the beginning of the process, nothing exists except an un-namable mess of the abject.

After the subject has expelled part of itself, it does not leave the rejected part as it is. Instead, through a conscious process of naming (by means of language and representation), the subject transforms the rejected part as the signifiable object in relation to the subject, so that the individual comes to establish his or her identity as the subject. This is a process not of being but of becoming a subject. According to Kristeva, the subject's rejection of the abject—or, more accurately, the signifiable object—contributes to the formation of the subjectivity of the self. The process affirms that the subject is alive: "There, I am at the border of my condition as a living being. My body extricates itself, as being alive, from that border. Such wastes drop so that I might live, until, from loss to loss, nothing remains in me and my entire body falls beyond the limit—*cadere*, cadaver."[23] The abject is a border or boundary that marks the threshold between the subject and the object and consequently guarantees and sustains the identity of the self.

I am interested in using Kristeva's concept of the abject to work with the representation of rubbish and the scavengers in Wang's *Beijing Besieged by Waste*. The latter can be considered a documentary of abjection. Kristeva explains that the self-rejection of the abject constitutes the subject and the abject. Through the process of naming, the abject is turned into the signifiable object, thereby taming and domesticating its horror. In fact, a similar process is at work in the documentary. The consumer produces the rubbish. However, the rubbish as the abject is rendered safe through visual representation (or what Kristeva calls naming). The documentary form functions as a screen to mediate the viewer's relationship to the rubbish, which appears uncanny and horrifying.

In her imagination, Kristeva regards the corpse as the ultimate abject of human experience. She asserts: "The corpse . . . is the utmost of abjection. It is death infecting life."[24] The corpse is the site where the Real may erupt into our lives. Similar to the Kantian sublime that has the potentiality to shatter the subject, the corpse conjures up intense fear—the fear of castration, for example—and jouissance. For Kristeva, it is the most intense form of waste: "If dung signifies the other side of the border, the place where I am not and which permits me to be, the corpse, the most sickening of wastes, is a border that has encroached upon everything. It is no longer I who expel, 'I' is expelled. The border has become an object. How can I be without border?"[25] According to Kristeva, the corpse is horrifying to the person who looks at it because the dead body breaks down the stable categories of life and death.[26]

Deviating from Kristeva's idea that the corpse is the ultimate horror of human life, I suggest that rubbish and the scavengers can be regarded as the abject in Wang's documentary. The abjected rubbish is fear-provoking because it disturbs our sense of the system and the border. In particular, rubbish breaks down our established idea of the inside and the outside. In theory, rubbish should be located outside our lives. It should be condensed in the management centers and displaced to the dumps and landfills. However, similar to our dreams, the slip of the tongue, and literature, which Freud regards as ways in which our repressed desire returns, the documentary betrays the insistent force of the repressed. *Beijing Besieged by Waste* reminds us that the repressed rubbish turns out to be inside our lives. The rubbish is not too far away from us. In addition, the rubbish as a transformed object has already returned. The rubbish exists in the form of a circle, a ring (the seventh ring of Beijing), a wall (the new Great Wall of China), and a border between the urban and rural areas. It is also rapidly accumulating. The transformed rubbish can be found in the marriage photo we take, the food we eat, and the water we drink. The rubbish may also appear on the shelves of the supermarket where we do our grocery shopping. In short, the repressed rubbish has already returned in disguised forms. Rather than coming back to us in the future, what is really frightening is that it has already returned in unanticipated forms. Disturbingly, Beijing—and, by extension, the city in which we live—is already a rubbish dump. Disturbingly, we are already surrounded by rubbish. Disturbingly, we are already scavengers.

This brings us to the idea of the scavenger as an abject of Chinese consumer culture. The documentary portrays the scavengers in a somewhat horrifying way. When they are first introduced, the atmosphere is somewhat gothic-like: the air is foggy, steamy, misty, and vaporous. The scavengers appear as mysterious and dangerous figures. Because they wear hoods and caps and have their mouths covered, we cannot see their faces. Because they wear baggy clothes, we cannot see their bodies. It is not possible to tell whether they are men or women. Some of them also work as herdsmen. The sheep that they care for eat rubbish. Some scavengers eat rubbish too. To confirm their humanity (or the lack of it), we look at the self-representation of the female scavengers in this documentary.

Female scavengers are featured twice in *Beijing Besieged by Waste*. In the first instance, one of them asks the documentarian not to film her while she is busy sorting out rubbish. She does not want people to know that she works in the dumps.

WOMAN 1: The trash does not look good on the camera. Film more of Ms. Liu!

WOMAN 2: We old ladies collecting trash do not look good on the camera.

WOMAN 1: Don't film us. We don't look good. We'll be ashamed if people from our village see us on TV.

WOMAN 2: We don't tell our families that our job in Beijing is to collect trash. People will laugh at us if they know we work in the rubbish dump.

WOMAN 3: Even our parents do not know that we collect trash for a living. We tell them we work in Beijing. None of us tell people we collect trash in the dump. We told them we have a job, not this!

WOMAN 4: To pick garbage. To pick broken stuff.

These scavengers are not proud of their job. They think that working with rubbish makes them less respectable. The job of sorting out garbage has rendered them less human. In the second instance, a female scavenger boldly presents herself in front of the camera and tells us her life as a scavenger.

We built houses with the bricks from the dump. It's been over ten years. I've spent over ten years in this house. The clothes they [i.e., the other female scavengers] wear, nine out of ten were found in the dump. I am not kidding you. This silk scarf I am wearing was also found in the dump. I thought it looked nice, so I washed it and put it on. As for them, all of their clothes were from the dump. I am not afraid if you laugh at us. All we wear was found in the dump, including the underwear. Some rich people from high-end residential areas like throwing things out. Sometimes we find brand new clothes, one pack after another. . . . Most of what we eat is from the trash. That's true, especially my elder sister. If she finds something not so bad, like sprouting potatoes, she takes it home, removes the bad part, and eats the good part. People in Chaoyang and Tongzhou districts look down on us because we are not from Beijing. They look down on us. They don't even want to talk to [us]. They say [we] are filthy. They won't even eat what you cook. They don't think it's clean.

This scene raises questions about the humanity of the scavengers. On the one hand, they are human beings and are like us. But on the other hand, they are unlike us in that they live in rubbish-houses, wear rubbish-clothes, and eat rubbish-food. Because of their living and working conditions, they have been deprived of their humanity. To the viewer, they simultaneously appear human and inhuman. It is possible to say that these scavengers are human-but-not-quite, but quite-alike. They are alterity. (However, what complicates the issue is that one of the scavengers turns back to the camera to confidently reassert her humanity: "I am not afraid if you laugh at us." This is the moment when we realize that she is more human and less passive than we think she is.)

The fact that the humanity of the scavenger cannot be easily identified may cause distress, even fear, in the viewer. What adds to the horror is that we are confronted with the idea that if we keep consuming and producing rubbish, our society will become dumps. To the documentary viewer, the ultimate horror is that we will be besieged by rubbish and become scavengers ourselves. We will have to live in rubbish-houses, wear rubbish-clothes, and eat rubbish-food. In a more frightening way, we have already been surrounded by rubbish and become scavengers.

Rubbish: The Utopian Impulse

Fredric Jameson's concept of the utopian impulse can be applied to the portrayal of rubbish and the scavengers in Wang's *Beijing Besieged by Waste*.[27] In his influential essay "Reification and Utopia in Mass Culture" (1979), Jameson asks students of cultural studies to look at mass cultural productions more dialectically. Critiquing the reified ways in which commercialized mass and popular culture (e.g., the culture industry) have been analyzed, he proposes that ideology and utopian impulse coexist in the form of mass culture. Theorizing in relation to the pulse of history, he suggests that "the works of mass culture cannot be ideological without at one and the same time being implicitly or explicitly Utopian as well: they cannot manipulate unless they offer some genuine shred of content as a fantasy bribe to the public about to be so manipulated."[28] In addition, "the works of mass culture, even if their function lies in the legitimation of the existing order . . . cannot do their job without deflecting in the latter's service the deepest and most fundamental hopes and fantasies of the collectivity."[29] This poses a difficult challenge for the cultural critic: the critique of ideology and the discovery of utopian impulse have to be simultaneously pursued. If one practices ideological analysis of mass culture without attending to the utopian components, the criticism may devolve into an easy denunciation of the ruling class's manipulation of the working class through cultural hegemony. Conversely, if one explores utopian desire and fantasy while overlooking ideological critique, the analysis may become myth criticism, devoid of the determinations of historical situations.

In the conclusion of *The Political Unconscious* (1981), Jameson provides a similar theoretical assertion. Rather than simply equating ideology with false consciousness, class bias, ideological programming, and the structural limits of the values and attitudes of particular social classes in a simplistic and mechanical way, he suggests that cultural critics can also find their inspirations from the positive hermeneutic in the Marxist genealogy. Such a genealogy includes "Ernst Bloch's idea of hope or of the Utopian impulse," "Mikhail Bakhtin's notion of the dialogical as a rupture of the one-dimensional text of bourgeois narrative, as a carnivalesque dispersal of the hegemonic order of a dominant culture," and "the Frankfurt School's conception of strong memory of that *promesse de bonheur* most immediately inscribed in the aesthetic text."[30] Jameson proposes a completely new way to interpret the politics of mass culture. He insists that a negative hermeneutic must be exercised simultaneously with a positive hermeneutic, and that a Marxist practice of ideological analysis can simultaneously be a decipherment of the repressed utopian impulse.[31] Taking up Jameson's call, I investigate the dialectic of ideology and utopian desire in the figuration of rubbish and the scavengers in Wang's documentary. While it is convincing to argue for the ideology of rubbish as a product of consumption, how is it permeated with an unconscious desire called utopia? If rubbish is reactionary, how can it be revolutionary?

There are several ways to detect the utopian impulse in rubbish. First, rubbish is relational. Rubbish is produced by modern consumer culture as much as the proletariat is produced by the capitalistic mode of production. Such a relation—the relation between rubbish and the consumer, and the relation between the proletariat and the bourgeoisie—is unidirectional. Similar to the distinction that Georg Lukács makes with respect to the standpoints of the proletariat and the bourgeoisie in *History and Class Consciousness*, the standpoints of rubbish and the consumer are decidedly different. When we adopt the consumer's perspective, we can only see ourselves as the consumer. However, if we adopt the garbage's viewpoint, then we can observe the world from the perspective of garbage and from the perspective of consumer; we can also see the distance between us (rubbish) and them (the consumer). If we occupy the standpoint of rubbish, we will have the epistemic privilege to see the world differently.

Similar to the proletariat and the multitude, rubbish is inherently collective. Rubbish is rarely alone; it tends to congregate. Similar to a magnet, rubbish likes to be with other rubbish; it feels safe in a pile or heap.[32] In addition, rubbish is not countable. It is not possible to speak of one rubbish, two rubbishes, three rubbishes, and so on. One can only say a pile of rubbish or a heap of rubbish. Rubbish rejects bourgeois individualism and embraces proletarian collectivity. Moreover, the rubbish collective exhibits signs of equality and democracy. For example, it is absurd to say that an obsolete plastic bag is more rubbish than a pile of industrial waste. It is equally strange to say that an old-fashioned iPod is less rubbish than leftovers from last night's dinner. Instead, they are equally rubbish. In other words, rejecting hierarchy and embracing reciprocity, rubbish embodies an equalizing, democratic, and utopian impulse. Moving further, rubbish exemplifies the spirit of the proletarian multitude in the sense that rubbish allows for the expression of sameness and difference, and singularity and multiplicity, at the same time. For example, we can still recognize the identity of a rotten apple within a pile of rubbish. The fact that the rotten apple has been rendered rubbish (sameness) does not in itself mean that the identity of the rotten apple is lost. On the contrary, its identity as a rotten apple (difference) is maintained and preserved when it is embedded in the pile of rubbish. The rotten apple will not necessarily lose its individual identity when it becomes a member of the larger collective. The rubbish collective is not one but many.

In addition to rubbish, the scavenger is also a productive site to think about the utopian impulse. The previous section on Kristeva's theory argues that rubbish and the scavengers in Wang's *Beijing Besieged by Waste* can be considered as the abject. Kristeva asserts that there is no essence to the abject or abjection. The latter is relational and dependent on the subject's perspective. I explain this by making reference to three entities—the human being, the plant, and cow dung. From the human being's perspective, the cow dung is abject waste. However, from the plant's perspective, the cow dung is not abject waste but nutritious food. The abjectness of the cow dung is not absolute but relative. It is dependent on what the subject is. To relate the abjectness of the cow dung to rubbish and the scavenger, we can imagine that the consumer is the human being, the scavenger is the plant, and rubbish is the cow dung. From the consumer's perspective, rubbish is the abject. It is the object of abjection. However, from the scavenger's perspective, rubbish is not the abject; it is not the object of abjection; instead, it can be potentially useful. This analogy allows us to see that the scavenger's relationship with rubbish is different from the consumer's relationship with rubbish.

To be sure, the scavenger consumes. However, in the rubbish dumps, how the scavenger consumes is not the same as how the consumer consumes. According to the scavenger, "some rich people from the high-end residential areas like throwing things out. Sometimes we find brand new clothes, one pack after another." The attitude that the consumer adopts is one of disposability and waste. In contrast, the scavenger reuses the materials that they find in the dumps. The scavenger says: "We built houses with the bricks from the dump." "The clothes we wear were found in the dump." "Most of what we eat is from the trash." (The scavenger uses the word "we"—it is the gendered collective of the "we"—but not the "I" of the individualistic consumer.) The attitude that the scavengers adopt to consumption is one of thrift and frugality. The scavengers make a living by sorting out materials in the dumps. While some scavengers pick up leftovers from the dumps and salvage them, other scavengers recycle useless materials from the scrap yards, rework them, and turn them into something useful. By reusing, recycling, reducing, repairing, and repurposing rubbish, the scavengers reverse and redirect the linearity of the progress narrative of consumption. Adopting the commodity-as-rubbish, the scavenger transforms what is (perceived to be) useless into something useful, and in this process, reverses consumption-time. The scavenger also disrespects exchange-value and tries to create a new kind of use-value. In addition, as opposed to the consumer who pays to buy the commodity that will eventually become rubbish, the scavenger can acquire the commodities in the rubbish dumps for free. In other words, there is a communizing impulse in how the scavenger works with the rubbish commodities. While trying not to idealize or romanticize their poverty, the scavenger embodies faint traces of the utopian impulse. This figure allegorizes our unconscious desire for a radical break from the current economic, political, and social system in which we live. The scavenger also gestures toward a new kind of communizing subjectivity that is already happening in the global capitalistic consumer society.

CONCLUSION: RUBBISH TIME

Indeed, what will happen if we place Wang's documentary alongside the official representations, such as Zhao Huayong (趙化勇) and colleagues' TV documentaries *The Rise of Great Nations* (*Daguo jueqi* 大國崛起) (2006) and *The Road to Revival* (*Fuxing zhilu* 復興之路) (2007), that glorify the rise of China on the global stage in the early twenty-first century? What will happen if we juxtapose the representation of rubbish, the polluted environment, the scarred landscape, the exploited labor, and the disposable scavengers in *Beijing Besieged by Waste* with the unprecedented economic transformations of neoliberal China? How do rubbish and the scavenger enable us to think about contemporary China's consumer culture differently? Moreover, should the rubbish piling up not slow down, unsettle, intervene, and disrupt the speed of capitalistic development in China now?

Indeed, the representation of rubbish and time—or, one may say "rubbish time"—in Wang's documentary challenges the monolithic temporality, or what Benjamin calls the "homogeneous and empty time," of the Chinese nation-state, the middle class, and the ideology of consumer culture. To be sure, rubbish time in this documentary is not singular but multiple. It is similar to Benjamin's idea of constellation in *The Arcades Project*. If a constellation is made up of a number of stars both near and afar, it is only from the perspective of the now that these stars take on a particular shape and configuration. This is also true for the rubbish in *Beijing Besieged by Waste*. Every component of the rubbish heap brings its own temporality— history, memory, and story—to the dump. In addition, the rate of each item's decay and decomposition is different. Together, they form a rubbish constellation. Indeed, the multiplicity of temporalities embodied in this rubbish constellation disturbs and unsettles the monolithic and hegemonic progress narrative; this constellated image insists that there are different ways to look at China's rise on the global stage. In short, Wang's documentary not only reveals the problem of waste in neoliberal China but also offers a substantial critique of the evolutionary idea of history and progress that the party-state and the global and national capitals deploy to justify their political ideologies and economic interests.

NOTES

INTRODUCTION

1. Selected books include Jie Chen, *A Middle Class Without Democracy: Economic Growth and the Prospects for Democratization in China* (New York: Oxford University Press, 2013); Minglu Chen and David S. G. Goodman, eds., *Middle Class China: Identity and Behavior* (Cheltenham, U.K.: Edward Elgar, 2013); David S. G. Goodman, ed., *The New Rich in China: Future Rules, Present Live* (New York: Routledge, 2008); Hsin-Huang Michael Hsiao, ed., *Chinese Middle Classes: Taiwan, Hong Kong, Macao and China* (New York: Routledge, 2013); Cheng Li, ed., *China's Emerging Middle Class: Beyond Economic Transformation* (Washington, D.C.: Brookings Institution Press, 2010); Ying Miao, *Being Middle Class in China: Identity, Attitudes and Behavior* (Abingdon, Oxon: Routledge, 2017); Hai Ren, *The Middle Class in Neoliberal China: Governing Risk, Life-Building, and Themed Spaces* (New York: Routledge, 2012); Jean-Louis Rocca, *The Making of the Chinese Middle Class: Small Comfort and Great Expectations* (New York: Palgrave Macmillan, 2016); Eileen Yuk-Ha Tsang, *The New Middle Class in China: Consumption, Politics and the Market Economy* (New York: Palgrave Macmillan, 2014); and Jun Zhang, *Driving Toward Modernity: Cars and the Lives of the Middle Class in Contemporary China* (Ithaca, N.Y.: Cornell University Press, 2019).

2. Adding to Zhou's observation, I think the co-emergence of the old and new middle classes is a result of compressed and accelerated postmodernity. However, this phenomenon is not distinctively Chinese. The materialization of the old and new middle classes at more or less the same time can also be observed in the economies of Asia's "four little dragons"—Hong Kong, Taiwan, Singapore, and South Korea—in the 1970s and 1980s. This is a condition of global capitalism and postmodernity in East Asia.

3. See Zhou Xiaohong (周曉虹), "Introduction: History and Current Situation of the Chinese Middle Class" (*Daoyan: zhongguo zhongchan jieceng de lishi he xianzhuang* 導言:中國中產階層的歷史和現狀), in *Survey of the Chinese Middle Classes* (*Zhongguo zhongchan jieji diaocha* 中國中產階級調查), ed. Zhou Xiaohong (周曉虹) (Beijing 北京: Shehui kexue wenxian chubanshe 社會科學文獻出版社, 2005).

4. This view is confirmed by anthropologist Ann Anagnost, who suggests that the reports on social stratification can have anticipatory functions and effects. She writes: "What is most striking about the literature on social stratification is its anticipatory nature, as if mapping out the emerging categories of social difference could produce their emergence in fact." She continues:

> This discourse simultaneously incites a certain insecurity on the part of urban-educated subjects about where they are to locate themselves, given the tremendous fluidity in mobility structures and the shrinking social safety net, while also providing a grid in which these subjects may locate themselves and their aspirations. It should come as no surprise, then, to discover that what presents itself as an objective scientific social analysis often spills over into the realm of marketing, where the incitement of anxiety is transformed into desire for the commodity as a sign of middle-classness. The acquisition of the particular commodity becomes a way of 'fixing' one's location in the grid of newly possible social positions.

Ann Anagnost, "From 'Class' to 'Social Strata': Grasping the Social Totality in Reform-era China," *Third World Quarterly* 29, no. 3 (2008): 508.

5. Mao Tse-tung, "Analysis of the Classes in Chinese Society," in *Selected Works of Mao Tse-tung*, March 1926, Marxists Internet Archive, https://www.marxists.org/reference/archive/mao/selected-works/volume-1/mswv1_1.htm.

6. Mao divides the petty bourgeoisie into three groups: the right wing, the middle wing, and the left wing. He also points out the difference in their attitudes toward the Chinese revolution. Mao writes: "In normal times, these three sections of the petty bourgeoisie differ in their attitude to the revolution [i.e., the left-wing section will support the revolution whereas the right-wing section will oppose it]. But in times of war, that is, when the tide of the revolution runs high and the dawn of victory is in sight [the three sections of petty bourgeoisie] will have to go along with the revolution." See Mao Tse-tung, "Analysis of the Classes in Chinese Society."

7. This can be seen in one particular scene in Feng Xiaogang's (馮小剛) film *Youth* (*Fanghua* 芳華) (Hong Kong 香港: Yugao yule youxian gongsi 域高娛樂有限公司, 2018).

8. According to contemporary Chinese film director Jia Zhangke (賈樟柯), Taiwanese cinema, such as Hou Hsiao-Hsien's (Hou Xiaoxian 侯孝賢) film *Boys from Fengkuei* (*Fenggui laide ren* 風櫃來的人) (1983) had a huge impact on mainland Chinese film viewers like him. In contrast to the Cultural Revolution model works, which emphasize collective identification, these foreign films stress individual experience. See Jia Zhangke (賈樟柯), *Cinema, Thinking, and Solutions* (*Dianying xiangfa he banfe* 電影,想法和辦法) (Beijing 北京: Zhongguo renmin daxue chubanshe 中國人民大學出版社, 2000s).

9. Dai Jinhua, "Invisible Writing: The Politics of Mass Culture in the 1990s," in *Cinema and Desire: Feminist Marxism and Cultural Politics in the Work of Dai Jinhua*, ed. Jing Wang and Tani Barlow (London: Verso, 2002), 222.

10. Cultural critic Shaohua Guo shares Dai's view. She writes: "urban professionals' obsession with middle class lifestyles precedes the recent rise of the middle class . . . the cultural realm from the mid-1990s onward has witnessed an inundation of fashion magazines, leisure newspaper and bestsellers aiming at educating urban readers on how to quality as a member of the middle class." See Shaohua Guo, "Acting Through the Camera Lens: The Global Imaginary and Middle Class Aspirations in Chinese Urban Cinema," *Journal of Contemporary China* 26, no. 104 (2017): 312.

11. Chinese fashion magazine *Fashion* (时尚) was founded in 1993. In 1997 the female edition called *Yiren* (伊人) and the male edition called *Xiansheng* (先生) were published. In 1998 the female edition of *Fashion* collaborated with American female fashion magazine *Cosmopolitan*; and in 1999 the male edition of *Fashion* collaborated with American male fashion magazine *Esquire*. This Chinese fashion magazine became both local and global.

12. Mei Yuanmei (梅園棐), "An Anonymous Leader: The Cultural Meaning of *Fashion* Magazine" (*Niming de yindaozhe: shishang zazhi de wenhua yiwei* 匿名的引导者—《时尚》杂志的文化意味), in *Writing Cultural Hero: Cultural Studies at the Turn of the Century* (*Shuxie wenhua yingxiong: shiji zhijiao de wenhua yanjiu* 書寫文化英雄: 世紀之交的文化研究), ed. Dai Jinhua (戴錦華) (Nanjing 南京: Jiangsu ren min chu ban she 江蘇人民出版社, 2000), 264 (my translation).

13. Mei, "An Anonymous Leader," 265.

14. In fact, this can also be observed in Chinese middle-class magazines, such as *Sanlian Life Weekly* (*Sanlian shenghuo zhoukan* 三聯生活週刊). In the early and mid-2000s, this magazine featured articles about the Chinese middle class. Selected topics include "The Middle Class and Automobile" (*zhongchan jieji yu qiche* 中產階級與汽車) (2002); "Bobos [Bourgeois Bohemians] and the 'New Cultural Movement'" (*bobozu yu xinwenhua yundong* 波波族與'新文化運動') (2003); "60,000 [yuan]: The Threshold of 'Middle Class?'" (*liuwan zhongchan de menkan* 六萬:「中產」的門檻) (2005); and "The Anxiety and Desire of the Middle Class" (*zhongchanzhe de jialü yu kewang* 中產者的焦慮與渴望) (2007).

15. Wang Dan, Li Minqi, and Wang Chaohua, "A Dialogue on the Future of China," in *One China, Many Paths*, ed. Wang Chaohua (New York: Verso, 2003), 325–27.

16. Wang, Li, and Wang, "A Dialogue on the Future of China," 325–26.

17. Wang, Li, and Wang, "A Dialogue on the Future of China," 326.

18. Wang, Li, and Wang, "A Dialogue on the Future of China," 326.

19. Wang, Li, and Wang, "A Dialogue on the Future of China," 326–27.

20. Wang, Li, and Wang, "A Dialogue on the Future of China," 327.

21. Wang, Li, and Wang, "A Dialogue on the Future of China," 327.

22. Xie Jin's (謝晉) film *Hibiscus Town* (*Furongzhen* 芙蓉鎮) (1986), an adaptation of Gu Hua's (古華) novel with the same title, also features the small business owner. In this film, the couple sells tofu on the street and provides very good service to the local customers.

23. For the connection between 1989 (the Tiananmen Square movement) and 1992 (the beginning of China's neoliberalism), see Wang Hui, "The 1989 Social Movement and

the Historical Roots of China's Neoliberalism," trans. Theodore Huters, in Wang Hui, *China's New Order: Society, Politics, and Economy in Transition*, ed. Theodore Huters (Cambridge, Mass.: Harvard University Press, 2003).

24. Raymond Lotta, "China's Rise in the World Economy," *Economic and Political Weekly* 44, no. 8 (2009): 33.

25. Li Tuo (李陀), "The New Petty Bourgeoisie and the Transfer of Cultural Hegemony" (*Xin xiaozi he wenhua lingdaoquan de zhuanyi* "新小資"和文化領導權的轉移), *Changjiang Literature and Art* (*Changjiang Wenyi* 長江文藝) 12 (2013): 76–89.

26. Li Tuo, preface to *Bo dong* (波動) by Bei Dao (北島) (Beijing 北京: San lian shu dian 三聯書店, 2010).

27. Li Tuo, 84 (my translation).

28. Li Tuo, 86 (my translation).

29. Li Tuo, 86 (my translation).

30. Li Tuo, 87 (my translation).

31. Mao Jian (毛尖), "Pale: Speaking from a Petty-Bourgeois Adjective" (*Cangbai: congyige xiaozide xinrongci tanqi* 蒼白:從一個小資的形容詞談起), *Southern Literary Forum* (*Nanfang Wentan* 南方文壇) 1 (2013): 36.

32. See Paul Fussell, *Class: A Guide through the American Status System* (New York: Summit Books, 1983). For the translation of this book from English to Chinese, see Baoluo Fusai'er (Paul Fussell 保羅 福塞爾), *Taste: Social Status and Lifestyle* (*Gediao: shehui dengji yu shenghuo pinwei* 格調: 社會等級與生活品味) (Beijing 北京: Zhonghuo shehui kexue chubanshe 中國社會科學出版社, 1998). It is interesting to note that the English title is *Class* whereas the Chinese title is *Taste*.

33. Walter Benjamin, "The Work of Art in the Age of Its Technological Reproducibility" (1937), in *Walter Benjamin: Selected Writings*, ed. Marcus Bullock and Michael W. Jennings (Cambridge, Mass.: Belknap Press, 1996–2003), 129n24.

34. Roland Barthes, *Mythologies* (New York: Hill and Wang, 1972), 153.

35. According to my interpretation of Deng Xiaoping, the PRC in the age of economic reforms and opening up is also a "neither/nor" political-economic formation: neither socialism nor capitalism, but "socialism with Chinese characteristics." Marxist geographer David Harvey calls it "neo-liberalism with Chinese characteristics." See David Harvey, *A History of Neoliberalism* (New York: Oxford University Press, 2005), 120–51.

36. Mao wrote the poem "To the Female Soldiers" (*Wei nüminbing tizhao* 為女民兵題照) in 1961. The poem is:

颯爽英姿五尺槍，　Five-foot rifles, flashing bravely,
曙光初照演兵場。　On the training ground, at the break of the day,
中華兒女多奇志，　How remarkable the spirit of Chinese women,
不愛紅裝愛武裝。　They love the martial dress, not the red dress.

For this English translation, see Antonia Finnane, *Changing Clothes in China: Fashion, History, Nation* (New York: Columbia University Press, 2008), 231.

37. Fredric Jameson, "Reification and Utopia in Mass Culture." *Social Text*, no. 1 (1979): 130–48.

38. In fact, the way I present my arguments is consistent with the three levels of interpretation proposed by Jameson. According to Jameson, the first level is political

history. When he uses the word "history," he means the chronicle-like sequence of happenings and punctual events in time. The second level is the social, and the smallest unit of class langue is ideologeme. The third level is the mode of production. Jameson produces the concept of the ideology of form to study the mode of production. He considers form as sediment content, carrying with it latent ideological message which is not the same as the manifest message. Jameson writes: "[Formal] specification and description can, in a given . . . text, be transformed into the detection of a host of distinct [formal] messages—some of them objectified survivals from older modes of cultural production, some anticipatory, but all together projecting a formal conjuncture through which the 'conjuncture' of coexisting modes of production at a given historical moment can be detected and allegorically articulated." Fredric Jameson, *The Political Unconscious: Narrative as a Socially Symbolic Act* (Ithaca, N.Y.: Cornell University Press, 1981), 99.

1. DIRTY FASHION

1. Jia Zhangke (賈樟柯), *Jia Thinks* (*Jia Xiang 1996–2008: Jia Zhangke dianying shouji* 賈想 1996–2008: 賈樟柯電影手記) (Beijing 北京: Beijing daxue chubanshe 北京大學 出版社, 2009), 233.
2. For fashion and class distinction, see Georg Simmel, "Fashion," *International Quarterly* 10 (1904): 130–55; and Thorstein Veblen, *The Theory of the Leisure Class* (1898; repr., New York: Oxford University Press, 2007). For the cultural theories of fashion, see Walter Benjamin, "Fashion," in *The Arcades Project* (Cambridge, Mass.: Belknap Press, 1999), 62–81. For secondary sources on Benjamin's works, see Susan Buck-Morss, *The Dialectics of Seeing: Walter Benjamin and The Arcades Project* (Cambridge, Mass.: MIT Press, 1989). See also Roland Barthes's works on fashion and semiotics, including *The Fashion System* (New York: Hill and Wang, 1983) and *The Language of Fashion*, ed. Andy Stafford and Michael Carter (New York: Berg, 2006).
3. For the website, see Ma Ke, "*Wuyong* [*Useless*]," Ma Ke, accessed May 15, 2013, http://www.wuyonguseless.com/. For the recording of Ma's *Useless* art exhibit at London's Victoria and Albert (V&A) Museum in May 2008, see Victoria and Albert Museum, "Fashion in Motion: Ma Ke Wuyong," accessed March 12, 2021, https://www.vam.ac.uk/articles/fashion-in-motion-ma-ke.
4. Jia, *Jia Thinks*, 229.
5. For the website, see Ma Ke, "Liwai [Exception]," accessed May 15, 2013, http://www.mixmind.com.cn/.
6. According to Ma, Exception is defined by its exceptionality. However, she does not explain what is distinctively exceptional about her fashion design. Is it the content or the form that is exceptional? In addition, she has not explained how it is exceptional to the norm. One should be cautious regarding how exceptional Exception can be.
7. The Paris Fashion Week includes three categories: men's wear, haute couture, and ready-to-wear. Ma presented *Useless* in the ready-to-wear section. However, it can be more convincing to regard *Useless* as haute couture. An *Edelweiss* journalist once asked Ma why she did not choose to present *Useless* in the couture section. In her reply, Ma emphasized that *Useless* is neither couture nor ready-to-wear. The existing

fashion categories, she insisted, cannot adequately capture the uniqueness of her *Useless* design. According to Ma:

> It is very difficult to define *Wuyong* (*Useless*). It can be everything or nothing. On the one hand, it is about anything related to every individual's life. Thus, it finds wide application in ready-to-wear. On the other hand, its uniqueness and the fact that its design cannot be copied make it more like couture. Anyway, it is what it is. It is not anything that already exists. So, it doesn't matter whether it was shown as haute couture or ready-to-wear. (*Edelweiss* May 2007, http://www.wuyong.org/Uploads/ArtFile/20140910 /20140910093240_3394.pdf; my translation)

Although *Useless* can move between couture and ready-to-wear, Exception is, strictly speaking, ready-to-wear. It is not couture. Fashion is situated between commodity and art, and between mass/popular culture and high culture.

8. Ma Ke, "*Wuyong* [*Useless*]."
9. Ma Ke, "*Wuyong* [*Useless*]."
10. Ma Ke, "*Wuyong* [*Useless*]."
11. Ma Ke, "*Wuyong* [*Useless*]."
12. Ma Ke, "*Wuyong* [*Useless*]."
13. In fact, Ma was not the first Chinese fashion designer to present in the Paris Fashion Week. Frankie Xie (Xie Feng 謝鋒) had presented Jefen (吉芬) in the 2006 Paris Fashion Week. To symbolize China's opening up to the fashion world, Xie adopted the sign of "Chinese door" in his fashion collection.
14. For contemporary designs from Shenzhen, Shanghai, and Beijing, see Zhang Hongxing and Lauren Parker, eds. *China Design Now* (London: V&A Pub., 2008). This book catalogs the *China Design Now* exhibition at London's Victoria and Albert (V&A) Museum in March–July 2007.
15. In fact, *Useless/The Earth* was the first part, and probably the most famous part, of Ma's *Useless* series. In July 2008 Ma was invited to present a variation of the same theme *Useless/Frugality* (*Wuyong/Qing Ping* 無用/清貧) at the Jardin du Palais-Royal in Paris, France. Her fashion was similarly regarded as "antifashion" by the Western media. This fashion show was presented in a public outdoor setting. It showcased modern dances, martial artists, and tai chi practitioners. Their dance performances were choreographed by Shen Wei (沈偉).
16. One should question the gendered implication of Ma's narrative, which can be politically conservative. In her first example, it is the woman who stays at home and does the stitching and knitting, and it is the man who travels and enjoys the product of woman's manual labor. In her second example, it is the man who has the privilege to participate in the construction of stories. In Ma's narrative, women are not given any opportunities to create histories or memories.
17. Ma does not specify whether she is referring to capitalistic or socialist modernity. There were also machines in socialism as well.
18. Interestingly, Ma Ke's (馬可) name sounds like Marx or, in Chinese, Ma Ke Si (馬克思).
19. In fact, a handloom can also be a machine.
20. Ma takes pain to emphasize that *Useless* is not a mass-produced commodity. However, to what extent is her claim legitimate? When Ma says that *Useless* is not a

commodity, what she means is that *Useless* is not mass produced. However, her understanding of the commodity is not the same as Marx's theorization of the commodity. Marx emphasizes the qualitative, rather than the quantitative, dimension of commodification. The fact that *Useless* is not mass produced does not in itself mean that it is not a commodity. Because *Useless* is historically embedded in the context of global capitalism, its handmade dimension is also underwritten by the logic of commodification. In other words, *Useless* is the opposite of what Ma claims it is: *Useless*, a commodity that claims itself not a commodity, is, in fact, a handmade commodity.

21. Is Ma's design genuinely antifashion? It seems that her work is less antifashion than it is a different type of fashion. Ma's antifashion is, at most, alter-fashion.

22. See Li Yang's (李陽) film *Blind Shaft* (*Mang Jing* 盲井) (Kowloon: 星寶集團有限公司 Xingbao jituan youxian gongsi, 2003), which examines the lives of coal miners in the context of neoliberal China.

23. Rather than seeing these individuals' behaviors as an expression of what Marx calls "commodity fetishism" (the fact that these individuals focus on consumption and endow meanings onto their commodities does not necessarily mean that they cannot see how consumption is related to production), it may be more useful to ask how Arjun Appadurai's theory of "the social life of things" (or commodities) can help one evaluate Ma's idea. Arjun Appadurai, ed., *The Social Life of Things: Commodities in Cultural Perspective* (New York: Cambridge University Press, 1986). For "commodity fetishism," see Karl Marx, *Capital: A Critique of Political Economy*, 3 vols. (New York: Penguin, 1990–1991). See also David Harvey, *A Companion to Marx's Capital* (New York: Verso, 2010).

24. In fact, this is also true for the fashion models posing in Ma's *Useless* show. Before the show begins, the models are busy reading, texting, or playing games on their cell phones. One can imagine that after the fashion show, they would like to get rid of the dirt as soon as possible and return home.

25. This section ("Montage as Ideology Critique") thinks with Jia's documentary film to unravel the ideology of Ma's fashion idea. My critique echoes the title of Jia's writings. In 2009 Jia published a collection of Chinese essays titled *Jia Thinks* (賈想 *Jia Xiang*). In fact, the Chinese title is a pun. Although the pronunciation of Jia (賈) is the same as that of another word *jia* (假), their meanings are different. The former Jia (賈) refers to the director's surname whereas the latter *jia* (假) means falsehood (ideology). When *jia* is combined with *xiang* (想), which means "to think," *Jia xiang* (賈想) can mean "Jia thinks" or "the reflections of Jia." However, *Jia xiang* (假想) can also mean "what if" in subjunctive mood. The book title is filled with utopian longings. From the last name Jia (賈) to the falsehood *jia* (假), from "Jia thinks" (賈想) to "what if" (假想), one can relate the pun of Jia's book title to Fredric Jameson's theorization of the dialectic of ideology (假: falsehood) and utopian desire (假想: what if) in mass culture. See Fredric Jameson, "Reification and Utopia in Mass Culture," *Social Text* 1, no. 1 (1979): 130–48. In this chapter, I show that Jia's documentary film allows one to see the ideology of Ma's fashion. One can also detect the traces of utopian impulse in her fashion. Such a desire for equality can be observed in the representation of the naked and dirty bodies.

26. Xudong Zhang, "Market Socialism and Its Discontent: Jia Zhangke's Cinematic Narrative of China's Transition in the Age of Global Capital," in *Neoliberalism and*

Global Cinema: Capital, Culture, and Marxist Critique, ed. Jyotsna Kapur and Keith B. Wagner (New York: Routledge, 2011), 141.

27. For "cognitive mapping," see Fredric Jameson, "Cognitive Mapping," in *Marxism and the Interpretation of Culture*, ed. Cary Nelson and Lawrence Grossberg (Urbana: University of Illinois Press, 1988). See also Fredric Jameson, *Postmodernism; or, the Cultural Logic of Late Capitalism* (Durham, N.C.: Duke University Press, 1991); and Fredric Jameson, *The Geopolitical Aesthetic: Cinema and Space in the World System* (Bloomington: Indiana University Press, 1992).

28. Zhang, "Market Socialism and Its Discontent," 142.

29. Zhang, "Market Socialism and Its Discontent," 142, 143.

30. Jia, *Jia Thinks*, 231.

31. Jia, *Jia Thinks*, 231–32.

2. THE HIGH-QUALITY SUIT, CLASS STRUGGLE, AND CULTURAL REVOLUTION

1. Chen Yu (陳煜), *The Memory of Chinese Life: The Past Livelihood of the 60 Years of the Founding of the Nation (Zhongguo shenghuo jiyi: jianguo 60 nian minsheng wangshi* 中國生活記憶: 建國60年民生往事) (Beijing 北京: Zhongguo qinggongye chubanshe 中國輕工業出版社, 2009), 70.

2. "Shanghai People Actively Participated in the Discussions About Resisting Strange-looking Clothes; Develop the Good Tradition of the Proletariat, Oppose the Thinking and Behavior of the Bourgeoisie" (Shanghai guangda renmin jiji danjia dizhi qizhuang yifu de taolun fayang wuchan jieji youliang chuantong fandui zichan jieji sixiang zuofeng 上海廣大人民積極參加抵制奇裝異服的討論 發揚無產階級優良傳統反對資產階級思想作風), *People's Daily (Renmin ribao* 人民日報), November 14, 1964.

3. Cai Xiang's book in Chinese was published in 2010. The English translation came out in 2016. For the book in Chinese, see Cai Xiang (蔡翔), *Revolution/Narration: China's Socialist Literary and Cultural Imaginaries (1949–1966) (Geming/Xushu: Zhongguo shehui zhuyi wenxue—wenhua xianxiang* [1949–1966] 革命/敘述:中國社會主義文學—文化想象 [1949-1966]) (Beijing 北京: Beijing daxue chubanshe 北京大學出版社, 2010). For the book in English, see Cai Xiang, *Revolution and Its Narratives: China's Socialist Literary and Cultural Imaginaries, 1949–1966*, ed. Rebecca Karl and Xueping Zhong (Durham, N.C.: Duke University Press, 2016).

4. Yu Feng's and Jiang Qing's dress reforms can be compared with the Soviet constructivist movement in the 1920s. According to Christina Kiaer, some Soviet artists attempted to imagine everyday socialist objects, such as pots, pans, overcoats, stoves, fashions, textiles, packaging, advertisements, and the interiors of workers' club, as their comrades. These objects can be called "objects-as-comrades" or "comradely objects." What is intriguing is that these artists attempted to "imagine no possessions." To them, what needed to be eliminated was one's possessive relation to the objects, not the object as such. See Christina Kiaer's book *Imagine No Possessions: The Socialist Objects of Russian Constructivism* (Cambridge, Mass.: MIT Press, 2005). I thank Roy Chan for bringing this book to my attention.

5. Emily Honig and Gail Hershatter, *Personal Voices: Chinese Women in the 1980's* (Stanford, Calif.: Stanford University Press, 1988), 42.

6. However, there is no simple, causal relationship between the Western suit and bourgeois ideologies, between the Chinese *qipao* and feudalism, and between the Soviet-style *bulaji* dress and revisionism. Those who radically critiqued the ideological dimension of clothes had not satisfactorily explained the complex mediations among fashion, social class, ideology, and political economy. Furthermore, it is useful to distinguish between the high-cut *qipao* (*qipao gao kaicha* 旗袍高開叉) and low-cut *qipao* (*qipao di kaicha* 旗袍低開叉). During the seventeen years of the PRC (1949–1966), the low-cut *qipao* was not severely condemned. What was critiqued was the high-cut *qipao* because this kind of dress turns women into sexual objects for the male gaze.

7. Paul Clark, *Chinese Cinema: Culture and Politics Since 1949* (New York: Cambridge University Press, 1987). For a summary of this book, see Paul Clark, "Artists, Cadres, and Audiences," in *A Companion to Chinese Cinema*, ed. Yingjin Zhang (Malden, Mass.: Wiley-Blackwell, 2012).

8. Zhuoyi Wang, *Revolutionary Cycles in Chinese Cinema, 1951–1979* (New York: Palgrave Macmillan, 2014). See also Yomi Braester and Tina Mai Chen, "Film in the People's Republic of China, 1949–1979: The Missing Years?" *Journal of Chinese Cinemas* 5, no. 1 (2011): 5–12. See also Julian Ward, "The Remodeling of a National Cinema: Chinese Films of the Seventeen Years (1949–66)," in *The Chinese Cinema Book*, ed. Song Hwee Lim and Julian Ward (New York: Palgrave Macmillan; and London: British Film Institute, 2011).

9. See Clark, *Chinese Cinema*, chap. 4.

10. Xie Tieli directed the following works in the 1960s and 1970s: *A Prodigious Storm* (*Baofeng zhouyu* 暴風驟雨) (1961), *Early Spring February* (*Zaochun eryue* 早春二月) (1963), *Never Forget* (*Qianwan buyao wangji* 千萬不要忘記) (1964), *Revolutionary Model Work: Taking Tiger Mountain by Strategy* (*Zhiqu weihushan* 智取威虎山) (1970), *Revolutionary Model Work: Glory to the Long Jiang* (*Longjiangsong* 龍江頌) (1972), *The Harbor* (or, *On the Docks*) (*Haigang* 海港) (1972), and *Azalea Mountain* (*Dujuanshan* 杜鵑山) (1974). In fact, Xie had directed the controversial film *Early Spring in February* (1963) before *Never Forget* (1964). For this controversy, see Wang, *Revolutionary Cycles*, chap. 6.

11. For cultural criticism of *The Young Generation*, see Xiaobing Tang, *Chinese Modern: The Heroic and the Quotidian* (Durham, N.C.: Duke University Press, 2000), 163–195.

12. Lei Feng (雷鋒). *The Diary of Lei Feng* (*Leifeng riji* 雷鋒日記) (Beijing 北京: Jiefangjun wenyi she 解放軍文藝社, 1964), April 17, 1962 (my translation).

13. The motif of education is part of the socialist education campaign in the PRC in the early 1960s. It encompassed the "Learn from Chairman Mao" campaign. The *Quotations of Chairman Mao* was published in 1964. This socialist education campaign also included the "Learn from Workers, Peasants, and Army" campaigns. While the Daqing (大慶) oil field was praised as exemplary of industrial production, the Dazhai (大寨) commune was promoted as an agricultural model. The young generation was also encouraged to learn from comrade Lei Feng. This campaign then evolved to become the "Learn from the People's Liberation Army" campaign. In addition, the discussions concerning the young people's attitude toward happiness (*Qingnian yinggaiyou shenmeyang de xingfu guan* 青年應該有什麼樣的幸福觀)

in the *China Youth* (*Zhongguo qingnian* 中國青年) magazine in 1963–1965 were also part of the discourse of socialist education.

14. Cong Shen (叢深), *Never Forget* (*Qianwan buyao wangji* 千萬不要忘記) (Beijing 北京: Zhongguo xiju chubanshe 中國戲劇出版社, 1964), 11.

15. Cai, *Revolution and Its Narratives*, 378.

16. Cong, *Never Forget*, 78–79.

17. Cong, *Never Forget*, 84.

18. Cong, *Never Forget*, 90–91.

19. In Cong's play, Ding Haikuan vividly describes the class struggle between the proletariat and bourgeoisie. This class struggle is expressed as the struggle for the hegemony over the education of children. Ding Haikuan says: "While our children are wearing a red scarf, someone would like them to wear a black scarf! We tell them how glorious it is to labor and serve as a model worker, but someone says to them 'you cannot fill up your stomach by being a model worker!' We educate them not to care about reward, however, someone asks them: 'How much money you are making?'" Cong, *Never Forget*, 71–72. This scene is missing in the film.

20. Cong, *Never Forget*, 97–98.

21. Cong Shen (叢深), "The Formation of the Theme of *Never Forget*" (Qianwan buyao wangji zhuti de xingcheng 〈千萬不要忘記〉主題的形成), *Drama* (*Xiju bao* 戲劇報) 4 (1964): 27–28 (my translation).

22. Here, addiction is linked to consumption, not production. In the film (and the play), Ji works all the time. It can be said that he is addicted to factory labor. However, his addiction to work is not problematized in the narrative. How should one deal with socialist workaholism?

23. This quote comes from the film, not the play. Meanwhile, in the play, Ding Haikuan says:

> Shaochun, the question is not what you wear or what you eat. The question is what you think, what you desire, and what you aspire towards! My child! In this world, there are thousands and millions of people who don't have proper clothes to wear! If you are thinking about the high-quality uniform only, if you are thinking about shooting a few more wild birds, then you will forget closing the machine door, you will forget going to work, you will forget the fact that our country needs to make more progress, and you will forget world revolution! (84)

24. Shen, "The Formation of the Theme," 27–28.

25. Another example can be found in Fu Chaowu's (傅超武) film *Family Problems* (*Jiating wenti* 家庭問題) (1964). In the beginning of the story, Master Du chooses a moderately good-looking hat (rather than the most old-fashioned hat) for his son, Du Fumin. Similar to Ding Haikuan, Master Du endorses a mild and moderate degree of fashion within the socialist context.

26. Mao Zedong, *Yan'an Talks on Literature and Art* (*Zai yan'an wenyi zuotanhui shang de jianghua* 在延安文藝座談會上的講話) (Beijing 北京: Renmin chubanshe 人民出版社, 1975).

27. Cai, *Revolution and Its Narratives*, 386.

28. This can also be seen in Lu Ren's (魯韌) film *Today Is My Day Off* (*Jintian woxiuxi* 今天我休息) (1959). In this praising comedy (*gesongxing xiju* 歌頌性喜劇) film,

policeman Ma Tianming (馬天明), played by actor Zhong Xinghuo (仲星火), volunteers to help his fellow citizens during his day off. For a summary of *Today Is My Day Off*, see Krista Van Fleit Hang, *Literature the People Love: Reading Chinese Texts from the Early Maoist Period (1949–1966)* (New York: Palgrave Macmillan, 2013).

29. Tang Xiaobing (唐小兵), "The Historical Meaning of *Never Forget*—The Anxiety of the Everyday Life and Modernity" (*Qianwan buyao wangji de lishi yiyi—guanyu richang shenghuo de jiaolü jiqi xiandaixing* 《千萬不要忘記》的歷史意義—關於日常生活的焦慮及其現代性), *Reinterpretations* (*Zai jiedu* 再解讀), ed. Tang Xiaobing (唐小兵) (Xianggang 香港: Niujin daxue chubanshe 牛津大學出版社, 1993), 228–29. This edited book was reprinted by Beijing Daxue chubanshe 北京大學出版社 in 2007. In fact, 再解讀 (*zai jiedu*), which means reinterpretation, has the same pronunciation as 再解毒 (*zai jiedu*), which means detoxification. To reinterpret socialist cultural productions through the lens of critical and cultural theory is to remove the toxin that is mainstream ideology.

30. Fredric Jameson, *The Political Unconscious: Narrative as a Socially Symbolic Act* (Ithaca, N.Y.: Cornell University Press, 1981), 99.

31. "The Temptation of Fashion" (*Shishang de youhuo* 時尚的誘惑), The Blog of Zhang Yiwu, May 29, 2007 (Zhang yiwu de boke 張頤武的博客), accessed May 15, 2013 (my translation). Zhang Yiwu continues: "The contradiction has been written into the culture of fashion: on the one hand, it is considered as something to be achieved, but on the other hand, it is repressed, denied, and overcome in the everyday life. This is the reason why fashion is perceived to be a source of unease and anxiety within the context of the socialist planned economy" (my translation).

32. Tina Mai Chen, "Proletarian White and Working Bodies in Mao's China," *positions: east asia cultures critique* 11, no. 2 (2003): 363–64.

33. In fact, the high-quality suit that Shaochun has purchased, or the suit that the engineer Shao wore on the day when Mother Yao saw him off at the airport, can also be regarded as a proletarian white suit. This suit also reveals the socialist contradiction of proletarianization and modernization.

34. Tina Mai Chen's idea can be related to Mao's dialectic of popularization and raising standard in his famous talk called "Yan'an Talks on Literature and Arts" in 1942.

35. Tang, "The Historical Meaning of *Never Forget*," 229 (my translation).

36. Raymond Williams, *Marxism and Literature* (Oxford: Oxford University Press, 1977), 121–27.

37. Tang, "The Historical Meaning of *Never Forget*," 233 (my translation).

38. Adding to Tang's idea, one can also think about what the text does not do or has not done. On the one hand, *Never Forget* does not attempt to envision what the everyday life in socialist industrialized modernity can potentially look like. The text does not try to imagine how socialist consumption and leisure can be different from, or even better than, its capitalist counterpart. On the other hand, the text has oversimplified and under-analyzed capitalism and ideology. Rather than presenting the complexity of bourgeois and revisionist hegemony, the text simply condemns it with a moralistic judgment.

39. Maurice Meisner, *Mao's China and After: A History of the People's Republic* (New York: Free Press, 1999), 308. See also Richard Kraus, *Class Conflicts in Chinese Socialism* (New York: Columbia University Press, 1981), 89–143.

40. Cai, *Revolution and Its Narratives*, 364. In fact, cultural critic Kang Liu has also highlighted the contradiction between revolution and construction. He writes:

> Of all the contradictions, the twofold goal of consolidating revolutionary hegemony and reconstructing China's society—from economic infrastructure to political and cultural institutions—presented the greatest challenge. Building a revolutionary hegemony required that cultural revolution be ceaselessly continued and renewed. Yet continued revolution inevitably entailed destabilization and disruption of the routine, institutional practices necessary for the construction and maintenance of the country's economic and social structures. On the other hand, the tasks of consolidation and reconstruction dictated the establishment of an ideological orthodoxy or ideological state apparatuses to ensure the normativity and regularity of social life. These two conflicting goals remained central to China's project of an alternative modernity.

Kang Liu, *Aesthetics and Marxism: Chinese Aesthetic Marxists and their Western Contemporaries* (Durham, N.C.: Duke University Press, 2000), 111.

41. Cai, *Revolution and Its Narratives*, 20.

42. Cai, *Revolution and Its Narratives*, 390–91.

43. Meng Yue (孟悅), "*White-Haired Girl* and the Historical Complexities of Yan'an Literature" (*Bai maonü yu yan'an wenxue de lishi fuzaxing* 《白毛女》與「延安文學」的歷史複雜性), *Reinterpretations* (*Zai jiedu* 再解讀), ed. Tang Xiaobing (唐小兵) (Xianggang 香港: Niujin daxue chubanshe 牛津大學出版社, 1993), 176–81.

44. Meng, "*White-Haired Girl*," 181–86.

45. Meng, "*White-Haired Girl*," 186–87.

46. Meng Yue, "Female Images and National Myth," in *Gender Politics in Modern China: Writing and Feminism*, ed. Tani Barlow (Durham, NC: Duke University Press, 1993), 118.

47. Ban Wang, "Desire and Pleasure in Revolutionary Cinema," in *The Sublime Figure of History: Aesthetics and Politics in Twentieth Century China* (Stanford, Calif.: Stanford University Press, 1997), 123–54.

48. See Ban Wang's discussion of Žižek in his chapter "Desire and Pleasure in Revolutionary Cinema."

49. Wang, "Desire and Pleasure in Revolutionary Cinema," 134.

50. Jianmei Liu, "Love Cannot Be Forgotten," in *Revolution Plus Love: Literary History, Women's Bodies, and Thematic Repetition in Twentieth-Century Chinese Fiction* (Honolulu: University of Hawaii Press, 2003), 164.

51. Liu, "Love Cannot be Forgotten," 164.

52. Liu, "Love Cannot be Forgotten," 165.

53. Ma Lunpeng (馬綸鵬), "A Study of 'Career Women Films' of the Seventeen Years (1949–66)" (*Shiqinian (1949–1966) zhiye funü yingxiang chutan—jianlun zhongguo xiandai dainyingzhong de funü yingxiang* <<十七年(1949–1966)職業婦女影像初探——兼論中國現代電影中的婦女影像>>), *Film Research* (*Dianying Yanjiu* 電影研究) (2015): 61–75.

54. Xie Fengsong (謝逢松). "A Letter to Younger Sister—Discussing the Film *Shanghai Girls*" (*Jigei meimei dexin—tan yingpian shanghai guniang* 寄給妹妹的信—談影片'上海姑娘), *Beijing Art* (*Beijing Wenyi* 北京文藝) 3 (1959): 25. According to Ma Junxiang

(馬軍驤), the constructions and receptions of female characters in selected Chinese socialist films are different from the representation of women as sexual objects in classical Hollywood cinema. He argues that *Shanghai Girls* represents a socialist attempt to devise a film language not dominated by the male voyeurism that Laura Mulvey analyzes in "Visual Pleasure and Narrative Cinema," in *Movies and Methods*, vol. 2, ed. Bill Nichols, 303–15 (Berkeley: University of California Press, 1985). See Ma Junxiang, "*Shanghai Girls*—Revolutionary Women and the Question of Looking" (*Shanghai guniang—geming nüxing ji guangkan wenti* 《上海姑娘》—革命女性及「觀看」問題), *Reinterpretations* (*Zai jiedu* 再解讀), ed. Tang Xiaobing (唐小兵) (Xianggang 香港: Niujin daxue chubanshe 牛津大學出版社, 1993), 176–91. Similarly, Chris Berry has also made a point concerning Lu Ren's film *Li Shuangshuang* (李雙雙). Berry argues that the viewing subject is collective in Chinese socialist cinema. See Chris Berry, "*Sexual Difference and the Viewing Subject in* Li Shuangshuang *and* The In-Laws," in *Perspectives on Chinese Cinema*, ed. Chris Berry (London: British Film Institute, 1991).

55. Tian Fanghua (天方畫), "Discussing 'The Aesthetics of Waste'" (*Tan langfei meixue* 談'浪費美學'), *Film Art* (*Dianying yishu* 電影藝術) 3 (1958): 68.

56. This film is an adaptation of Chen Yun's (陳雲) play *The Young Generation* (*Nianqing de yidai* 年青的一代) (1964).

57. This film is an adaptation of Hu Wanchun's (胡萬春) short story *Family Problems* (*Jiating wenti* 家庭問題) (Shanghai 上海: Zuojia chubanshe 作家出版社, 1964).

58. This film is an adaptation of Shen Ximeng's (沈西蒙) play *Sentinels Under the Neon Lights* (*Nihong dengxia de shaobing* 霓虹燈下的哨兵) (Beijing 北京: Jiefangjun wenyishe 解放軍文藝社, 1963).

59. This can be compared to Lei Feng's frugal attitude toward his old, worn-out socks in the film *Lei Feng* (*Leifeng* 雷鋒) (1964) directed by Dong Zhaoqi (董兆琪).

60. Other examples include the purchase of sunglasses and leather shoes in Zhou Yu's (周予) film *Road Examination* (*Lukao* 路考) (1965), which is an adaptation of Zhang Tianmin's (張天民) short story "Road Examination" (*Lukao* 路考) (1963).

61. The remake of *The Young Generation*, directed by Ling Zhihao (凌之浩) and Zhang Huijun (張惠均), came out in 1976. The remake is also called *The Young Generation*.

62. For the English translation of the original play, see Chen Yun, "The Young Generation," in *The Columbia Anthology of Modern Chinese Drama*, ed. Xiaomei Chen (New York: Columbia University Press, 2014), 466. In this chapter's conclusion, I refer to the film. I also include the page numbers of the play so the reader can refer to the play while engaging with my analysis.

63. Chen Yun, "The Young Generation," 473.

64. Chen Yun, "The Young Generation," 463.

65. Chen Yun, "The Young Generation," 466.

66. Chen Yun, "The Young Generation," 500.

67. Chen Yun, "The Young Generation," 501.

68. Chen Yun, "The Young Generation," 502.

69. Chen Yun, "The Young Generation," 501.

70. Chen Yun, "The Young Generation," 502.

71. Chen Yun, "The Young Generation," 502.

72. Chen Yun, "The Young Generation," 506.

73. Chen Yun, "The Young Generation," 507.

3. "MAO'S CHILDREN ARE WEARING FASHION!"

1. China Photographers Association, *China's Thirty Years* (*Jianzheng: Gaige kaifang sanshinian* 見證: 改革開放三十年), ed. Wang Miao and Liu Yang (New York: Oxford University Press, 2009), 65.

2. Anthropologist Lisa Rofel calls this "post-socialist allegory." See Lisa Rofel, *Other Modernities: Gendered Yearnings in China after Socialism* (Berkeley: University of California Press, 1999); and Lisa Rofel, *Desiring China: Experiments in Neoliberalism, Sexuality, and Public Culture* (Durham, N.C.: Duke University Press, 2007).

3. The revisionists characterize the socialist period as one filled with drab and monotonous colors. This is the viewpoint offered by Gong Yan (龔彥), the host of Chinese TV show "風言鋒語: 六十年代精典記憶:時尚" (*Fengyan fengyu: Liushi niandai jingdian jiyi: shishang*). Yi Zhongtian (易中天) provides an interesting response to this revisionist argument. He thinks that such "sameness" should be appreciated as neatness or tidiness instead.

    GONG YAN: In the beginning of the founding of the PRC, Chinese people's clothes had so few colors. You can count them with your fingers. Blue, gray, white, green, and black. That's all, right? Yi Laoshi [Teacher], don't you think it is monotonous?

    YI ZHONGTIAN: It depends on how you look at it. At that time, we felt it was neat and tidy! . . . It was a form of identification. I could be one member of this society. As a member of the revolutionary, I was recognized.

    See Youku.com (*Youku wang* 優酷網), "*Fengyan fengyu: Liushi niandai jingdian jiyi: shishang* 風言鋒語: 六十年代精典記憶:時尚," Youku, updated September 21, 2009, accessed May 15, 2013, http://v.youku.com/v_show/id_XMTIwMzYiNTQ4.html.

4. Arguably, Bao Zhifang's (鮑芝芳) film *Black Dragonfly* (*Hei qingting* 黑蜻蜓) (1984) is one of the first PRC films to feature fashion designers and fashion models. Other films that deal with similar subject matter include (but are not limited to) Tian Zhuangzhuang's (田壯壯) film *Rock Kids* (*Yaogun qingnian* 搖滾青年) (1988) and Wang Binglin's (王秉林) film *A Model's Story* (*Nümote de fengbo* 女模特的風波) (1989). Scenes of fashion shows also appear in Mi Jiashan's (米家山) film *The Troubles-Shooters* (*Wanzhu* 頑主) (1988) and Wei Shaohong (衛兆紅) and Chang Yan's (常彥) film *The Temptation of Beauty* (*Meide youhuo* 美的誘惑) (1992).

5. Emily Honig and Gail Hershatter, *Personal Voices: Chinese Women in the 1980s* (Stanford, CA: Stanford University Press, 1988), chap. 2.

6. Michel Foucault, *The History of Sexuality*, vol. 1: *An Introduction* (New York: Vintage Books, 1990), 103.

7. Wang Hui (汪暉), *Depoliticized Politics: The End of the Short Twentieth Century and the 1990s (Qu zhengzhihua de zhengzhi: duan ershi shiji de zhongjie yu jiushi niandai* 去政治化的政治: 短20世紀的終結與90年代) (Beijing 北京: Sanlian shudian 三聯書店, 2008). See also Wang Hui, *The End of the Revolution: China and the Limits of Modernity* (New York: Verso, 2009).

8. According to some Chinese viewers and critics, some parts of the story may not be completely convincing. First, the love relationship between Geng Hua and Zhou Yun lacks a solid foundation. Given the difference in their backgrounds and upbringings, their love for China and for the richness of Chinese culture and history are insufficient to bring these two individuals together. Second, it is not likely that Geng

Hua, the son of a victim of the Cultural Revolution, chooses to fall in love with and marry the daughter of a former military commander in the Nationalist Party. At that time it was uncommon for a mainland Chinese man to have a love relationship with someone from overseas.

9. Chris Berry, *Postsocialist Cinema in Post-Mao China: The Cultural Revolution After the Cultural Revolution* (New York: Routledge, 2004), 120–21.

10. Bryan Johnson, "Marching Peasants Are out in New Chinese Films," *Globe and Mail*, November 7, 1980, 8.

11. Sina.com.cn (*Xinlang wang* 新浪網) "Sishui liunian," episode 20, "Fashion (Part I)" (《似水流年》第20集《時尚》（上）), sina.com.cn (*Xinlang wang* 新浪網), accessed May 15, 2013, http://video.sina.com.cn/ent/m/c/2009-01-04/160231865.shtml.

12. In the newspaper article titled "My Views Regarding Several Films with Love Themes" ("對幾部愛情題材影片的意見"), the author writes: "Fashion and props should be used according to the development of the plot. The changes of clothes are too frequent—the actress wears a new set of fashionable clothes in every scene, and she continuously has her clothes changed during her trip. This is not logical or necessary. Such a choice weakens people's appreciation of the film. It is a pity that the actress becomes the fashion model for advertisement."

13. Situ Beichen (司徒北辰) and Li Zhao (李兆), "Pierre Cardin: 'A Crazy Man' from France" (*Pi'er kadan: cong faguo laide fengzi* 皮爾·卡丹: 從法國來的'瘋子'), *China News Weekly* (*Zhongguo xinwen zhoukan* 中國新聞週刊) 44 (2008).

14. According to the CCTV website, originally, Xinhuashe journalist Li Anding (李安定) was about to publish a news article about Pierre Cardin's fashion show in Beijing and Shanghai. Just before the article was released, *Reference News* (《參考消息》) had reprinted a commentary article in a Hong Kong newspaper, which inquired whether it was reasonable for Chinese people to appreciate Cardin's fashion shows when some Chinese people did not even have the most basic clothing to wear. This article expressed the dissatisfaction of some members in the socialist administration. Therefore, the Xinhuashe article could not be published. See CCTV.com (*Yangshi wang* 央視網), "Economic Reforms and Opening Up: The Changes of Fashion During the Past 30 Years" (Gaige kaifang: fuzhuang biange 30 nian 改革開放: 服裝變革30年), accessed May 15, 2013, http://news.cctv.com/society/20081112/101903.shtml.

15. CCTV.com (*Yangshi wang* 央視網), "Phenomenon 1980: First Episode: Catwalk" (*Xianxiang 1980:diyiji: tianqiao* 現象1980第一集:天橋), accessed May 15, 2013, http://jishi.cntv.cn/xianxiang1980/classpage/video/20110826/100095.shtml.

16. CCTV.com, "Phenomenon 1980."

17. Liu Fang (流芳), "Liberate Thinking; Be Bold and Innovative" (*Jiefang shixiang dadan chuangxin* 解放思想大膽創新) *Fashion* (*Shizhuang* 時裝) 2 (1983): 6 (my translation).

18. In Jia Zhangke's (賈樟柯) documentary film *24 City* (*Ershisichengji* 二十四城記) (2008), character Song Weidong (宋衛東), played by Chinese actor Chen Jianbing (陳建斌), recalls his former love relationship in high school in an interview. His ex-girlfriend had the same hairstyle as Sachiko (幸子) in the Japanese TV melodrama *Red Suspicion* (*Xueyi* 血疑). By the end of the interview, the viewer can hear "Thank You" (謝謝你), the theme song of this melodrama, sung by actress Momoe Yamaguchi (山口百惠). She plays the role of Sachiko in *Red Suspicion*.

19. Rey Chow, "Fetish Power Unbound: A Small History of 'Woman' in Chinese Cinema," in *The Oxford Handbook of Chinese Cinemas*, ed. Carlos Rojas and Eileen Cheng-Yin-Chow (New York: Oxford University Press, 2013), 492. In fact, cultural critic Mao Jian has made a similar observation. See Mao Jian (毛尖), "The Crisis of Sexual Politics and Socialist Aesthetics—Beginning with the Room in *Woman Basketball Player Number 5*" (*Xingbie zhengzhi he shehui zhuyi meixue de weiji- cong nülan wuhao de fangjian shuoqi* 性別政治和社會主義美學的危機—從《女籃5號》的房間說起), *Chinese Modern Literature Research Series* (*Zhongguo xiandai wenxue yanjiu congkan* 中國現代文學研究叢刊) 3 (2010): 29–37.

20. Chow points out the contradiction in Wu Yonggang's (吳永剛) film *The Goddess* (1934) and Zhang Yimou's (張藝謀) early films. She writes: "Material deprivation and social oppression are typically dramatized on screen with breathtakingly adorable female faces and bodies." Chow, "Fetish Power Unbound," 495. In my understanding, this observation is based on the Shanghai filmmaking tradition that was later taken up in Hong Kong and Taiwan. How about the Yan'an tradition influenced by the Soviet filmmaking practices (e.g., montage, fragmentation, estrangement)?

21. Chow, "Fetish Power Unbound," 500.

22. Chow, "Fetish Power Unbound," 495.

23. Michael Berry, "The Absent American: Figuring the United States in Chinese Cinema of the Reform Era," in *A Companion to Chinese Cinema*, ed. Yingjin Zhang (Malden, Mass.: Wiley-Blackwell, 2012), 574.

24. The lyrics to "Fly Toward the Homeland from Far Away" are as follows: "Wild geese, wild geese, when spring comes, Fly, fly, fly toward the homeland far away! La la la la la. Wild geese, wild geese, when spring comes, Fly, fly, fly toward the homeland far away! Homeland, Homeland!" The lyrics to "Oh! Homeland!" are as follows: "When the full moon rises, when it rises, I miss my homeland so dearly. There is beautiful water and mountain. That is the place I grow up. When the festival comes, I miss my homeland dearly. It's like being able to see the blossom of the flowers and smell the fragrance of the soil in my homeland. Oh, homeland, my dear homeland, Oh, homeland, my dear homeland, I wish I could be the clouds on the sky, to ride the wind and float toward your side."

25. Berry, "The Absent American," 556.

26. It is useful to juxtapose this Chinese feminist revisionist argument with the Western feminist poststructuralist theory. Interestingly, what the Chinese revisionists demanded is not the deconstruction of gender but the reconstruction of it. These revisionists argued for more, rather than less, gender difference and femininity for Chinese women. For a complex theorization of this disjuncture between Chinese historical reality and Western poststructuralist theory, see Mayfair Mei-hui Yang, "From Gender Erasure to Gender Difference: State Feminism, Consumer Sexuality, and Women's Public Sphere in China," in *Spaces of Their Own: Women's Public Sphere in Transnational China*, ed. Mayfair Mei-hui Yang (Minneapolis: University of Minnesota Press, 1999).

27. Here Zha tries to make two claims. First, Chinese women's femininities were erased during the revolutionary period. Second, Chinese women resisted the state-imposed masculinization of their bodies by making minor adjustments to their clothes; by doing so, they made themselves look more feminine. However, what Zha expresses can also be used to undo her own argument. When she says that the women sewed

in their uniforms so that they could have a waistline, she was already pointing to the presence of gender differences in women's clothes. Femininities were not entirely erased during the socialist period.

28. Ai Hua (Harriet Evans 艾華) and Li Yinhe (李銀河), "Dialogue About Feminism" (*Guanyu nüxing zhuyi de duihua* 關於女性主義的對話), *Sociological Research* (*Shehuixue yanjiu* 社會學研究) 4 (2001): 122 (my translation).

29. Ai Hua and Li Yinhe, "Dialogue About Feminism," 122.

30. Juanjuan Wu, *Chinese Fashion: From Mao to Now* (New York: Berg, 2009), 37.

31. Wu, *Chinese Fashion*, 3.

32. Wu, *Chinese Fashion*, 4.

33. For a photograph showing the difference between women's and men's clothing, see Liu Xiangcheng (Liu, Heungshing 劉香成), *Post-Mao China 1976–1983* (*Mao yihou de zhongguo 1976–1983*毛以後的中國1976–1983) (Beijing 北京: Shijie tushu chuban gongsi Beijing gongsi 世界圖書出版公司北京公司, 2011), 175.

34. Wu, *Chinese Fashion*, 4.

35. For socialist androgyny, see Marilyn Young, "Chicken Little in China: Some Reflections on Women," in *Marxism and the Chinese Experience: Issues in Contemporary Chinese Socialism*, ed. Arif Dirlik and Maurice Meisner (Armonk, N.Y.: M. E. Sharpe, 1989), 253–68.

36. Xiaomei Chen, "Growing Up with Posters in the Maoist Era," in *Picturing Power in the People's Republic of China: Posters of the Cultural Revolution*, ed. Harriet Evans and Stephanie Donald (Lanham, Md.: Rowman & Littlefield, 1999).

37. It is possible to do more theoretical work about sex and gender, sameness and difference, and equality and inequality. Indeed, a feminist utopia should be one that recognizes multiple forms of sexes (e.g., men and women) and genders (e.g., masculinities and femininities) rather than one that eradicates sex or gender. This feminist utopia should be a privilege-less society in which the sex or gender of an individual should not be regarded as the determining factor of the organization of society. On the one hand, one should oppose essentialism or biological determinism—that is, the idea that sex and gender can serve to ground and legitimize hierarchical and oppressive social norms that put the sexual and gender other(s) in disadvantageous positions. On the other hand, one should also reject nominalism that considers the sexual and gender other as abstract, idealist, and disembodied creatures. In my opinion, what one should demand is not the eradication of sex and gender as such but rather the abolition of the determining effect of sex and gender. When one approaches the issue from this perspective, then, what one should radically critique is not sex or gender (or sexual or gender difference) but rather sex or gender determinism.

4. IMAG(IN)ING THE CHINESE MIDDLE-CLASS CULTURE

1. For an analysis of Chinese workplace novels, see Grace Hui-chuan Wu, "The Making of the New Global Middle Class: China's Workplace Novels," *Concentric: Literary and Cultural Studies*, 43 no. 1 (2017): 299–327.

2. The 2010 TV drama is Chen Mingzhang (陳銘章). *A Story of Lala's Promotion* (*Dulala shengzhiji* 杜拉拉升職記). [Shanghai 上海]: Shanghai luxiang gongsi 上海錄像公司,

2010. The later adaptations are An Zhujian (安竹間), *Go! Lala Go! 2* (*Dulala zhui-hunqi* 杜拉拉追婚記) (Guangzhou 廣州: Guangdong yinxiang chuban youxian gongsi 廣東音像出版有限公司, 2015); and Liu Junjie (劉俊傑), *Still Lala* (*Woshi Dulala* 我是杜拉拉) (Jiangsu weishi 江蘇衛視, 2016).

3. The narrative tells how Du becomes what some Chinese people humorously call the *baigujing* (白骨精), a monster character in the *Journeys to the West* novel. Regarding the *baigujing*, *bai* means *bailing* (white collar 白領), *gu* means *gugan* (backbone [of the company] 骨幹), and *jing* means *jingying* (elite 精英).

4. Li Ke (李可), *Chronicle of Du Lala's Promotion* (*Du Lala shengzhi ji* 杜拉拉升職記) (Xi'an 西安: Xi'an shifan daxue chuban she 西安師範大學出版社, 2007), 20.

5. Li, *Chronicle of Du Lala's Promotion*, 130.

6. Li, *Chronicle of Du Lala's Promotion*, 19.

7. Li, *Chronicle of Du Lala's Promotion*, 255.

8. Li, *Chronicle of Du Lala's Promotion*, 255.

9. Interestingly, Du's ex-boyfriend uses the SWOT formula to evaluate their love relationship. Later he breaks up with her.

10. Quoted in Fredric Jameson, "Imaginary and Symbolic in Lacan," in *The Ideologies of Theory: Essays 1971–1986*, vol. 1: *Situations of Theory* (Minneapolis: University of Minnesota Press, 1988), 85.

11. Jameson, "Imaginary and Symbolic in Lacan," 85.

12. Jane Gallop, *Reading Lacan* (Ithaca, N.Y.: Cornell University Press, 1985), 77.

13. Gallop, *Reading Lacan*, 78.

14. Gallop, *Reading Lacan*, 81.

15. Gallop, *Reading Lacan*, 82. In "Discourse of Rome," Jacques Lacan writes: "What realizes itself in my history is not the past definite of what was since it is no longer, nor even the present perfect of what has been in what I am, but the future perfect of what I will have been for what I am in the process of becoming." See Gallop, *Reading Lacan*, 81–82.

16. Cultural critic Eva Chen suggests that this novel series "offers useful tips on office politics and desirable Western business practices for young, educated, upwardly mobile urban women." They also "inculcate sartorial and consuming practices as a crucial technology to construct an ideal cosmopolitan femininity." Eva Chen, "Fashioning the Cosmopolitan Girl: Sartorial Display and Technologies of Femininity in the Chinese Bestseller *Du Lala* (2007–11)," *Fashion Theory: The Journal of Dress. Body & Culture* 17, no. 5 (2013): 553–78.

17. Wang Xiaoming (王曉明), *Zai xinyishi xingtai de longzhao xia: 90 niandai de wenhua he wenxue fenxi* 在新意識形態的籠罩下: 90年代的文化和文學分析 (Nanjing 南京: Jiangsu renmin chubanshe 江蘇人民出版社, 2000), 30–31.

18. Wang, *Zai xinyishi xingtai de longzhao xia*, 31.

19. Wang, *Zai xinyishi xingtai de longzhao xia*, 31 (my translation).

20. Wang, *Zai xinyishi xingtai de longzhao xia*, 33 (my translation).

21. Louis Althusser, "Marxism and Humanism," in *For Marx* (New York: Verso, 2006), 231.

22. Althusser, "Marxism and Humanism," 231.

23. Althusser, "Marxism and Humanism," 233.

24. Louis Althusser, "Ideology and Ideological State Apparatus (Notes Towards an Investigation)," in *Lenin and Philosophy, and Other Essays* (New York: Monthly Review Press, 2001), 107–9.

25. Althusser, "Ideology and Ideological State Apparatus," 109–12.

26. Althusser, "Ideology and Ideological State Apparatus," 112–15.

27. Althusser, "Ideology and Ideological State Apparatus," 115–20.

28. Althusser, "Ideology and Ideological State Apparatus," 118.

29. Althusser, "Ideology and Ideological State Apparatus," 118.

30. Althusser, "Ideology and Ideological State Apparatus," 118–19.

31. Warren Montag, *Althusser and His Contemporaries: Philosophy's Perpetual War* (Durham, N.C.: Duke University Press, 2013), 138.

32. Mladen Dolar, "Beyond Interpellation," *Qui Parle* 6, no. 2 (1993): 77–78.

33. Montag, *Althusser and His Contemporaries*, 138.

34. See Marco Fumian, "*Chronicle of Du Lala's Promotion*: Exemplary Literature, the Middle Class, and the Socialist Market," *Modern Chinese Literature and Culture* 28, no. 1 (2016): 78–128. See also Wu, "The Making of the New Global Middle Class"; and Yi Zheng, *Contemporary Chinese Print Media: Cultivating Middle Class Taste* (Abingdon, Oxon: Routledge, 2014), 79–104.

35. Fumian, "*Chronicle of Du Lala's Promotion*," 78–128. For the quote, see the article abstract at the MCLC Resource Center, Ohio State University, https://u.osu.edu /mclc/journal/abstracts/fumian2/.

36. Fumian, "*Chronicle of Du Lala's Promotion*," 108.

37. Fumian, "*Chronicle of Du Lala's Promotion*," 109.

38. Fumian, "*Chronicle of Du Lala's Promotion*," 110–11.

39. Critic Hai Ren suggests that "the Chinese middle class . . . is a state project of managing risks in Chinese society." He points out that the development of the Chinese middle class coincides with the party-state's attempt to build what President Hu Jintao calls a "harmonious society" (*hexie shehui* 和諧社會). See Hai Ren, *The Middle Class in Neoliberal China: Governing Risk, Life-building, and Themed Spaces* (New York: Routledge, 2012), 9.

40. The romance between Wang Wei (David) and Lala is mentioned in the novel. Compared with its representation in the film, the novel's depiction is much more subdued. In the novel, Wang Wei's ex-girlfriend is Daisy, not Rose.

41. In fact, the film *Go! Lala Go!* was sponsored by Thailand's Tourism Authority, hence the advertisement of Pattaya. This strategy of product placement (Pattaya as a commodity) proves to be quite successful. For example, Feng Xiaogang's (馮小剛) film *If You Are the One* (*Feicheng wurao* 非誠勿擾) (2008) features the Xixi Wetland in Suzhou, China, and Hokkaido in Japan; see Feng Xiaogang, *If You Are the One* (*Feicheng wurao* 非誠勿擾) (Yunnan 雲南: Yunnan yinxiang chuanshe 雲南音像出版社, 2008) (with Chinese subtitles) or Feng Xiaogang, *If You Are the One: Love & Marriage* (New York: New Video, 2011) (with English subtitles). Meanwhile, *If You Are the One 2* (*Feicheng wurao 2* 非誠勿擾2) (2010) features Sanya in Hainan, China. After these two commercial films had been released, the local tourism boards reported many-fold increase of visits by Chinese tourists. For a survey of product placement in contemporary China's commercial films, see Wing-Fai Leung, "Product Placement with 'Chinese Characteristics':

Feng Xiaogang's films and *Go! Lala Go!*" *Journal of Chinese Cinemas* 9, no. 2 (2015): 125–40.

42. According to the credits, the film was sponsored by the FAW Mazda Motor Sales Co., Ltd.

43. Li, *Chronicle of Du Lala's Promotion*, 175, 252.

44. See the credits for the film's sponsors.

45. Eileen Chang (Zhang Ailing 張愛玲), "A Chronicle of Changing Clothes," in *Written on Water* (New York: Columbia University Press, 2005), 66.

46. For an exaggerated version of product placement in Chinese cinema, see Feng Xiaogang's film *Big Shots Funeral* (*Dawan* 大腕) (2001).

47. This translation is from Antonia Finnane's *Changing Clothes in China: Fashion, History, Nation* (New York: Columbia University Press, 2008), 231.

48. Harriet Evans, "Fashions and Feminine Consumption," in *Consuming China: Approaches to Cultural Change in Contemporary China*, ed. Kevin Latham, Stuart Thompson, and Jakob Klein (New York: Routledge, 2006), 179.

49. Susan Willis, *A Primer for Daily Life* (New York: Routledge, 1991), 73, 75.

50. Willis, *A Primer for Daily Life*, 75.

51. Willis, *A Primer for Daily Life*, 77.

52. See the section titled "She Is Wearing Her Body on Her Clothes" (*Tazai yifu shang chuandai zhe shengti* 她在衣服上穿戴著身體) in Calvin Hui, "'Mao's Children Are Wearing Fashion!'" in *The Changing Landscape of China's Consumerism*, ed. Alison Hulme. Kidlington, Oxford: Chandos, 2014.

5. BETWEEN PRODUCTION AND CONSUMPTION

1. Ho Chao-ti has directed and produced several documentary films about fashion and consumption. In 2009 she released a documentary titled *Wandering Island* (*Chuanzai zhongtudao* 穿在中途島). It consists of six related parts, including *Bras* (*Xiongzhao* 胸罩), *Dresses* (*Yangzhuang* 洋裝), *Designers* (*Qiuzhuang shangshi* 秋裝上市), *Blue Jeans* (*Niüzaiku* 牛仔褲), *Shoes* (*Xiezi* 鞋子), and *El Salvador Journal* (*Sa'er waduo riji* 薩爾瓦多日記). See "Wandering Island," Taiwan Public Television Service, accessed May 15, 2013, http://web.pts.org.tw/~web01/dress/about.htm.

2. The last part of the documentary film features the skinning of calves at the border of China and Russia. See Sheldon Lu, "Introduction: Chinese-Language Ecocinema," *Journal of Chinese Cinemas* 11 no. 1 (2017): 1–12.

3. Concerning the Chinese term *nongmingong* (農民工): *nongmin* (農民) refers to peasants, *mingong* (民工) refers to migrant workers, and *gongren* (工人) refers to workers. Taken together, *nongmingong* refers to the Chinese migrant peasant-workers who move from the rural to the urban areas to work.

4. Wanning Sun, *Subaltern China: Rural Migrants, Media, and Cultural Practices* (Lanham, Md.: Rowman & Littlefield, 2014), 15.

5. For an ethnography of Chinese construction workers, see Sarah Swider, *Building China: Informal Work and the New Precariat* (Ithaca, N.Y.: Cornell University Press, 2015).

6. Sun, *Subaltern China*, 16.

7. Sun, *Subaltern China*, 16.

8. Sun, *Subaltern China*, 16.
9. Sun, *Subaltern China*, 17–18.
10. For an early representation of the Chinese migrant factory workers in Chinese television, see Cheng Hao's (成浩) *Foreign Girls* (*Wai Lai Mei* 外來妹) (Guangzhou 廣州: Xinshidai yingyin gongsi 新時代影音公司, 1999).
11. In this chapter I focus on female migrant factory workers. For a study of migrant workers and masculinity, see Susanne Yuk-Ping Choi and Yinni Peng, *Masculine Compromise: Migration, Family, and Gender in China* (Oakland: University of California Press, 2016).
12. There are several documentary films about the production of fashion commodities in the context of twenty-first-century China. One is Micha Peled's documentary film *China Blue* (2005), which focuses on the production of blue jeans in the Lifeng factory in Shaxi, Guangdong, China. The director presents the lived experience of three young women workers—Jasmine is a thread cutter, Liping is a seamstress, and Orchid is a zipper installer—from Sichuan, in southwest China. Peled describes the exploitative working conditions that confronted these migrant factory workers. He also emphasizes how the workers try to imagine different futures in their everyday lives. Focusing on the making of blue jeans within the context of global capitalism, the director presents how the lives of Chinese migrant factory workers are fundamentally shaped by the collaboration among the transnational and national capitals, the state, and their local apparatuses. Similar to blues, a musical genre that expresses the sadness and melancholy of former African American slaves in the United States, the director suggests that the Chinese migrant factory workers also work like slaves. Their lives can be called a China blues. See Micha X. Peled, *China Blue* (Oley, Penn.: Bullfrog Films, 2005).
13. Xu Lizhi's poem is as follows: "I swallowed an iron moon / they called it a screw / I swallowed industrial wastewater and unemployment forms / bent over machines, our youth died young / I swallowed labor, I swallowed poverty / swallowed pedestrian bridges, swallowed this rusted-out life / I can't swallow any more / everything I've swallowed roils up in my throat / I spread across my country / a poem of shame." See Qin Xiaoyu (秦曉宇), ed., *Iron Moon: An Anthology of Chinese Migrant Worker Poetry* (Buffalo, N.Y.: White Pine Press, 2016).
14. Pun Ngai, "Subsumption or Consumption? The Phantom of Consumer Revolution in 'Globalizing' China," *Cultural Anthropology* 18, no. 4 (2003): 470.
15. Pun, "Subsumption or Consumption?," 475.
16. Pun, "Subsumption or Consumption?," 478, 486.
17. Pun Ngai, *Made in China: Women Factory Workers in a Global Workplace* (Durham, N.C.: Duke University Press, 2005), 143.
18. Eileen Otis, *Markets and Bodies: Women, Service Work, and the Making of Inequality in China* (Stanford, Calif.: Stanford University Press, 2012), 143.
19. Otis's observation is also made by Roberta Zavoretti. See Zavoretti, *Rural Origins, City Lives: Class and Place in Contemporary China* (Seattle: University of Washington Press, 2016), chap. 4.
20. Pun, "Subsumption or Consumption?," 485. *Dagongmei* (打工妹), from the Cantonese term *dagong* (打工), refers to young women who work for the bosses.
21. Pun, "Subsumption or Consumption?," 485.
22. Pun, *Made in China*, 160.

23. Pun, *Made in China*, 160. *Waishengmei* is an abject term for girls from foreign provinces, in this case, outside of Guangdong Province.

24. Anthropologist Lisa Rofel discusses the significance of the places where her Chinese informants would like to meet her. She writes about their desires to become urban and cosmopolitan: "While in China, it did not strike me at first as an ethnographic insight that the vast majority of the young professional women I spoke with wanted to meet me in American or American-style fast-food restaurants: A&W, McDonald's, and others. Only afterward did I think about the significance of our meeting places as I began to realize that the creation of a consumer identity domesticates cosmopolitanism even as the goal of such a creation is to transcend place." Lisa Rofel, *Desiring China: Experiments in Neoliberalism, Sexuality, and Public China* (Durham, N.C.: Duke University Press, 2007), 120. In fact, similar impulses can be observed in the behaviors of Pun's subjects. The spaces that Pun's fellow migrant factory workers visited—theme parks, supermarkets (rather than local family-owned grocery stores), and cafes—are also symbolic spaces of modernity, urbanity, and cosmopolitanism.

25. Yan Hairong, *New Masters, New Servants: Migration, Development, and Women Workers in China* (Durham, N.C.: Duke University Press, 2008), 172, 177.

26. Yan, *New Masters, New Servants*, 176.

27. Lisa Rofel, "Temporal-Spatial Migration: Workers in Transnational Supply-Chain Factories," *Ghost Protocol: Development and Displacement in Global China*, ed. Carlos Rojas and Ralph Litzinger (Durham, N.C.: Duke University Press, 2016), 186.

28. Rofel, "Temporal-Spatial Migration," 169.

29. In Cantonese, *dagong* (打工) means working for the boss; meanwhile, *mei* (妹) refers to sisters or girls.

30. Wanning Sun, *Maid in China: Media, Morality, and the Cultural Politics of Boundaries* (New York: Routledge, 2008), 106–7.

31. Sun, *Maid in China*, 112.

32. Sun, *Maid in China*, 118, 120.

33. In *Anti-Oedipus*, Gilles Deleuze and Félix Guattari critique Freudian psychoanalysis. Contrary to psychoanalysis that considers the unconscious as a theater representing Hamlet and Oedipus, they see the unconscious as a factory that produces. As opposed to psychoanalysis that focuses on the family ("daddy, mommy, and me"), their idea of desire is "geographical-political" and is linked to the world. For them, desire is also collective and multiple, rather than individual. Gilles Deleuze and Félix Guattari, *Anti-Oedipus: Capitalism and Schizophrenia* (Minneapolis: University of Minnesota Press, 1983). See also "D as in Desire" in Pierre-André Boutang, *Gilles Deleuze from A to Z* (Los Angeles: Semiotext(e); Cambridge, Mass.: MIT Press, 2012). This film is also called *ABC Primer*. For the website, see "'Gilles Deleuze's ABC Primer, with Claire Parnet.' Directed by Pierre-André Boutang (1996)," accessed May 15, 2013, http://www.langlab.wayne.edu/cstivale/d-g/abc1.html.

34. "'Gilles Deleuze's ABC Primer, with Claire Parnet.'"

35. Lauren Berlant, *Cruel Optimism* (Durham, N.C.: Duke University Press, 2011), 1.

36. Berlant, *Cruel Optimism*, 27.

37. David Redmon, *Beads, Bodies, and Trash: Public Sex, Global Labor, and the Disposability of Mardi Gras* (New York: Routledge, 2015), 19.

38. Laura Mulvey, "Visual Pleasure and Narrative Cinema," in *Movies and Methods*, vol. 2, ed. Bill Nichols, 303–15 (Berkeley and Los Angeles: University of California Press, 1985).

39. The Chinese names (whose pinyin is not entirely correct) come from the *Mardi Gras* documentary. I follow the spelling in this documentary.

40. Michel de Certeau, *The Practice of Everyday Life* (Berkeley: University of California Press, 1984). See also John Fiske, *Understanding Popular Culture* (New York: Routledge, 2010).

41. An interesting character in the *Mardi Gras* documentary film is a middle-aged Catholic priest. While looking at the women flashing their breasts, he claims that he does not look at them. However, if he does not plan to look, why does he attend the Mardi Gras carnival to begin with?

42. Slavoj Žižek, *The Sublime Object of Ideology* (New York: Verso, 1989), 29, 33.

43. Gilles Deleuze, "Postscript on the Societies of Control," *October* 59 (1992): 3–7. According to Foucault, the "disciplinary society" succeeded the "society of sovereignty." The function of the "society of sovereignty" is to tax rather than organize production, and to rule on death rather than administer life.

44. Deleuze, "Postscript on the Societies of Control," 4.

45. Deleuze, "Postscript on the Societies of Control," 4–5. For modulation, Deleuze uses salary (e.g., "salary according to merit") and education as examples. For the education, he writes that "just as the corporation replaces the factory, perpetual training tends to replace the school, and continuous control to replace the examination."

46. Deleuze, "Postscript on the Societies of Control," 5.

47. Deleuze, "Postscript on the Societies of Control," 5. Deleuze gives the example of money to distinguish between disciplinary society and society of control. He writes: "Discipline always referred back to minted money that locks gold in as numerical standard, while control relates to floating rates of exchange, modulated according to a rate established by a set of standard currencies."

48. According to Deleuze, the machines in society of sovereignty are simple machines (e.g., levers, pulleys, and clocks)."

49. Deleuze, "Postscript on the Societies of Control," 6.

50. For a comparable reading of Deleuze, see Cara Wallis, *Technomobility in China: Young Migrant Women and Mobile Phones* (New York: New York University Press, 2013). For a different perspective, Fredric Jameson historicizes and periodizes capitalism into three stages: classical capitalism; monopoly capitalism, or what Lenin calls imperialism; and late capitalism (or global or transnational capitalism). Corresponding to these three stages are the cultural expressions of realism, modernism, and postmodernism. See Jameson, *Postmodernism; or, the Cultural Logics of Late Capitalism* (Durham, N.C.: Duke University Press, 1991).

51. See Pun, *Made in China*. See also Ching Kwan Lee, *Gender and the South China Miracle: Two Worlds of Factory Women* (Berkeley: University of California Press, 1998).

52. Yan Hairong focuses on migrant domestic workers, not migrant factory workers. See Yan, *New Masters, New Servants*.

53. Yan Hairong, "Neoliberal Governmentality and Neohumanism: Organizing Suzhi/Value Flow through Labor Recruitment Networks," *Cultural Anthropology* 18, no. 4 (2003): 494.

54. Yan, "Neoliberal Governmentality and Neohumanism," 494.

55. Yan, "Neoliberal Governmentality and Neohumanism," 494–95.

56. Aihwa Ong, *Neoliberalism as Exception: Mutations in Citizenship and Sovereignty.* (Durham, N.C.: Duke University Press, 2006), 122.

57. Aihwa Ong, *Flexible Citizenship: The Cultural Logics of Transnationality* (Durham, N.C.: Duke University Press, 1999).

58. Ong, *Neoliberalism as Exception,* 124.

6. THE PSYCHIC LIFE OF RUBBISH

1. Walter Benjamin, *Illuminations,* ed. Hannah Arendt (New York: Schocken, 1968), 217–252 (Part VII and Part XVI).

2. Benjamin, *Illuminations,* 217–252 (Part XIV).

3. Benjamin, *Illuminations,* 217–252 (Part XVI).

4. Benjamin, *Illuminations,* 217–252 (Part V and VI).

5. Benjamin, *Illuminations,* 217–252 (Part XVII and Part III). In *The Arcades Project,* Walter Benjamin also explains the dialectical image as "what has been comes together in a flash with the now to form a constellation" (N2a,3). See Walter Benjamin, *The Arcades Project* (Cambridge, Mass.: Belknap Press, 1999), 462.

6. Benjamin, *Illuminations,* 217–252 (Part II).

7. Benjamin, *Illuminations,* 217–252 (Part IX).

8. In fact, Wang's documentary film *Beijing Besieged by Waste* is part of the discourse of eco-cinema and eco-documentary in China. Other documentary films also point to contemporary China's ecology in distress. These works include (but are not limited to): Jennifer Baicjwal, *Manufactured Landscapes* (New York: Zeitgeist Video, 2007); Huaqing Jin, *Heavy Metal* (Wheeling, Ill.: Film Ideas, 2012); Gary Marcuse, *Waking the Green Tiger: Rise of a Green Movement in China* (Vancouver, B.C.: Face to Face Media, distributed by Video Project, San Francisco, Calif., 2011); Ruby Yang, *The Warriors of Qiugang* (*Qiugang weishi* 仇崗衛士) (New York: Cinema Guild, 2010); and Liang Zhao, *A Farmer's Struggle* (Montréal, Québec: CinéFête, 2009). These works chronicle how different kinds of waste, including electronic waste, are shipped from the first to the third world. The diasporic rubbish upsets the well-being of the local habitats.

9. Chen Xuelin (陳雪蓮) and Tao Hong (陶虹), "Rubbish Doesn't Surround the City, But the City Surrounds the Rubbish" (*Bushi laji baowei chengshi, ershi chengshi baowei laji* 不是垃圾包圍城市 而是城市包圍垃圾), *Guo ji xian qu dao bao* 國際先驅導報, June 8, 2011, http://www.solidwaste.com.cn/news/184505.html (my translation).

10. For an ethnography of the scavengers in Beijing's rubbish dumps, see Hu Jiaming (胡嘉明) and Zhang Jieying's (張劼穎) Chinese-language ethnography, *Wasted Lives: The Economy, Community, and Space of Rubbish Dumps* (*Feipin shenghuo: lajichang de jingji, shequn yu kongjian* 廢品生活:垃圾場的經濟、社群與空間) (Xianggang 香港: Xianggang zhongwen daxue chubanshe:香港中文大學出版社), 2016.

11. Jia Zhangke (賈樟柯), Hao Jian (郝建), and Wu Dan (吳丹), "Conversations About *Xiaoshan Going Home* and *Xiao Wu*" (*Guanyu xiaoshan huijia xiaowu de duihua* 關於 "小山回家," "小武" 的對話). *Yellow River* (*Huanghe* 黃河) 4 (1999): 146–66.

12. *The Supermarket* series is similar to Andreas Gursky's photographic series *99 Cent II Diptychon*, a chromogenic color print (2001), https://www.andreasgursky.com/en /works/2001/cent-ii-diptychon.

13. Ye Zi, "Central Leaders Pay Attention to *Beijing Besieged by Waste* Images, Instruct the Rectification of Beijing Rubbish Dumps" (*Zhongyang lingdao guanzhu laji weicheng zhaopian pishi Beijing lajichang zhengzhi* 中央領導關注垃圾圍城照片 批示 北京垃圾場整治), China Photographer's Association (*Zhongguo shying xiehui* 中國攝 影協會), June 9, 2011, http://www.cpanet.org.cn/detail_news_78837.html.

14. Fenghuang shipin (鳳凰視頻). "Traveling with Dreams: *Beijing Besieged by Waste* Photographer Wang Jiuliang." ("Yu mengxiang tonghang: Laji weicheng sheying shi Wang Jiuliang" 與夢想同行: 垃圾圍城 攝影師王久良). Accessed May 15, 2013, http://v .ifeng.com/history/renwujingdian/201111/d67e9026-4830-4976-8b1b-ac836d8bf491 .shtml.

15. Wang Jiuliang (王久良), "Beijing Besieged by Garbage," *Cross-Currents: East Asian History and Culture Review*, no. 1 (December 2011), accessed May 15, 2013, https:// cross-currents.berkeley.edu/e-journal/photo-essay/beijing-besieged-garbage /statement.

16. On "lightness," see Paola Voci, *China on Video: Small-Screen Realities* (New York: Routledge, 2010).

17. For DV and contemporary Chinese documentary films, see Zhang Zhen and Angela Zito, eds., *DV-Made China: Digital Subjects and Social Transformations After Independent Film* (Honolulu: University of Hawaii Press, 2015).

18. In the documentary, Wang shows that Beijing is surrounded by rubbish. Adding to the director's discovery, it is possible to read the geography of Beijing, comprising of concentric circles, as a toilet. Indeed, the way in which the rubbish, the excrement of capitalistic consumer culture, surrounds Beijing is similar to the way in which the excrement of human beings surrounds the toilet. In fact, cultural critic Slavoj Žižek has made a similar point concerning the ideology of toilet. His observation of the relationship between the architecture of toilet, on the one hand, and European philosophy and politics, on the other hand, can help one look at Beijing as a city-toilet. In a book review, Žižek explains how the designs of the French, English, and German toilets reflect the cultural and political ideologies of these countries. He writes:

> In a traditional German toilet, the hole into which shit disappears after we flush is right at the front, so that shit is first laid out for us to sniff and inspect for traces of illness. In the typical French toilet, on the contrary, the hole is at the back, i.e., shit is supposed to disappear as quickly as possible. Finally, the American (Anglo-Saxon) toilet presents a synthesis, a mediation between these opposites: the toilet basin is full of water, so that the shit floats in it, visible, but not to be inspected. . . . It is clear that none of these versions can be accounted for in purely utilitarian terms: each involves a certain ideological perception of how the subject should relate to excrement. Hegel was among the first to see in the geographical triad of Germany, France and England an expression of three different existential attitudes: reflective thoroughness (German), revolutionary hastiness (French), utilitarian pragmatism (English). In political terms, this triad can be read as German conservatism,

French revolutionary radicalism and English liberalism. In terms of the pre-dominance of one sphere of social life, it is German metaphysics and poetry versus French politics and English economics. The point about toilets is that they enable us not only to discern this triad in the most intimate domain, but also to identify its underlying mechanism in the three different attitudes toward excremental excess: an ambiguous contemplative fascination; a wish to get rid of it as fast as possible; a pragmatic decision to treat it as ordinary and dispose of it in an appropriate way. It is easy for an academic at a round table to claim that we live in a post-ideological universe, but the moment he visits the lavatory after the heated discussion, he is again knee-deep in ideology.

See Slavoj Žižek, "Knee-Deep," *London Review of Books* 26 no. 17 (2004): 12–13. How is it possible to see the Chinese squatter toilet, as opposed to the sitting toilet, as an ideological expression of Chinese culture and politics?

19. Jacques Derrida, *Specters of Marx: The State of the Debt, the Work of Mourning, and the New International* (New York: Routledge, 1994), 63. See also Sigmund Freud, "The 'Uncanny,'" in *Standard Edition of the Complete Psychological Works of Sigmund Freud*, vol. 17: *An Infantile Neurosis and Other Works (1917–1919)*, ed. James Strachey (London: Hogarth Press and the Institute of Psychoanalysis, 1955); and Sigmund Freud, *The Interpretation of Dreams*, ed. James Strachey (New York: Basic Books, 2010).
20. Julia Kristeva, *Powers of Horror: An Essay on Abjection* (New York: Columbia University Press, 1982), 1.
21. Kristeva, *Powers of Horror*, 4.
22. Kristeva, *Powers of Horror*, 3.
23. Kristeva, *Powers of Horror*, 3.
24. Kristeva, *Powers of Horror*, 4.
25. Kristeva, *Powers of Horror*, 3–4.
26. I thank Xiaoying Wang for introducing Kristeva's work to me.
27. Jameson makes the distinction between utopian program and utopian impulse. He is interested in the utopian impulse in mass culture. See Fredric Jameson, *Archaeologies of the Future: The Desire Called Utopia and Other Science Fiction* (London: Verso, 2005), 1–9.
28. Fredric Jameson, "Reification and Utopia in Mass Culture," *Social Text* 1, no.1 (1979): 144.
29. Jameson, "Reification and Utopia in Mass Culture," 144.
30. Fredric Jameson, *The Political Unconscious: Narrative as a Socially Symbolic Act* (Ithaca, N.Y.: Cornell University Press, 1981), 285.
31. Jameson, *The Political Unconscious*, 296.
32. Cultural critic Wang Min'an has made a similar point. See Wang Min'an (汪民安), "On Rubbish" (*Lun laji* 論垃圾), in *What Is the Contemporary (Shenme shi dangdai* 什麼是當代) (Beijing 北京: Xinxingn chubanshe 新星出版社, 2014), 147–61.

WORKS CITED

SOURCES IN ENGLISH

Althusser, Louis. "Ideology and Ideological State Apparatus (Notes Towards an Investigation)." In *Lenin and Philosophy, and Other Essays*. New York: Monthly Review Press, 2001.

——. "Marxism and Humanism." In *For Marx*. New York: Verso, 2006.

Anagnost, Ann. "From 'Class' to 'Social Strata': Grasping the Social Totality in Reform-Era China." *Third World Quarterly* 29, no. 3 (2008): 497–519.

Appadurai, Arjun, ed. *The Social Life of Things: Commodities in Cultural Perspective*. New York: Cambridge University Press, 1986.

Bahrani, Ramin. *Plastic Bag* (2009). Accessed May 15, 2013. https://vimeo.com/144928861.

Baicjwal, Jennifer. *Manufactured Landscapes*. New York: Zeitgeist Video, 2007.

Barthes, Roland. *The Fashion System*. New York: Hill and Wang, 1983.

——. *The Language of Fashion*, ed. Andy Stafford and Michael Carter. New York: Berg, 2006.

——. *Mythologies*. New York: Hill and Wang, 1972.

Baudrillard, Jean. *Simulacra and Simulation*. Ann Arbor: University of Michigan Press, 1994.

Benjamin, Walter. *The Arcades Project*. Cambridge, Mass.: Belknap Press, 1999.

——. *Illuminations*, ed. Hannah Arendt. New York: Schocken, 1968.

——. "The Work of Art in the Age of Its Technological Reproducibility" (1937). In *Walter Benjamin: Selected Writings*, ed. Marcus Bullock and Michael W. Jennings. Cambridge, Mass.: Belknap Press, 1996–2003.

Berlant, Lauren. *Cruel Optimism*. Durham, N.C.: Duke University Press, 2011.

Berry, Chris. *Postsocialist Cinema in Post-Mao China: The Cultural Revolution After the Cultural Revolution*. New York: Routledge, 2004.

——. "Sexual Difference and the Viewing Subject in *Li Shuangshuang* and *The In-Laws*." In *Perspectives on Chinese Cinema*, ed. Chris Berry. London: British Film Institute, 1991.

Berry, Michael. "The Absent American: Figuring the United States in Chinese Cinema of the Reform Era." In *A Companion to Chinese Cinema*, ed. Yingjin Zhang. Malden, Mass.: Wiley-Blackwell, 2012.

Bourdieu, Pierre. *Distinction: A Social Critique of the Judgement of Taste*. Cambridge, Mass.: Harvard University Press, 1984.

Boutang, Pierre-Andre. *Gilles Deleuze From A to Z*. Los Angeles: Semiotext(e); Cambridge, Mass.: MIT Press, 2012.

Braester, Yomi, and Tina Mai Chen. "Film in the People's Republic of China, 1949–1979: The Missing Years?" *Journal of Chinese Cinemas* 5, no. 1 (2011): 5–12.

Buchanan, Ian. *A Dictionary of Critical Theory*. Oxford: Oxford University Press, 2010. .

Buck-Morss, Susan. *The Dialectics of Seeing: Walter Benjamin and The Arcades Project*. Cambridge, Mass.: MIT Press, 1989.

Cai Xiang. *Revolution and Its Narratives: China's Socialist Literary and Cultural Imaginaries, 1949–1966*, ed. Rebecca Karl and Xueping Zhong. Durham, N.C.: Duke University Press, 2016.

Canadian Broadcasting Corporation. *China's Sexual Revolution*. Montréal: Galafilm Productions, 2007.

Chang, Eileen (Zhang Ailing 張愛玲). "A Chronicle of Changing Clothes." In *Written on Water*. New York: Columbia University Press, 2005.

Chen, Eva. "Fashioning the Cosmopolitan Girl: Sartorial Display and Technologies of Femininity in the Chinese Bestseller *Du Lala* (2007–11)." *Fashion Theory: The Journal of Dress. Body & Culture* 17, no. 5 (2013): 553–78.

Chen, Jie. *A Middle Class Without Democracy: Economic Growth and the Prospects for Democratization in China*. New York: Oxford University Press, 2013.

Chen, Minglu, and David S. G. Goodman, eds. *Middle Class China: Identity and Behavior*. Cheltenham, U.K.: Edward Elgar, 2013.

Chen, Tina Mai. "Proletarian White and Working Bodies in Mao's China." *positions: east asia cultures critique* 11, no. 2 (2003): 361–93.

Chen, Xiaomei. "Growing Up with Posters in the Maoist Era." In *Picturing Power in the People's Republic of China: Posters of the Cultural Revolution*, ed. Harriet Evans and Stephanie Donald. Lanham, Md.: Rowman & Littlefield, 1999.

——. *Occidentalism: A Theory of Counter-Discourse in Post-Mao China*. New York: Oxford University Press, 1995.

Chen, Yun. "The Young Generation." In *The Columbia Anthology of Modern Chinese Drama*, ed. Xiaomei Chen. New York: Columbia University Press, 2014.

China Photographers Association. *China's Thirty Years* (*Jianzheng: Gaige kaifang sanshinian* 見證:改革開放三十年), ed. Wang Miao and Liu Yang. New York: Oxford University Press, 2009.

Choi, Susanne Yuk-Ping, and Yinni Peng. *Masculine Compromise: Migration, Family, and Gender in China*. Oakland: University of California Press, 2016.

Chow, Rey. "Fetish Power Unbound: A Small History of 'Woman' in Chinese Cinema." *The Oxford Handbook of Chinese Cinemas*, ed. Carlos Rojas and Eileen Cheng-Yin-Chow. New York: Oxford University Press, 2013.

——. *Primitive Passions: Visuality, Sexuality, Ethnography, and Contemporary Chinese Cinema*. New York: Columbia University Press, 1995.

Clark, Paul. "Artists, Cadres, and Audiences." In *A Companion to Chinese Cinema*, ed. Yingjin Zhang. Malden, Mass.: Wiley-Blackwell, 2012.

——. *Chinese Cinema: Culture and Politics Since 1949*. New York: Cambridge University Press, 1987.

Dai Jinhua. "Invisible Writing: The Politics of Mass Culture in the 1990s." In *Cinema and Desire: Feminist Marxism and Cultural Politics in the Work of Dai Jinhua*, ed. Jing Wang and Tani Barlow. London: Verso, 2002.

De Certeau, Michel. *The Practice of Everyday Life*. Berkeley: University of California Press, 1984.

Deleuze, Gilles. *Logic of Sense*, ed. Constantin V. Boundas. New York: Columbia University Press, 1990.

——. "Postscript on the Societies of Control." *October* 59 (1992): 3–7.

Deleuze, Gilles, and Félix Guattari. *Anti-Oedipus: Capitalism and Schizophrenia*. Minneapolis: University of Minnesota Press, 1983.

Derrida, Jacques. *Specters of Marx: The State of the Debt, the Work of Mourning, and the New International*. New York: Routledge, 1994.

Dolar, Mladen. "Beyond Interpellation." *Qui Parle* 6, no. 2 (1993): 75–96.

Evans, Harriet. "Fashions and Feminine Consumption." In *Consuming China: Approaches to Cultural Change in Contemporary China*, ed. Kevin Latham, Stuart Thompson, and Jakob Klein. New York: Routledge, 2006.

Finnane, Antonia. *Changing Clothes in China: Fashion, History, Nation*. New York: Columbia University Press, 2008.

Fiske, John. *Understanding Popular Culture*. New York: Routledge, 2010.

Foucault, Michel. *The History of Sexuality*. Vol. 1: *An Introduction*. New York: Vintage, 1990.

Freud, Sigmund. *The Interpretation of Dreams*, ed. James Strachey. New York: Basic Books, 2010.

——. "The 'Uncanny.'" In *Standard Edition of the Complete Psychological Works of Sigmund Freud*. Vol. 17: *An Infantile Neurosis and Other Works (1917–1919)*, ed. James Strachey. London: Hogarth Press and the Institute of Psychoanalysis, 1955.

Fumian, Marco. "*Chronicle of Du Lala's Promotion*: Exemplary Literature, the Middle Class, and the Socialist Market." *Modern Chinese Literature and Culture* 28, no. 1 (2016): 78–128.

Fussell, Paul. *Class: A Guide Through the American Status System*. New York: Summit, 1983.

Gallop, Jane. *Reading Lacan*. Ithaca, N.Y.: Cornell University Press, 1985.

Goodman, David S. G., ed. *The New Rich in China: Future Rules, Present Lives*. New York: Routledge, 2008.

Guo, Shaohua. "Acting Through the Camera Lens: The Global Imaginary and Middle Class Aspirations in Chinese Urban Cinema." *Journal of Contemporary China* 26, no. 104 (2017): 311–24.

Gursky, Andreas. *99 Cent II Diptychon*. Chromogenic color print. 2001. https://www
.andreasgursky.com/en/works/2001/cent-ii-diptychon.

Harvey, David. *A Companion to Marx's Capital*. New York: Verso, 2010.

——. *A History of Neoliberalism*. New York: Oxford University Press, 2005.

Hinton, Carma, Geremie R. Barmé, and Richard Gordon. *Morning Sun (Bajiu dianzhong de taiyang* 八九點鐘的太陽). Brookline, Mass.: Long Bow, 2005.

Honig, Emily, and Gail Hershatter. *Personal Voices: Chinese Women in the 1980's*. Stanford, CA: Stanford University Press, 1988.

Hsiao, Hsin-Huang Michael, ed. *Chinese Middle Classes: Taiwan, Hong Kong, Macao
and China*. New York: Routledge, 2013.

Hui, Calvin. "Dirty Fashion: Ma Ke's Fashion 'Useless,' Jia Zhangke's Documentary
Useless, and Cognitive Mapping." *Journal of Chinese Cinemas* 9, no. 3 (2015): 253–70.

——. "Mao's Children Are Wearing Fashion!" In *The Changing Landscape of China's
Consumerism*, ed. Alison Hulme. Kidlington, Oxford: Chandos, 2014.

——. "Socks and Revolution: The Politics of Consumption in *Sentinels Under the Neon
Lights* (1964)." In *The Cold War and Asian Cinema*, ed. Poshek Fu and Man-Fung
Yip, 158–73. New York: Routledge, 2020.

Jameson, Fredric. *Archaeologies of the Future: The Desire Called Utopia and Other Science Fictions*. London: Verso, 2007.

——. "Cognitive Mapping." In *Marxism and the Interpretation of Culture*, ed. Cary
Nelson and Lawrence Grossberg. Urbana: University of Illinois Press, 1988.

——. *The Geopolitical Aesthetic: Cinema and Space in the World System*. Bloomington:
Indiana University Press, 1992.

——. "Imaginary and Symbolic in Lacan." In *The Ideologies of Theory: Essays 1971–
1986*. Vol. 1: *Situations of Theory*. Minneapolis: University of Minnesota Press, 1988.

——. *The Political Unconscious: Narrative as a Socially Symbolic Act*. Ithaca, N.Y.: Cornell University Press, 1981.

——. *Postmodernism, or the Cultural Logic of Late Capitalism*. Durham, N.C.: Duke
University Press, 1991.

——. "Reification and Utopia in Mass Culture." *Social Text* 1, no. 1 (1979): 130–48.

Jin, Huaqing. *Heavy Metal*. Wheeling, Ill.: Film Ideas, 2012.

Johnson, Bryan. "Marching Peasants Are out in New Chinese Films." *Globe and Mail*,
November 7, 1980.

Katzin, Lee H. *The Man from Atlantis*. Burbank, Calif.: Hanna-Barbera and Warner
Bros., 2011.

Kiaer, Christina. *Imagine No Possessions: The Socialist Objects of Russian Constructivism*. Cambridge, Mass.: MIT Press, 2005.

Kraus, Richard Curt. *Class Conflict in Chinese Socialism*. New York: Columbia University Press, 1981.

Kristeva, Julia. *Powers of Horror: An Essay on Abjection*. New York: Columbia University Press, 1982.

Lacan, Jacques. "The Mirror Stage as Formative of the 'I' Function as Revealed in Psychoanalytical Experience." In *Ecrits*. New York: Norton, 2006.

Lee, Ching Kwan. *Gender and the South China Miracle: Two Worlds of Factory Women*.
Berkeley: University of California Press, 1998.

Leung, Wing-Fai, "Product Placement with 'Chinese Characteristics': Feng Xiaogang's
Films and *Go! Lala Go!*" *Journal of Chinese Cinemas* 9, no. 2 (2015): 125–40.

Li, Cheng, ed. *China's Emerging Middle Class: Beyond Economic Transformation*. Washington, DC: Brookings Institution Press, 2010.

Liu, Jianmei. "Love Cannot Be Forgotten." In *Revolution Plus Love: Literary History, Women's Bodies, and Thematic Repetition in Twentieth-Century Chinese Fiction*. Honolulu: University of Hawaii Press, 2003.

Liu, Kang. *Aesthetics and Marxism: Chinese Aesthetic Marxists and Their Western Contemporaries*. Durham, N.C.: Duke University Press, 2000.

Louie, Kam. "The Meaning of Love and Marriage in China, 1978–1981." In *Between Fact and Fiction: Essays on Post-Mao Chinese Literature and Society*. Broadway, Australia: Wild Peony, 1989.

Lukács, Georg. *History and Class Consciousness*. Cambridge, Mass.: MIT Press, 1971.

Lotta, Raymond. "China's Rise in the World Economy." *Economic and Political Weekly* 44, no. 8 (2009): 29–34.

Lu, Sheldon. "Introduction: Chinese-Language Ecocinema." *Journal of Chinese Cinemas* 11, no. 1 (2017): 1–12.

Marcuse, Gary. *Waking the Green Tiger: Rise of a Green Movement in China*. Vancouver, B.C.: Face to Face Media; distributed by Video Project, San Francisco, Calif., 2011.

Mao Tse-tung. "Analysis of the Classes in Chinese Society" In *Selected Works of Mao Tse-tung*. March 1926. Marxists Internet Archive. https://www.marxists.org/reference/archive/mao/selected-works/volume-1/mswv1_1.htm.

Mao Zedong. "Analysis of the Classes in Chinese Society" (*Zhongguo shehui gejieji de fenxi* 中國社會各階級的分析) (March 1926). In *Selected Works of Mao Tse-tung*, 13–21. Peking: Foreign Languages Press, 1967. Prepared for the Internet by David J. Romagnolo, May 1997. http://marx2mao.com/Mao/AC26.html.

Marx, Karl. *Capital: A Critique of Political Economy*. 3 vols. New York: Penguin, 1990–1991.

McGrath, Jason. "Communists Have More Fun! The Dialectics of Fulfillment in Cinema of the People's Republic of China." *World Picture* 3 (2009).

Meisner, Maurice. *Mao's China and After: A History of the People's Republic*. New York: Free Press, 1999.

Meng Yue. "Female Images and National Myth." In *Gender Politics in Modern China: Writing and Feminism*, ed. Tani Barlow. Durham, N.C.: Duke University Press, 1993.

Miao, Ying. *Being Middle Class in China: Identity, Attitudes and Behavior*. Abingdon, Oxon: Routledge, 2017.

Montag, Warren. *Althusser and His Contemporaries: Philosophy's Perpetual War*. Durham, N.C.: Duke University Press, 2013.

Mulvey, Laura. "Visual Pleasure and Narrative Cinema." In *Movies and Methods*, vol. 2, ed. Bill Nichols, 303–15. Berkeley and Los Angeles: University of California Press, 1985.

Ong, Aihwa. *Flexible Citizenship: The Cultural Logics of Transnationality*. Durham, N.C.: Duke University Press, 1999.

——. *Neoliberalism as Exception: Mutations in Citizenship and Sovereignty*. Durham, N.C.: Duke University Press, 2006.

Otis, Eileen. *Markets and Bodies: Women, Service Work, and the Making of Inequality in China*. Stanford, Calif.: Stanford University Press, 2012.

"Paris Fashions Go to Peking [Beijing] with Cardin's Couture, a Great Leap Sexward." *Time* 113, no. 7 (February 12, 1979): 70.

Peled, Micha X. *China Blue*. Oley, Penn.: Bullfrog Films, 2005.

Pun Ngai. *Made in China: Women Factory Workers in a Global Workplace*. Durham, N.C.: Duke University Press, 2005.

——. *Migrant Labor in China*. Cambridge: Polity, 2016.

——. "Subsumption or Consumption? The Phantom of Consumer Revolution in 'Globalizing' China." *Cultural Anthropology* 18, no. 4 (2003): 469–92.

Qin Xiaoyu, ed. *Iron Moon: An Anthology of Chinese Migrant Worker Poetry*. Trans. Eleanor Goodman. Buffalo, N.Y.: White Pine Press, 2016.

Redmon, David. *Beads, Bodies, and Trash: Public Sex, Global Labor, and the Disposability of Mardi Gras*. New York: Routledge, 2015.

——. *Mardi Gras: Made in China*. Brooklyn: Carnivalesque Films, 2008.

Ren, Hai. *The Middle Class in Neoliberal China: Governing Risk, Life-Building, and Themed Spaces*. New York: Routledge, 2012.

Rocca, Jean-Louis. *The Making of the Chinese Middle Class: Small Comfort and Great Expectations*. New York: Palgrave Macmillan, 2016.

Rofel, Lisa. *Desiring China: Experiments in Neoliberalism, Sexuality, and Public China*. Durham, N.C.: Duke University Press, 2007.

——. *Other Modernities: Gendered Yearnings in China after Socialism*. Berkeley: University of California Press, 1999.

——. "Temporal-Spatial Migration: Workers in Transnational Supply-Chain Factories." In *Ghost Protocol: Development and Displacement in Global China*, ed. Carlos Rojas and Ralph Litzinger. Durham, N.C.: Duke University Press, 2016.

Ross, Kristin. *Fast Cars, Clean Bodies: Decolonization and the Reordering of French Culture*. Cambridge, Mass.: MIT Press, 1995.

Simmel, Georg. "Fashion." *International Quarterly* 10 (1904): 130–55.

Sun, Wanning. *Maid in China: Media, Morality, and the Cultural Politics of Boundaries*. New York: Routledge, 2008.

——. *Subaltern China: Rural Migrants, Media, and Cultural Practices*. Lanham, Md.: Rowman & Littlefield, 2014.

Swider, Sarah. *Building China: Informal Work and the New Precariat*. Ithaca, N.Y.: Cornell University Press, 2015.

Tang, Xiaobing. *Chinese Modern: The Heroic and the Quotidian*. Durham, N.C.: Duke University Press, 2000.

Tsang, Eileen Yuk-Ha. *The New Middle Class in China: Consumption, Politics and the Market Economy*. New York: Palgrave Macmillan, 2014.

Van Fleit Hang, Krista. *Literature the People Love: Reading Chinese Texts from the Early Maoist Period (1949–1966)*. New York: Palgrave Macmillan, 2013.

Veblen, Thorstein. *The Theory of the Leisure Class*. 1898. Reprint, New York: Oxford University Press, 2007.

Victoria and Albert Museum. "Fashion in Motion: Ma Ke Wuyong." Accessed May 15, 2013. https://web.archive.org/web/20090129143951/http://www.vam.ac.uk/collections/fashion/fashion_motion/ma_ke/vidoe/index.html.

Voci, Paola. *China on Video: Small-Screen Realities*. New York: Routledge, 2010.

Wallis, Cara. *Technomobility in China: Young Migrant Women and Mobile Phones*. New York: New York University Press, 2013.

Wang, Ban. "Desire and Pleasure in Revolutionary Cinema." In *The Sublime Figure of History: Aesthetics and Politics in Twentieth-Century China*. Stanford, Calif.: Stanford University Press, 1997.

Wang Dan, Li Minqi, and Wang Chaohua. "A Dialogue on the Future of China." In *One China, Many Paths*, ed. Wang Chaohua. New York: Verso, 2003.

Wang Hui. *The End of the Revolution: China and the Limits of Modernity*. New York: Verso, 2009.

——. "The 1989 Social Movement and the Historical Roots of China's Neoliberalism," trans. Theodore Huters. In *China's New Order: Society, Politics, and Economy in Transition*, ed. Theodore Huters. Cambridge, Mass.: Harvard University Press, 2003.

Wang, Jing. *High Culture Fever: Politics, Aesthetics, and Ideology in Deng's China*. Berkeley: California University Press, 1996.

Wang Jiuliang (王久良). "Beijing Besieged by Garbage." *Cross-Currents: East Asian History and Culture Review*, no. 1 (December 2011). https://cross-currents.berkeley.edu/e-journal/photo-essay/beijing-besieged-garbage/statement.

Wang, Zhuoyi. *Revolutionary Cycles in Chinese Cinema, 1951–1979*. New York: Palgrave Macmillan, 2014.

Ward, Julian. "The Remodeling of a National Cinema: Chinese Films of the Seventeen Years (1949–66)." In *The Chinese Cinema Book*, ed. Song Hwee Lim and Julian Ward. New York: Palgrave Macmillan; and London: British Film Institute, 2011.

Williams, Raymond. *Marxism and Literature*. Oxford: Oxford University Press, 1977.

Willis, Susan. *A Primer for Daily Life*. New York: Routledge, 1991.

Wu, Grace Hui-chuan. "The Making of the New Global Middle Class: China's Workplace Novels." *Concentric: Literary and Cultural Studies* 43, no. 1 (2017): 299–327.

Wu, Juanjuan. *Chinese Fashion: From Mao to Now*. New York: Berg, 2009.

Yan Hairong. "Neoliberal Governmentality and Neohumanism: Organizing Suzhi/Value Flow through Labor Recruitment Networks." *Cultural Anthropology* 18, no. 4 (2003): 493–523.

——. *New Masters, New Servants: Migration, Development, and Women Workers in China*. Durham, N.C.: Duke University Press, 2008.

Yang, Mayfair Mei-hui. "From Gender Erasure to Gender Difference: State Feminism, Consumer Sexuality, and Women's Public Sphere in China." In *Spaces of Their Own: Women's Public Sphere in Transnational China*, ed. Mayfair Mei-hui Yang. Minneapolis: University of Minnesota Press, 1999.

Yang, Ruby. *The Warriors of Qiugang (Qiugang weishi* 仇岗衛士). New York: Cinema Guild, 2010.

Young, Marilyn. "Chicken Little in China: Some Reflections on Women." In *Marxism and the Chinese Experience: Issues in Contemporary Chinese Socialism*, ed. Arif Dirlik and Maurice Meisner. Armonk, N.Y.: M. E. Sharpe, 1989.

Zavoretti, Roberta. *Rural Origins, City Lives: Class and Place in Contemporary China*. Seattle: University of Washington Press, 2016.

Zhang Hongxing and Lauren Parker, eds. *China Design Now*. London: V&A Pub., 2008.

Zhang, Jun. *Driving Toward Modernity: Cars and the Lives of the Middle Class in Contemporary China*. Ithaca, N.Y.: Cornell University Press, 2019.

Zhang, Xudong. *Chinese Modernism in the Era of Reforms: Cultural Fever, Avant-Garde Fiction, and the New Chinese Cinema*. Durham, N.C.: Duke University Press, 1997.

——. "Market Socialism and Its Discontent: Jia Zhangke's Cinematic Narrative of China's Transition in the Age of Global Capital." In *Neoliberalism and Global Cinema: Capital, Culture, and Marxist Critique*, ed. Jyotsna Kapur and Keith B. Wagner. New York: Routledge, 2011.

Zhang Zhen and Angela Zito, eds. *DV-Made China: Digital Subjects and Social Transformations After Independent Film*. Honolulu: University of Hawaii Press, 2015.

Zhao, Liang. *A Farmer's Struggle*. Montréal, Québec: CinéFête, 2009.

Zheng, Yi. *Contemporary Chinese Print Media: Cultivating Middle Class Taste*. Abingdon, Oxon: Routledge, 2014.

Zhong, Xueping. *Masculinity Besieged? Issues of Modernity and Male Subjectivity in Chinese Literature of the Late Twentieth Century*. Durham, N.C.: Duke University Press, 2000.

Žižek, Slavoj. "Knee-Deep." *London Review of Books* 26, no. 17 (2004): 12–13.

——. *The Sublime Object of Ideology*. New York: Verso, 1989.

SOURCES IN CHINESE

Ai, Hua (Harriet Evans 艾華) and Li Yinhe (李銀河). "Dialogue About Feminism" (*Guanyu nüxing zhuyi de duihua* 關於女性主義的對話). *Sociological Research* (*Shehuixue yanjiu* 社會學研究) 4 (2001): 118–25.

An Zhujie (安竹間). *Go! Lala Go! 2* (*Dulala zhuihunqi* 杜拉拉追婚記). Guangzhou 廣州: Guangdong yinxiang chuban youxian gongsi 廣東音像出版有限公司, 2015.

Antonioni, Michelangelo, *Chung Kuo Cina* (*Zhongguo* 中國). Translated from Italian to Chinese. Roma: Rai Trade; Milano: Feltrinelli. China: Jiangxi wenhua yinxiang chubanshe 江西文化音像出版社, 2007.

Bao Zhifang (鮑芝芳). *Black Dragonfly* (*Hei qingting* 黑蜻蜓). 1984.

Cai Xiang (蔡翔). *Revolution/Narration: China's Socialist Literary and Cultural Imaginaries (1949–1966)* (*Geming/Xushu: Zhongguo shehui zhuyi wenxue—wenhua xianxiang* [1949–1966] 革命/敘述:中國社會主義文學—文化想象 [1949–1966]). Beijing 北京: Beijing daxue chubanshe 北京大學出版社, 2010.

CCTV.com (Yangshi wang 央視網). "Economic Reforms and Opening Up: The Changes of Fashion During the Past 30 Years" (*Gaige kaifang: fuzhuang biange 30 nian* 改革開放: 服裝變革30年). Accessed May 15, 2013. http://news.cctv.com/society/20081112/101903.shtml.

——. "Phenomenon 1980: First Episode: Catwalk" (*Xianxiang 1980:diyiji: tianqiao* 現象1980第一集:天橋). Accessed May 15, 2013. http://jishi.cntv.cn/xianxiang1980/classpage/video/20110826/100095.shtml.

Chan, Peter Ho-sun (Chen Kexin 陳可辛). *American Dreams in China* (*Zhongguo hehuoren* 中國合伙人). Hong Kong: Edko Films, 2013.

Chen Mingzhang (陳銘章). *A Story of Lala's Promotion* (*Dulala shengzhiji* 杜拉拉升職記). [Shanghai 上海]: Shanghai luxiang gongsi 上海錄像公司, 2010.

Chen Peisi (陳佩斯) and Ding Xuan (丁喧). *Father and Son Open a Bar* (*Ye'erliang Kaigeting* 爺兒倆開歌廳). Hangzhou 杭州: Zhejiang wenyi yinxiang chubanshe 浙江文藝音像出版社, 1992.

Chen Xuelin (陳雪蓮) and Tao Hong (陶虹). "Rubbish Doesn't Surround the City, But the City Surrounds the Rubbish" (*Bushi laji baowei chengshi, ershi chengshi baowei laji* 不是垃圾包圍城市 而是城市包圍垃圾). *Guo ji xian qu dao bao* 國際先驅導報, June 8, 2011. http://www.solidwaste.com.cn/news/184505.html.

Chen Yu (陳煜). *The Memory of Chinese Life: The Past Livelihood of the 60 Years of the Founding of the Nation* (*Zhongguo shenghuo jiyi: jianguo 60 nian minsheng wangshi* 中國生活記憶: 建國60年民生往事). Beijing 北京: Zhongguo qinggongye chubanshe 中國輕工業出版社, 2009.

Chen Yun (陳耘). *The Young Generation* (*Nianqing de yidai* 年青的一代). Beijing 北京: Zhongguo xiju chubanshe 中國戲劇出版社, 1964.

Cheng Hao (成浩). *Foreign Girls* (*Wai Lai Mei* 外來妹). Guangzhou 廣州: Xinshidai yingyin gongsi 新時代影音公司, 1999.

Cheng Yin (成蔭). *Shanghai Girls* (*Shanghai guniang* 上海姑娘). Beijing 北京: Zhongying yinxiang chubanshe 中影音像出版社, 2004.

Cong Shen (叢深). "The Formation of the Theme of *Never Forget*" (*Qianwan buyao wangji zhuti de xingcheng* 〈千萬不要忘記〉主題的形成). *Drama* (*Xiju bao* 戲劇報) 4 (1964): 27–28.

——. *Never Forget* (*Qianwan buyao wangji* 千萬不要忘記). Beijing 北京: Zhongguo xiju chubanshe 中國戲劇出版社, 1964.

Cui Manli (崔曼莉). *Floating and Sinking* (*Fuchen* 浮沈). Xi'an 西安: Shanxi shi fan da xue chu ban she 陝西師範大學出版社, 2008.

Cui Wei (崔嵬). *Song of Youth* (*Qingchun zhige* 青春之歌). Beijing 北京: Zhongying yinxiang chubanshe 中影音像出版社, 2005.

Deng Youmei (鄧友梅). *On the Cliff* (*Zai xuanya shang* 在懸崖上). Nanchang 南昌: Ershi shiji chubanshe 二十世紀出版社, 2013.

Dong Zhaoqi (董兆琪). *Lei Feng* (*Leifeng* 雷鋒). Beijing 北京: Zhongguo sanhuan yinxiangshe 中國三環音像社, 2005.

Fan Lixin (范立欣). *Last Train Home* (*Guitu lieche* 歸途列車). New York: Zeitgeist Video, 2011.

Fang Ying (方熒). *So Passionate* (*Ruci duoqing* 如此多情). Changchun 長春: Changchun dianying zhipianchang yinsheng chubanse 長春電影製片廠銀聲音像出版社, 2003.

Feng Gong (馮鞏). *Eat Hot Tofu Slowly* (*Xinji chibuliao redoufu* 心急吃不了熱豆腐). Ha'erbin 哈爾濱: Heilongjiang wenhua yinxiang chubanshe 黑龍江文化音像出版社, 2005.

Feng Xiaogang (馮小剛). *Big Shots Funeral* (Dawan). Culver City, Calif.: Columbia Tri-Star Home Entertainment, 2003.

——. *If You Are the One* (*Feicheng wurao* 非誠勿擾). Yunnan 雲南: Yunnan yinxiang chubanshe 雲南音像出版社, 2008.

——. *If You Are the One 2* (*Feicheng wurao 2* 非誠勿擾 2). Guangdong 廣東: Guangdong yinxiang chubanshe 廣東音像出版, 2010.

——. *If You Are the One: Love & Marriage*. New York: New Video, 2011.

——. *Youth* (*Fanghua* 芳華). Hong Kong 香港: Yugao yule youxian gongsi 域高娛樂有限公司, 2018.

Fenghuang shipin (鳳凰視頻). "Traveling with Dreams: *Beijing Besieged by Waste* photographer Wang Jiuliang" ("Yu mengxiang tonghang: Laji weicheng sheying shi Wang Jiuliang" 與夢想同行: 垃圾圍城 攝影師王久良). Accessed May 15, 2013. http://so .v.ifeng.com/video?q=%E4%B8%8E%E6%A2%A6%E6%83%B3%E5%90%8C%E8%A1%8C%20%E5%9E%83%E5%9C%BE%E5%9B%B4%E5%9F%8E%E6%91%84%E5%BD%B1%E5%B8%88%E7%8E%8B%E4%B9%85%E8%89%AF&c=5.

Fenghuang shipin (鳳凰視頻). "The Real Meaning of *Beijing Besieged by Waste*" (*Laji weicheng de xianshi yiyi* 《垃圾圍城》的現實意義). Accessed May 15, 2013. Website lost.

Fu Chaowu (傅超武). *Family Problems* (*Jiating wenti* 家庭問題). Shenzhen 深圳: Shenzhen yinxiang gongsi 深圳音像公司, 2011.

Fu Yao (付遙). *Lose or Win* (*Shuying* 輸贏). Beijing 北京: Beijing daxue chubanshe 北京大學出版社, 2011.

Fusai'er, Baoluo (Fussell, Paul 福塞爾,保羅). *Taste: Social Status and Lifestyle* (*Gediao: shehui dengji yu shenghuo pinwei* 格調: 社會等級與生活品味). Beijing 北京: Zhonghuo shehui kexue chubanshe 中國社會科學出版社, 1998.

Gu Hua (古華). *Hibiscus Town* (*Furong zhen* 芙蓉鎮). Beijing 北京: Renmin wenxue chuban she 人民文學出版社, 1981.

Guo Jingming (郭敬明). *Tiny Times* (*Xiaoshidai* 小時代). AV-Jet International Media, 2013.

Guo Wei (郭維). *Blooming Flowers and the Full Moon* (*Huahao yueyuan* 花好月圓). Beijing 北京: Zhongguo wencai shengxiang chuban gongsi 中國文採聲像出版公司, 2005.

Ho Chao-ti (He Zhaoti 賀照緹). *My Fancy High Heels* (*Wo'ai gaogenxie* 我愛高跟鞋). Taipei 台北: Gonggong dianshi 公共電視, 2010.

Hu Jiaming (胡嘉明) and Zhang Jieying (張劼穎). *Wasted Lives: The Economy, Community, and Space of the Rubbish Dumps* (*Feipin shenghuo: lajichang de jingji, shequn yu kongjian* 廢品生活:垃圾場的經濟、社群與空間). Xianggang 香港: Xianggang zhongwen daxue chubanshe: 香港中文大學出版社), 2016.

Hu Wanchun (胡萬春). *Family Problems* (*Jiating wenti* 家庭問題). Shanghai 上海: Zuojia chubanshe 作家出版社, 1964.

Huang Zumo (黃祖模). *Romance on Lu Mountain* (*Lushanlian* 廬山戀). Guangzhou 廣州: Guangzhou yin xiang chu ban she 廣州音像出版社, 1980.

Huo Jianqi (霍建起). *Life Show* (*Shenghuoxiu* 生活秀). Beverly Hills, Calif.: Razor Digital Entertainment, 2002.

Jia Zhangke (賈樟柯). *24 City* (*Ershisi chengji* 二十四城記). Guangzhou 廣州: Guangdong yinxiang chubanshe 廣東音像出版社, 2009.

——. *Cinema, Thinking, and Solutions* (*Dianying xiangfa he banfe* 電影,想法和辦法). Beijing 北京: Zhongguo renmin daxue chubanshe 中國人民大學出版社. 200-?.

——. *Dong* (*Dong* 東). New York: dGenerate Films, 2008.

——. *Jia Thinks* (*Jia Xiang 1996–2008: Jia Zhangke dianying shouji* 賈想1996–2008: 賈樟柯電影手記). Beijing 北京: Beijing daxue chubanshe 北京大學出版社, 2009.

——. *Platform* (*Zhantai* 站台). London: Artificial Eye, 2002.

——. *Still Life* (*Sanxia Haoren* 三峽好人). New York: New York Video, 2008.

——. *Unknown Pleasures* (*Renxiaoyao* 任逍遙). London: Artificial Eye, 2004.

——. *Useless* (*Wuyong* 無用). Seoul: SYComad, 2010.

——. *The World* (*Shijie* 世界). Guangzhou 廣州: Guangzhou yinxiang chubanshe 廣州音像出版社, 2004.

——. *The World* (*Shijie* 世界). New York: Zeitgeist Films, 2005.

——. *Xiaowu* (*Xiaowu* 小武). London: Artificial Eye, 2004.

Jia Zhangke (賈樟柯), Hao Jian (郝建), Wu Dan (吳丹). "Conversations About *Xiaoshan Going Home* and *Xiao Wu*" (*Guanyu xiaoshan huijia xiaowu de duihua* 關於 "小山回家," "小武" 的對話). *Yellow River* (*Huanghe* 黃河) 4 (1999): 146–66.

Kong Sheng (孔笙) and Jian Chuanhe (簡川訸). *Ode to Joy* (*Huanlesong* 歡樂頌). Chang-sha 長沙: Hunan jinfeng yinxiang chubanshe youxian gongsi 湖南金蜂音像出版社有限公司, 2016.

Lei Feng (雷鋒). *The Diary of Lei Feng* (*Leifeng riji* 雷鋒日記). Beijing 北京: Jiefangjun wenyi she 解放軍文藝社, 1964.

Li Ke (李可). *Chronicle of Du Lala's Promotion* (*Du Lala shengzhi ji* 杜拉拉升職記). Xi'an 西安: Xi'an shifan daxue chuban she 西安師範大學出版社, 2007.

——. *Dulala 2* (*Du Lala 2* 杜拉拉2). Xi'an 西安: Shanxi shifan daxue chubanshe, 陝西師範大學出版社, 2009.

——. *Dulala 3: Fighting for Flying.* (*Du Lal 3: Wozai zhe zhandou de yinian li* 我在這戰鬥的一年裏). Nanjing 南京: Jiangsu wenyi chubanshe 江蘇文藝出版社, 2010.

——. *Du Lala Finale: Follow Your Hearts, Follow Your Dreams* (*Dulala da jieju: yu lixiang youguan* 杜拉拉大結局:與理想有). Changsha 長沙: Huanan wenyi chubanshe 湖南文艺出版社, 2011.

Li Tuo (李陀). "The New Petty Bourgeoisie and the Transfer of Cultural Hegemony" (*Xin xiaozi he wenhua lingdaoquan de zhuanyi* "新小資"和文化領導權的轉移). *Changjiang Literature and Art* (*Changjiang Wenyi* 長江文藝) 12 (2013): 76–89.

——. Preface to *Bo dong* (波動), by Bei Dao (北島). Beijing 北京: San lian shu dian 三聯書店, 2010.

Li Yang (李楊). *Blind Shaft* (*Mangjing* 盲井). Kowloon: 星寶集團有限公司 Xingbao jituan youxian gongsi, 2003.

Li Yunlei (李雲雷). "The Proletarianization of the New Petty Bourgeoisie and the Question of Cultural Hegemony" (*Xin xiaozide dicenghua yu wenhua lingdaoquan wenti* 新小資的"底層化"與文化領導權問題). *Southern Literary Forum* (*Nanfang Wentan* 南方文壇) 1 (2013): 39–41.

Ling Zhihao (凌之浩) and Zhang Huijun (張慧鈞). *The Young Generation* (Nianqing de yidai 年青的一代). Jinan 濟南: Qilu yinxiang chubanshe 齊魯電子音像出版社, 2005.

Liu Fang (流芳). "Liberate Thinking; Be Bold and Innovative" (*Jiefang shixiang dadan chuangxin* 解放思想大膽創新) *Fashion* (*Shizhuang* 時裝) 2 (1983): 6.

Liu Junjie (劉俊傑). *Still Lala* (*Woshi Dulala* 我是杜拉拉). Jiangsu weishi 江蘇衛視, 2016.

Liu Xiangcheng (Liu, Heung Shing 劉香成). *Post-Mao China 1976–1983* (*Mao yihou de zhongguo 1976–1983* 毛以後的中國 1976–1983). Beijing 北京: Shijie tushu chuban gongsi Beijing gongsi 世界圖書出版公司北京公司, 2011.

Liu Xinwu (劉心武). "The Place of Love" (*Aiqing de weizhi* 愛情的位置). In *Selected Novellas by Liu Xinwu* (*Liu xinwu duanpian xiaoshuo xuan* 劉心武短篇小說選). Beijing 北京: Beijing chubanshe 北京出版社, 1980.

Lu Ling (路翎). *Battle of the Lowlands* (*Wadishang de zhanyi* 窪地上的戰役). Guangzhou 廣州: Huangcheng chubanshe 花城出版社, 2009.

Lu Ren (魯韌). *Li Shuangshuang* (*Li Shuangshuang* 李雙雙). [Jinan 濟南]: Qilu yinxiang chubanshe 齊魯音像出版社, 2004.

——. *Today Is My Day Off* (*Jintian woxiuxi* 今天我休息). Jinan 濟南: Qilu yinxiang chubanshe 齊魯音像出版社, 2004.

Lu Xiaoya (陸小雅). *The Girl in Red* (*Hongyi shaonü* 紅衣少女). Jinan 濟南: Qilu yinxiang chubanshe 齊魯音像出版社, 2005.

Lu Xueyi (陸學藝), ed. *Research Report on Contemporary Chinese Social Strata* (*Dangdai zhongguo shehui jieceng yanjiu baogao* 當代中國社會階層研究報告). Beijing 北京: shehui kexue wenxian chubanshe 社會科學文獻出版社, 2002.

Lü Ban (呂班). *The Unfinished Comedies* (*Meiyou wancheng de xiju* 沒有完成的喜劇). China: Bandao yinxiang chubanshe 半島音像出版社, 2009.

Ma Junxiang (馬軍驤). "*Shanghai Girls*—Revolutionary Women and the Question of Looking" (*Shanghai guniang—geming nüxing ji guangkan wenti* 《上海姑娘》—革命女性及「觀看」問題). *Reinterpretations* (*Zai jiedu* 再解讀), ed. Tang Xiaobing (唐小兵). Xianggang 香港: Niujin daxue chubanshe 牛津大學出版社, 1993.

Ma Ke (馬可). Exception (*Liwai* 例外). 1996.

——. "Exception de Mixmind" (*Liwai* 例外). Accessed May 15, 2013. http://www .mixmind.com.

——. Useless (*Wuyong* 無用). Paris: Paris Fashion Week, 2007.

Ma Lunpeng (馬綸鵬). "A Study of 'Career Women Films' of the Seventeen Years (1949–66)" (*Shiqinian (1949–1966) zhiye funü yingxiang chutan—jianlun zhong-guo xiandai dainyingzhong de funü yingxiang* 十七年(1949–1966)職業婦女影像初探——兼論中國現代電影中的婦女影像). *Film Research* (*Dianying Yanjiu* 電影研究) (2015): 61–75.

Mao Jian (毛尖). "The Crisis of Sexual Politics and Socialist Aesthetics—Beginning with the Room in *Woman Basketball Player Number 5*" (*Xingbie zhengzhi he shehui zhuyi meixue de weiji- cong nülan wuhao de fangjian shuoqi* 性別政治和社會主義美學的危機—從《女籃5號》的房間說起). *Chinese Modern Literature Research Series* (*Zhongguo xiandai wenxue yanjiu congkan* 中國現代文學研究叢刊) 3 (2010): 29–37.

——. "Pale: Speaking from a Petty-Bourgeois Adjective" (*Cangbai: congyige xiaozide xinrongci tanqi* 蒼白:從一個小資的形容詞談起). *Southern Literary Forum* (*Nanfang Wentan* 南方文壇) 1 (2013): 36–38.

Mao Zedong (毛澤東). *Yan'an Talks on Literature and Art* (*Zai yan'an wenyi zuotan-hui shang de jianghua* 在延安文藝座談會上的講話). Beijing 北京: Renmin chubanshe 人民出版社, 1975.

Mei Yuanmei (梅園縣). "An Anonymous Leader: The Cultural Meaning of *Fashion* Magazine" (*Niming de yindaozhe: shishang zazhi de wenhua yiwei* 匿名的引导者—《时尚》杂志的文化意味). In *Writing Cultural Hero: Cultural Studies at the Turn of the Century* (*Shuxie wenhua yingxiong: shiji zhijiao de wenhua yanjiu* 書寫文化英雄: 世紀之交的文化研究), ed. Dai Jinhua (戴錦華). Nanjing 南京: Jiangsu ren min chu ban she 江蘇人民出版社, 2000.

Meng Yue (孟悅). "*White-Haired Girl* and the Historical Complexities of Yan'an Literature" (*Bai maonü yu yan'an wenxue de lishi fuzaxing*《白毛女》與 「延安文學」的歷史複雜性). *Reinterpretations* (*Zai jiedu* 再解讀), ed. Tang Xiaobing (唐小兵). Xianggang 香港: Niujin daxue chubanshe 牛津大學出版社, 1993.

Mi Jiashan (米家山). *The Trouble-Shooters* (*Wanzhu* 頑主). Guangzhou 廣州: Guangzhou qiaojiaren wenhua chuanbo youxian gongsi 廣州俏佳人文化傳播有限公司, 2005.

Qi Xingjia (齊興家). *Red Dress Is in Fashion* (*Jieshang liuxing hongqunzi* 街上流行红裙子). Beijing 北京: Bandao yinxiang chubanshe 半島音像出版社, 2002.

Qian Zhongshu (錢鍾書). *Fortress Besieged* (*Weicheng* 圍城). Beijing 北京: Renmin wenxue chubanshe 人民文學出版社, 1991.

Qin Xiaoyu (秦曉宇), ed. *Wode shipian: dangdai gongren shidian* 我的詩篇:當代工人詩典. Beijing 北京: Zuojia chubanshe 作家出版社, 2015.

Qin Xiaoyu (秦曉宇), and Wu Feiyue (吳飛躍). *Iron Moon* (*Wode shipian* 我的詩篇). Shanghai 上海: Shanghai yiteng yingshi wenhua youxian gongsi 上海易騰影視文化有限公司, 2015.

Ouyang Shan (歐陽山). *Three-Family Lane* (*Sanjiaxiang* 三家巷). Beijing 北京: Renmin wenxue chubanshe 人民文學出版社, 1999.

Research on China's Cultural Revolution. (*Zhongguo wenge yanjiuwang* 中國文革研究網). Accessed May 15, 2013. http://www.wengewang.org/.

Sanpu Youhe (三浦友和) and Shankou Baihui (山口百惠). *Red Suspicion* (*Xueyi: Riben jingdian dianshi lianxuju* 血疑: 日本經典電視連續劇). Translated from Japanese to Chinese. Fujian 福建: Fujian wenyi yinxiang chubanshe 福建文藝音像出版社, 2002.

"Shanghai People Actively Participated in the Discussions About Resisting Strange-looking Clothes; Develop the Good Tradition of the Proletariat, Oppose the Thinking and Behavior of the Bourgeoisie" (Shanghai guangda renmin jiji danjia dizhi qizhuang yifu de taolun fayang wuchan jieji youliang chuantong fandui zichan jieji sixiang zuofeng 上海廣大人民積極參加抵制奇裝異服的討論 發揚無產階級優良傳統反對資產階級思想作風). *People's Daily* (*Renmin ribao* 人民日報), November 14, 1964.

Shen Ximeng (沈西蒙). *Sentinels Under the Neon Lights* (*Nihong dengxia de shaobing* 霓虹燈下的哨兵). Beijing 北京: Jiefangjun wenyishe 解放軍文藝社, 1963.

Shen Yan (沈嚴). *The First Half of My Life* (*Wode qianbansheng* 我的前半生). Xinli dianshi wenhua touzi youxian gongsi 新麗電視文化投資有限公司, 2017.

Sina.com.cn (*Xinlang wang* 新浪網). "Sishui liunian" Episode 20 "Fashion" (Part I). (《似水流年》第20集《時尚》上). Accessed May 15, 2013. http://video.sina.com.cn/ent /m/c/2009-01-04/160231865.shtml.

Situ Beichen (司徒北辰) and Li Zhao (李兆). "Pierre Cardin: 'A Crazy Man' from France" (*Pi'er kadan: cong faguo laide fengzi* 皮爾·卡丹: 從法國來的 '瘋子') *China News Weekly* (*Zhongguo xinwen zhoukan* 中國新聞週刊) 44 (2008).

Sun Yu (孫瑜). *The Life of Wu Xun* (*Wuxun chuan* 武訓傳). Shenzhen 深圳: Shenzhen yinxiang chubanshe 深圳影像出版社, 2011.

Tang Xiaobing (唐小兵). "The Historical Meaning of *Never Forget*—The Anxiety of the Everyday Life and Modernity" (*Qianwan buyao wangji de lishi yiyi—guanyu richang shenghuo de jiaolü jiqi xiandaixing* 《千萬不要忘記》的歷史意義—關於日常生活的焦慮及其現代性). *Reinterpretations* (*Zai jiedu* 再解讀), ed. Tang Xiaobing (唐小兵). Xianggang 香港: Niujin daxue chubanshe 牛津大學出版社, 1993.

Tao Jin (陶金). *The Nurse's Diary* (*Hushi riji* 護士日記). Beijing 北京: Beijing beiying luyin luxiang gongsi 北京北影錄音錄像公司, 1999.

Teng Huatao (滕華濤). *Dwelling Narrowness* (*Woju* 蝸居). Guangzhou 廣州: Gunagdong yinxiang 廣東音像, 2009.

——. *Love Is Not Blind* (*Shilian 33 tian* 失戀33天). Guangzhou 廣州: Guangdong yinxiang 廣東音像, 2011.

Tian Fanghua (天方畫). "Discussing 'The Aesthetics of Waste'" (*Tan langfei meixue* 談 '浪費美學'). *Film Art* (*Dianying yishu* 電影藝術) 3 (1958): 68.

Tian Zhuangzhuang (田壯壯). *Rock Kids* (*Yaogun qingnian* 搖滾青年). Hong Kong 香港: Meiya leishe yingdie youxian gongsi 美亞鐳射影碟有限公司, 1997.

Tie Ning (鐵凝). *The Red Shirt That Does Not Have Buttons* (*Meiyou niukou de hongchenshan* 沒有紐扣的紅襯衫). Changchun 長春: Shidai wenyi chubanshe 時代文藝出版社, 1992.

Wang Bin (王濱) and Shui Hua (水華). *White-Haired Girl* (*Baimaonü* 白毛女). Jinan 濟南: Qilu dianzi yinxiang chubanshe 齊魯電子音像出版社, 2004.

Wang Binglin (王秉林). *Erzi Has a Little Hotel* (*Erzi kaidian* 二子開店). Jinan 濟南: Qilu yinxiang chubanshe 齊魯音像出版社, 1987.

——. *A Model's Story* (*Nümote de fengbo* 女模特的風波). Tianjin 天津: Tianjin wenyi yishu yinxiang 天津文化藝術音像, 2005.

Wang Hui (汪暉). *Depoliticized Politics: The End of the Short Twentieth Century and the 1990s* (*Qu zhengzhihua de zhengzhi: duan ershi shiji de zhongjie yu jiushi niandai* 去政治化的政治:短20世紀的終結與90年代). Beijing 北京: Sanlian shudian 三聯書店, 2008.

Wang Jiuliang (王久良). *Absolute Happiness* (*Jile* 極樂). 2008. [Photographic series.]

——. *Beijing Besieged by Waste* (*Laji weicheng* 垃圾圍城). 2008–2010. [Photographic series.]

——. *Beijing Besieged by Waste* (*Laji weicheng* 垃圾圍城). New York: dGenerateFilms and Icarus Films, 2010.

——. *Beijing Hotels* (*Beijing fandian* 北京飯店). Songzhuang Art Center, Beijing, 2010. [Photographic series.]

——. *The Fringes of the City* (*Chengbian* 城邊). 2009. [Photographic series.]

——. *Fruity Coffee* (*Guoka* 果咖). Songzhuang Art Center, Beijing, 2010.

——. *Plastic China* (*Suliao wangguo* 塑料王國). Beijing: CNEX Foundation, 2016.

——. *Previous Lives* (*Wangsheng* 往生). 2007–2008. [Photographic series.]

——. *Rituals and Souls* (*Li hun* 禮魂). 2008. [Photographic series.]

Wang Min'an (汪民安). "On Rubbish." (*Lun laji* 論垃圾) In *What Is the Contemporary* (*Shenme shi dangdai* 什麼是當代). Beijing 北京: Xinxing chubanshe 新星出版社, 2014.

Wang Ping (王蘋) and Ge Xin (葛鑫). *Sentinels Under the Neon Lights* (*Nihong dengxia de shaobing* 霓虹燈下的哨兵). Beijing 北京: Beijing beiying luyin luxiang gongsi 北京北影錄音錄像公司, 1964.

Wang Qiang (王強). *Circles and Traps* (*Quanzi quantao* 圈子圈套). Beijing 北京: Qinghua daxue chubanshe 清華大學出版社, 2006.

Wang Xiaoming (王曉明). *Zai xinyishi xingtai de longzhao xia: 90 niandai de wenhua he wenxue fenxi* 在新意識形態的籠罩下: 90年代的文化和文學分析. Nanjing 南京: Jiangsu renmin chubanshe 江蘇人民 出版社, 2000.

Wei Shaohong (衛兆紅) and Chang Yan (常彥). *The Temptation of Beauty* (*Meide youhuo* 美的誘惑). 1992.

Wong Kar-wai (Wang Jiawei 王家衛). *In the Mood for Love* (*Huayang nianhua* 花樣年華). New York: The Criterion Collection, 2002.

Wu Yonggang (吳永剛). *The Goddess* (*Shennü* 神女). Jinan 濟南: Qilu yinxiang chubanshe 齊魯音像出版社, 2006.

Xiao Yemu (蕭也牧). *Between Me and My Wife* (*Women fufu zhijian* 我們夫婦之間). Guangzhou 廣州: Huangcheng chubanshe 花城出版社, 2010.

Xie Fengsong (謝逢松). "A Letter to Younger Sister—Discussing the Film *Shanghai Girls*" (*Jigei meimei dexin—tan yingpian shanghai guniang* 寄給妹妹的信—谈影片'上海姑娘). *Beijing Art* (*Beijing Wenyi* 北京文藝) 3 (1959): 25.

Xie Jin (謝晉). *Hibiscus Town* (*Furong zhen* 芙蓉鎮). Shenzhen 深圳: Shenzhen yinxiang 深圳音像, 1986.

——. *The Red Detachment of Women* (*Hongse niangzijun* 紅色娘子軍). Jinan 濟南: Qilu dianzi yinxiang chubanshe 齊魯電子音像出版社, 2004.

Xie Tieli (謝鐵驪). *Azalea Mountain* (*Du Juan Shan* 杜鵑山). Beijing 北京: Zhongguo changpian zong gongsi 中國唱片總公司, 1998.

——. *Early Spring in February* (*Zaochun eryue* 早春二月). Beijing 北京: Zhongying yinxiang chubanshe 中影音像出版社, 2005.

——. *Never Forget* (*Qianwan buyao wangji* 千萬不要忘記). Beijing 北京: Beiying luyin luxiang 北影錄音錄像, 1964.

——. *On the Docks* (*Hai Gang* 海港). Jinan 濟南: Qilu yinxiang chubanshe 齊魯音像出版社, 2004.

——. *A Prodigious Storm* (*Baofeng zhouyu* 暴風驟雨). Beijing 北京: Zhongying yinxiang chubanshe 中影音像出版社, 2005.

——. *Revolutionary Model Work: Glory to the Long Jiang* (*Geming yangbanxi: Long Jiang Song* 革命樣板戲:龍江頌). Beijing 北京: Zhongying yinxiang chubanshe 中影音像出版社, 2008.

——. *Revolutionary Model Work: Taking Tiger Mountain by Strategy* (*Geming yangbanxi: zhiqu weihushan* 革命樣板戲: 智取威虎山). Beijing 北京: Zhongying yinxiang chubanshe 中影音像出版社, 2009.

Xu Jinglei (徐靜蕾). *Go! Lala Go!* (*Du Lala shengzhi ji* 杜拉拉升職記). Guangzhou 廣州: Guangdong hongyi wenhua chuanbo youxian giongsi 廣東弘藝文化傳播有限公司, 2010.

Xu Tongjun (許同均). *Zhenzhen's Hair Salon* (*Zhenzhen de fawu* 珍珍的髮屋). China: [Publisher not identified], 1987.

Yan Jizhou (嚴寄洲) and Hao Guang (郝光). *Intrepid Hero* (*Yingxiong hudan* 英雄虎膽). Beijing 北京: Zhongguo sanhuan yinxiang she 中國三環音像出版社, 1958.

Yan Ting Yuen. *Yang Ban Xi: The 8 Model Works* (*Yangbanxi* 樣板戲). Chatsworth, Calif.: Image Entertainment, 2007.

Yang Qingxiang (楊慶祥). "The Age of the Petty Bourgeoisie Is Dead" (*Siqu lede xiaozi shidai* 死去了的小資時代). *Southern Literary Forum* (*Nanfang Wentan* 南方文壇) 1 (2013): 42–44.

Ye Zi. "Central Leaders Pay Attention to *Beijing Besieged by Waste* Images, Instruct the Rectification of Beijing Rubbish Dumps" (*Zhongyang lingdao guanzhu laji weicheng zhaopian pishi Beijing lajichang zhengzhi* 中央領導關注垃圾圍城照片 批示北京垃圾場整治). China Photographer's Association (*Zhongguo shying xiehui* 中國攝影協會), June 9, 2011. http://www.cpanet.org.cn/detail_news_78837.html.

Youku.com (*Youku wang* 優酷網), "*Fengyan fengyu: Liushi niandai jingdian jiyi: shishang* 風言鋒語:六十年代精典記憶:時尚." Youku, updated September 21, 2009. Accessed May 15, 2013. http://v.youku.com/v_show/id_XMTIwMzY1NTQ4.html.

Zhang Jie (張潔). *Love Must Not Be Forgotten* (*Ai, shi buneng wangjide* 愛,是不能忘記的). Guangzhou 廣州: Guangdong renmin chubanshe 廣東人民出版社, 1980.

Zhang Kangkang (張抗抗). *The Right to Love* (*Aide quanli* 愛的權利). Guiyang 貴陽: Guizhou renmin chubanshe 貴州人民出版社, 1996.

Zhang Liang (張良). *A Woman's Street* (*Nürenjie* 女人街), 1989.

——. *Yamaha Fish Stall* (*Yamaha yudang* 雅馬哈魚檔). Guangzhou 廣州: Zhuying bai tian'e yinxiang chubanshe 珠影白天鵝音像出版社, 1984.

Zhang Qi (張其) and Li Yalin (李亞林). *The Corner Forgotten by Love* (*Bei Aiqing Yiwang de Jiaoluo* 被愛情遺忘的角落). Jinan 濟南: Qilu yinxiang chubanshe 齊魯音像出版社, 2004.

Zhang Tianmin (張天民). "Road Examination" (*Lukao* 路考). *People's Literature* (*Renmin wenxue* 人民文學) 3 (1963): 13–21.

Zhang Yimou (張藝謀). *Ju Dou* (*Judou* 菊豆). Studio City, Calif.: Razor Digital Entertainment; Los Angeles: MagicPlay Entertainment, 1990.

——. *Raise the Red Lantern* (*Dahong denglong gaogaogua* 大紅燈籠高高掛). Beverly Hills, Calif.: Twentieth Century Fox Home Entertainment, 1991.

——. *Red Sorghum* (*Hong gaoliang* 紅高粱). New York: New Yorker Video, 1987.

Zhang Yiwu (張頤武). "The Temptation of Fashion" (*Shishang de youhuo* 時尚的誘惑). The Blog of Zhang Yiwu, May 29, 2007 (Zhang yiwu de boke 張頤武的博客). Accessed May 15, 2013. http://blog.sina.com.cn/s/blog_47383f2d010008x1.html.

Zhao Baogang (趙寶剛) and Wang Ying (王迎). *Struggle* (*Fendou* 奮鬥). Guangzhou 廣州: Guangdong yin xiang 廣東音像, 2007.

Zhao Huayong (趙化勇), Luo Ming (羅明), Yuan Zhengming (袁正明), Ren Xue'an (任學安), Tan Jianghai (譚江海), Zhang Ning (張寧), and Wei Zi (巍子). *The Road to Revival* (*Fuxing Zhilu* 復興之路). Beijing 北京: Zhongguo guoji dianshi zong gongsi 中國國際電視總公司, 2007.

Zhao Huayong (趙化勇), Sun Zhanshan (孫占山), Luo Ming (羅明), Yuan Zhengming (袁正明), Mai Tianshu (麥天樞), Ren Xue'an (任學安), Chen Jin (陳晉), and Pan Dawei (潘大為). *The Rise of Great Nations* (*Daguo jueqi* 大國崛起). Beijing: Zhongguo guoji dianshi zong gongsi 中國國際電視總公司, 2006.

Zhao Ming (趙明). *The Young Generation* (*Nianqing de yidai* 年青的一代). Beijing 北京: Beijing bei ying lu yin lu xiang going si 北影錄音錄像公司, 1965.

——. *The Young Generation* (*Nianqing de yidai* 年青的一代). Jinan 濟南: Qilu yinxiang chubanshe 齊魯音像出版社, 2005.

Zhao Shuli (趙樹理). *Sanlian Village* (*Sanliwan* 三里灣). Beijing 北京: Renmin wenxue chubanshe 人民文學出版社, 2005.

Zheng Junli (鄭君里). *Nie Er* (*Nie'er* 聶耳). Jinan 濟南: Qilu yinxiang chubanshe 齊魯音像出版社, 2004.

Zheng Junli (鄭君里), and Sun Yu (孫瑜). *Song Jingshi* (*Song Jingshi* 宋景詩). Beijing 北京: Beijing beiying luyin luxiang 北京北影錄音錄像, 1957.

Zhou Xiaohong (周曉虹). "The Chinese Middle Class: Reality or Illusion?" (*Zhongguo zhongchan jieji xianshi yihuo huangxiang* 中國中產階級現實抑或幻想). "The Century Forum" (*Shiji dajiangtang* 世紀大講堂). Shenzhen, China: Phoenix TV (*Fenghuang weishi* 鳳凰衛視), 2005.

——. "Introduction: History and Current Situation of the Chinese Middle Class" (*Daoyan: zhongguo zhongchan jieceng de lishi he xianzhuang* 導言:中國中產階層的歷史和現狀). In *Survey of the Chinese Middle Classes* (*Zhongguo zhongchan jieji diaocha* 中國中產階級調查). Beijing 北京: Shehui kexue wenxian chubanshe 社會科學文獻出版社, 2005.

——, ed. *Survey of the Chinese Middle Classes* (*Zhongguo zhongchan jieji diaocha* 中國中產階級調查). Beijing 北京: Shehui kexue wenxian chubanshe 社會科學文獻出版社, 2005.

——, ed. *Report of Middle Classes in the World* (*Quanqiu zhongchan jieji baogao* 全球中產階級報告). Beijing 北京: Shehui kexue wenxian chubanshe 社會科學文獻出版社, 2005.

Zhou Yu (周予). *Road Examination* (*Lukao* 路考). Shenzhen 深圳: Shenzhen yinxiang gongsi 深圳音像公司, 2013.

Zong Pu (宗璞). *Red Beans. Hongdou* 紅豆. Guangzhou 廣州: Huacheng chubanshe 花城出版社, 2010.

INDEX